MW00816801

RACE AND TRANSNATIONALISM IN THE AMERICAS

PITT LATIN AMERICAN SERIES
CATHERINE M. CONAGHAN, EDITOR

RACE
AND TRANSNATIONALISM
IN THE AMERICAS

EDITED BY BENJAMIN BRYCE
AND DAVID M. K. SHEININ

UNIVERSITY OF PITTSBURGH PRESS

Published by the University of Pittsburgh Press, Pittsburgh, Pa., 15260
Copyright © 2021, University of Pittsburgh Press
All rights reserved
Manufactured in the United States of America
Printed on acid-free paper
10 9 8 7 6 5 4 3 2 1

Library of Congress Cataloging-in-Publication Data

Names: Bryce, Benjamin, editor. | Sheinin, David, editor.
Title: Race and transnationalism in the Americas / edited by Benjamin Bryce
    and David M.K. Sheinin.
Description: Pittsburgh, Pa. : University of Pittsburgh Press, 2021. |
    Series: Pitt Latin American series | Includes bibliographical references
    and index.
Identifiers: LCCN 2020053062 | ISBN 9780822946717 (cloth) | ISBN
    9780822988168 (ebook)
Subjects: LCSH: America—Race relations. | Group identity—America. |
    Minorities—Race identity—America. | Indigenous peoples—Race
    identity—America. | Nationalism—Social aspects—America. |
    Transnationalism. | Race.
Classification: LCC E29.A1 R325 2021 | DDC 305.80097—dc23
LC record available at https://lccn.loc.gov/2020053062

Cover art: Ealy Mays, *Birth of the Mestizo Warrior*. Licensed under CC BY-SA 3.0.
Cover design: Melissa Dias-Mandoly

For Gabriela and Gabriel

CONTENTS

Acknowledgments   ix

INTRODUCTION. Toward New Coordinates?   3

MARC HERTZMAN

CHAPTER ONE. Asian Migration, Racial Hierarchies, and Exclusion in Argentina, 1890–1920   20

BENJAMIN BRYCE

CHAPTER TWO. Intersections, Barriers, and Borders in Gregorio Titiriku's Republic of Qullasuyu   37

WASKAR ARI-CHACHAKI

CHAPTER THREE. Race and Political Rights: Constructions of Citizenship among British Caribbeans inside and outside the British Empire, 1918–1962   56

LARA PUTNAM

CHAPTER FOUR. Crossing the Border at the Primer Congreso Indigenista Interamericano, 1940   74

ALEXANDER DAWSON

CHAPTER FIVE. No Place in the Cosmic Race? The False Promises of *Mestizaje* and *Indigenismo* in Postrevolutionary Mexico   91

STEPHEN LEWIS

CHAPTER SIX. Creating False Analogies: Race and Drug Wars 1930s to 1950s   106

ELAINE CAREY

CHAPTER SEVEN. Baseball and the Categorization of Race in
Venezuela   121

DAVID M. K. SHEININ

CHAPTER EIGHT. Making Their Own Mahatma: Salvador's Filhos de Gandhy
and the Local History of a Global Phenomenon   140

MARC HERTZMAN

CHAPTER NINE. Reading the Caribbean and United States through
Panamanian *reggae en español*   159

SONJA STEPHENSON WATSON

CHAPTER TEN. The Tortuous Road toward the Building of a Mosque
in Buenos Aires: Overcoming Racial Stereotypes under Populist
Governments   177

RAANAN REIN

CHAPTER ELEVEN. Buried: Race, Photography, and Memory in *Damiana
Kryygi*   192

KEVIN COLEMAN WITH JULIA IRION MARTINS

EPILOGUE. Overcoming the National   214

BENJAMIN BRYCE AND DAVID M. K. SHEININ

Notes   221
About the Contributors   285
Index   289

ACKNOWLEDGMENTS

We would like to thank our editor, Josh Shanholtzer, for his professional and generous support throughout this project. It has been a pleasure working with him. Tulie O'Connor did a wonderful job picking up all sorts of errors and polishing the text in the copyediting stage. Many others behind the scenes at the University of Pittsburgh Press did an excellent job turning this manuscript into a book, and for all of their help we are very thankful. Two peer reviewers offered very helpful suggestions on all of the chapters.

Chapter 3, written by Lara Putnam, appeared in a different form in the *Journal of British Studies* (2014). We would like to thank the editors of the *Journal of British Studies* for allowing us to publish a revised version in this volume.

RACE AND TRANSNATIONALISM IN THE AMERICAS

INTRODUCTION

TOWARD NEW COORDINATES?

Marc Hertzman

Nearly three decades in, the "transnational turn" continues to pull at historians' spatial moorings. The impetus to look beyond the boundaries of the nation-state, combined with new directions in Atlantic, global, and Pacific history, has led many scholars to cast their empirical nets wide. This, combined with the rise of powerful digital tools, has created opportunity as well as peril. For all the important intellectual and political reasons to trace history across national borders, doing so can risk losing sight of local and national details, sending scholars scrambling to trace "the most far-flung circuit plausible."[1] Despite concerted efforts to bridge north-south divides, Latin American-based scholars tend to eye transnational history more skeptically than their counterparts in North America. Where, then, does Latin American history as a field stand amid the blowing winds of transnationalism? What is the place of the nation-state in transnational scholarship? And to address the specific focus of this book, how have race and the categorization of race functioned as mechanisms or organizing frameworks for cultural, political, and social inclusion in the Americas? In the context of inclusion, how have such frameworks transcended the national (where authors contemplate "nation" amply)?

Though the answers to these questions vary by author, collectively *Race and Transnationalism* emphasizes the importance of the local, even while remaining attentive to global forces and phenomena, and to the very important and useful ways that transnational inquiry has decentered the nation and forced scholars to think in new ways about borders and history itself. The questions posed above carry unique challenges, amplified by the productive ambiguity that marks "transnational," a concept that hovers between a category of analysis and a methodology.[2] Understood as the former, "transnational" functions as a means to see and explore histories that cross national boundaries. Defined as the latter, things get murky. One scholar writes, "Transnational history does not designate either a theory or a discrete method . . . and instead a perspective, a manner of casting a gaze on an object of study."[3] To two others, transnationalism, "still continues to suffer from confusion over what distinguishes it from the related concepts of globalization and migration."[4] Pamela Voekel and Elliott Young, two of the founders of the Tepoztlán Institute for the Transnational History of the Americas, an innovative workshop-collective dedicated to debate and collaboration among US- and Latin American-based scholars, call transnational a "deliberately vague moniker."[5]

Race and Transnationalism both inhabits and seeks to break free from the ambiguities of transnational history. Understanding transnational history to be a category (or manner of casting a gaze) more than a fixed or defined methodology, the authors of this volume trace stories across borders but also highlight local and national particularities. In every instance, race plays a disruptive role, simultaneously holding history captive to the nation-state, and demanding historians to look beyond it. Because national governments create legal and penal regimes, censuses, and other tools that codify race and its categories, it would be all but impossible to study race without attention to the nation-state. At the same time, those tools—and the less concrete but equally important cultural pathways along which race is created and challenged—are invariably in contact with conversations, debates, politics, commodities, and spheres of influence that go far beyond national borders. Accordingly, this book takes as a given that transnational forces have fundamentally shaped visions of racial difference and ideas of race and national belonging throughout the Americas, from the late nineteenth century to the present.

To probe the relationships of race, nation, and the transnational flow of ideas, people, and capital, the authors of this book examine exclusionary immigration policies, government attempts to colonize internal "others," indigenous and Black decolonization movements as well as sport, drugs, music, populism, and film. They focus on the Americas, from New York to Buenos Aires, from the US-Mexican borderlands to Bolivia, and along the coasts of Brazil, Venezuela, Panama, and Jamaica. In so doing, *Race and Transnationalism* engages in broad debates about race, citizenship, and national belonging in the Americas and suggests multiple and new ways to think about the intertwined histories of North America, South America, Central America, and the Caribbean.

FROM THE ATLANTIC TO THE PACIFIC . . . AND BEYOND?

Latin Americanist transnational scholarship has developed in dialogue with two central lines of analysis that marked earlier generations of historical work, especially that focused on slavery. First, transnationalism evolved in part as a response to comparative history, embodied by Frank Tannenbaum's *Slave and Citizen* (1947), which helped set in place a comparative template for largely English-language studies of slavery and race in the Americas.[6] Second, Latin Americanist transnational analysis has built on generations of scholarship about links between Africa and the Americas. This was pioneered by Gonzalo Aguirre Beltrán, Melville Herskovits, Fernando Ortiz, and Raimundo Nina Rodrigues, and others who studied African contributions to their respective national "characters."[7] More recently, scholars have built on but also rejected central premises of Tannenbaum's inter-American comparative methodology, favoring transnational inquiry over comparison, while also discarding the paternalism and outright racism that marked some of the pioneering scholarship produced by Rodrigues and his peers.[8]

Transnational scholars are also indebted to nineteenth- and twentieth-century Caribbean and Latin American intellectuals who wrote anticolonial and anti-imperial works that prefigured today's transnational scholarship.[9] Lisa Lowe's *The Intimacy of Four Continents* (2015), an expansive global history and critique of liberalism, begins in the Caribbean with references to Ortiz and C. L. R. James. Both Ortiz and James located Caribbean national origins in "the intimacies of four continents," a heretofore underexplored set of entanglements linking the Americas, Africa, Asia, and Europe.[10] The anticolonial and anti-imperial roots of transnational scholarship lives on in the shared intention among many current scholars to not only rescue "history from the nation" but also to think about in new ways imperial domination in the global North and South, as well as international solidarity networks meant to counter imperialism and other forms of violence and exclusion.[11]

A key link between earlier and contemporary scholarship is Paul Gilroy's *The Black Atlantic: Modernity and Double-Consciousness* (1993), which helped reject the Atlantic as a white-European space.[12] Having appeared just as the "transnational turn" was revving into gear, the book centers all the same on the North Atlantic and erases most of the rest of the hemisphere. Nonetheless, Gilroy's work has been generative in numerous ways, including the somewhat recent move to conceptualize and better understand the meanings and forms of Blackness on Latin America's western coast, and a movement among some (Latin) Americanists to envision a Black Pacific to complement Gilroy's Black Atlantic. The give-and-take that the move to the Pacific entails is embodied in a provocative map that frames *Decolonizing Native Histories*, a 2012 collection about indigenous history and activism in the Americas and the Pacific that seeks to "decenter" the (Latin) Americanist gaze and extend it west.[13] In order to include Hawai'i and other points in the South Pacific, the book's mapmaker had to slice off the eastern half of Brazil and most of French Guiana. As the map vividly shows, each change in our spatial coordinates has the potential, depending on where one stands, to expand or diminish the horizon.

Gilroy's impact is evident in Heidi Feldman's *Black Rhythms of Peru: Reviving African Musical Heritage in the Black Pacific* (2006), which extends Gilroy's project to write histories of Blackness and Black modernity into the Atlantic world to the western coast of South America, where Blackness has repeatedly been erased.[14] *Black Rhythms of Peru* traces the mid- and late twentieth-century construction of Peruvian Black musical and cultural identities, long subsumed and marginalized to a *mestizo* identity that valorized whiteness and grudgingly included certain aspects of indigeneity. One of the book's more remarkable stories involves the relationship that Nicomedes de Santa Cruz, an Afro-Peruvian musician-activist at the heart of the "revival," developed with Edison Carneiro, a prolific, though often overlooked, polymath Black Brazilian scholar.[15] Santa Cruz met Carneiro when he traveled to Brazil in the early 1960s. After returning, he proposed a genesis of Peruvian *landó* music that ran through *lundu*, a Black Atlantic creation with its own tangled genealogy and which, according to Santa Cruz, traveled from Africa to Brazil to Peru.[16] Though not historically accurate, Santa Cruz's Brazil-inspired genealogy is an exemplary case of cross-border community making and artistic and intellectual creation.

Feldman's reconstruction and analysis of the Africa-Brazil-Peru route proposed by Santa Cruz illustrates how recent transnational Latin Americanist scholarship has expanded and recentered the maps charted by previous generations. The expansion and recentering has taken place across vast spaces, as in the case of Santa Cruz, and also in more compact ones, such as the Caribbean, the site of exciting recent works that trace the flow of ideas and people across smaller but no less significant geographic boundaries than those studied by Feldman. In conversations with recent work on "trans-imperial" colonial histories, Anne Eller and Ada Ferrer have examined how race and nation formed before, during, and after independence in Cuba, the Dominican Republic, and Haiti.[17] Focusing on the first half of the twentieth century, Lara Putnam shows the remarkable ways that migrants, music, goods, and ideas zigzagged across space, helping create a circum-Caribbean whose borders extended all the way to New York.[18] In this volume, Putnam traces similarly vibrant paths even further, demonstrating how British West Indians coped with increasingly exclusionary definitions of citizenship that shaped their lives and defined struggles across (and beyond) the British Empire.

Mainly focused on people of African descent, the works mentioned above have helped galvanize shifts in other areas of study. Tatiana Seijas's *Asian Slaves in Colonial Mexico: From Chinos to Indians* narrates the history of slaves taken to Mexico during the sixteenth and seventeenth centuries from Southeast and South Asia, a diverse set of communities lumped together upon arrival in America as *chinos*.[19] Whereas books about the African diaspora in Latin America build on (and also struggle against) previous generations of scholarship on comparative slavery, Seijas's work is one of the only extended considerations of Asian slavery during the colonial period, though there is, of course, a large, developed literature on the rise of so-called coolie labor in Latin America.[20] Significantly, that ugly slur originated in South Asia, and over time came to be used as a racist gloss to refer to Asians from all over the continent, much like "chino."[21]

Transnational gazes have also shaped recent work on indigenous peoples in Latin America. Rebecca Earle's *The Return of the Native: Indians and Myth-Making in Spanish America, 1810–1930*, embraces a hemispheric approach to studying the discursive construction of indigeneity among Latin American elites during the "long nineteenth century."[22] In ways that resemble what Jace Weaver calls the "Red Atlantic," Nancy E. van Deusen and José Carlos de la Puente Luna examine the West-to-East flow of indigenous people to Europe during the colonial period.[23] Focused more on the genesis of ideas than the circulation of people, James E. Sanders and Mark Thurner trace similarly innovative routes across time and space into the national period. Both Sanders and Turner stretch the maps that van Deusen and de la Puente Luna expanded east across the Atlantic back to Latin America, where they reveal hidden American origins of liberalism and historicism.[24]

Though often treated in isolation, scholarship on indigenous peoples and the African and Asian diasporas in America share important points of contact and dialogue with each other, as well as with literature on Jewish and European immigration and diasporas. Jeffrey Lesser's work has pushed Brazilianist scholars to expand their cognitive maps by exploring East Asian and Middle Eastern origins, influences on, and connections to Brazil, much as Ranaan Rein's work in this volume (and elsewhere) has done in Argentina.[25] Andre Kobayashi Deckrow builds on Lesser's work while taking the story in new directions by using Japanese archives and Japanese-language sources in Brazil to reveal novel insights about Japanese imperialism and its surprising relationship with Brazil.[26] By centering a substantial amount of research in the Pacific, Deckrow helps redirect narratives of nation and belonging in Brazil, and in the process bolsters the importance of following transnational histories not only within the Americas or toward Europe or Africa but also across the Pacific.

In different ways, all of these works raise questions about the intellectual horizon: How far west should we travel? Should our maps extend even beyond Hawai'i, the Philippines, and East Asia into the Indian Ocean? The questions, in turn, point to a central challenge raised by transnational history: how to travel beyond the boundaries of the nation-state without losing sight of the local, and without spinning out of control into an never-ending search for every global connection imaginable. South Asia, which appears in two chapters of this volume, offers a case in point. Whereas there is significant literature on South Asian indentured labor and migration to the Caribbean and the northern coast of South America, very little is known about the rest of Latin America. Benjamin Bryce's contribution to this volume helps address that lacuna and also illustrates how even a relatively small group of migrants, such as the six hundred Sikh workers who arrived in Argentina in 1912, can cast "light on some of the latent contours" of larger racial dynamics.[27] As Bryce shows, the erasure of South and East Asians from Argentine historiography distorts our understanding of politics and the nature of racism. Contrary to prevailing wisdom, Bryce shows that early in the twentieth century Argentine officials were intimately concerned with Asian immigration.

If Bryce's chapter suggests why it can, indeed, be fruitful to expand the map even beyond the Pacific, Marc Hertzman's exploration of the Filhos de Gandhy, a Carnival group founded by Black port workers in Bahia inspired by Mohandas Gandhi, leads toward another conclusion. Whereas Bryce conjures a map framed on one end by South Asia and the other by South America (and provides a separate map that highlights Europe), the Filhos de Gandhy could be illustrated through two different cartographic representations: one of the entire globe to account not only for India but also Gandhi's time, impact, and reception in Africa, as well as in England, where striking British port workers helped inspire the Brazilian stevedores who founded the Filhos de Gandhy. The second map would be much smaller and would magnify Salvador, its unique history, and the political and cultural moment there that gave birth to the Filhos de Gandhy. Together, Bryce's and Hertzman's chapters suggest that although expanding and decentering the map sometimes makes sense, in other cases transnational flows anchor the story in the local, often a repository of audaciously global and heterogeneous influences that ultimately, and perhaps ironically, root us ever more deeply at home. The collective takeaway is to avoid endlessly stretching, decentering, and recentering the map in a relentless search for one more "hidden" global connection or group and to instead craft studies that first and foremost honor and understand local and national subtleties and complexities, and that then proceed to approach the transnational and the global not as obvious realities but rather as subjects meant to be studied, questioned, and challenged.

CONNECTIONS, DISCONNECTIONS, AND DIVISIONS

Our book proposes new scales and methods for studying transnationalism and illustrates why multiple lenses are necessary for understanding local manifestations of transnational histories of race. In *The Intimacy of Four Continents*, Lowe shows how the indelible links between capitalism and racism run the gamut from intimate to global. In a similar spirit, *Race and Transnationalism* maneuvers across macro and micro dimensions, in the process splintering the United States and the world binary that still defines much of transnational history and dislodging the nation-state and migration as the principal scales for comprehending transnational flows. Many of those flows, the contributors demonstrate, have become entrenched through surprising practices and experiences that often present more obviously as local, national, and everyday.

Slavery, indentured labor, voluntary migration, commerce, culture, and other forces that brought individuals from across the world to the Americas in turn helped generate connections, return routes, and other lines of contact and exchange that traversed national boundaries, as did racial, indigenous, feminist, LGBTQ, labor, environmental, and other forms of activism. Though such connections are central to transnational history, one of the most influential recent Latin Americanist works, Heidi Tinsman's *Buying into the Regime: Grapes and Consumption in Cold War Chile and the United States* (2014), provides a cautionary note. As tantalizing as commonalities, bonds, and links can be, Tinsman emphasizes "the importance of studying *disconnections* as well as connections."[28]

What kinds of connections and disconnections mark the transnational histories of race in the Americas? In this volume, Alexander Dawson argues that during the 1940s in Mexico and the United States "a transnational indigenista project was simply impossible," and Stephen Lewis details an inward-looking gaze of Mexican national racial projects that nonetheless resonate in remarkable ways with related projects across the hemisphere.[29] Waskar Ari-Chachaki shows how racism, as much as racial solidarity, flowed into Bolivia along transnational pathways, a powerful counterpoint to examples of cross-border solidarity and resistance.[30] These examples illustrate the book's project to engage and explore the tension between connection and disconnection, and each contributor's mindfulness of transnationalism's potential to threaten political and intellectual projects that, by choice or by force, retain the nation-state as a central point of reference.

Music and other cultural forms, what Putnam calls the "non-material lines of transnational connection," provide especially rich material for exploring these dynamics. Cultural products, Putnam writes, "circulate and overlap, reflecting past lines of connection and new ones."[31] Those products also have the capacity to differentiate and delineate—to disconnect. Music, for instance, so often and so easily travels beyond national boundaries, and yet it is also frequently held up as a symbol of unique and even insular national identities. In chapter nine of this volume, Sonja Stephenson Watson shows how "transnational circuits of cultural, racial, and linguistic exchange" shaped Panamanian *Reggae en español*. Like Putnam before her,

Watson expands reggae's map, introducing coordinates far west of Jamaica that challenge earlier narratives.[32]

Studies of music often link and flatten out musical traditions across the African diaspora, though a closer look reveals a more complex picture. The Charleston, which took the United States and other parts of the world by storm in the 1920s, is an exemplary case. Flávio Gomes and Petrônio Domingues show that although the music enjoyed success in Brazil, Black communities there had multiple reactions to it, sometimes embracing the dance and other times rejecting it in favor of national music.[33] In addition to reaffirming the importance of local and the national subtleties, Gomes and Domingues challenge the notion advanced in Pierre Bourdieu and Loïc Wacquant's ill-conceived and widely discussed essay that Afro-Brazilians were "mere receptacles and passive reproducers of foreign influences."[34] By tracing the global flows of music in ways that also pay serious attention to local realities, Gomes and Domingues exemplify how the best transnational scholarship not only looks past national borders but also keeps a close eye on what is happening inside them, in the process contributing to larger debates about history and power.

Those debates have taken different directions across the Americas. In general, US- and Canada-based academics have adopted transnationalism more eagerly and more explicitly than their counterparts in Latin America, though that divide can be misleading considering the way that C. R. L. James and others helped lay the groundwork for the "transnational turn." The Tepoztlán Institute and other North-South collaborations further blur the line, as do books such as Ricardo Salvatore's edited collection, *Los lugares del saber: Contextos locales y redes transnacionales en la formación del conocimiento moderno*, Diego Galeano's *Criminosos viajantes: circulações transnacionais entre Rio de Janeiro e Buenos Aires, 1890–1930*, and Catherine Vézina's *Diplomacia Migratoria: una historia transnacional del Programa Bracero, 1947–1952*.[35] Salvatore's volume examines the ways that international currents shaped the production of knowledge—cultural, scientific, political, legal, and more. Galeano's innovative study uses archives in Argentina and Brazil to show how policing models and stereotypes flowed across borders. Vézina examines the renegotiation of the Bracero Program, providing insights not only about high politics but also much more local concerns. By rooting the book in Guanajuato, one of the main sending states for Mexican laborers who went to the United States, and California, a principal US "consumer" of those laborers, Vézina uses a transnational lens to write an also deeply local history.[36]

These examples do not mean that the North-South divide is not real. Voekel and Young relate that one Central American participant at Tepoztlán rejected an initial invitation "because the term *transnacional* evokes multinational corporations for Spanish speakers: she feared that we were gathering to celebrate neoliberal globalization."[37] Barbara Weinstein implores "scholars following the transnational turn . . . to consider the drawbacks of a historical approach that attenuates connections to scholars in Latin America whose main analytical references is still the national context."[38] Similar concerns have been raised by indigenous scholars, who point out the significance that the nation-state retains for indigenous communities seeking to gain rights from it.[39] In Latin America, suspicion also derives from early transnational works that seemed to do little more than place the United States at the center of histories that expanded outward to the "rest" of the world. It is for good and multiple reasons, then, that transnational method is often viewed with skepticism in Latin America.

REIMAGINING THE ATLANTIC (AGAIN) AND THE POLITICS OF RACE AND LABOR

To Galeano, borders represent the grist of transnationalism's intellectual mill. "Transnational history," he writes, "attempts to make visible the fissures that open along nations' borders."[40] Keila Grinberg examines such fissures, in the process expanding and also complicating a central insight about colonial and imperial borders—that slaves crossed them to escape bondage and to take advantage of imperial rivalries and competing legal regimes—with a series of innovative arguments about what Silmei de Sant-Ana Petiz calls Brazil's history "beyond the border."[41] People often moved across Brazil's southern border to pursue freedom, but in so doing also helped create "a new frontier of enslavement" for Brazilian slave catchers, who targeted Blacks in Uruguay and Argentina while pursuing slaves who had fled Brazil.[42] Cross-border movement also "established unprecedented diplomatic situations" and "led to the creation of a new jurisprudence in the domain of international law."[43] By blending micro-history and the stories of individual slaves and runaways with larger legal regimes and international politics and law, Grinberg reveals transnationalism to be a means for centering marginalized and forgotten histories and also for reimagining the creation of national borders and the shape of international diplomacy and justice.[44]

Transnational scholarship has also helped counter North-heavy interpretations of the Atlantic world, a larger project encapsulated in a special issue of the *Luso-Brazilian Review* dedicated to "ReCapricorning the Atlantic."[45] That cartographic reorientation not only gestures South but also emphasizes the kind of East-West back-and-forth across the Atlantic highlighted by other scholars of the African diaspora and the "Red Atlantic." Anchored in Bahia and Yorùbáland, J. Lorand Matory shows that Black "travelers, scholars, writers, pilgrims, merchants, and priests" cannot be understood within the confines of a single country. "Since the mid-19th century," he writes, individuals in Brazil and elsewhere have acted "in defense of their own interests, and who, in so doing, have sagaciously interpreted forces far beyond any single country of origin or country of destination."[46] Expanding, decentering, and "ReCapricorning" the Atlantic also means questioning the relationship between nation and diaspora, and the shape of both.[47] Lauren Derby makes related points about Haitian Vodou, though by orienting our gaze not only toward Africa but also Europe and the United States. Although the story she tells is undeniably transnational, it is driven toward understanding the forging of a Haitian national identity that engaged, appropriated, and repelled foreign threats in a way that gave rise to a "martial ethos . . . as a renegade nation that forged its identity against the world through the barrel of a gun."[48] Together, Derby and Matory illustrate how transnational studies of diasporic religion may at once counter and account for US and European hegemony, while alternately centering and traversing the nation.

Haiti, the world's first "Black republic," and Brazil, held by many (including its current president) to be a mythical "racial democracy," represent just two points in a larger American kaleidoscope of racial configurations and racialized national mythologies.[49] Many, perhaps all, were forged in conversation with and in the shadow of a purportedly "white" Europe and United States. In chapter seven of this volume, David M. K. Sheinin writes about Venezuela, whose citizens "have at times constructed a distinct, parallel vision of US Blackness based on a binary US segregationism, with a range of cultural implications that include distinguishing a putatively less racist Venezuelan society (absent segregation and other violent US discriminatory forms) from the United States."[50] Similar comparisons and claims of racial exceptionalism are found throughout the Americas. Revealing the lie behind apocryphal national stories of racial harmony helped dislodge comparison as a lens of analysis and imbue transnationalism with extra appeal.

Labor history has also become increasingly focused on global and transnational questions, sometimes in dialogue with histories of race and gender, though gender, it is worth noting, is often conspicuously absent from transnational scholarship.[51] As slavery was abolished throughout the Americas, schemes to bring in different kinds of laborers—especially Asian and European—came to the fore, almost always accompanied by discourses about how those foreign laborers would improve the racial composition of the nation. But whereas there is a sizeable literature, for example, on the large-scale projects to bring Asian laborers to Cuba, Peru, and Brazil, other national case studies of such migrations have fallen by the wayside. One such history is the construction of the Madeira-Mamoré rail line in the Amazon, made possible by more than twenty one thousand immigrant workers from more than thirty different countries. Many came from the Antilles, whose experiences have been "completely forgotten within Brazilian working-class and immigration history."[52]

Closely related to labor is the history of Marxism and radical leftist politics in the Americas, a body of literature increasingly attuned to transnationalism. In *Indians and Leftists in the Making of Ecuador's Modern Indigenous Movements* (2008), Marc Becker writes, "From its beginnings in the 1920s . . . Indigenous activism must be understood and contextualized within international trends."[53] Jaymie Heilman similarly frames her account of politics and indigenous activism in rural Ayacucho within global events such as the Mexican and Bolshevik Revolutions.[54] Although attentive to global flows of movements and ideas, both Becker and Heilman root themselves deeply within their respective national contexts, and for good reason—most of the people they study did, too.

The Bolivian-based French sociologist Hervé Do Alto shows how Evo Morales's Movimiento al Socialismo (Movement for Socialism, MAS) creatively and effectively brought together Marxism and "*indianismo*" under a nationalist umbrella.[55] The achievement, Do Alto shows, is especially remarkable when considered in a larger context. Bolivia, after all, was the site of Che Guevara's death, a grim reminder of the way that local and national realities can trump transnational links and collaborations. But that does not suggest a zero-sum game: MAS successfully incorporated into its iconography figures as diverse as the Argentine-born-cum-Cuban revolutionary Che; Túpac Katari, the famous eighteenth-century Aymara leader; and Marcelo Quiroga Santa Cruz, a prominent late twentieth-century Bolivian socialist.[56]

In some cases, local and national affiliations have helped generate strategic differentiation among members of diasporas. Arlindo J. Viega dos Santos, the founder of the Black Brazilian Front (FNB, Frente Negra Brasileira), rejected "any sort of alliance with foreign blacks," Paulina Alberto writes, and shunned ties with Africa altogether.[57] Jessica Graham's *Shifting the Meaning of Democracy: Race, Politics, and Culture in the United States and Brazil* (2019) highlights conversations and exchanges among and about Black political actors in the United States and Brazil. Eschewing the false choice between comparative and transnational models, Graham employs both approaches, tracing cross-border exchange while also contextualizing and comparing her case studies. The result is an unprecedented accounting of the ways in which Black political actors in both countries shaped and were shaped by entreaties from Communists and Fascists, and ever-louder (though still empty) proclamations of racial democracy and equality.[58] Aruã Lima casts his research net even wider, incorporating archives in Brazil, the United States, Russia, and Finland into a research itinerary that yields new insights about the Comintern, and race and radicalism in Brazil.[59] Just as

Communists sought to make good on Comintern directives to recruit more Black Brazilians, so too, Graham and Kim Butler show, did fascists and the Ação Integralista Brasileira (Brazilian Integralist Action).[60] The remarkable, if also limited and sometimes strained, mutual affinity between Brazilian integralists and the Frente Negra takes Tinsman's admonition to account for disconnections a step further, underscoring the importance of also accounting for previously unseen connections and alliances that run against the scholarly grain.

TOWARD A TRANSNATIONAL HISTORY OF RACE IN THE AMERICAS

In the pages that follow, twelve scholars explore a fascinating collection of histories, some of which were previously neglected, and others that have received attention but merit reconsideration. Together, the essays cover a broad area and place in conversation histories of indigeneity, the African diaspora, and Asia, and in doing so serve as a rejoinder to some of the more stubbornly calcified epistemological categories of Latin American Studies. The volume opens with Bryce's chapter on race and immigration in Argentina. In addition to the South Asians previously referenced, Bryce shows how from 1890 to 1920 Argentine writers, politicians, and officials sought to use political and labor market maneuvering to prevent immigration from South and East Asia. The chapter demonstrates the presence of Asian immigrants in Argentina much earlier than is often suggested and shows that race-based immigration exclusion also predates the typical chronology. While stretching the conceptual map across and beyond the Pacific (with an eye also on Europe, and a fascinating Argentine government map of it), Bryce connects the flow of global migration to Argentine racial ideology, demonstrating the kind of productive back-and-forth that can occur when our guiding coordinates are thought of as an open question rather than as a fixed border.

Borders are a central concern of chapter two, where Waskar Ari-Chachaki explores and attempts to create an "Indian Republic" alongside a "white Republic" in 1920s and 1930s Bolivia. Of special interest is Gregorio Titiriku, an indigenous intellectual who helped advocate for the recognition and implementation of "Indian Law," a set of ideas and concepts meant to integrate views of and beliefs about mother earth with colonial and republican legal precepts. While the Bolivian state repressed and segregated indigenous people, Titiriku and others in the network of Alcaldes Mayores Particulares (AMPs), or major autonomous mayors, creatively and subversively appropriated the colonial idea of "two nations." Calling Bolivia an "Aymara land," Titiriku advocated for the creation of the Republic of Qullasuyu. Indigenous people, he maintained, were imbued with the right to create the borders of such a republic because, unlike the white "guests" who ran Bolivia, he and his fellow native people "were in their own country."[61] Though his project did not come to fruition, it anticipated and helped lay the groundwork for future mobilizations and provided a forceful rebuke of the main flows of transnational racism through eugenics, mestizaje ideology, and the memory of Indian removal in various parts of the continent.[62] Titiriku's "two republics" project also vividly illustrates both the power and limits of transnationalism. By resisting continental traditions of racist ideology and by seeking to literally redraw Bolivian borders, Titiriku clearly transgressed national boundaries. At the same time, much of his project's genius lay in its clever utilization of national structures and ideals, a clear illustration of how the very idea of transnationalism can seem anachronistic or even threatening.

In chapter three, Lara Putnam provides an intriguing counterpoint that includes significant contrasts and also remarkable similarities with Ari-Chachaki's chapter. With a sprawling map that illustrates the incredible expanse of the circum-Caribbean, and a story that travels beyond the Americas to the seat of the British Empire and back, Putnam describes how in the aftermath of World War I, race and nation conspired to marginalize Black British West Indians in multiple locales. In Costa Rica, Cuba, Panama, the United States, Venezuela, and other American republics, white nationalist legislators marginalized British West Indian laborers, who found themselves increasingly denied access to a large spectrum of political, social, and economic rights and privileges, and increasingly left on the outside looking in when it came to establishing residence, finding work, and even entering a given country. Across and beyond the British Empire, "race and racism set the boundaries of belonging," invariably shutting out people of African descent.[63] Hopes that the British state would provide support or assistance were dashed at every turn. As in the Bolivian case, here the nation functioned as a bitter and repressive reality, even if the borders of this story were multiple, distant, and fully discernible only when studied transnationally.

Although the physical US-Mexico border is seen to be easily crossed and in some cases almost irrelevant in chapter four, Dawson also shows the ideological and political lines separating the two countries to have been so extreme as to have short-circuited an attempted cross-border *indigenista* project. Focusing on the 1940 Primer Congreso Interamericano Indígena (First Inter-American Congress on Indian Life), Dawson describes how *indigenismo* remained forcefully and indelibly shaped by national particularities. This is made clear through the case of peyote, a cactus with hallucinogenic powers. During the early twentieth century, a significant amount of the peyote used in the United States was gathered in Mexico, making peyote "a material expression of transnationalism."[64] Nonetheless, both peyote and its religious uses were understood in dramatically different ways on each side of the border, making it an illustrative example of how and why the Pan-American indigenist project failed, and serving as one more reminder of the stubborn persistence and significance of the nation-state.

Although the Primer Congreso Interamericano Indígena ultimately failed to galvanize transnational indigenist collaborations and networks, the 1951 founding of a pilot coordinating center in Chiapas under the aegis of Mexico's National Indigenist Institute (Instituto Nacional Indigenista, or INI) floundered in different ways. As Stephen Lewis shows in chapter five, the INI's goal of integrating Tseltal and Tsostil Maya communities into the nation was unsuccessful. Some of Mexico's most influential indigenistas and social scientists came to Chiapas, implementing policies and programs meant to serve as an international model for development and "integration" policies. By 1970, the programs had had little effect, and Tesltals and Tsotsils remained excluded from the nation in every meaningful way. As Lewis shows, the failed project illustrates the emptiness of Mexican *mestizaje* discourses, which praise distant historical contributions of indigenous culture while making clear that living and breathing native people have no place in a nation bent on chasing Europeanized ideals of modernity and progress. Considered together with Gregorio Titiriku's unrealized "two republics" project in Bolivia, Lewis's chapter also illustrates how a nation's internal borders—in this case, the lines separating Chiapas from wealthier regions, and those that trapped Mayans in poverty—can be as important as its external ones.

Keeping one foot in Mexico and placing the other in the United States, chapter six, by Elaine Carey, explores how US policy makers employed racial stereotypes to marginalize and criminalize Mexican Americans and Mexicans in the United States. Almost since its creation, the US-Mexico border has witnessed and helped create oppositional categories of US whiteness and Mexican otherness. Throughout the US Southwest, racist definitions and policies were used to limit Mexican access to economic and political resources. Starting in the 1930s, the US Federal Bureau of Narcotics launched an antidrug campaign to demonize Mexicans as deviants who trafficked in drugs and violence, a template that continues to shape contemporary drug policy (not to mention presidential campaigns and political platforms). As Carey shows, the drug wars that took place between the 1930s and 1950s helped reify white supremacy and marginalize and stigmatize Mexican-Americans on the border and throughout the United States, all while dismissing any responsibility or role in the drug trade of white US citizens. Ultimately, Carey shows that it is all but impossible to understand the intertwined histories of drug policy and racism—not only during the 1930s through the 1950s but also today—without traveling to and beyond the border.

A different kind of cross-border exchange involving the United States and Latin America is the focus of chapter seven, where Sheinin explores the dynamic paths blazed by Afro-Venezuelan baseball players in the United States, and African American players in Venezuela, who altered understandings and depictions of Blackness and Latin Americanness in both countries. The making of a Venezuelan *criollo* identity affected the ways that race was understood and represented, Sheinin argues, though that hardly translated romantic ideas about racial harmony into reality or signaled improved quality of life for Afro-Venezuelans. Venezuelan racial categories are more complex and numerous than the stark Black-white dichotomy typified by the infamous "one-drop rule" in the United States, a point that Venezuelans (like counterparts elsewhere in Latin America) often use to suggest an absence of racism at home. Sheinin not only shows the emptiness of that myth but also suggests how the transnational movement of baseball players and flow of news and ideas about baseball helped simultaneously prop up and challenge the idea of a democratic Venezuelan mestizaje.

Chapter eight, by Marc Hertzman, asks why the Filhos de Gandhy Carnival group chose the Mahatma as their namesake and what the group's early history may tell us about the relationship between Bahian politics and culture, and the global circulation of Gandhi as an icon and an ideal. Combining Orientalist imagery and symbols with leftist ideology and eventually Afro-Bahian religion, the Black stevedores who founded the group made Gandhi into something distinctly Brazilian and Bahian. Their creation, the chapter shows, is legible only through historical lenses focused both on the creation and contestation of "Global Gandhi" and local and national politics and culture in Salvador. To create their own Gandhi, the stevedores also drew on longstanding masculinist tropes that were mainly at odds, but also at times surprisingly in line, with Gandhian gender ideals. By tracing the local history of a global icon, the chapter illustrates the complex ways that local and national racial categories and fantasies interact with transnational phenomena.

In chapter nine, Sonja Stephenson Watson examines transnational and transcultural webs of exchange linking the United States, the Caribbean islands, and Panama since the 1960s. With Panamanian *reggae en español* as her lens, Stephenson Watson shows how culture "hybridized and transculturated" as it traversed national and also local boundaries. The story of reggae en español is one that highlights transnational connectivity and exemplifies how the African diaspora crosses national boundaries and forges bonds among Black people throughout the Americas. By tracing these contours, Stephenson Watson shows how music helped Black Panamanians redefine, reimagine, and reinterpret nationalism and national culture.

In chapter ten, working with a different diaspora—Muslims in Argentina—Raanan Rein reconstructs the project to create a mosque in Buenos Aires beginning in the 1940s, during Juan Perón's first presidency, through the "grandiose materialization of the project" in the 1990s under the Carlos Menem administration.[65] In the 1940s, Arab Argentines were stereotyped and demonized, before eventually being typecast in a slightly more positive light as well integrated and financially savvy. Like Jews and the Irish in the United States, over time Arab Argentines became "white," or something close to it. A crucial moment in this transformation came when Perón described Spain's Islamic history as a means for justifying the presence of Muslims in Argentina. As a group understood to be not-African, not-indigenous, and not-mestizo, Arab Argentines complicate the binary categories that pervade much of the public and scholarly discussion of race in Argentina. The successful completion of the Buenos Aires mosque is an example of how a group once stigmatized and marginalized as outsiders to the nation effectively leveraged what Rein calls "racial ambiguity" within Argentina, as well as international ties to Saudi Arabia, which would eventually provide financial support for the mosque. Here, once again, we see the national, the local, and the transnational working not only in concert but also sometimes at different paces and in different ways.

The volume concludes with an evocative piece by Kevin Coleman, in collaboration with Julia Irion Martins, about *Damiana Kryygi*, a 2015 documentary directed by Alejandro Fernández Mouján and set in Argentina, Paraguay, and Germany. The film tells the story of Damiana Kryygi, an indigenous child who survived an 1896 massacre at the hands of mestizo settlers in Paraguay. Ten years later she was sent to a mental hospital in Argentina where she died. A German anthropologist, Robert Lehmann-Nitsche, measured and photographed her before she perished, and in 2010, Paraguay's Aché people claimed her remains from the Museo de La Plata and repatriated them. The film documents how members of her community transformed the artifacts of scientific racism into powerful objects of memory and mobilization. By connecting the history of Paraguayan frontiersmen and European scientists who plundered and expropriated Aché land, culture, and life with the reclaiming a century later of the child's remains, Coleman treats *Damiana Kryygi* as a provocative model of how history and historical knowledge can—and might one day—be made. The film not only connects events across time and national borders but also shows how violence became naturalized as progress, and how that violence was then, in turn, exhumed from the archives so that new historical memories might be generated. Damiana Kryygi's story provides a fitting last chapter to this book and a salient complement and also counterpoint to the maps that pull our spatial coordinates in new directions while decentering nations, regions, and continents. After stretching the narrative to Germany and Argentina, the story—and more crucially, Damiana Kryygi's remains—returns to a now marginalized local center: indigenous land at the heart of generations of expropriation, struggle, and triumph.

CHAPTER ONE

ASIAN MIGRATION, RACIAL HIERARCHIES, AND EXCLUSION IN ARGENTINA, 1890–1920

Benjamin Bryce

I understood them to say that they drew the line at "Turks and Austrians,"
but why they made that discrimination I was unable to discover.

—REGINALD TOWER, BRITISH MINISTER PLENIPOTENTIARY
TO THE ARGENTINE REPUBLIC, FEBRUARY 1912

Silvestre de Marchi arrived in Paris in March 1910. The Argentine chargé
d'affaires and his family had spent a little more than a month traveling by
rail from his post in Tokyo via Russia. In France, a telegram from Victorino
de la Plaza, the Argentine minister of foreign affairs, was waiting for him.
De la Plaza wanted answers for what de Marchi described in his defense
as "the crude and malevolent invention of the newspapers."[1] De la Plaza
had read reports in the *Japan Times*, the *New York Herald*, and the largest
Argentine daily, *La Prensa*, about a speech that de Marchi had given in
his farewell address before setting out on his westward journey to Buenos
Aires. The *Japan Times* had reported that de Marchi spoke of the "vast prospects of his country and the beneficial results of closer intercourse between
the Argentine and Japan."[2] Making reference to the informal gentlemen's
agreement between Japan and the United States signed in 1908 whereby
the Japanese government agreed to limit emigration, de Marchi—reported
the *Japan Times*—claimed that unlike "the great Power in North America which closed its doors," his country was "open to all the rest of the
world and existing for the entire world."[3] *La Prensa*'s editor, Ezequiel Paz,
sounded alarm bells that de Marchi's actions would "channel the stream of
Japanese emigration and Asian emigration in general toward the Argentine
Republic."[4] And he claimed that Argentine policies oppose the "incorporation of ethnic elements that upset the homogeneity of our population."[5] The
paper asserted that "Europeanization" (*la europeización*) was the "supreme

ideal of the Latin American world"[6] and that "we are not the enemies of the yellow race, whose abilities the prosperous and strong Japan has plainly shown: we only want to note that because of the form of its civilization, it is not suitable to meld with the nationalities of the Americas. . . . Not even the ashes of the men of the [Asian] race should perpetually rest far from their homeland."[7]

The outburst in early 1910 was part of a more general anxiety about the perils of Asian immigration shared by journalists, politicians, and officials in Argentina. Starting in the 1890s and into the 1910s, the Directorate General of Immigration and lawmakers looked for ways to prevent Japanese, South Asian, and Chinese immigration through a combination of diplomacy, legislation, and labor market exclusion. This chapter argues that immigration from East and South Asia was a central concern for Argentine officials, lawmakers, and the foreign ministry in the late nineteenth and early twentieth centuries. It demonstrates that Argentina had both a history of Asian immigration and of race-based exclusion before the First World War. In so doing, this chapter casts light on some of the latent contours of Argentine racial thought. Asian migration to Argentina is something often associated with the second half of the twentieth century, and race-based exclusion in the era of mass European immigration has been largely overlooked in the existing historiography.[8] Focusing on the efforts to create both formal and informal methods to enforce race-based exclusion, the concerns about Japanese and South Asian immigrants, and European immigrants' ideas about whiteness and belonging, this chapter contributes to broader discussions about how global migration and local racial ideologies intersected.

In the early twentieth century, Argentine intellectuals, politicians, and immigration officials discussed the nation in racial terms. They asserted it was a white, European, Hispanic nation. Paradoxically, however, they also recognized the presence of a diverse population, which included indigenous peoples, mestizos, and Afro-Argentines.[9] For example, when discussing Argentina in *El porvenir de la América Española* (1910), Manuel Ugarte—an anti-imperialist, socialist writer, and politician—wrote, "The bulk of our population is comprised of the white race of Hispanic origin and that that white race is the essential core, the first base around which the multicolored materials assemble and which have come from all countries from the four corners of the earth."[10] In *Nuestra América* (1903), Carlos Octavio Bunge had a different take on race in his analysis of the national "psychology" of various Spanish American republics. In his diatribe against politicians and the political systems of many countries, he highlighted the racial diversity of Argentina. He described Buenos Aires as "today maybe the most European [city], in terms of race, climate, and customs, of all of Spanish

America," but he also stressed that "indigenous blood abounds in certain semi-white populations of the interior of the Argentine Republic."[11] In noting the demographic decline of Afro-Argentines in the city of Buenos Aires, he explained that "they have mixed [*se han mestizado*], and the white race, as the more vigorous, predominates in mixes of people who see themselves as white."[12] Both Ugarte and Bunge asserted that Argentina was European and also not.

Discussions of the country's whiteness were shaped by popular racial thinking that lauded the transformative power of European immigration and its ability to dilute the preexisting populations through mixing. Yet as Gastón Gordillo notes, the vision of a European nation has long been seen by Argentines as "a haunted and ever-incomplete project, a whiteness that feels under siege, for it permanently confronts the evidence that millions of Argentine citizens bear in their bodies the traces of the non-European substratum of the nation."[13] The growing discussions of potential East and South Asian immigration emerged in this context. A small number of people had arrived, but the majority of this discourse was focused on the imagined potential of future immigration. Between 1902 and 1913, only 759 Japanese and 290 Chinese immigrated to Argentina. In 1912, 612 British subjects from India entered the country.[14] Between 1881 and 1930, more than 5.8 million immigrants entered Argentina.[15] Partially as a result of this massive influx, the population quadrupled between 1869 and 1914, rising from 1.8 million to 7.9 million.[16]

Marilyn Lake and Henry Reynolds have demonstrated how a "global color line" emerged in the late nineteenth century, which demarcated where people—particularly from China, India, and Japan—could and could not migrate.[17] Several historians have illustrated how the United States and the British Empire collaborated in order to stanch what they perceived as an emerging threat to white settler societies.[18] Despite potential consequences to diplomatic relationships, Argentine officials' insistence on the undesirability of Japanese subjects and British subjects from India illustrates how adamant they were that Asian migration and international diplomacy would not place their country on the other side of a global color line.

One cause of the (albeit small) increase in East and South Asian immigration to Argentina included policy changes and stricter exclusion laws elsewhere.[19] The United States and Canada struck separate accords with imperial Japan between late 1907 and early 1908, and the Japanese government agreed to prevent emigration to North America.[20] Similarly in 1908, the Canadian government passed legislation requiring all immigrants to come to the country directly on a "continuous journey" from their country of origin, which was a convoluted way to specifically exclude fellow British subjects from South Asia and for Ottawa to walk a fine line between imperial interests in London and pressures from British Columbian exclusion-ists.[21] In direct response to the Canadian legislation, the US government also ramped up its unofficial policies of South Asian exclusion, but it did not formalize that exclusion until the 1917 Immigration Act that estab-lished an "Asiatic Barred Zone."[22]

Coinciding with the North American gentlemen's agreements, Japanese immigration to Argentina increased from twenty-eight arrivals in 1908 to 251 in 1909.[23] In neighboring Brazil, the first Japanese immigrants in São Paulo came in 1908, and 15,543 people arrived between 1908 and 1914.[24] Similar ripple effects were felt in Peru despite a longer history of Japanese (and Chinese) immigration. The number of Japanese arrivals in Peru more than doubled from approximately 1,250 in 1907 to 2,900 in 1909.[25] One reason that the flows from Japan to different parts of the Americas were connected was that private emigration companies played a large role in re-cruiting workers to send abroad. By 1908 there were more than fifty such companies.[26]

There was an increase in Indian migration to Canada starting in 1907 when the Canadian Pacific Railway specifically promoted immigration from South Asia in response to fears about restrictions of Japanese labor-ers.[27] The swift response of the Canadian government in 1908 and of the US government in 1909 to limit Indian immigration seems to have set the stage for increases in South Asian migration to Argentina. North Ameri-can policies had other global repercussions. In late 1907, German shipping companies sought permission from the German Foreign Office to open a new shipping line between Japan and Argentina. Nevertheless, the German Foreign Office, driven by its own goal of fostering more German-speaking migration to the Southern Cone and concerns about growing Asian in-fluence in world affairs,[28] responded, "We have no interest in Argentina becoming the destination of Japanese emigration," reasoning that such a shipping line "in essence would only serve to encourage emigration from Japan to Argentina."[29]

CALLS FOR EXCLUSION

From the 1890s onward, there were growing efforts in Argentina to exclude East Asian immigrants. Indeed, in Argentina as elsewhere, raced-based ex-clusion, alongside health and gender concerns related to fears about disease and about female morality, gave rise to modern systems of immigration control.[30] Understanding how the Argentine state implemented exclusion-ary ideas and its motivation for doing so adds another dimension to racial ideologies prevalent in the country in the late nineteenth and early twen-tieth centuries. The perceived threat of Asian immigration led most Ar-gentine politicians, officials, and intellectuals to become more entrenched than ever in their view that their country should be populated with only European peoples.

In 1893, Juan Alsina, the director general of immigration, wrote an extensive report about East Asian immigration to other countries in South America, particularly Peru and Brazil, and he outlined the reasons why these migrants should not find their way to Argentina. As Carl Solberg notes, "A man of national influence, Alsina composed reports that were widely read and that were regularly cited in newspaper articles and editorials."[31] Alsina worried about companies importing Chinese workers as cheap labor, and he asserted, "They are not suited to the Argentine Republic."[32] He added, "The Republic receives the European . . . because we have created a nation whose purpose is to maintain Christian civilization and make it prosper, rejecting therefore any human race that could introduce seeds to the contrary and rejecting the arrival of that disadvantageous condition in which Asians entered the United States, Peru, or Brazil, which was to replace slaves and not to be citizens."[33] Indeed, Alsina and others often focused on the unsuitability of Chinese laborers and they cited other examples in the Americas—in addition to the desire to attract only European immigrants—as the reason to deny entry.

Alsina continued to write about the dangers of non-European immigration for the next two decades. In 1903, as Japanese emigration companies began to contact Argentine officials about sending laborers to Argentina, Alsina wrote to the minister of foreign affairs, that "indeed we have a fundamental interest in preventing the incorporation and assimilation of those elements, which in general could be considered as inferior to the average European."[34] Taking aim at potential Japanese migrants, Alsina added, "Although certain Asian peoples have reached a high level of civilization . . . [they remain] nonetheless inferior to European civilization. . . . That does not change the fundamental principle of inferiority or, if one prefers, of unfavorable difference between the average Europeans and the most advanced Asians."[35] In his 1910 book, *La inmigración en el primer siglo de la independencia* (Immigration in the first century after independence), Alsina articulated more clearly than before a desire to select immigrants based on country of origin in order to maintain "the homogeneity of the Argentine population."[36] In his view, indigenous peoples from Peru, Bolivia, and Brazil, along with people of African origin, could not come to Argentina, "nor could we permit Asians to enter as a numerous group because that would alter the homogeneity of our population, which is clearly prescribed and which should be only of European origin."[37]

Alsina's concerns about Asian and other non-European immigrants had antecedents in the very formation of Argentina's pro-immigration policies of the nineteenth century. In a revised preface to his 1852 *Bases y puntos de partida para la organización política de la República Argentina*, Juan Bautista Alberdi warned in 1873,

> If the population of six million [*sic*] Anglo-Americans who began the Republic of the United States, instead of growing through immigration from the free and civilized Europe, had instead populated the country with Chinese or Asiatic Indians, or with Africans, or with Ottomans, would it be the same country of free men that it is today? There is no soil so blessed as to be able, with its own virtue, to turn grass into wheat. Good wheat can grow out of bad wheat, but not from barley. To govern is to populate, but without forgetting that to populate can also bring pestilence and ignorance and enslave, depending on what population is transplanted, if instead of being civilized immigrants are backward, poor, or corrupt.[38]

In addition to lauding the transformative benefits that immigrants from the United Kingdom, Germany, France, and Switzerland would bring to Argentina, Alberdi staked out an early vision for future exclusionary policies.[39]

Another example of Argentine concerns about the dangers of Asian migration and calls to exclude came in April 1912, against the backdrop of increasing South Asian immigration. *La Nación*, one of Buenos Aires's main daily newspapers, published an article about the immigration restriction taking place in the United States, and the author, Alfredo Elías, flagged that country as an instructive model for Argentina. Drawing on the ideas of Jeremiah Jenks, board member of the United States Immigration Commission, Elías bluntly said, "The Chinese do not fit in US social and political institutions and it is better for them, the North Americans, and for the Chinese and for the entire world, that Asians stay put where they came from."[40]

In August of the same year, *La Prensa* reported that the Directorate General of Immigration had received a request from Colombo, Ceylon, about "the possibility of giving work to over 5,000 natives."[41] The paper reported that it informed the "Ceylonese institution" about "the terms of our laws that encourage immigration, which refer exclusively the European races" and the recent stance of Argentine authorities "regarding immigration of another origin, such as Hindu immigration, an antecedent that can help avoid an unnecessary trip for the Ceylonese."[42] One of the city's main German-language newspapers, the *Argentinisches Tageblatt*, also reported on this possible immigration, and it concluded that "we cannot make use of this sort of people; our origins (*Völkerkarte*) are already colorful enough."[43]

Argentine anxieties about East and South Asian immigration could be seen in other ways. In an interview with *La Nación* in July 1910, an Argentine journalist asked a visiting Japanese government minister about his country's intention to send emigrants abroad because it had an excess of population. The minister responded that China had 400 million people,

Russia 160 million, and the United States 100 million. Revealing an air of imperial competition, he added, "Surrounded by such powerful nations, it is essential that the population of the empire reach 100 million. That population should not be scattered over the face of the earth but rather be concentrated, as much as possible, in the vicinity of one and the same place."[44] The reporter sought assurances that that meant there would be no Japanese immigration to Argentina, to which the minister responded, "Even if there were, it would very insignificant."[45] It is worth noting that Japanese immigration made up only a fraction of a percentage of the total influx of foreigners to the country over the preceding decade.[46] Nonetheless, the topic attracted as much attention as economic relations in the interview with the visiting dignitary.

In the decade before the First World War, Japanese emigration agencies and the Japanese foreign ministry in fact did begin to inquire with Argentine officials about the possibility of fostering Japanese emigration to the country. These inquiries and the arrival of some Japanese laborers sparked several behind the scenes efforts in the Directorate General of Immigration and the Argentine foreign ministry. In one request, N. Okoshi, representing the Japanese Society of South America, asked the Argentine consul in Tokyo if the state would give a large land concession somewhere in the territories of Formosa, Misiones, or Chaco in northern Argentina to cultivate rice, tea, and silkworms. Okoshi suggested that in these semitropical zones, "perhaps there could be two harvests per year, like in our Formosa [Taiwan]."[47] In 1906, Herbert Shepherd, the Japanese consul in Argentina (likely a British merchant or Anglo-Argentine representing the country rather than a Japanese national), reported that he had arranged for a contract for thirty workers, noting, "This contract is the outcome of my propaganda in favor of the employment of Japanese in certain spheres of activity in aiding the progress of this country [Argentina] and is drawn up in favorable terms for the prospective immigrants, who by its provisions, are not only on par with workmen of other nationalities but the condition of their arrival and placing are more advantageous than that of other immigrants.[48]

In the early twentieth century, Argentine officials in Japan sent reports to Buenos Aires about the potential threat of Japanese emigration. In 1903, Alfonso de Laferrère, the consul general in Yokohama (Japan's largest port), raised concerns about an emigration project destined for Argentina. He notified his foreign minister that a representative from the Transoceanic Immigration Company had set sail for Buenos Aires "with the goal of establishing a stream of Japanese immigration to Argentina," something he considered "a serious danger for our country."[49] Making a direct link between the benefits of European immigration and the dangers of Japanese immigration, he asserted, "While all other Argentine consulates abroad encourage European emigration toward the country, this one needs to dedicate all of its attention and zeal in the complete opposite direction."[50]

Juan Alsina followed up on Laferrère's warning with the Argentine foreign minister, writing, "it seems, in fact, that the emigration companies in that country have directed their attention to our Republic."[51] He noted that he had received other inquiries, and he contended that "Asians, particularly the Chinese and Japanese, are frugal . . . they can meet their necessities with low salaries, much below those needed by European workers. That is to say, for businessmen it will be cheaper to employ Japanese and Chinese workers than Europeans."[52] He warned, "Therefore Japanese workers and farmers would be a source of overwhelming competition for Europeans and would displace them entirely."[53]

In 1907 the Argentine vice-consul in Yokohama made a similar argument, warning that such immigration to Argentina "would be harmful; the European, no matter how restrained and frugal he may be, as is the case with Italian and Spanish workers, could never live with the infinitely little that a Japanese worker can live. Moreover, while stressing that I am beyond any form of discrimination against any race, I believe that the contact between whites and yellows, of an inferior class, would easily produce conflicts, as is the case in the United States and as recently occurred in English Canada as well."[54] He concluded, "I do not dare, by the way, to resolve such a serious question and whose implications we need to consider calmly. I can only say that the Japanese would love to direct their emigration toward Argentina. Thousands of Japanese are ready to depart, only waiting for word that they can come."[55]

In all of these discussions, Argentine officials merged concerns about Chinese and Japanese immigration as one and the same problem. On occasion, they created explanations for recent industrial progress in Japan but as part of an ongoing effort to construct an "Asiatic" danger. Those fears about East Asia would soon expand to include British colonial subjects from South Asia. Argentine officials, politicians, and newspaper editors made little, if any, distinction between these groups. In both the public sphere and the foreign ministry, Argentina began to lay the foundations for race-based policies of exclusion even though they did not formalize them with legislation.[56]

THE BOUNDARIES OF INCLUSION

By 1912 other groups of migrants began to catch the eye of Argentine immigration officials and appear in the press. Over the course of the year, 612 Sikh laborers arrived, which was almost as many as the total number of Japanese laborers in the previous decade. A small group of Austro-Hungarian subjects that Argentine officials labeled as "gypsies" also came in July 1912, and they were denied entry to the country.[57] In the case of South Asians, officials and employers used a mix of border control, labor market discrimination, and diplomatic solutions. These new approaches marked a policy shift compared to the previous concerns over Japanese and Chinese immigration. The growing presence of Ottoman subjects shaped the British and Austrian response to this exclusion; they took particular issue with the boundaries of inclusion and exclusion that Argentine officials were drawing. While immigration from the Ottoman Empire had a longer history, 115,217 Ottoman subjects entered Argentina between 1904 and 1913.[58] These migrants came mainly from Syria, Lebanon, and Palestine and were overwhelmingly Eastern Christians.[59]

The first Sikh men arrived in Buenos Aires aboard an Italian steamer in late January 1912.[60] Word of mouth about high wages, available land, and open immigration policies in Argentina as well as reports in Punjabi newspapers attracted these men to the southwest Atlantic.[61] *La Nación* reported that although these fifty-nine men "do not comply with the respective laws regarding nothing more than European immigration, they have been permitted to enter, under the express condition that this does not create a precedent for another occasion."[62] Immigration officials denied the first and all subsequent arrivals access to the Hotel of Immigrants, a facility that provided new arrivals free lodging and food for five days, access to work placement opportunities, telegraph and mail services to facilitate employment, and medical care so as to ensure their success in the country.[63] The British minister plenipotentiary, Reginald Tower, wrote, "Owing to the refusal of the Argentine authorities to allow these men to enjoy the privileges granted to all immigrants by the laws in force, viz., lodging in the Immigrants' Hotel and free transportation up country, it has been a matter of considerable difficulty to find work for these men."[64] Argentine employers also regularly denied employment opportunities to South Asians. Turning a cold shoulder to South Asian jobseekers in fact appeared to be part of the Argentine approach to exclusion; after months of closing doors on Sikh laborers, Ernesto Bosch told Tower in July 1912 that "it was so evident that they could not find employment in this country that the only solution appeared to be that the Indian Government should repatriate all those now in Argentina."[65]

In mid-1912, Manuel Cigorraga, Alsina's replacement as director general of immigration, sent a circular to every shipping company represented in the city.[66] He urged them to refuse passages to any Asians seeking to immigrate to Argentina.[67] According to Cigorraga, the authors of the mid-nineteenth-century constitution knew well that "the European-Asian cross produced bad physical outcomes, and even worse moral outcomes."[68] He reasoned, "The recently arrived Indians cannot find permanent work because of their ineptitude and innate spirit of idleness."[69] Ezequiel Paz, in

La Prensa, praised Cigorraga, writing, "The exotic characteristics of Asian morality, so obviously distant from our own ethics, means that these individuals are not adaptable to our society, reason enough to make sure that they do not come to our country."[70] The editor of *La Nación* worried that the approach was not strong enough and that the companies could appeal the rejection. It asserted that, "Hindu immigration is, in fact, pernicious and antagonistic to our national type. Their idle habits and their ethnic deficiencies make them unsuitable for a country that seeks its development through immigrants whose physical and moral conditions are suitable for assimilation."[71]

Argentine officials were relatively successful at stopping South Asian immigration while Japanese immigration continued. For example, according to Argentine records, only 111 *Hindúes* arrived between 1921 and 1924, whereas 1,253 Japanese and 71 Chinese arrived.[72] One reason for this difference was the support that British imperial authorities offered to help stop emigration at the source. The diplomatic (and economic) connections that existed between Argentina and the United Kingdom surely helped. Argentine ministers had a close relationship with the British representative, Reginald Tower, in a way that they did not with the Japanese consul, and the United Kingdom was Argentina's most important trading partner and foreign investor.[73] Those personal relationships and economic interests appear to have had an impact on the extent that Argentina could prevent certain migratory groups. One tangible way that the British government took an active role in deterring emigration is that the India Office decided to stop issuing passports to those planning on leaving India for Argentina.[74]

In July 1912, in the midst of the concerns over South Asian immigration, a group of twenty-eight Roma from Bielcza in the Austro-Hungarian Empire (a city in present-day Poland sixty-five kilometers [forty miles] east of Krakow) were turned away at the port of Buenos Aires.[75] Cigorraga justified his decision by contending that "European countries reject gypsies, and it would not be possible to allow this co-existence (*convivencia*) in our country, which seeks to increase its population and mold it with elements that are homogeneous in their habits and moral tendencies. We cannot accept what the civilized peoples of Europe repudiate."[76] *La Prensa* supported Cigorraga, and took aim not only at the Roma but also the recent South Asian immigration, writing that Argentina did not need "elements of races and civilizations that are incapable of feeling, thinking and living like Argentines."[77]

The German-language newspaper published in Buenos Aires that took aim at possible Ceylonese immigrants took a similar, exclusionary stance against these Roma. It warned that the supposed boilermakers and tinkers would soon return to their "wandering spirit" and would encourage oth-

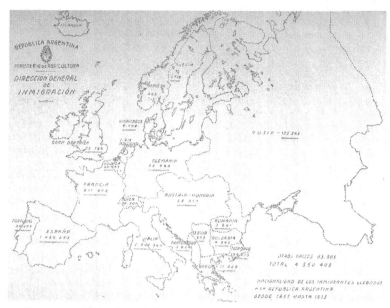

FIGURE I.I. Nationality of the Immigrants Arrived in the Argentine Republic, 1857–1913. Dirección General de Inmigración, *Memoria de la Dirección General de Inmigración correspondiente al año 1913* (Buenos Aires: Talleres Gráficos del Ministerio de Agricultura, 1915), 51.

er members of their race (*Stammesgenossen*) to come. The editors asserted, "Argentina is not a country that needs to accept small tribes (*Völkerreste*), especially those whose history and lack of adaptation to other peoples can been seen over centuries."[78] The opinions of European immigrants in a city made up of so many foreign-born residents are particularly relevant. Indeed, 46 percent of the 1.2 million residents of Buenos Aires in 1910 were foreign nationals.[79] The views expressed in the ethnic press show the role of immigrants in supporting the aims of Argentine elites in making a white Argentina.

The 1912 arrival of South Asians—and the potential that that first trickle would become a steady flow—made Argentine officials reflect on the acceptability of the growing numbers of Ottoman immigrants, and by and large they decided that there was a marked difference between these migrants from the eastern Mediterranean (western Asia) and those from South and East Asia. The presence of British subjects from India, and British and Anglo-Argentine efforts to support them, forced Argentine immigration officials and politicians to discuss more explicitly the boundaries of whiteness that they applied in fostering European immigration. Until then, Ottomans were geographically one step further than eastern and southern European immigrants. Yet, as new migration from South Asia appeared more likely, Ottomans' geographic origins and religious differences became a sort of conceptual borderland between Europe and Asia.

In response to new South Asian immigration, officials at the Directorate General of Immigration bent over backward to assert that Ottoman subjects were European. In its 1912 annual report, for example, the Directorate General included all Ottomans who arrived that year in the category of "Europeans" but the Persian, Indian, Chinese, and Japanese arrivals in the category of "Asians."[80] The map, included in the 1913 annual report, went out of its way to assert that Ottoman subjects were European, and it was surely a response to the recent arrival of British subjects from South Asia. The total number of immigrants from each country since 1857 is written beside or below the country's name. All 130,939 Ottoman subjects were crunched into the empire's European territory on the border with Bulgaria and Greece, and unlike the previous year, their nationality was listed as Turkish rather than Ottoman.

With the growing diversity of migratory groups in the decade before the First World War, Argentine officials felt compelled to redefine their goal of fostering wide-scale European immigration. Ottoman subjects, who had been arriving for decades, were included within the boundaries of Europeanness, at least compared to others from South and East Asia. Roma, like South Asians, were excluded, and various proposals for legislative reform singled out Roma as an unwelcome group.[81]

ANGLO-ARGENTINES AND "UNDESIRABLE" IMMIGRATION

In Buenos Aires, Anglo-Argentines—both British immigrants and the Argentine-born children or grandchildren of those immigrants—and the British minister plenipotentiary were critical of the Argentine opposition to the new influx of Indian migrants in 1912. Ottoman subjects became a particular target of scorn, largely because they were admitted in large numbers, whereas British subjects from India were rejected on the grounds of not being European. Anglo-Argentines navigated between Argentine national and British imperial identities. They argued for the superiority of Sikhs over Ottomans, and they founded their case on how that racial and cultural vision would benefit Argentina. In several articles in English-language newspapers in the city, Anglo-Argentines argued that Sikhs were Aryans and Caucasians, and therefore whiter and more attractive for Argentina than Ottoman Syrians. The views of Anglo-Argentines offer a helpful case study to understand how preferred immigrant groups thought about other groups (in addition to the previously discussed case of German speakers' views of Ceylonese and Roma immigration). In an era of cultural pluralism, it was the negotiation between all members of Argentine society that set the boundaries of belonging.[82] The views of one group—which took a special interest in South Asian migration because of their shared British subjecthood—reveal some of the racial ideologies that existed in Buenos Aires in this period. Their perspective adds depth to how whiteness was a multidimensional and changing construction in the early twentieth century.

The complaints of Anglo-Argentines and the British minister about Ottoman immigration and their initial defense of South Asians brought the language of anthropological, racial science to the forefront of discussions about immigrant selection in Argentina. The Anglo-Argentine stance also illustrated how they thought of themselves as both Argentines and British imperial subjects. In the beginning, they lauded the value of British colonial subjects for Argentine society and in particular when compared to other groups coming to the country. Nevertheless, as more South Asians arrived over the course of 1912, many English-speaking immigrants and Argentines of British heritage came down on the side of Argentine elites, talking about the reasons why future South Asian immigration should be cut off at the source.

Despite initial support, the city's two English-language dailies soon worried that British colonial subjects and Argentine opposition to them would negatively affect other British interests in the country. Describing the first Sikhs who arrived in January 1912 as "of the Aryan type," the editors of the *Standard*, one of the city's two main English-language newspapers, argued that "the people of the North West are in culture, morality and industry quite as good as the mass of the 'white' immigrants received and often fairer skinned and redder haired."[83] It added, "Except for a turban they dress in European style and are hardly more exotic than the Naps[84] and Syrians we have already."[85]

The paper also contended, "Immigrants from Northern India especially Afghans and Sikhs are more likely to merge with the Argentine nation and to bring in stricter ideas of honesty and morality than yellow men and some of the races of the Mediterranean."[86] The editors advocated for South Asians and against other groups for the apparent benefit of Argentina. They pitched to their readers an idea uncommon in the United Kingdom about the racial superiority and whiteness of Punjabis. Yet in the context of Argentina, and against the backdrop of growing Ottoman immigration, it was the stance that both the *Standard* and the *Buenos Aires Herald* initially took.

The South Asian arrivals brought to light a specific constellation of Argentine ideas about racial mixing and whitening the national body. M. A. Farías, who according to British officials was involved in recruiting South Asians to Argentina,[87] published an article in English in the *Buenos Aires Herald*, denouncing the Directorate General of Immigration's treatment of Sikhs. He relied on the trope of South Asians as superior to Ottoman subjects and to some European immigrants. In denying the first South Asians access to the Hotel of Immigrants when they arrived in late January 1912, the directorate—in Farías's view—"neglected to give them that hospitality which is afforded to other nationalities, including the Turks, Arabs, Syrians, and the very offscouring of the international sewers of Europe. This is a scandal of the first magnitude . . . [and] for the fair name of the Argentine Republic."[88] The editor of the *Standard* similarly argued that "the Department of Immigration does not in any way oppose the influx of a large and increasing number of Syrians, who in considerable proportion wander over the Republic as pedlars, and who, though as industrious and thrifty as the Hindoos, are certainly inferior, in some respects, to the latter in their habits and moral qualities." [89] A concern about mobility, which likely drew from a longer tradition of deriding indigenous mobility, was at the core of the *Standard*'s complaints about the unsuitability of Ottoman migrants to Argentina.

The *Standard* also complained that "the [shipping] agents might also remind the Director that Asiatics from all parts of Asia, besides British India, as well as from Africa, are freely admitted into this country."[90] Thomas Bell, the editor of the *Buenos Aires Herald*, pointed out that over the past decades, "Chinese, Japanese, Negroes, Negroids, Turks, and Tartars have come to this port and landed without question. But, when a troop of British subjects, seduced by Argentine propaganda-mongers, arrive on these shores, they are left to starve."[91] These Anglo-Argentines raised an interesting point about race-based exclusion; although there were some behind the scenes efforts to prevent Japanese immigration, in 1912 the Argentine state did indeed come down harder against South Asian immigrants. Nonetheless, these papers advocated a contradictory stance. They opposed race-based exclusion when applied to British colonial subjects but appeared to welcome it when it came to East Asians, Ottomans, Africans, and Tartars.

In addition to the comparisons with Ottoman immigration made by English-language, Buenos Aires newspapers, the British minister in the capital city often criticized the Argentine rejection of South Asians but acceptance of Ottoman subjects. In his early correspondence about how Manuel Cigorraga denied Sikh laborers access to the Hotel of Immigrants, Tower quipped to London: "I refrained from pointing out to Dr Bosch [the Argentine foreign minister] the obvious inconsequence of the attitude of the Argentine Republic in allowing large numbers of Ottoman subjects, Syrians etc. to enter without restriction, and, as far as I know, to use the Immigrants' Hotel without cavil."[92] That comment and the situation it described brings to light both Argentine and British ideas of whiteness (but not necessarily Anglo-Argentine ones). Tower reasoned that since Argentina welcomed Ottoman immigrants, Sikhs were hardly any different. Argentine policy makers' openness to Ottoman subjects but rejection of British ones (from South Asia) upended Tower's vision of the European order.

It is worth noting that Tower's first diplomatic posting was in Constantinople (1885–1892), and he surely carried with him ideas about European political and racial hierarchies to his new posts in Latin America (first in Mexico starting in 1906 and then Argentina in 1910).[93] The *Standard* summed up Tower's position regarding Cigorraga's denying South Asians entry to the Hotel of Immigrants, writing, "The British position is that since Turkish Asiatics not of the Caucasian but Semitic race, and Moslems, as well as Moors, Algerians, Egyptians and other non-Europeans not so closely related to the white races as the Indo-Germanic[94] people of Northern India, are admitted, there is no reason why these not quite so dark Aryans should be rejected."[95]

Despite their initial support of South Asian immigration (and their criticism of Ottomans), the city's two English-language newspapers within months of their praise of Sikhs began instead to advocate for exclusion at the borders and the repatriation of any already in the country. Speaking of an "Indian invasion" in June 1912, the editor of the *Standard* wrote, "We have previously expressed the opinion that this class of immigrant is totally unsuited to this country. They are British subjects, and on that account the British community is being urged to come to their aid. The truth must be confessed, however, that these sons of India are not welcomed in any English-speaking country. Australia will have none of them, they are banned from South Africa, the doors of Canada are shut against them."[96] It is interesting to note that the paper linked Argentina to several British settler societies, highlighting three British dominions but not the British colonies of Trinidad, Guyana, and Jamaica, which were much more common destinations for South Asian migrants, albeit primarily indentured, Hindu laborers.

The competing positions held by Argentine and British officials and by Anglo-Argentines illustrate what Matthew Frye Jacobson has described as the "seemingly natural but finally unstable logic of race."[97] The debates about Ottomans' and South Asians' degree of undesirability highlight the fluidity of racial categories in Argentina. In addition, the racial ideologies that these groups followed—Anglo-Argentines first accepting then opposing South Asians, Argentine elites rejecting South Asians more than Japanese, or state officials turning away Austro-Hungarian Roma but accepting Ottoman Syrians—were inconsistent. Yet slippage and inconsistencies are in fact common occurrences.

The *Standard* made a series of climatic arguments in an attempt to galvanize the support of Anglo-Argentines behind its position and to put pressure on Reginald Tower to enlist the British government to help Argentine authorities prevent future emigration from India.[98] It wrote that "the 'mild Hindoo' compares favourably, in obedience to authority and in general character, with a large proportion of the immigrants from Europe and Syria . . . we are, however, of the opinion that, in the interest of the Hindoos themselves, the British authorities in India should endeavour to prevent their emigration to this country, by making it generally known among them that this is not a place for people of their race."[99] Discussing a group who had come into particularly tough times and for which many Anglo-Argentines were raising funds to relieve their distress, the paper unsympathetically countered that the "Hindoos...have discovered that they are unable to adapt themselves to the conditions of the country; the climate, especially at this time of the year, is uncongenial for them, the work for which immigrants are needed differs greatly from that to which they are accustomed and for which they are fitted, and the peculiar regulations relative to the 'caste' to which they are subjected creates difficulties for them as regards the means of subsistence and prevents their assimilation or intimate association with other inhabitants of the Republic."[100] It is worth noting that the South Asians were having difficulties in the climate of the Argentine winter because they were without shelter; any person born in Britain would have surely struggled outside in Buenos Aires in late June (winter) as well.

The next week, the *Standard*'s editor added that rather than linguistic or religious differences, "the chief objection to this class of immigration is their unsuitability to our climatic conditions. As farm labourers they would quickly succumb to the rain, cold and sudden changes of temperature which do not exist in India."[101] Yet the editor also quickly returned to more explicit racial arguments, pointing out that South Asians "would be willing to accept work in this country at a rate of pay on which Europeans or their descendants could not manage to exist."[102] He concluded, "They are not in some ways as big a menace as the 'Yellow Peril,' but the very fact that their arrival in wholesale quantities would tend to lower the present rate of wages, the fact that whatever money they manage to save will not be spent in Argentina, but carried back to their own land makes them undesirable."[103] Considering the widespread practice of Italian sojourning in Argentina, with the express purpose of saving money and returning to Italy (or remitting it while working), to which Argentines did not seem to object, the critique of South Asians, who showed no inclination of wanting to return to India, seems like a thinly veiled attempt to conceal racial prejudice.

THE MAKING OF A WHITE ARGENTINA

By expanding the historiographic conversation about immigration to Argentina to include racialized groups from Asia and discussions about the very boundaries of Asia and Europe, this chapter highlights an important strand of Argentine racial thought in the early twentieth century. How Argentines discussed the suitability of Japanese, South Asian, Chinese, and Ottoman migrants for a country that was receiving millions of European laborers sheds light on competing racial ideologies and ideas about racial "improvement" through immigration. Paying attention to small groups of Asians and the fears that they could increase in number casts new light on the well-explored elite visions about the relationship between European immigration and indigenous, mestizo, and Afro-Argentines. It offers a broader picture of how racial ideologies influenced and fed off debates about immigration to the country.

For most Argentine politicians, intellectuals, and officials, the realization that the same forces that brought mass immigration from Europe could also bring growing waves of immigration from Asia solidified their views that their country was and should be populated by Europeans. They feared that non-European immigrants would undermine the supposed benefits of wide-scale European immigration, which according to Argentine elites would stamp out the mestizo, indigenous, and colonial legacies of the country.[104] As a result, from the 1890s to the 1910s, immigration officials and the foreign ministry worked to discourage or prevent emigrants from leaving Japan and India. Those who did come, however, also shaped the discussions about the boundaries of inclusion and exclusion. Responding in particular to British pressure over the rights of colonial subjects, Argentine officials drew a line east of the Ottoman Empire beyond which future citizens should not come.

Across the Americas, the language of selection and racial improvement came to influence immigration policies as national borders hardened between the 1880s and outbreak of the First World War.[105] In Argentina, this did not lead to formal legislation banning or limiting certain groups based on country of origin or race. Yet Asian migration was an important concern for Argentine officials, journalists, and the foreign ministry. In instances when it appeared that there would be an increase in the number of a given group—because a small contingent arrived or because an emigration agency contacted the Argentine state—politicians and bureaucrats took steps to informally deter Asian immigration. The concerns about Asian immigration reveals that for Argentine elites in the early twentieth century, mass migration could not only help transform and whiten the national body but also undermine that very project.

INTERSECTIONS, BARRIERS, AND BORDERS IN GREGORIO TITIRIKU'S REPUBLIC OF QULLASUYU

Waskar Ari-Chachaki

On the morning of August 1, 1925, Gregorio Titiriku discovered that he could not enter La Paz's main plaza because he was an Indian. Accompanied by ten Indian *apoderados* (indigenous legal representatives) from Potosí and Chuquisaca, he was on his way to meet with his lawyer about a lawsuit against the landlord of a hacienda. Titiriku was an indigenous intellectual who represented the concerns and struggles of many peasants. He was also a member of the Alcaldes Mayores Particulares (AMP), or major autonomous mayors, a large network of indigenous activists who promoted "Indian Law." It was an amorphous concept that the AMP invented to incorporate their views of mother earth with their ideas about older colonial and republican legislation. It reflected traditional legal concepts related to land, territory, nation, faith, religion, and rights. It was never adopted by the Bolivian state. A policeman stopped Titiriku on the street and told him that he could go no further dressed as an Indian. Titiriku explained that he was unaware of any new regulations, and furthermore, the Potosí Indians had traveled twenty days on foot and by train from their local village to get to La Paz.[1] When Titiriku insisted on continuing toward the main plaza, he was taken to the police station and charged with "attempting to break the law."[2]

It was not new or unusual for indigenous people in Bolivian cities to experience this type of harassment. The segregation of plazas had begun in colonial times, and it continued in many postcolonial Bolivian towns and cities. It had also been frequently resisted.[3] In the 1920s, municipal and national laws institutionalized this de facto segregation. President Bautista Saavedra—the leader the Republican Party—signed an executive order forbidding indigenous peoples from "walk[ing] in the main plaza," particularly because he did not want Indians to be visible during the 1925 celebration of Bolivia's first centennial of independence.[4] Alcides Arguedas, the most influential elite Bolivian intellectual of the time, argued that this type of segregation was the best way to "achieve modernity and progress."[5]

The emergence of legislated segregation in Bolivia represented a quest for modernity that was expressed through practices that included prohibiting Indians and *cholas* (mostly urban indigenous women) from riding streetcars, banning Indians from the central plaza, prohibiting Indian street vendors, and controlling the overall circulation of indigenous people in the cities. Through such policies, the ruling elite attempted to domesticate the country's populace, the vast majority of which was indigenous. The elite developed an authoritarian version of modernity that denigrated Indianness and could be used as an instrument of domestication and self-empowerment for the white-mestizo minority. These policies and their historical context reveal intersections, barriers, and borders of race. This was Titiriku's negative experience of urban life in La Paz; rejected in multiple contexts, he also saw other AMP activists and indigenous people being degraded. La Paz was deeply mired in the colonial legacy, and elites in the city viewed the Indian population as inferior to other groups of people.

Titiriku helped position ethnic politics and anti-racial activism at the core of indigenous political struggles during the first half of the twentieth century. In this chapter, I illustrate how he represents a distinct kind of indigenous activist motivated not by class concerns but by an interest in creating an ethnic, cultural, and spiritual revival of Indians. Although Titiriku wanted to assert his and others' agency through Indian Law, he was also providing a vehicle to indigenous peoples to deal with racism. He epitomizes the work of an AMP activist before the 1952 National Revolution, focusing on ethnic politics when other movements, many of them Marxist, attempted to erase indigeneity in the interest of class-based politics. Titiriku and the other AMPs were the precursors to the ethnic revival of the 1990s, which in turn led to the rise of Evo Morales and the formal creation of a plurinational state in Bolivia.

Born in the ayllus (autonomous economic and political indigenous local governments) at the shores of Lake Titikaka, Titiriku went to the city of La Paz to serve the goals of the apoderado and *cacique* movement in the 1920s. In contrast to the dominant idea that only elite and educated people were fit for modernity,[6] Titiriku argued that modernity did not conform to a single model and that Indians should have their own modernization project since most Bolivians perceived themselves particularly sidelined in a region already marginalized by nonindigenous elites in the Americas and beyond. Those elites tied modernity to whiteness, in stark contrast to native cultures. Although constantly contested and supported only weakly through state policies during most of the twentieth century, segregation was highly effective in shaping the lives of subaltern groups. An important aspect of Titiriku's decolonization project was his reinforcement of the notion of an Indian nation, which he referred to as a nation of *jaqis* (indigenous peoples) or Qullas, and he called for the creation of the Republic of Qullasuyu. "We should enforce the border of the Republic of Qullasuyu," he stated, suggesting that Indians had a special right to create such borders because they "were in their own country" unlike the "*q'aras* [whites] who were there as guests."[7] This was a reaction to the power that people of Spanish ancestry wielded and that drew from centuries of oppression of Aymara and other indigenous peoples.

Titiriku nonetheless contemplated anti-racism more as a cultural revolution than as separatism. For Titiriku, "Qullasuyu is the land of jaqis and because of that we have the right to speak and we should not let q'aras dominate us." The proposal that Titiriku promoted portrayed a struggle between jaqis and q'aras, between dominant and subordinate groups in which race was a defining feature. Questioning segregationist policies, the activist intellectual AMPs addressed the "racial regulatory system" embedded in Bolivian society from a subaltern perspective.[8]

To ilustate his anti-racism Titiriku insisted that Bolivia consisted of two entities, the "white Republic" and the "Indian Republic." This discourse contributed to the construction of a strong fraternity among the networks of the AMP.[9] Operating within the ideological context of the 1920s and 1930s, the AMP mobilized the discourse of two republics based on ideas of Indian Law and equality, both of which were already being widely used and discussed by Santos Marka T'ula's indigenous network, another group of indigenous activists, especially after the 1932–1935 Chaco War.[10] Titiriku's discourse, however, was more explicit, using the idea of two republics to confront Bolivia's social inequality and to illustrate Indians' aspirations. Titiriku advocated for Indians and their lands to be defended and protected. He argued that some ideas from the sixteenth-century Laws of the Indies better represented indigenous rights in context of twentieth-century Bolivia. He thus blended elements from the Laws of the Indies and Republican laws with his own ideas to form a political discourse that he called the Indian Law.

Like Marka T'ula, Tititriku was interested in equality and anti-racism but with an Aymara worldview. Marka T'ula was one of the creators of an earlier indigenous network from which Tititriku would emerge in the 1930s. In opposing ideas inherent to the republican law, like individual property, the AMP made a clear choice to emphasize religion in Indian Law. Indeed, in a petition to the Ministry of Education and Indigenous Affairs, Tititriku asked indigenous communities to create *escuelas particulares* (autonomous indigenous schools), taught in Aymara or Quechua, to help first peoples' collective well-being (*el vivir bien de todos*). Titiriku sought equality in the context of education and opportunity but also emphasized the indigenous notion of collective well-being (*sumaqamaña*), which introduced traditional notions of justice, equality, and harmony with mother earth and nature.[11] Titiriku combined the liberal notion of equality with the Aymara notion of collective well-being.[12]

THE CHALLENGES OF "MODERN BOLIVIA"

Municipal and national segregation regulations are crucial to understanding Titiriku's life. Segregation in La Paz was often made visible on streetcars. When streetcars, owned by the British-run Bolivian General Enterprise, started to run in 1909, Indians were not allowed to board them.[13] As part of elite policies to segregate *cholos* (a term for those of mostly Indian heritage who embraced nonindigenous dress and rejected speaking Aymara in public) and Indians, the municipality of La Paz issued a regulation on the use of streetcars in 1925 that prohibited passengers from carrying bags in first and second class and exclusively reserved first class for *decent people* (meaning mostly whites). The 1925 municipal resolution did not focus on Indians, but rather on the maids, cooks, and other cholas who carried their bags onto streetcars. Ironically, not only were the maids and cooks working for elites but their bags often contained groceries for their employers. In response to these orders, the cooks' and maids' unions demonstrated outside the municipal offices. The protests were led, in part, by Aymara cholas.

Despite the rules, Gregorio Titiriku sometimes took the streetcar on Tuesdays when it had fewer passengers. He was allowed to ride in the very back of second class because his wife was an acquaintance of the driver's wife. The streetcar driver told him, "We are breaking the law, go to the back and make sure no one sees you." When Titiriku once tried to get onto a crowded downtown streetcar, the driver told him that "Indians do not take streetcars." Although he had the ten-cent fare, his indigenous clothing prohibited him from boarding. Other apoderados often changed their clothes so they could circulate freely, but Titiriku refused.[14]

Indians were not welcome in the city, or, as Titiriku used to call it, "white country."[15] Restaurants were restricted; Titiriku could not eat lunch on Calle Chirinos, near the San Francisco Church, because the owner, Gumercinda Huanca, who was probably a chola, argued that "she [could not] accept an Indian sitting in her restaurant," and "Indians eat at the *tambo* [house for Indian travelers]."[16] Despite these restrictions, Titiriku's strong sense of mission led him to resist and continue going to the city. "We [Aymaras] are in our land and we have the right to walk in the streets, the plaza, the parks, and take the streetcars, as well as to sit down on the city's broad avenues (*El Prado*) and watch the trucks and streetcars. No one has to stop doing that because we are the owner of these lands. This place is an Aymara land. We are not guests like the Spaniards are in these lands, we are not whites."[17] Employing the racial language of the era, Titiriku used "Spaniards" to mean "whites" as a racial category opposed to Indian and mestizos. At that time, Titiriku refused to address middle-class lawyers as *wiraxucha* (lord) or *caballero* (sir), and he would not stand up and hold his wool hat in his hands—a sign of respect—while speaking to them. As a man faithful to the Pachamama and the Achachilas, he refused to use the term "wiraxuchas" for whites because it referred to gods in the Aymara language.[18]

La Paz and Oruro provide excellent examples for understanding how segregation policies developed in relation to modernity and dress codes. Beginning in the early nineteenth century, some cholos had adopted western dress, whereas others preferred various types of ethnic dress. In 1925, Indians were banned from downtown La Paz, and some cholos, such as construction workers and carpenters, faced police aggression when they insisted on wearing their ponchos and ethnic pants, called "*calzones partidos,*" in the main plaza. Titiriku protested alongside them to defend the presence of indigenous clothing in the public arena.[19] The policemen tore off the cholos' *vicuña*-wool ponchos and told the men to sew the lower half of their pant legs together to accommodate this policy.[20] Consequently, people from La Paz began to be known as "*ch'uqutas*, the people who sewed their pants."[21] Oral histories frequently portray this period as the time when "Saavedra civilized the Aymaras of La Paz," and the years when *Paceños* abandoned their calzones partidos and started to wear "civilized pants."[22] Despite the fact that the state promoted and reinforced the de-indianization of cholos, many in La Paz and Oruro resisted. In La Paz and Oruro, people in power emphasized the value of suits made with European fabrics; indigenous and working-class people instead embraced local and handmade suits as an act of anti-racism.

The banning of Indians from certain spaces in an attempt to "modernize" society stemmed from the long-held opinions of public intellectuals. One of the first to address this topic was Manuel Rigoberto Paredes, who believed that the Indian race could become a modern people if they wore suits or other forms of western dress.[23] Other intellectuals, such as Alcides Arguedas, argued that the Turkish Revolution provided the best model for Bolivia to follow because Turkey was changing from Turkish and Muslim traditional ways of dressing in favor of European dress style for both men and women. It was also replacing Arabic characters with Latin characters for writing.[24] Whereas Bolivia had its own pattern of segregation and racialism that dated back to the colonial era, the global interconnections of the 1920s and 1930s made possible the circulation of other racialized events

such as the Turkish revolution as well as the structure of new forms of segregation based on dress.

The ban on Indian dress had the biggest impact in La Paz. Preparing
to celebrate the centenary of independence from Spain in 1925, Bolivia's
elite forbade Indians from participating in the public festivities. President
Saavedra issued an executive order banning Indians from downtown during
the official celebration of the centenary and encouraged other municipal
authorities to follow La Paz's example.[25] By pioneering the implementation
of modern segregation policies, president Saavedra nourished the idea that
cities were not proper places for Indians. Saavedra embraced international
ideas about white superiority, although he appreciated the role of indigenous peoples as laborers in the countryside.

When the municipality of La Paz constructed small indoor markets and
issued another order prohibiting women street vendors from selling outdoors, chola street vendors, who complained about the lack of space in the
new markets, continued to sell their wares in the streets. In the end, the police had to admit that they could not control the vendors[26] who created the
first women's union, the anarchist Federación Femenina Local.[27] Whereas
socialism became widely diffused among the cholo (male) working class,
anarchist activists were more effective at garnering support among chola
(female) cooks and flower sellers. The anarchists focused their activism in
the cities, whereas the socialists concentrated on mine workers; both shaped
Bolivian unionization in the first half of the twentieth century. Titiriku's
second wife, Rosa Ramos, and her mother, Anastacia Cutili, tried unsuc-
cessfully to join the anarchist women's association. Rosa Ramos was told
she should instead join the *caciques tituleros* group (traditional indigenous
leaders in La Paz slang), reserved for indigenous people. This and other experiences indicated to Titiriku that cholo labor institutions were closed to
Indians who wanted to retain or reassert their Indian heritage.[28]

Restrictive policies that municipal governments applied to cholos were
implemented mostly along gender lines, based on the idea that men were
the keepers of civilization, whereas women were more associated with nature and tradition.[29] In cities like La Paz, cholas were allowed to keep their
ethnic dress, which consisted of a wide skirt, a *mantilla* (long shawl), and
a derby hat.[30] Cholo men, on the other hand, were forced to give up ethnic
dress and don suits and hats. Both male and female indigenous peasants
were either kept outside urban centers or restricted from the downtown
core.

Municipal leaders in Oruro also developed racial segregation policies.
Thanks to mining prosperity, by the mid-1920s, Oruro hosted sixty-six international firms including an importer of Ford and other cars. In early
1926, many of these business owners wrote a letter to the municipality re-

questing that Indians be banned from downtown because, as the entrepreneur Serafín Ferrufino argued, "Indian llama drivers in the plaza and main streets are making foreign customers uncomfortable."[31] On July 9, 1928, shop owners won a municipal resolution modeled on the La Paz equivalent, banning indigenous people from Oruro's downtown.[32] Smaller towns followed that legislative lead. Wanuni banned indigenous people from walking in the plaza in 1929, demonstrating that segregation was widely instituted.[33]

Antonio García, an associate of Titiriku's, experienced this segregation when, as a young man, he left the hacienda of Suroma (Chuquisaca) and went to work in the mines of Oruro. In 1928, García was not allowed to enter Oruro's main plaza while wearing ethnic clothes, and the policemen told him that he needed to dress as a "civilized man with a suit and hat."[34] In other cases, this discrimination had more serious implications, such as when María Mamani was accused, in a charge based on her Indianness, of defecating in the bushes of the main plaza. Maria, who later became an indigenous activist associated with the AMP and worked for several years with Titiriku, was incarcerated in the Wanuni jail, where the police raped her several times.[35] Abuse of Indian women accused of littering or defecating in public places and restrictions on men entering cities became common features of Bolivian life in the late 1920s.

The emergence of segregation based on modernity and race was ironic. Elites saw clothing as a strong signifier of Indianness, which they believed stood in opposition to modernity. Starting in the 1920s and intensifying in the 1950s, the transnational flow of race and racism gave Bolivians of European heritage new ideas about mestizaje, which in turn shaped their ideas about white superiority. In Bolivian society, racism especially focused on eliminating indigenous culture, as expressed through language and clothing. In the same era, indigenous clothing in Peru, Mexico, and Guatemala became signifiers of backwardness, and indigenous peoples ended up marginalized and vulnerable to polices of racialization. In other words, the Bolivian case had many similarities with other countries with large indigenous populations: The goal was to eliminate ethnic or indigenous identity and assimilate them.[36] Although colonial practice mandated that Indians and whites must occupy different physical space, this practice was constantly contested. By the 1920s, elites were using transnational ideas about segregation and dress to reinforce their position in various Bolivian cities. Thus, by promoting the ban on Indians in downtown areas, elites reinforced the colonial idea of two republics. La Paz was most strongly affected by this segregation because it had the country's largest indigenous community. Despite Bolivia's profound regional variations at the time, the case of La Paz had an impact on other parts of the country. In the years to come, segregationist policies gradually spread to the rest of country, as the cases of Oruro and Wanuni illustrate.[37] Although ordinances were imposed and enforced at different times, they were all grounded in ideas about separate places for Indians and Spaniards in modern Bolivia. This situation only partially changed after the 1932–1935 Chaco War between Bolivia and Paraguay. By then, president Salamanca was so alarmed by the cholo labor movement that he sent many Indian and cholo leaders to the front as a way to eliminate Indian rebellions and working-class movements.[38] During the war, at least fifty thousand Bolivians, mostly indigenous peoples, died.[39]

SUPERIMPOSITION OF THE INDIGENOUS NATION ON THE MODERN NATION

Titiriku challenged both elites and cholos. He experienced similar forms of discrimination from both groups, though most cholos were of Indian heritage. Ideas about race shaped class categories in the Bolivian social hierarchy of the 1920s. In Titiriku's racial imaginary, q'aras—whites and mestizos who shared a common commitment to a universal modernizing process—were indeed at the top of the social structure. Below them were cholos, who represented the working class, artisans, mineworkers, and others associated with urban blue-collar jobs. Although cholos developed a strong class identity, they typically had a weak Aymara or Quechua ethnic identity (although there were exceptions). Ch'utas, or new cholos, straddled the frontier between Indian and cholo identities. The majority of the population consisted of Indians who had strong Aymara or Quechua ethnic identities and often organized around ayllu or hacienda peons' representatives.

Most cholos had lived in the cities for one or two generations by this period, had mostly Indian ancestors, and frequently still spoke Aymara or Quechua as well as Spanish. Yet cholos defined themselves as neither Indian nor white. Bolivian literature presented fantasies of cholas' love and sex lives with elite men (white and mestizo). These stories reveal how white and mestizo men perceived cholas, and document the rise in inequality between different racial segments of the Bolivian social structure. In an unequal world, where women had an especially precarious position, cholas who were involved with white men, and mestizos were often able to empower themselves.[40]

Cholos comprised the majority of the emerging working class in the new urban economy, which was closely linked to the mining industry. In La Paz, the most prosperous cholos lived in San Pedro, their own segregated neighborhood, where they owned restaurants and printing shops and also worked in banks. However, most cholos worked as carpenters, construction workers, tailors, shoemakers, maids, flower and street vendors, leather tanners, railroad workers, and print shop workers.[41] In several parts of the country, such as Sucre and Potosí, ch'utas often came from the surrounding countryside to sell milk, fruit, and vegetables in urban areas. They were considered different from rural cholos and Indians because they wore shoes rather than sandals.[42]

Cholos' power varied significantly by region. The majority of cholos in La Paz and Oruro were of Aymara heritage, and through leading the labor movement, they were at the head of the counter-hegemonic forces of the country. In Sucre and Potosí, Quechua cholos were governed by their own elite, but working-class cholos followed leftist whites in the late 1920s. One of these leftists was Tristán Marof, who was from Sucre and founded the Partido Socialista Revolutionario, the country's first socialist party.[43]

In the 1920s, La Paz and Oruro cholos created a vibrant labor movement that contested existing racial policies based mainly on anarchist ideology. In La Paz, cholos had a strong sense of group identity within the larger society, which led them to reject the leftist white elite and instead foster their own intellectuals. Luis Cusicanqui, who came from this milieu, defined himself as an urban "Aymara Indian," which was something unusual for a cholo during that time. Cusicanqui founded the most influential anarchist organization, "La Antorcha," and the largest labor organization in La Paz, the Federación Obrera Local.[44] As they slowly became empowered by the new anarchist and labor movements, cholos were continuously condemned by the Bolivian elite. Alcides Arguedas argued that the country was in a "terminally ill condition" because Bolivian society was becoming "dominated by cholos."[45] In Arguedas's view, the hybrid role of cholos in history represented a struggle between "civilization" and "barbarism."[46] Similarly, although Franz Tamayo, a politician and intellectual of this period, defended the Indian race, he was disturbed by the "pervasive role" of cholos in Bolivian society.[47] Thus, during the 1920s, Arguedas and Tamayo expressed the white elite's hatred of cholos for breaking up the binary caste system in Bolivia and for following threatening and counter-hegemonic ideologies.

While Titiriku was attending to the apoderados' issues, he also worked in temporary blue-collar jobs at a slaughterhouse and a small bakery that put him in touch with the urban working class. However, he always returned to the countryside, especially during harvests, to work in his community's fields. Moving between country and city, he got the impression that cholos were largely anti-Indian. For instance, in 1931, a group of cholos at his job in the market told Titiriku: "If you want to stay among us, you have to become civilized, . . . buy pants, wear a hat, and get a shirt. You could at least buy *ch'uta* clothes. People from the other groups will ask themselves why we let you stay among us."[48] Because of these attitudes and their refusal to speak Aymara, Titiriku often clashed with the cholo working class.[49] In later years, Titiriku recalled refusing to speak Spanish in response to cholos who did not want to speak Aymara. Titiriku eventually decided to leave his blue-collar jobs and concentrate on his activist work. He advanced his own project of modernity through education, the revalorization of native languages, and giving a political meaning to the dresscodes being imposed on indigenous people.[50]

During Titiriku's lifetime, political parties manipulated measures of literacy. Beginning in 1905, Education Minister Juan Misael Saracho created a law that paid instructors three bolivianos for every *indígena alfabetizado* (literate Indian) they taught, which essentially meant someone who knew how to sign his name. Since every literate man in the early twentieth century counted as a citizen under Bolivian law, Liberals and Republicans competed for votes by promoting literacy for Indians and cholos. In the mid-1920s, this became particularly important because candidates could sway the results of national elections by signing up just a small number of new voters. At one point, the majority of the Republican Party was comprised of cholos, some of whom had recently become literate. This phenomenon was especially important in Jach'aqhachi, where the Republicans won in 1925 for the first time. However, the Liberal elite refused to acknowledge this new type of citizen, calling them the "sheep of Jach'aqhachi" for blindly following the Republicans.[51] The Liberals thought that because these new citizens were Indians and cholos, they could not have rational reasons for supporting the Republican Party. Their fears seemed confirmed by several cases in which cholos and Indians received cash to vote for the Republicans. Titiriku recognized this manipulative practice for what it was and condemned the client-oriented relationship that linked literacy with political participation. Some of Titiriku's Indian friends became cholos in the 1920s by moving to Jach'aqhachi, working urban jobs, and learning Spanish. In the 1920s, ethnic identity was defined from a class perspective through work categories. Jach'aqhachi became known for its hat-making industry, and it provided rural Aymaras with supplies for rituals in the vast region of the Qulla or Umasuyus Aymara nation.[52] By the mid-1920s, Jach'aqhachi had a huge number of cholos or ch'utas, groups that Titiriku referred to as "whitened Indians" (*vueltos en blancos*).[53] In the late 1930s, he frequently mentioned that, "while Indians are dying in Paqajaqis and Potosí, here the Indians in Jach'aqhachi want to become white, and they dress like cholos."[54] The killing of Aymaras in the massacre of Jesús de Machaqa in 1921 (Paqajaqis) and the 1927 massacre of Indians in Chayanta (Potosí) justified his rejection of both mainstream political parties, particularly the Republicans, which had vast support among cholos. During this time, President Bautista Saavedra was known widely as "cholo Saavedra" because of his background and his strong support among cholos. From Titiriku's perspective, cholos, mestizos, and whites could not be trusted and were all part of the "white republic." Titiriku became increasingly convinced of the merit of Miranda and Marasa's (both crucial indigenous activists in the context of the AMP) confrontational demand for a "Republic of Indians," which sought a fully and exclusively Indian country, separate from white Bolivia.[55] At that time, society was so unequal that he could not imagine an integrated nation that did not require Indians to "cholify" [*cholificar*] and reject their heritage. Titiriku's personal experience of moving back and forth from the countryside to the city made him aware of the whitening process that was taking place, so he devoted most of his life to denouncing it and to offering an alternate vision of the nation.

Not until the 1970s, long after the 1952 National Revolution, did the *katarista* and *indianista* movements take up Titiriku's concerns and denounce the discrimination that a new generation of Aymaras and Quechuas were facing. The Indianistas argued that the Indian agenda should be to fight oppression as a nation; the Kataristas instead insisted that Indian peasants were oppressed as both a class and a nation. They promulgated the Tiwanaku manifesto, arguing that "a nation cannot be free if it oppresses another nation." Whereas Titiriku's experience epitomizes racialization before the 1952 National Revolution, the conflicts between Indians and cholos belong to a larger story of the struggle for and resistance to whitening, "modernity," and "civilization," where whites discriminated against mestizos, mestizos against cholos, and cholos against Indians. These racial dynamics reveal the superimposition of the modern nation in a conflictual relationship with the indigenous nation, where language and indigenous dress constituted a significant barrier to equality. Cholos and ch'utas are on the border of the modern nation and also show that the intersections of the modern nation and the indigenous nation were heavily racialized.

DOCUMENTING THE INDIAN LAW AND ITS CONTEXT

In response to the political turmoil of the 1920s and the effects of the Great Depression on Bolivian politics and the labor movement, Titiriku promoted the AMP's ideas about the Indian Law and religion by emphasizing faith in the Pachamama and the Achachilas. In 1926, Titiriku urged several apoderados, including Francisco Condori and Juan Iquiapaza from Laxa and Jach'aqhachi, to study the connections between the Law of the Indies and what was then known as the Indian Law, which was already a point of reference before Titiriku and Miranda appropriated it. Indian Law had a variety of meanings and uses: as an alternative way to refer to the Law of the Indies, as a name for the struggle for legal recognition of indigenous rights, and as a term that referred to the Indian lifestyle or worldview.[56] But it is only with Miranda, Titiriku, and other AMP activists that the Indian Law emerged as something separate or different from the Law of the Indies, that is, a discourse that addressed dimensions of racialization by responding to the dehumanization of indigenous peoples, and by articulating an agenda of decolonization. Of all the AMP members, Titiriku was most involved in drawing up a more structured doctrine with political and religious arguments.[57]

Titiriku frequently brought multiple volumes of the Law of the Indies to apoderado meetings and tried to explain its content in Aymara.[58] He was especially interested in the articles related to the protection of Indians and their possessions. Ideas for a special judicial system for Indians, separate authorities, and penalties for abuses against Indians also appealed to Titiriku. They coincided more with the Aymara concept of *sumaqamaña*, which the AMP promoted.[59] In this sense, he saw that colonial law had the potential to be more beneficial to Indians than Republican law because it helped to better promote their goal of collective well-being and because it overlapped with Aymara religious beliefs.

Indigenous peoples and activists who worked with them, especially the apoderados in southern Bolivia (Potosí and Chuquisaca), were eager to learn about the AMP and Titiriku's new interpretation of the Republic of Qullasuyu, which differed from other contemporary conceptions, such as those of Santos Marka T'ula and Eduardo Nina Quispe. Although Santos Marka T'ula also sought a law for Indians that incorporated some colonial law, his concept was primarily based on Republican law. On the other hand, Eduardo Nina Quispe believed that education was the key to protecting Indians from colonial abuses and ultimately strove for the full incorporation, or assimilation, of Indians into Bolivia, calling this process the "renovation of Bolivia." Titiriku promoted the Indian Law in a more holistic sense of sumaqamaña and grounded it in colonial law in order to explicitly reject the Republican Law, which, in Titiriku's opinion, was inadequate. He wanted to establish an Indian nation.

In the 1930s, Titiriku intensified his activism by interweaving his Aymara religious views with his political perspective while he began to create his own networks of AMP in different regions of the country. The fragility of Bolivia's political system, weakened by defeat in the Chaco War, was an important factor in this shift. The apoderado movement had been destroyed by the war since many of its leaders either were sent to the front lines or faced persecution. Supporting the ideas of Feliciano Inka Marasa and Toribio Miranda after the war, Titiriku tried to reorganize the movement; however, he argued that, instead of apoderados, indigenous activists should call themselves "Alcaldes Mayores Particulares" because this better expressed their goal of leading an Indian nation as an *alcalde* (mayor) does.[60] Titiriku insisted, however, that the AMP should distinguish themselves from the *alcaldes escolares* (school mayors) or *alcaldes del campo* (field mayors), who were cholos who worked with the government in rural areas. Thus, they became *alcaldes particulares* (particular mayors) because they had a "particular cause," namely, to impose the Indian Law.

By 1936, Titiriku was already a prestigious apoderado and was especially well-known among the Indians and apoderados of Potosí and Chuquisaca because of his connections with Marasa and Miranda.[61] Although they were in many ways critical of aspects of Santos Marka T'ula's doctrine, both Titiriku and Miranda had been active in his indigenous movement of the apoderados mallkus for more than two decades. Since the mid-1920s, Titiriku and his allies Miranda and Marasa questioned Santos Marka T'ula's leadership, but they started to write petitions separate from Marka T'ula only in the mid-1930s. Titiriku did not publicly criticize Marka T'ula until an apoderados mass meeting in 1937, when he said: "The spirits of [colonial] titles did not bring any result. The blood of *Qullasuyu* [the Indian nation] is still crying. We give our money, we give our time and our hope to this worthless endeavor."[62] These meetings became an arena for confrontations between the two bands of indigenous activists. Many apoderados who sided with Santos Marka T'ula did not accept Miranda and Titiriku's questioning of his work. Titiriku, however, argued that indigenous activists should follow the Achachilas and the Pachamama rather than Marka T'ula's paper titles.[63]

In 1936, Titiriku began periodically publishing a document that he and most of the AMP called the Indian Law, but was also known as a *garantía*. Over time, this document came to symbolize the AMP's discourse. This does not mean that the Indian Law was codified in a single document; it became more of a template for articulating indigenous rights and culture. The document contained selected passages from the Law of the Indies, the colonial legal code, and portions of Titiriku's own petitions to Bolivian Ministers and Congress. Even though Titiriku had not received a formal education (he did not attend elementary school), literacy played an important role in the AMP indigenous movement's decolonization project and, in fact, functioned as a way to legitimize Titiriku's project because of the prestige that written documents already had in indigenous communities. In all of Titiriku's garantías, the essence of the text was the same; they referenced the Law of the Indies and enumerated certain rights based on their status as "first peoples." One passage, for example, states: "We report in this present certificate that . . . we have read the Law of the Indies and by the way of it understand that . . . [you whites] should not take our lands away; we were here because of the will of the virgin mother earth. We are Indians, the first peoples. . . . Our languages are Aymara and Quechua."[64] This is an example of how the Indian Law was a way of resisting the force of transnational flows of white superiority in Bolivia. Indeed, the making of the Bolivian

nation-state and the tensions over racial categories in the 1920s was shaped
by both local and international ideas of race. According to Titiriku, AMP
discourse and the Indian Law were also legitimized by religious contents
that drew on both Catholic and indigenous backgrounds.

Indigenous peoples used this document in many different ways: For
instance, Juan Wallpa from the community of Churumumu (Chuquisaca)
used the "Indian Law document" against the local hacienda to argue that
according to "this document I cannot be obligated [to work] or [be] punish[ed] because I do not pay rent. . . . According this document, I am the
owner because I am the blood of these lands, so no Spaniard [white man]
should punish me."[65] Like him, many other peons refused to pay rent; this
situation led to widespread rebellion in 1947. Most of the AMP indigenous
activists, including Melitón Gallardo, Toribio Miranda, and many others
in the Andrés Jach'aqullu's later generation, carried copies of this "Indian
Law" in order to contest the hacienda owners and the rural elite.

In another case, Eustaquio Philly, an AMP activist in Wayllamarka (La
Paz), rejected demands to provide free labor for the construction of another
church based on the same garantía.[66] In addition, Philly used the Indian
Law decree to argue that they should not work for the church, which he
said was the voice of Spain.[67] Titiriku argued at meetings that because they
held indigenous ceremonies for weddings and baptisms, Indians no longer
had to make requests to the Catholic Church.[68] Based on the same law,
Pedro Ilaquita, in Santiago Pampa (La Paz), also refused to provide free
labor on a new highway between Jach'aqhachi and Ambana.[69] People living
in both ayllus and haciendas felt that this document was useful in their
struggles. For people in the countryside and indigenous villages, the idea
that Indians could no longer be subjected to "forced" labor was the document's principal message. Indigenous peoples were interested in the AMP's
Indian Law because it showed that Indians had some recourse and some
sort of legal support during these difficult times. Titiriku's audience liked
to listen to a translated version of the AMP's Indian Law documents, which
were originally written in Spanish. The idea that the AMP's activism was
inspired by the Aymara gods and the Pachamama was also attractive to his
indigenous audience.[70] Although there were many indigenous activists who
presented their arguments in liberal, populist, and leftist frames, only the
AMP and Titiriku based their ideas on indigenous religiosity and culture
in this period.

In 1945, the priest of Sacaca, Potosí, complained during the Sunday
mass that since the AMP were now in the region, some Indians were choos-
ing not to marry in the church and were instead traveling to Oruro and
Potosí in order to marry under false priests.[71] He was offended that these
Indians preferred to marry near the *wak'as* (Indian deities) instead of the

church and asked that they be punished.[72] Soon after, Claudio Pacheco and Celso Paye were detained by the local police and their houses were searched for evidence of their connections to false priests.[73] The police found certain documents that Paye identified as the garantías. Pacheco argued that "they indeed follow the Indian Law" and complained that the Bolivian laws only teach people to follow Spaniards' laws, which meant "whitening laws."[74] Pacheco also admitted that they married and performed baptisms according to indigenous traditions. Implying that the AMP was helping them practice their culture, he added that with the "Indian Law a time has come in which they are truly free."[75] After Pacheco and Paye had been in detention for eight days, the jilaqatas of the Saqaqa region pressured the authorities to set the men free.[76]

In another case, Antonio García and his group of indigenous activists, apoderados, and jilaqatas from Chuquisaca and Potosí tried to enter the main plaza of Oruro in 1937 and were subsequently taken to the police station. The police told them that if they were so interested in using the main plaza, they should go as "a civilized man with a suit and hat . . . and follow the law."[77] García responded that "we follow our Indian Law," and thus should dress according to their traditions and those of their ancestors.[78] These documents, then, were not only used to address labor abuse and land issues but also to affirm their right to practice their indigenous religion and to wear their own clothes, and consequently reaffirming their anti-racist stance. In some areas, community members and peons organized fundraising meetings, or *ramas*, where indigenous peasants gave contributions, presented their views, and requested support for their causes. In return for their contribution, indigenous peoples would receive copies of the Indian Law. Although most participants were illiterate, these texts were read during community meetings by the all-important Aymara scribes and thus were orally transmitted for use as ammunition in confrontations with the white elite. According to the testimony of Juan Pari from Chuqurasi (Oruro), Indian Law documents became handy reference tools when indigenous communities suffered different kinds of abuse from the state, the church, and *hacendados* (white or mestizo owners of large estates. For Titiriku, this was all part of a larger effort to decolonize the indigenous communities and unify them into a separate Indian republic, a nation of their own. Education, he came to believe, was also critical to this new Indian republic. The Indian Law had its anti-racist dimension and used to confront transnational racism.

RELIGION, INDIGENOUS EDUCATION, AND THE NEW QULLASUYU

Both the struggle for education and the expansion of Protestant missionary activities took place in Titiriku's native Umasuyus during the 1930s, which profoundly shaped his activism. Groups of Adventists and Methodists carried out literacy programs in Janqulaimes. Methodists and Adventists were part of a form of transnational evangelism, which reinforced dominant patterns of white superiority. Preachers were a representation of power in the indigenous context, reinforcing ideas that associated whites with modernity and superiority. Their work strongly influenced Titiriku, who joined the Methodist Church for a short time in 1926. Titiriku and other indigenous people did not find it difficult to embrace the church during this time because of their commitment to Christian beliefs and recognition of the benefits of combining aspects of Protestantism with traditional Aymara beliefs, such as the worship of the Pachamama.[79] These churches either ignored or tried to control this syncretism. Although the Methodist Church, for instance, gradually changed its view about permitting indigenous peoples' belief systems, during the 1930s, it encouraged commitment to the official church doctrine.

In the 1930s, the Methodist Church expanded into several communities of Janqulaimes and began prohibiting its parishioners from worshiping both the Pachamama and the Christian God. Titiriku's brother Lorenzo Titiriku and his cousin José María Titiriku, who founded the Methodist Church in the Lake Titikaka region, slowly stopped supporting the apoderado movements, and the AMP movement in particular, because of their personal adherence to the church. In 1935, Titiriku confronted them, arguing that they were "forgetting the good tradition of serving the Pachamama, worshiping our lord lightning [qixuqixu wiraxucha] and our mother the water [uma taika]" and were "devoting themselves to the 'Evangelical God.'" Despite his initial involvement with the church, Titiriku strongly disapproved of the Protestant Church's teaching people to reject Aymara gods and goddesses. During August of 1935, the month of special worship of the Pachamama and the wak'as (ancient tombs of the spirits of the ancestors), he discovered, much to his dismay, that rituals such as the waxt'a (sweet offerings to Pachamama) and luxt'a (llama sacrifices to the Achachilas, the gods in the mountains) had declined in the region of Janqulaimes because the new converts to Methodism were no longer worshipping the Pachamama.[80] One way to revive these traditional practices was to make sure that they were reincorporated into community teachings through indigenous schools.

A related factor that influenced Titiriku's activism in the 1930s was the dramatic transformation of the Warisata School that was located in his native Umasuyus. Founded by Elizardo Pérez, Raúl Pérez, and local Aymara activist Avelino Siñani, Warista's administration and most of its expenses were in the hands of indigenous communities from 1934 to 1939.[81] The founding of this first indigenous school was an act of disobedience against the white ruling elite, which perceived it as threatening the power of hacienda owners of the region.[82] Only the ayllus's defense of the school and the firm decision of the apoderados and other Aymara chiefs of the region to support it allowed this project to survive. Titiriku thought that the Warisata experience could "help our race to flourish."[83] Because of his commitment to the network of Santos Marka T'ula, in the late 1920s he believed that the politics of literacy could help indigenous peoples. However, the failure of this strategy made Titiriku change his opinion by the late 1930s.

When Warisata became a clear success in 1939, the national government took over the school. This stemmed from a new belief, supported by the left and later by President Gualberto Villarroel, who was in a political alliance with the Nationalist Revolutionary Movement (Movimiento Nacionalista Revolucionario) that indigenous people should have state-sponsored education.[84] The Warisata School seemed like a good place to start, since the government argued that the communities could no longer support it financially. Under state sponsorship, the school became a symbol of dependency on the state, making a mockery of its original purpose: to enhance communal autonomy.[85] This situation disappointed Titiriku, who compared it to "the colonial Spanish who came to rob our lands and nation. The public school will damage us in the same way."[86] He believed that the government was not providing public schools unconditionally and that it would later request that communities "pay back" their expenses. Urging indigenous communities to reject public schools, he argued: "Spaniards do not give anything for free. If you do not believe it, ask our grandparents. We are selling ourselves out. The whites will come back as owners of not only your lands, but also of yourselves."[87]

Titiriku saw the assimilationist policies that would put Bolivia under one school system as a mistake. He preferred a segregationist system of autonomous indigenous schools (*escuelas particulares*), which would be small, private, and experimental schools that would offer autonomy for Indians. As the idea of establishing schools became popular with indigenous people, Titiriku proposed that "we should create *escuelas particulares*, and they will prepare the people to achieve our dream . . . to organize the Republic of Qullasuyu. The good spirits [Achachilas] and our mother earth, the virgin, will rejoice in happiness seeing how we rise again."[88] Titiriku argued that the best way to promote this policy was to publicize President Germán Busch's 1936 decree, which ordered hacienda owners to promote education for Indians by founding and financially supporting elementary schools (*escuelas particulares*). Titiriku discovered this decree as soon it was published thanks to his frequent visits to the National Public Office for Information, known as the *Gaceta Pública*. Although the decree was vague and not widely disseminated, Titiriku considered it useful for legally supporting community-controlled schools. In other words, for AMP indigenous activists such as Titiriku, "escuelas particulares" meant autonomous indigenous schools, whereas for the government the term meant elementary schools controlled by the state. Titiriku thus subverted governmental discourse and imbued it with his own meaning, to his own ends.[89]

In the 1930s, the rural elite believed that the very the idea of escuelas particulares was dangerous. Hacendados were opposed to the idea of educating Indians, and earlier schools in the countryside had been considered "seriously subversive."[90] It was not until the 1940s that some white public intellectuals admitted that Indians should be educated; however, they believed this education should focus on the skills essential for fieldwork rather than on providing training that would allow Indians to become doctors or lawyers. These intellectuals argued that Indians would be good for industrial labor but not intellectual or professional endeavors.[91] Titiriku, on the other hand, used the 1936 law and the AMP organization to promote schools throughout the countryside, and in the process to discuss the Indian Law and faith in the Pachamama and the Achachilas.[92]

Indeed, with the escuelas particulares, Titiriku sought to enhance Indian activism and to teach "the path of Qullasuyu peoples." Although Toribio Miranda, the founder of the AMP, started promoting escuelas particulares, Titiriku imbued them with a clear indigenous content, calling on them to "empower the blood of Qullasuyu." In contrast to Miranda, Titiriku did not just want the escuelas particulares to teach in indigenous languages but also to promote Indianness.[93] In other words, he wanted the schools to teach the Indian Law and its anti-racist perspective. Titiriku argued that "we should pray with faith and devotion to the good spirits [Achachilas] on the tops of mountains where the wak'as are, and say, Achachilas and mother Pachamama, give light to our hearts and fortify us with your will. . . . Only you will make us strong. We are your children poor and crying . . . we are the blood of Qullasuyu."[94]

Titiriku believed that making requests on the top of the mountains to the Pachamama and the Achachilas would "fortify" Indians to construct the "Republic of Qullasuyu" and confront the whites of Bolivia as well as his agenda.[95] To lead the new schools, he started to appoint alcaldes particulares in different parts of the country. By 1944, 489 communities and ayllus throughout the country had founded escuelas particulares under Titiriku's sponsorship. Although few of them really achieved the goal of teaching reading and writing skills, their existence reflected the impact of his discourse on indigenous communities and the way that the idea of separate educational systems made sense to Titiriku's audience in the communities. Based on the ideas of early Indian nationalists such as Zárate Willka, which he learned from Toribio Miranda and Feliciano Inka Marasa, Titiriku insisted that the Qullasuyu should be reorganized into nations.

ANTI-RACISM AND TRANSNATIONALISM IN MID-TWENTIETH-CENTURY BOLIVIA

Titiriku's ideas about the Republic of Qullasuyu (an anti-racist place where Indians would no longer be discredited, racialized, and victims of oppression or hate) had a wide audience among the indigenous peoples of southern Bolivia during the first half of the twentieth century. Titiriku's ideas responded to the transnational flows of racism in the form of mestizaje ideology, politics of assimilation, and the removal of indigenous peoples in various parts of the Americas. Titiriku's ideas were a grassroots response to the elite discourse that argued that only educated people were fit for modernity. Bolivian elites were especially worried about indigenous peoples migrating to cities and thus emphasized some actors as fit and others as not fit for the construction of a modern Bolivia. The Republic of Qullasuyu was a strategic ideological construction to discuss modernity from an indigenous perspective, an anti-racist coalition, and its arguments confronted the transnational flow of ideas about race and racism in modern Latin America. Titiriku lived at the intersection of these two projects; he suffered the barriers and he challenged the boundaries of transnational racism.

CHAPTER THREE

RACE AND POLITICAL RIGHTS

CONSTRUCTIONS OF CITIZENSHIP AMONG BRITISH CARIBBEANS INSIDE AND OUTSIDE THE BRITISH EMPIRE, 1918–1962

Lara Putnam

This chapter explores debates over political membership and rights among British Caribbeans in the interwar era and its aftermath. I track the multiple meanings of the word "citizen." I also trace the concerns "citizen" and "citizenship" came to invoke, which were clustered around civic participation, political voice, and mobility rights. The role of racial hierarchy in undercutting state protection for colonial subjects' rights was debated more and more explicitly as the era wore on. The interwar nationalisms British West Indian migrants encountered abroad were not solely about race, but their racial coordinates were unmistakable. Nationalist legislators explicitly named those of "black race" as "undesirable." Britishers of color were barred and vilified even as white Britishers remained welcome. British West Indian commentators read these events as part of a global pattern of white supremacist state-making. And gazing out at the broader world, they observed racial discrimination within the British Empire—from the immigration laws of Australia and Canada to the treatment of Black seamen in British ports—that suggested their own governing state was part of the problem, rather than part of the solution.

Thus British Caribbean debates over race, belonging, and exclusion reflected experiences far outside their home islands. By 1930, over 170,000 individuals born in the British West Indies resided outside of British territory in circum-Caribbean republics, from Venezuela to Panama to the United States. Each and every one of these lands imposed anti-Black immigration laws in the late 1920s and 1930s. Was this the future the modern world held for subjects of color? In overseas communities and among activists and observers back home, the era saw passionate debates over the costs of political disenfranchisement, the need for territorial belonging, and the role of racism in the modern world order. These debates took place not just among elites but across the social spaces working-class transnational migrants made their own: on street corners, in rum shops, at Universal Negro Improvement Association halls, and in a print public sphere that linked home islands to receiving rimlands via newspapers read by scores of thousands.[1]

Where would these debates lead? Let us glance ahead to London, 1948, noting the juxtaposition of three events apparently quite distinct in their origins and significance. On June 22, 1948, the former troop transport *Empire Windrush* docked in London, carrying 493 British West Indians planning to work. Though hardly the first arrivals from the colonies to British shores, these would prove to be harbingers of the first mass labor migration in that direction. The decade that followed would see over 150,000 British Caribbeans arrive to take part in the rebuilding of postwar United Kingdom.[2] On July 22, 1948, Parliament concluded debate on the British Nationality Act, creating the unprecedented category of "Citizen of the United Kingdom and the Colonies." And at the London School of Economics, pioneering sociologist T. H. Marshall was preparing notes for a lecture he would deliver in 1949 and publish in 1950 entitled "Citizenship and Social Class." Each of these events has great significance in scholarly consideration of the evolution of political belonging in modern Britain. But to understand their interrelation we must look beyond Britain's shores.

Stepping back in time and away from London reveals the entanglement of the processes that produced the *Windrush* arrivals, the Nationality Act, and the insights and absences of T. H. Marshall's view of citizenship. The entangled backstory of these three events reflected a generation-long international process in which the growth of Populist politics, the centering of popular welfare, and the consolidation of racialized borders were fundamentally fused. In nation after nation, the entitlements citizens could claim were expanding, in the form of nascent welfare states and pro-employment policies, while the access accorded non-citizens was shrinking. By the 1930s, mobility rights had joined political and civil rights as privileges that individuals could not claim without the support of their governing state.

Although Marshall and the members of parliament who drafted the 1948 Nationality Act seemed almost willfully blind to the tensions these international trends created for an imperial Britain, men and women in the British Caribbean had been grappling explicitly with the tensions for a full generation. They had a detailed understanding of the racialized hierarchies that made rights unequal, in practice, even within nominally color-blind policies. And they had developed a vernacular theorization of imperial citizenship as an ideal continually betrayed.

The imperial citizenship they believed theirs by right did not legally exist for them or any other British subject. Nor did "British citizenship" as a state-recognized category. That did not stop British subjects from arguing about citizenship then, and it has not stopped scholars from using the concept since. I begin this chapter by establishing the turn-of-the-century baseline from which interwar debates took off, noting the role of race-based disparity in precluding formal codification of citizenship on the one hand and the routine use of the term "citizen" by British West Indians to recognize virtuous participants in the civic community on the other. I next address the impact on British Caribbeans of the hemisphere-wide consolidation of mobility control in the 1920s, a process that confronted sojourners in Panama, Cuba, the United States, and beyond with an implacable new legal status under that same label, citizen. Turning back to the islands, I note the accelerating invocation of citizens' rights in the 1930s by reformers demanding political rights within colonies, in part with explicit reference to race-based exclusion abroad. Then I widen the view, showing that conflicts over who counted as citizens echoed across Britannia's realms in those years, as the common aspirational phrase "citizen of empire" allowed distant disputes to become evidence in local debates. Finally, I move forward a decade to the immediate postwar era, analyzing the insights and blind spots of ideas about citizenship offered by metropolitan intellectuals in precisely the years when Caribbean labor migrants, for the first time, headed toward their governing state's home terrain.

Much of my analysis will rely on local newspapers published by and for British West Indians of color, which flourished in the interwar years in rimland-receiving societies and island-sending societies alike. Newspapers like the Grenada-based *West Indian*, the Barbados *Weekly Herald*, the *Panama Tribune*, and the *Searchlight* from Limón, Costa Rica, were each read by thousands of people, with subscribers near and far.[3] Impassioned readers' letters about issues local and global, personal and political filled their pages. This space was not limited to a small elite. Literacy among working-class British West Indian emigrants was particularly high: 80 to 90 percent in Panama and Costa Rica and higher still in Harlem and Brooklyn.[4] These understated, overlooked local newspapers capture a transnational conversation of vital import.

It took place in a migratory sphere created by the travels of Jamaicans, Barbadians, and other British Caribbeans in the generations after emancipation. Panama's cities and canal works were the foremost destination in the first decade of the century, Cuba's canfields followed after the Great War, and New York City's burgeoning service economy surpassed them in the 1920s. By the end of that decade, over 170,000 British West Indies-born sojourners resided outside of British territory. That total does not include those who had worked abroad and returned home or those who lost their lives "in foreign." Meanwhile, if we count not only island-born immigrants but their locally born children (or in some cases, by 1930, grandchildren),

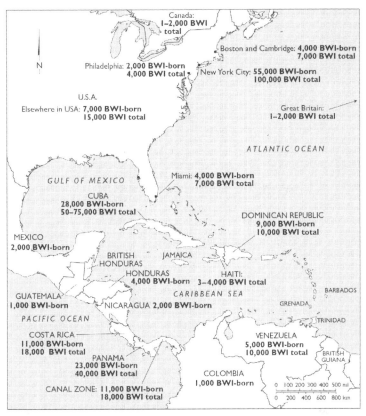

MAP 1. British West Indian immigrants and total British West Indian community sizes, circa. 1930. Drawn by Bill Nelson; data and design by Lara Putnam.

the size of the British West Indian diaspora circa 1930 rises to over three hundred thousand (see Map 1).[5]

The decade from 1924 onward saw anti-Black immigration bans enacted by every one of the significant receiving societies where those three hundred thousand dwelled—including Venezuela, Colombia, Panama, Costa Rica, Nicaragua, Honduras, Guatemala, Mexico, Cuba, the Dominican Republic, and the United Sates—as scientific racism among national elites and protectionist demands by national workers converged to make xenophobia an irresistible political platform.[6] All around the Greater Caribbean, British West Indians found visas denied, bribes demanded, employment barred, and family cut off at hundreds of sites they had previously called home. And meanwhile, in the only places where they could claim native status—the British colonies where they or their parents were born—their ability to claim full political and civil rights was compromised by racial hierarchies that were no less real for being (usually) unspoken.

RACE AND THE DILEMMA OF IMPERIAL RIGHTS

The challenge of squaring the rhetoric of race-blind imperial subjecthood with a colonial system dependent on deep inequality was not new in the 1920s. Indeed it was this underlying dilemma that underlay the failure to create either "British citizen" or "imperial citizen" as a formal status before 1948. The populaces of the United Kingdom, the dominions, and the dependent colonies had remained, by law, British subjects (the nonwhite among them sometimes specified as "non-European British subjects"), whereas the populaces of the Empire's other territories were classed as British Protected Persons.[7]

The absence of a "citizen" status was out of step with modern state norms, but it persisted for a reason. In the Imperial Conference of 1911, Home Secretary Winston Churchill called for formalization of "a uniform and world-wide status of British citizenship which shall protect the holder of that certificate wherever he may be."[8] But how could such a status be applied only to white British subjects—as Churchill clearly intended—without making racial barriers explicit? The challenge echoed a policy dilemma that repeatedly placed Whitehall at odds with dominion legislatures. Australia, Canada, and South Africa kept insisting on banning the entry of nonwhite migrants regardless of British subjecthood, and nonwhite British subjects kept objecting. Any formal category of imperial citizenship would need to reconcile citizenship's promise of the right of abode with the continuance of race-based exclusion.

A 1912 debate among imperial bureaucrats explored the questions raised by Churchill's proposal. The former governor of New Zealand called for a straightforward race-based bar: "In my view full British citizenship, 'good' for any and every part of the Empire and entitled to recognition by foreign States, cannot be given to British subjects of colour." In contrast, he continued, all individuals of "pure white stock" should have easy access to "full British citizenship," be it from birth or, for foreign-born whites, through naturalization after brief residence.[9] Such an open embrace of racial bars was rare among the administrators of empire. Far more common was the forbearance exemplified by Walter Hely-Hutchinson, who acknowledged obliquely that "certain categories of British subjects" faced "special disabilities as regards franchise, admission to certain portions of the Empire, and so forth," but insisted "it would be a grave mistake to label British subjects who suffer under such disabilities, with a name, connoting inferiority, different to that borne by their fellow-citizens: to say to them, in effect, 'You are not a British citizen; you are only a subject.'"[10]

The ambiguities surrounding "imperial," "British," or other subsets of "citizenship" within empire stemmed not just from Great Britain's lack of a written constitution but from the utility of ambiguity itself. At the end of the day, the debate's convener summed up, the diverse local laws and regulations that could be said to comprise implicit imperial citizenship drew "a much broader distinction between persons of European and non-European descent than between subject and alien."[11] This was not a truth empire's boosters could speak.

CITIZENSHIP IN THE GREATER CARIBBEAN: ATTAINABLE MERIT VERSUS IMPLACABLE CREDENTIAL

Yet if a good portion of the men who ran the Empire presumed "British subjects of colour" to be categorically excluded from citizenship, a good portion of those subjects never doubted that citizenship was theirs. Among English-speaking Afro-Caribbeans, as among English speakers across the anglophone world, "citizen" had long been used to denote meritorious membership in the local community. For instance, since the mid-nineteenth century, parish-specific "Citizens' Associations" in Jamaica had hosted speakers and sponsored civic initiatives. Newspapers in Jamaica and Trinidad often carried complaints about the need to safeguard "respectable citizens" or "peaceful citizens" from this or that noisy urban nuisance.[12] This usage continued as British West Indians settled in lands far from home, where there was no question that the governing states considered them foreigners rather than members. Thus, a Jamaican-run newspaper in Bocas del Toro, Panama, described one local as a "native of Portland, Jamaica, who left Jamaica since 1904 via Costa Rica, thence to Colon and then to Bocas in the year 1905 [and] was settled here as a law abiding citizen until 1916."[13] Similarly, on islands and rimlands alike, those concerned with child welfare often argued for the importance of youth as "the citizens of tomorrow"; as one enthusiast in a British West Indian settlement in Costa Rica explained in 1930, "good boy scouts in a locality is a sign of good citizenship among the rising generations."[14] As in these examples, the term "citizen" conveyed well-earned merit and public respect. As such, it was particularly resonant for those arguing that character transcended racial divides.

As the interwar era wore on, even as the term "citizen" persisted as a rhetorical signal of civic virtue and inclusion among British Caribbeans, the same label increasingly confronted them as a formal credential that created exclusion. The years after the Great War saw the consolidation of an international shift, as nation-states systematized birth certificates, passports, and visas and began to make access to employment and nascent social services contingent on these documentary proofs of belonging. Welfare states and border regimes were together in the making.[15]

In this new international system, "citizenship" was not a portmanteau term for civic virtue but a requisite component of individual identity, one that only state action conferred. Sojourners sensed rumblings afoot. In January 1919, one British West Indian worker in the Canal Zone wrote to the British consul in Colón, "Is it true that by the termination of the war the status of the British subjects have been changed, and that we are no longer British subjects but citizens of Britain?" The consul seemed blithely confident in response: "There is no foundation whatever for the supposition that the status of British subjects will be changed as a result of the War."[16] But although the formalities of empire had not changed, international practices of governance were changing, in ways that would impact British subjects' status, like it or not.

"EMIGRATION OF JAMAICANS TO U.S. STOPPED," ran the banner headline of Kingston's *Daily Gleaner* just five years later, as the local impact of the restrictionist US Johnson-Reed Act became suddenly, frighteningly clear. "The American Consul has received instructions not to visae any more passports and thus only American citizens will be able to go North."[17] "Citizen" as used in this sentence reflected nothing of local standing or civic worth. It was a legal status that states and only states could confer. Within the emergent regime of visas and passports, without documentary proof that citizenship had been conferred, it did not exist. Lacking citizenship, a visa was required for entry; lacking a visa, entry was denied. The Johnson-Reed Act brought the "non-self-governing" colonies of the Americas (e.g., the West Indies but not Canada) under quota-limited visa status for the first time, and the "quota control officer" at the US consulate in London cut visa allocation to the British West Indies to a trickle. Over ten thousand Afro-Caribbeans had entered the United States in the first six months of 1924; fewer than 250 did so under the British quota in the entirety of 1925.[18]

Citizenship in this new sense was not negotiated between popular and legal understandings. On the contrary, it could be legislated in Washington, regulated from London, and fracture families in Panama and Cuba, all without the restrictors having to negotiate anything—or even acknowledge that discrimination against colonials of color was underway. Newspapers published by and for British Caribbeans abroad in the late 1920s and 1930s reflect both the continued usage of "citizen" to reference the standing conferred by community participation and the new meaning of "citizen" as a legal category governing mobility.

The fraught new politics of territorial belonging made civic participation more vital than ever. So preached Sidney Young, the Jamaica-born founder of the *Panama Tribune* and a tireless crusader for the rights of British West Indians in Panama. Fighting the erosion of immigrants' rights by xenophobic Populism required active engagement at multiple levels, Young insisted, including community solidarity and economic self-help, assertion within empire, and supranational Black solidarity.[19] In steps from 1926 to 1928, the Panamanian legislature declared all those "of black race whose native language is not Spanish" undesirable aliens and limited their entry, employment, and birthright citizenship. Mass statelessness threatened. As British doctrine held, and local British diplomats gleefully (in private) confirmed, the two-thirds of locally born British West Indian children whose parents were not legally wed had no claim to British subject status.[20] How to ensure the future of these young men and women occupied hundreds of columns of ink in the newspaper sections Young published from the late 1920s onward.

Disputes over citizenship-as-state-status threatened to disrupt the forging of "citizens of tomorrow" in the rimlands. Responding to outcry in the Panamanian press in 1932 over local British West Indian Boy Scouts's use of the union jack in drills and ceremonies, Sidney Young reviewed the new panorama of laws governing "Panamanian citizenship" and the transmission of what Young termed "British citizenship" (that which British law deemed British subjecthood). Above all, Young exhorted, the vital project of scouting must not be put on hold until the fraught issues of national belonging were resolved, for what scouting offered was "training for usefulness as citizens and men," more vital now than ever.[21] The idea that citizenship as moral character transcended nationality was underlined the following week by local Scout Commissioner Clifford Bolt, who wrote that as he and others had founded scout troops over the past decade in Panama, "the question of nationality did not seriously occupy our attention, we were working for the benefit of our future men and endeavoring to make citizens fit for any country when they come to the age of maturity."[22] Citizenship here required communal roots but had cosmopolitan results: citizens must be made, but would be "fit for any country." Yet to fight state-mandated exclusion with civic participation was a battle of unequal arms.

"Why such animosity?" asked the editors of the Limón-based *Searchlight* in 1931, surveying the "hostile movements" threatening "coloured British subjects" around the region. "Cuba has had her turn, Honduras has had hers, Panama has had hers, Venezuela has had hers, Colombia also has put on the twitch, and now some sons of Costa Rica are thinking likewise."[23] The question of the status of the next generation was critical. Some receiving societies (like Panama) revoked birthright citizenship in these years, whereas others, like Costa Rica, had never recognized it—a legal reality not yet clear on the ground. In this same article, the *Searchlight* editors insisted it would be impossible to expel the "industrious coloured residents in Costa Rica," long settled, with "their own farms and houses as well as grown up children in this country who are all citizens of the Republic." In fact, Costa Rican law accorded those children no such status.[24]

Indeed, despite the savvy born of necessity, the editors and correspondents of the rimland papers made assertions about legal citizenship that were patently wrong, if understood as descriptions of the documentary regime now surrounding them. Their claims suggest a persistent moral economy of territorial rights that infused elements of the established notion of citizenship as civic merit into the new and intransigent legal term. Thus, in 1930 the Limón papers denounced Costa Rican government discrimination in public works hiring, which froze out "unfortunate people who actually form (whether by birth or length of years of residence) joint citizenship here."[25] In fact, neither long residence nor local birth "actually" conveyed Costa Rican citizenship, and no such thing as "joint citizenship" existed. Costa Rican citizenship could be claimed only through formal registration or formal naturalization, procedures only a tiny fraction of British West Indians living there pursued in this era.[26] The notion that long residence conveyed at least partial entitlement to things increasingly restricted by formal national membership—things like employment, aid when destitute, and a right of abode—was heard frequently among circum-Caribbean migrants in this era. Just as frequently, it was squashed by state authorities.

DIFFERENTIATED SUBJECTHOOD AND THE DUTY OF PATRIOTIC DISSENT

Facing race-based bars and mistreatment abroad, British West Indians demanded formal protection from the state to which they nominally belonged, the British imperial state. In theory, there was no doubt they were entitled to it: extending protection to crown subjects in foreign lands, whatever their ancestry, formed part of the Empire's raison d'être according to long tradition and copious rhetoric.[27] In 1921, the (near-white, elite) editors of Kingston's *Daily Gleaner* could trumpet the protective value to "the Jamaican abroad"—in Cuba and Panama, in this case—of "his British citizenship." "He is loyal by sentiment, he is also loyal because he recognizes that British citizenship is of real and sterling value."[28] A decade later and seven hundred miles to the west, that protection looked far less sterling. The lack of support from consuls and colonial officials for "the Coloured Britisher" in contrast to the "englishman" abroad was egregious, wrote the *Searchlight* editors from Costa Rica in 1930. State after state enacted race-based bans on entry (Panama, Nicaragua, Colombia) and employment (Costa Rica, Cuba), "and with all this prejudicial discrimination of the coloured subjects of the king in foreign parts, no protest is entered or suggested by the Consuls to Downing Street for the protection of his subjects." [29] Some crown representatives went further than sins of omission and publicly differentiated on the basis of race, "assert[ing] that they are not here to attend to coloured British subjects, only the British Shipping and Englishmen."[30] British West Indian commentators treated this as both common and appalling. If state agents declined to back rights in an era when state backing meant all, "what benefit does the black race obtain from being under the British Crown at home or abroad?"[31]

The term "citizen," carrying the affective charge of its older sense as meritorious civic membership alongside its new meaning as state-allocated status, served to denounce the betrayal with particular force. A 1924 editorial by Barbados-born, Panama-raised Eric Walrond in the Panama *Workman* suggested that although Latin American nativism was unsurprising, imperial silence in the face of "abuse, malignity and violence" was portentous. "How do West Indians stand in Central America? This question concerns the British Empire more than it does the Latin American Republics. The outspoken and evident antagonism to British West Indians is not only outrageous to the sufferers, but an insult to the British Government of which these people are bona fide citizens."[32] This declaration of "bona fide citizen" status, like the discussion of "joint citizenship" above, willfully ignored the fact that the legal status asserted was denied by the state empowered to grant it. Empire was betraying empire's core virtues, demanding response from below. A letter writer in Panama's British Caribbean press in 1927 linked the immigration laws of Canada and Australia, the exploitation in South Africa and Kenya, and the betrayal of Black soldiers in England. "Intelligent West Indians do not forget their duty to the Empire . . . but they also have not forgotten that they are a colored people."[33]

STATE RACISM ABROAD AND REFORM MOVEMENTS AT HOME

In the mid-1920s, Clennell Wickham's *Weekly Herald* championed the Democratic League, a new opposition party struggling to break the grip of white planters on Barbados's House of Assembly.[34] Reformers called for freedom of political speech, a broader franchise, investment in education and public health, and at least a beginning of labor protections. They made the case through constant reference to the rights of "citizens"—which, they insisted, all Barbadians were. In their renderings the term strengthened claims to the political rights denied them by local elites. "Representative Government" was Barbadians' "birthright" as "British citizens," wrote one correspondent. Citizenship derived from community membership. It could be ignored and insulted, but never erased.

The argument that popular citizenship demanded both political rights and social investment put Wickham and the Democratic League on a collision course with the island's plantocracy. The "callous indifference and naked greed of the wealthier classes" imposed "poverty, nakedness and disease," according to one letter writer. "They think it is no dishonour that our future citizens should be bred and rared [reared] like pigs in foul and overcrowded hovels."[35] But those future citizens would not suffer in silence forever, wrote another, self-described as a member of the enfranchised few. "There can be no desire on our part to have them true citizens without granting the status of citizens," he warned.[36] "True citizens" here meant loyal members of the polity; the "status of citizens" meant political rights within it. Passionate organizing won incremental change. The Democratic League finally elected several of its own to the House of Assembly in 1930, an unprecedented blow, wrote T. A. Marryshow from Grenada, against those white Barbadians who believed they had "inherited from their illustrious ancestors the right to regulate and ration a people's privileges of citizenship."[37] Marryshow's account of "privileges of citizenship" that no one had the right to "ration" still had faith in British political tradition. Yet gazing out at the region more broadly, it was hard to trust empire as the answer. For the rights of sojourners abroad were matters of high politics. And here, Britain was failing her subjects of color.[38]

Like Clennell Wickham and T. A. Marryshow, others in this era linked political rights within colonies to mobility and employment rights abroad. Lacking political voice within empire, they argued, West Indians were "nobody's child"—human beings without a backing state to substantiate their claims to basic protections. When Venezuela in 1930 began enforcing a law barring entry to all people "of black race," Port of Spain municipal councilor Tito Achong put the lack of state backing front and center. Just as the *Searchlight* editors would ask the following year, "What is the attitude of the British government toward her Negro Citizens?", Achong proclaimed that he and others "were primarily concerned about evaluating their rights as citizens of the British Empire." The evaluation was grim. Venezuelans in Trinidad "had the same domicillary rights as natives of Trinidad who had no rights of citizenship." Lack of mobility rights abroad compounded the lack of economic rights on the island: "West Indians were excluded from places abroad and at home. Foreigners were given the best jobs and West Indians had to work as day laborers." As the deputy mayor tried to cut him off for "straying from the subject," Achong named the racial coordinates of imperial rightlessness: "Venezuelans were citizens of Venezuela, whether white or black. A West Indian must be a negro with no rights."[39] In a single declamation, Achong had called for evaluation of West Indians' "rights as citizens" within empire and laid bare both their de jure lack of citizenship and de facto lack of political, economic, and mobility rights. Here as elsewhere, talk of citizenship within empire both declared a moral claim to race-blind state backing and measured the weight of its absence.

Increasingly it was as self-proclaimed citizens rather than self-described loyal subjects that colonials of color framed their pursuit of rights, even beyond the pages of the press. In the mid-1930s, Indo-Trinidadian activist Adrian Cola Rienzi founded first the "Citizens Welfare League" and later the "Trinidad Citizens League," while on the same island, Grenada-born organizer T. U. B. Butler named his (1936) movement the "British Empire Citizens' and Workers' Home Rule Party." The term "citizen" conveyed the goal of transforming civic participation into formal political voice. Moreover, the word grounded that claim in race-blind political belonging rather than the culturalist or communitarian claims around which others in the same era were attempting to rally—separately—Trinidad's East Indian and Afro-Creole masses.[40] It is not happenstance that Rienzi and Butler both sought to mobilize followers across lines of race and ethnicity: fellow citizens all.

Given these trends, we should not be surprised that in 1937 it was as self-described "citizens of Port-of-Spain" that members of the "Friends of Ethiopia Committee" demanded His Majesty's Government hear both "our claim for increased representation on the Legislative Council of Trinidad and Tobago" and "our continued indignation over the treatment of Ethiopia and Ethiopians," so contrary to British "obligations, as a member of the League of Nations."[41] What had Port of Spain civic life to do with the Italian invasion of Ethiopia on the one hand and Trinidadian legislative reform on the other? Everything. Political rights had local, regional, imperial, and international dimensions, as these "citizens of the world," "bona fide citizens," "true citizens," and "Negro citizens of empire"—who were legal citizens of no state at all—knew full well.

CITIZENS OF EMPIRE: INTERCOLONIAL OBSERVATION OF RACIAL BARS TO FULL RIGHTS

By the late 1920s the terms "citizen of empire," "imperial citizen," or, when used by subjects of color, "British citizen," summoned up the links between political rights within colonies and mobility rights abroad. They also asserted the existence of a single status of full state membership that all British subjects should share but that those of color did not. This nomenclature, I suggest, helped interwar colonials of color make analytic and rhetorical use of a resource increasingly available: news from other corners of empire.

The 1912 debate among the mandarins of empire over a possible "British citizenship" had warned that it was nonwhite subjects' ability to hear and transfer claims from one site to the next that made codifying citizenship so risky. "British Indians" in South Africa and Canada, for instance, had generated a "mass of documents" relying on "Such phrases as the 'rights of British citizenship,' or the 'rights of British subjects,' or the 'liberties' of one or other" to protest laws or acts that local colonial authorities deemed "perfectly legitimate."[42]

Two decades later, the growing circulation of local papers within and between colonies meant that news of "colour bars" or declarations of rights spread farther and faster than ever. T. A. Marryshow, setting out in Grenada in 1915 to channel the "voice of the people" and turn disempowered Grenadians into "citizens of the world" by means of the periodical press, had been part of an empire-wide trend. When colonials of color sought, in Tito Achong's phrase, to "evaluat[e] their rights as citizens of the British Empire," they now had access to a panoramic view of racist innovations and imperial responses. Those local developments that "br[ought] home to men that they had no status at all in the British Empire" now reverberated on an international stage.[43]

The attention of distant audiences might provide new kinds of leverage. When West Indian students in London protested in 1929 against the spreading "colour bar" in metropolitan restaurants and hotels, they demanded justice with reference to "our full rights of British citizenship" and pointedly reminded the secretary of state that "such acts of discrimination in Great Britain are likely to have far-reaching repercussive effects in different parts of the Empire."[44] They were not wrong: their petition was given prominent coverage in the *Panama Tribune*. The League of Coloured People, organized by Jamaican physician Harold Moody in London in 1931, likewise framed the fight against discrimination in Britain as part of a broader struggle. As Moody asked a gathering in 1932, "Why should it be so difficult for a Coloured British Citizen to earn his living in this country? If the Empire is to be kept together, this is one of the problems which must be solved." Moody was, he declared, "proud of my British citizenship. I am still more proud of my colour. I do not want to feel that my colour is robbing me of any of the privileges to which I am entitled as a British citizen."[45] Moody sent the text of his address to Afro-American leader Dr. Carter Woodson in Washington, DC, for publication in the *Journal of Negro History*.[46]

Where a "Coloured British Citizen" could "earn his living" was an increasingly urgent question. The rise of xenophobic Populism had closed every former migration outlet: the jobs and benefits of the region's emergent welfare states were reserved for those states' citizens alone. As remittances ended and returnees crowded home to the islands, the crisis became acute. "Labour rebellions"—strikes and riots met with deadly force—shook the region in the late 1930s. Great Britain sent a commission of inquiry expressly forbidden to consider "constitutional" questions like the electoral franchise and home rule, and played for time.

Distant war came to the rescue, putting political demands on hold and temporarily shifting the calculus regarding "alien labor." US naval base construction in Trinidad gave employment to thousands, including many from Grenada, Barbados, and other nearby islands.[47] A new guest worker program carried over one hundred thousand temporary laborers to the wartime United States.[48] Some ten thousand more traveled to England to meet the Royal Air Force's needs.[49] Yet once victory over Fascism was secured, the employment panorama reverted to its grim prewar norm. The US guest worker program was rewritten to ensure limited numbers and more limited rights.[50] Latin American republics jealously guarded their borders. Eager to travel and willing to sweat, where could coloured British citizens go?

THEORIZING CITIZENSHIP IN HOLBORN AND NOTTING HILL

The decades leading up to World War II had found hundreds of thousands of British West Indians in lands where working-class citizens were increasingly able to turn political rights into social entitlements. Nonwhite imperial subjects found themselves outside the borders, literal and figurative, in an era of expanding rights. The broad trajectory of expanding entitlements within evolving democracies that confronted them may sound familiar. For this was the history traced by Thomas Humphrey Marshall in a lecture at the London School of Economics in 1949, and published the following year as "Citizenship and Social Class."[51]

Certain elements with which Marshall (born 1893) was wrestling had been at the forefront of discussion among his contemporaries T. A. Marryshow (born 1887), Clennell Wickham (born 1895), Sidney Young (born 1898), and their fellow British Caribbean reformers for the previous three decades. Notably absent from Marshall's discussion, however, were precisely the two entwined issues that Marryshow, Wickham, Young, and their peers identified as at the crux of modern British rights: race and empire. Marshall did not address racial hierarchies of differentiated political belonging, nor did he mention territorial access, mobility, or right of abode. In colonial debates over "British citizenship," as we have seen, such issues were paramount. Marshall offered a narrower slice of the story.

Marshall argued that the centuries-long expansion of citizenship in Britain had been driven by demand from below—both the demands of new social sectors for inclusion as full members in the rights-bearing community, and demands that new realms of human need be incorporated under the umbrella of state obligation, securing first civil, then political, and finally social rights. The model would have resonated with Marryshow and Wickham, although in their experience struggles by working-class Caribbeans for civil, political, social rights—the "privileges of citizenship" and the prerogatives of "true citizens"—had been simultaneous and remained ongoing. Meanwhile, Marshall argued that town-based membership claims had been the building blocks for making demands of a consolidating national state. This echoed nonwhite subjects' trajectory from claiming merit as "an old respectable citizen" of Port Limón, to claiming voice as "citizens of Port of Spain," to protest marches in pursuit of the civil, political, and economic rights due "British citizens" across empire and beyond. Yet Marshall saw none of this history, although it had played out within his lifetime and was culminating in independence movements even as he spoke. Much less did he ask how this trajectory from the peripheries might be poised to shape developments in the metropole.

Poised it was. On July 22, 1948, Parliament created the formal category of Citizens of the United Kingdom and Colonies (CUKC), at one stroke giving eight hundred million British subjects worldwide nominally equal standing and equal rights of entry to Great Britain. Legislative proponents saw the maintenance of a shared imperial status as a matter of "mystical" rather than material import: "No one imagined," scholars report, that mass migration from the colonies might ensue.[52]

The notion that colonial citizenship could remain symbolic, or that the mobility rights reaffirmed by CUKC status did not matter, was starkly myopic. Even as the *Windrush* docked at Tilbury, the Jamaican public debated the prospects of the metropole as a new migrant outlet.[53] For the previous four generations, British West Indian societies had depended, to differing degrees, on emigration and remittances. Within recent memory, restrictionist laws in the republics of the Americas had barred doors and fractured families across the region, as we have seen spawning intense debate in the reformist press over exactly what imperial citizenship should mean. Parliament might have intended CUKC status to confer no new rights, but there was little chance Grenadians and Barbadians and Jamaicans would let it end there. They had long experience with the Sisyphean task of turning nominal commitments into substantive rights through active civic engagement. That is, they knew citizenship inside and out.

Like Clennell Wickham, Sidney Young, and T. H. Marshall, Claudia Jones and Hannah Arendt belonged to the same generation. From distant points of departure, each found her life marked by the efforts of states to control borders and shape populations in the 1930s and by the Cold War of the 1950s. Born in Germany in 1906, the Jewish Arendt fled the Nazis in the late 1930s and escaped to the United States on an illegally issued visa in 1941; she became a naturalized citizen in 1950 and began building a respected career as anti-Communist public intellectual. Claudia Jones was born in Trinidad in 1915. At the age of nine she traveled to New York to rejoin her parents, arriving just four months before the 1924 Johnson-Reed Act effectively barred further British Caribbean entry to the United States. She joined the American Communist Party in 1936 and by 1938 had become editor of the *Weekly Review*. In the same years in which Arendt found in New York a safe haven, Jones was harassed there and jailed along with hundreds of other activists from the Communist Party of the United States of America; like many of the foreign-born among them, she was refused naturalization and threatened with deportation. Jones was finally deported in 1955, and, when Trinidad refused her entry, ended up in London.[54] She arrived just as tensions got worse. British West Indians in circum-Caribbean receiving societies in the 1930s had found elite eugenicists and working-class Populists making common cause against them. Similarly, as new Commonwealth immigration accelerated, elites fretted over the impact on British "stock" of the arrival of "great quantities of negroes," while some working-class Britons, competing for housing and employ, judged the visible newcomers the cause of their straits.[55]

Whereas T. H. Marshall's account of citizenship saw only hard-won achievement when working-class natives claimed entitlements within states, Hannah Arendt clearly saw the systematic tension between popular sovereignty and "minorities'" standing. The emerging nation-state system created vicious, deadly rights shortfalls. Persons without state membership were rendered mere "human beings who, unprotected by any specific law or political convention, are nothing but human beings."[56] They were, as T. A. Marryshow put it a decade before, "nobody's child." As Arendt wrote in a seminal essay in 1951, "The Rights of Man, supposedly inalienable, proved unenforceable—even in countries whose constitutions were based upon them—whenever people appeared who were no longer citizens of any sovereign state."[57]

For Arendt, it was the dislocations and racial nationalisms that came with the dismantling of Europe's multi-ethnic empires in the wake of World War I that revealed the fierce cost of statelessness in the modern world. What she missed was the longer trajectory through which hundreds of thousands of (non-European) people "became aware" of the right to have rights and of the price of its absence. That history was entwined with race and racism—with color bars proclaimed by democracies and winked at by empire—in ways that escaped Marshall and Arendt alike.[58]

We can now analyze more clearly the convergence of events with which this chapter began: Marshall's 1949 encomium to expansive citizenship, Parliament's passage of the race-blind and inclusive 1948 Nationalities Act, and the arrival of the *Empire Windrush*. As Marshall recognized, a postwar consensus had emerged that held the state accountable for much-enhanced social citizenship for all Britons. As public investment in housing, health, and transportation boomed, Jamaicans, Barbadians, and other Caribbeans arrived by the thousands to find employment as laborers, nurses, and bus drivers. British West Indian migration to the United Kingdom was thus driven by consolidation of citizenship in two ways. On the one hand, jobs were created within the United Kingdom as public expenditure on social services grew; on the other hand, alternative receiving societies were now closed to British West Indian entry, precisely because those societies had consolidated their own border regimes as they built their own welfare states.

The fact that this did not end in a simple tale of labor relocation and political incorporation points to the need to understand what Marshall left out and Arendt recognized only as it affected white people: the history of citizenship as a state-backed credential, whose protections could be vitiated by racism and indeed could be taken away. Self-defined national communities were loath to give newcomers rights, and sojourners without full state backing were "nothing but human beings." As both colonial immigration and opposition to it swelled in the late 1950s, fervent organizing by Claudia Jones and her fellow British West Indian and British Communist activists proved fruitless. Tories wooed working-class votes with warnings that a vote for Labour meant "a nigger for a neighbour." Labour's leaders shifted from conflicted sympathy for immigration restriction to open embrace of the new nativism.[59] Only fourteen years after the 1948 act had created CUKC status, millions of Commonwealth citizens, British subjects at the moment of their birth, found the borders of Great Britain barred by the restrictive Commonwealth Immigration Act of 1962. The nominally race-neutral criteria of "patriality" differentiated between those of European and non-European ancestry quite as effectively as dictation tests, "continuous passage" requirements, and the Johnson-Reed Act's tidy visa allocation had done a generation before.[60]

Viewed only from the perspective of metropolitan laws, the 1962 act seems a sharp reversal. But viewed in a longer timeframe on an empire-wide scale, it seems the culmination of a half century's trends. Those years had seen non-European British subjects unable to claim white Britishers' rights to mobility across the dominions, had seen non-European British subjects' supposedly inviolable right to consular protection made mockery from Venezuela to Havana, and had seen citizens of Bridgetown and Port of Spain unable to leverage their local civic participation into electoral enfranchisement within empire.

The 1962 law that turned lifelong subjects into "non-patrials" with no right of abode, and the discriminatory practices that made British residents of color into (in Claudia Jones's term) "second class citizens," carried all the more insult because they coincided with British efforts to join the European Common Market. This choice was consistent with a long history in which, as the imperial bureaucrats' discussion had concluded in 1912, the diverse local laws and regulations that could be said to comprise imperial citizenship in toto drew "a much broader distinction between persons of European and non-European descent than between subject and alien."[61]

BRITISH CITIZENSHIP, FROM MARGINS TO METROPOLE

Sonya Rose suggests citizenship is most usefully defined as "a *discursive framework* explicating the juridical relationship between people and political community," which "provides the basis upon which people can make claims on the political community concerning juridical rights and duties, political and ethnical practices, and criteria of membership."[62] Neither imperial citizenship nor British citizenship existed as formal legal categories in the interwar era. As discursive framework, they clearly did, though just what comprised that framework was neither fixed nor constant. There was a multisited dialogue underway about the boundaries of belonging within empire, and which ones you saw depended in part on where you stood. British West Indian subjects summoned up a citizen status they insisted was theirs, regardless of official intent. They appealed to it with increasing frequency in the interwar years as international developments made claims in the name of citizenship weightier. Those who found themselves systematically excluded by the emerging international regime insisted on seeing themselves as full members of the modern world. They sought to turn local civic participation into portable state-backed rights through multiple routes: newspapers and new parties, petitions and protests. These processes, enacted at the margins of empire in the interwar era, would in the postwar era shift their stage to the metropolitan core on the one hand and postcolonial island nations on the other, for clear historical reasons: in the emergent international system, it was only in their "own" state that workers could stake a claim, or claim a stake. The ways race and racism set the boundaries of belonging were thrust out of the unspoken realm by the insistent travels of transnational subjects . . . and citizens.

CHAPTER FOUR

CROSSING THE BORDER AT THE PRIMER CONGRESO INDIGENISTA INTERAMERICANO, 1940

Alexander Dawson

Benjamin Bryce and David Sheinin asked the contributors to this volume to think about race and transnationalism in the Americas. This is an interesting request, as it forces us to situate our thinking about race outside of the narrow confines of the nation-state. Because we are historians, and because nation-states are often the authors of legal regimes that codify and concretize racial categories, historians of race are drawn to institutions and practices that produce race within specific legal and textual communities. More than this, because racial categories are invariably generated through reference to the "other," the national community is often a good place to start for understanding race as a concept. The United States has a long history in which representatives of the state have advanced a vague notion of the Mexican racial threat (as recently as 2015, then presidential candidate Donald Trump reiterated long-standing racial anxieties). These practices remind us of both the importance of the border in racial thinking and the seeming impossibility of something we would call transnational—that is, something that somehow transcends the border.[1] Furthermore, in crossing the border, Mexicans assume racial identities that they would not have possessed in their own country. Those south of the border who may think of themselves as white often become part of an undifferentiated racial other with their darker-skinned compatriots when they enter the United States, especially if they are poor or undocumented.

While Mexicans and Americans often fill the category "Indian" with local meanings (blood quotients, reservations, and a concept of tribal membership managed through the Bureau of Indian Affairs [BIA] in the United States, and a historic ambivalence that situates Indians simultaneously as nationalist icons and threats to progress in Mexico[2]), some elements of the category seem shared across the border. These include allusions to a pre-Columbian past, ties to post-colonialism, and the practices of paternalistic state agencies that claim to "help" indigenous populations. In recent decades the category has even taken a distinctly transnational quality, as the Declaration of Barbados, International Labour Organization Convention 169, and the Universal Declaration of the Rights of Indigenous Peoples have acted to promote the common cause of indigenous self-determination across the Americas. Conferences bringing native peoples from Latin America to the United States, and visits between North American Natives and their counterparts to the south have had the effect of highlighting the common interests (if not common culture) of indigenous peoples across the Americas and suggest that there is a common (read transnational) history of indigeneity in the Americas.

Some years ago, as I was finishing a monograph on *indigenismo*[3] in postrevolutionary Mexico, I found myself thinking about this question. The book included a chapter on the *internados indígenas*, Mexico's version of the Indian boarding/residential schools, and I was curious as to why institutions that were in some ways quite similar seemed to have produced such different histories in Mexico, Canada, and the United States. Was it that they were so different? Was it that the Mexican, US, and Canadian states were profoundly different when it came to indigenous peoples? Was it simply about the way that historians in three different countries approached these institutions? Was it possible that the very concept "Indian" simply had different connotations in these different contexts?[4]

While exploring these questions in the summer of 2006, I came across a file titled "Peyote" in the papers of John Collier (head of the US BIA from 1933 to 1945) at the US National Archives. Much of the file concerned a dispute on the Navajo Reservation over efforts to ban consumption of the hallucinogenic cactus, which was a component of the rituals of the Native American Church, but there was one particular document that caught my eye. It was an essay titled, "Peyotism as an Emergent Indian Culture," written by an American anthropologist named Vincent Petrullo, and prepared for the Primer Congreso Indigenista Interamericano (PCII, known in the United States as the First Inter-American Congress on Indian Life), which took place in Pátzcuaro, Mexico, in April 1940.[5] In the paper, Petrullo described a peyote cult whose origins lay in the experiences of Native Americans who had taken refuge in northern Mexico during the Indian Wars of the late nineteenth century. While hiding out in the mountains of Chihuahua, the refugees had been introduced to peyote, which grew in the borderlands and northern Mexico, and which the Tarahumaras (among others) worshipped as a deity. The refugees brought peyote devotion with them when they returned to the United States, and subsequent generations spread peyotism through the Indian boarding schools. From there it had become the most dynamic religion in the Native American community, a form of cultural rebirth and resurgence that nonetheless retained deep ties to the past.

The border between the United States and Mexico was incidental to Petrullo's account. He described a transcendent process in which communities that had long been oppressed by colonialism were reclaiming their right to exist. Indian peoples had been "swallowed up but not digested" by Euro-American society, their culture driven into the "unconscious," and peyotism represented that reassertion of their ancient values. And even if it seemed new in the United States, peyotism was really very old. It was clear proof of the resilience of indigenous peoples. He asserted: "When a people keeps its racio-cultural identity in spite of four and one-half centuries of military and cultural oppression, it offers common sense proof that it has a future."

American peyotism was thus "an excellent example of racial and cultural survival. . . . [We see] in peyotism one of the religious drives, racial and cultural in nature, which permit the Indian to reestablish some harmony between himself, the world, and God." It also represented a "continuity of Indian racial and cultural thought . . . one of the signs that the Indian race is still virile, still energetic, still potentially able to emerge as a living force in the future of America."

Petrullo offered still other reasons to celebrate peyote religions. Peyotism required "self-examination and great personal discipline" in a quest to find "the Indian's proper relationship to God" and "perfect harmony between men and the supreme deity of the universe." It fostered "harmony between man and nature." And although it was difficult for whites to understand peyotism because it had "sprung from the historical experiences of the Indian," he nonetheless envisioned it as "a religion for everyone," adding, "If meetings could be modified, perhaps by introducing mass singing or by limiting the singing to a chosen few, and they could be held in large structures, then indeed peyotism might develop into a mass religion, with mass participation." Peyotism was thus simultaneously ancient and modern.

Petrullo was wrong about certain particulars. It does not seem that peyotism entered the United States in the fashion that he described, and his prediction of a mass movement worshiping a hallucinogenic cactus was a little optimistic. Still, his paper at Pátzcuaro suggests that peyote offers a particularly interesting lens through which we might examine indigeneity and transnationalism. Petrullo made the connection between American peyotism and the Mexican variant explicit in his paper, and many of his colleagues at the conference were inclined to see other phenomena that transcended the border. More than this, many of the attendees at the Páztcuaro conference believed that a Pan-American approach to the "Indian Problem" was within reach. Delegates to the conference issued a number of declarations intended to shape a common hemispheric approach to indigenous policy, laid the groundwork for the creation of the Instituto Indigenista Interamericano (founded in Mexico City two years later), and seemed committed to a larger emancipatory project that would unite the best social science with a hemispheric emancipatory project rooted in indigenous self-determination.[6] Yet in the end, that vision never managed to come together in a meaningful way. The failure of that vision, and what peyote can tell us about the limits of that transnational indigenista project, are the subjects of this chapter.

In exploring the intersections and disjunctures of indigenista projects in the United States and Mexico in the years surrounding the PCII, I hope to illuminate both the ways in which a larger transnational project seemed possible and the ways in which indigenismos in both countries remained deeply rooted in national concerns. In part this can be seen through a series of unsurprising phenomena, including distinct but in some ways overlapping concerns about land tenure and restitution, and a fairly seamlessly connected set of assumptions about the need for scientific and social scientific expertise in addressing the "Indian Question." Peyote then, might seem to provide a curious lens through which to view these issues. However, as I will argue, it provides a useful means to contemplate the limitations of transnational indigenismo at the PCII. In the early twentieth century a good quantity of the peyote used by indigenous peyotists in the United States was collected in Mexico. As such, it is a material expression of transnationalism. And yet, peyote and peyotism were cast in profoundly different ways in Mexico and the United States during this era, a distinction that tells us a great deal about the ways in which a transnational indigenista project was simply impossible.

THE PRIMER CONGRESO INDIGENISTA INTERAMERICANO

The army of scholars, bureaucrats, and indigenous leaders from nineteen different countries that descended on Pátzcuaro for the PCII implicitly accepted the assumption that their "Indian problems" were not simply national or local phenomena rooted in particular histories; that *indigeneity* was instead a much more general experience best approached through commitments to indigenous rights, a rejection of racism, and universal principles that could be deduced through scientific knowledge.[7] Most of the ideas that circulated at the Congress were fairly predictable. Indians were desperately poor and needed government aid and tutelage. They needed schools, hospitals, land, and knowledge.[8] Delegates implored governments across the region to commit the resources and employ or train the experts needed to elevate indigenous peoples to a higher plane of civilization. A significant number of delegates asserted that Indians needed more than projects that would elevate their standards of living and incorporate them into modern nations—that the agenda of a Pan-American indigenismo should also focus on a series of rights: rights to land, rights to the rule of law, and in some cases, the right to self-determination.[9] This was not entirely new for the US delegation, which was led by John Collier. North Americans had always considered indigenous peoples separate nations, and self-determination had been official policy since 1934. But for Mexico's representatives, it was something altogether revolutionary.[10] When the Mexicans and Americans signed Pátzcuaro's Final Act, they committed themselves to a shared path that had not been seriously considered in Mexico since the 1850s.[11]

Mexico and the United States sent the largest delegations to the PCII, with Mexico's fifty delegates and technicians and thirty-two Indian delegates representing the largest (the United States, Mexico, and Panama were the only countries to send Indian delegates). The Mexican side was a who's who of the most important figures associated with indigenous issues in the country. Along with Luis Chávez Orozco, president of the PCII, and Moisés Sáenz, general secretary, this included persons of long-standing prominence, like Andrés Molina Enríquez, Elena Torres, Manuel Gamio (the father of Mexican anthropology), the award-winning novelist Gregorio López y Fuentes, and up-and-coming figures like Alfonso Caso (then director of the Instituto Nacional de Antropología e Historia) and Ramón C. Bonfil. Several foreigners, including Maurice Swadesh (an American linguist who was then leading a Mexican government-supported experiment in bilingual education called the Tarascan Project) and Paul Kirchoff (the German-born anthropologist who had been a founding member of the Escuela Nacional de Antropología e Historia in 1938) were also included in the Mexican delegation.

Led by John Collier, the United States delegation included forty-three delegates and technicians and fourteen Indian delegates. This included a number of important social scientists and scientists employed by the BIA. Anthropologists Sophie Aberle, Ralph Beals, and Esref Shevksy (who was trained in experimental medicine but was an aficionado of functionalist anthropology) joined Hugh Bennett and Allen Harper (experts in soil conservation), along with a collection of federal bureaucrats, including Oscar Chapman (denounced as a Communist by the House Un-American Activities Committee in 1939). The United States also brought along René d'Harnoncourt, who in the late 1930s was manager of the New Deal Indian Arts and Crafts Board, and would later direct the Museum of Modern Art in New York.

There were some fairly obvious lines of convergence between the US and Mexican delegations. Ties of friendship linked Collier and a number of his Mexican counterparts, and several in the US delegation had undertaken research or worked in Mexico. Several of the Mexicans were disciples of major US academics (notably Robert Redfield, who did not attend), or had earned advanced degrees at US universities (both Moisés Sáenz and Manuel Gamio studied at Columbia, Sáenz under John Dewey, and Gamio under Franz Boas). The Congress also saw the presentation of work from a major collaborative research project in Mexico's *meseta tarasca* between the University of California, Mexico's Instituto Politécnico Nacional, and the Mexican Departamento de Asuntos Indígenas.[12]

REFORM ERAS IN MEXICO AND THE UNITED STATES

In some ways the Mexican and US delegations told similar stories of significant transformations then underway in both countries. On the US side Collier, Bennett, Shevsky, and several others were among the architects of a new Indian policy, which was characterized by simultaneous efforts to restore tribal self-government and develop the economic resources of Indian communities.[13] The same could be said for the Mexican side, where Luis Chávez Orozco, Moisés Sáenz, Vicente Lombardo Toledano, Maurice Swadesh, and others had worked for years to produce tangible improvements in the material conditions in indigenous communities. In both countries this entailed putting land into the hands of indigenous peoples, along with efforts to tailor land reforms and government practices to the needs and interests of their indigenous clients.

In the United States, the Indian Reorganization Act (IRA) of 1934 was a critical reference point in these endeavors. As a signature piece of Roosevelt's New Deal legislation, the IRA promised to reverse many decades of assimilationist Indian policy by restoring tribal lands lost in the allotment process (mandated by the 1887 Dawes Act[14]) and restoring tribal self-government under federal guardianship. The IRA also opened positions in the Indian Service to Indians,[15] provided access to credit, and created a fund to help tribes purchase new lands. As a part of the reform effort, Collier also insisted that the Native American Church of North America, the principal indigenous peyotist church in the country, be allowed to practice its faith without interference from BIA officials on First Amendment grounds (Freedom of Religion). Though peyote had never been outlawed by the federal government (several states had state-level bans), and thus was technically legal on all federal Indian reservations, in the decades before the New Deal, BIA officials had used a series of legal and illegal means to impede the religion, which they saw as degenerate, dangerous to Indian bodies, and anathema to Christianity. Henceforth those efforts would cease.[16]

In Mexico, reform efforts were linked to the Cárdenas Administration (1934–1940), in which a number of previously neglected provisions included in the 1917 Constitution were vigorously implemented. Lázaro Cárdenas distributed forty-five million acres of land to Mexican peasants and undertook unprecedented social, economic, labor, and educational reforms in the countryside. The government increased the budgets of the Secretaría de Educación Pública and the Secretaría de Salud Pública and created an entirely new department devoted to Indian affairs, the Departamento Autónomo de Asuntos Indígenas. Federal officials also built special schools for Indians; launched three distinct (and theoretically integrated) major reform efforts targeted at indigenous Mexicans in the Yucatán, the Yaqui Valley, and Valle de Mezquital; promoted regional indigenous congresses; and developed programs that privileged indigenous languages and cultures.[17]

The Mexicans and North Americans at Pátzcuaro seemed to have similar views on the relationship of Indians to the land. Both imagined that communally owned land (whether in ejidos in Mexico or reservations in the United States) offered an antidote to the culturally devastating individualism and material precariousness that private holdings entailed; that communal land tenure offered an opportunity to rescue a sort of ancient Communism that distinguished Indians from whites. Whether this was seen as an opportunity to save the Indian (as in the United States) or a model for socialism on a national scale (as in Mexico), indigenistas in both societies actively supported a form of land reform that limited private ownership. They likewise imagined that the state had a powerful role to play in this arrangement, as the source of technical knowledge and other forms of expertise that could transform communal holdings into productive lands.

These concerns are clearly evident in the formal record of the US delegation at the PCII. Of the two publications prepared by the Americans, one offered a survey of Indian tribes in the United States (*Indians of the United States*), and the other was specifically devoted to the question of land (*Indians and the Land*). The latter was a compilation of six presentations from the Congress pertaining to Indian land tenure in the United States. All the papers in the volume linked indigeneity and pastoralism. As crystallized by the words of Allen Harper, the Americans believed that "if, as the [Roosevelt] administration believes, the Indians' future is on the land, then it follows that conservation of the land is a prerequisite of achieving that objective."[18]

The North Americans were happy to look to their southern neighbors in their search for the means to keep Indians on the land. Indeed, while the Mexicans at the Congress seemed largely uninterested in US Indian policy, Alida C. Bowler (superintendent at large, US Indian Service) directly addressed the ways in which a series of reforms in Mexico acted as potential models for the United States. In a paper focused on agricultural credit, she observed that crop deposit credit was being used successfully in Mexico, and she argued that because credit was given to Indians individually in the United States, the practice tended to pauperize them. She expressed admiration for a banking system connected to communally held lands because it gave credit to a committee (the comité ejidal) instead of individuals, describing it as a step toward an ideal "credit system in which the federal government deals with a democratically organized and managed credit society." In this she suggested that the system also needed to rely on Native American participation in planning, insisting that "when the government agency does play a controlling role in its loan clients' operations, it does so as a temporary expedient only." She also noted that in the United States during the previous five years "Indians have taken over management of their economic life in a far greater measure than ever before . . . a similar process may be seen going on in Mexico, where leaders chosen by the communities themselves are learning through participation in economic discussions."[19]

More than credit however, the American delegation was concerned about soil erosion. This should not be terribly surprising, given that a considerable number of the Indian tribes overseen by the BIA lived in the West and Southwest, which had been devastated in the dustbowl. If Indians were to remain on the land, they needed to find a way to mitigate the devastation of the previous decade through sound land management techniques. To these ends, Hugh H. Bennett (chief, Soil Conservation Service, US Department of Agriculture), who had made a career as a soil erosion expert, presented a paper about the critical need for expanded soil conservation on reservations. Surveying the long history of irrigation and agriculture, he concluded that centuries of poor farming in the western United States had produced a denuded landscape, and he called for a scientific transformation of the entire western landscape.[20]

Allen Harper (senior field representative, US Indian Service) echoed Bennett's concern about soil conservation but added to his presentation a concern for the need to expand reservation land holdings. Since the allotment of 1887, Indian lands had declined from 138 million acres to 52 million acres.[21] His narrative of land recovery was remarkably similar to the Mexican case. He and other US officials, like the Mexicans, framed the return of Indian lands as an act of restorative justice. Yet it was not a form of justice that came without strings attached. Harper insisted that without better management of the lands, few benefits would accrue to the Indians. Harper was particularly concerned about the need to reduce the number of livestock grazing on tribal lands, invoking his work with Bennett in the Mexican Springs Demonstration Area, where forty-three thousand acres had been under "strict and scientific control" for several years. He called it a "thrilling experience," but observed that "it would be misleading to leave the impression with the members of the Congress on Indian Life that the Navajos are pleased with the program which the government has asked them to adopt on their own. . . . It is a program . . . which goes contrary to a settled Navajo ideology; as for example, in the request for the reduction of useless, non productive horses." Harper insisted that the government needed to transform sheepherding and other livestock raising practices on the reservations, proposing numerous technical innovations (better sheep breeding and wool clipping, for example). Confident that these measures were critical to saving the land on the reservation, he dismissed Navajo demands that their values and practices be respected. "It is true that the Navajos are sometimes heard to grumble, and that, for a selfish reason, a few persons are able to influence them now and then to turn their backs on the program. But, nevertheless, the program goes forward, sometimes at half-desired speed, and sometimes not at all. But it goes on, and *must* go on." Harper's claims here represented a subtle dig at the likes of Collier and Shevky, who had been pressing since 1933 for a greater role for Navajo actors and for soil conservation programs that were more attuned to local beliefs and traditions. It was, however, hardly necessary because by this point Harper had already won the day. The entire soil conversation program was transferred from the BIA to the US Department of Agriculture in 1940, ensuring that a top-down technocratic approach that was little concerned with local beliefs and practices would prevail.[22]

The fact that Harper, Bennett, Collier, and Shevky all attended the PCII suggests that although these conflicts were serious, they did not result in intractable divisions within the federal government. In fact, Shevky, Collier, and their adversaries saw eye to eye on many issues. All agreed that Indian agriculture was in desperate need of improvement. All were of the opinion that the federal government had an important, paternal role to play in promoting soil conservation on Navajo lands. They all also seem to have agreed on the importance of livestock reduction, even if they differed on how to implement these changes. In this they were like many of their Mexican counterparts at the PCII, who clearly understood that their Indian problem could be resolved only by experts employed by the state. Irrigation projects (if not soil conservation, particularly) comprised an important element of the Mexican indigenista project in the 1930s and were extensively discussed at the PCII. One Mexican presentation went so far as to indicate that the sorts of technical improvements introduced by agronomists and engineers marked the difference between barbarism and modernity.[23]

THE VIEW FROM THE SOUTH

As that claim about barbarism and modernity suggests, in Mexico the stakes for a state-led program of economic, social, and cultural transformation were considerably higher than in the United States. South of the border the Indian represented a civilizational problem, a potential citizen who made up perhaps 40 percent of the national population and whose blood ran through the veins of nearly every citizen. The Indian was also a nationalist icon, representing either the potential greatness of Mexico or its inevitable downfall.[24] This perhaps explains the urgent words of president Cárdenas in his opening address to the PCII.

> Our Indian problem is not that of making the Indian "stay Indian," nor of Indianizing Mexico, but in Mexicanizing the Indian himself. If we respect his blood, and turn to account his emotional powers, his love of the soil and his unmistakable tenacity, we shall root national feeling more firmly and enrich it with moral qualities that will strengthen the spirit of patriotism, thus asserting Mexico's own personality. . . . It is not true that the Indian is opposed to improvement of his condition. . . . When a steadfast policy has succeeded in inspiring confidence, making the Indian realize that he can himself do something to raise his standards of living . . . then he responds with unshakable enthusiasm, the more when he becomes convinced that the authorities are exercising the powers vested in them as a means to secure his redemption.

In this speech Cárdenas explicitly attacked both racists and advocates of self-determination, arguing that the Indian was in no way a child, or a race apart, but was "a member of a social class taking part in the collective task of production." "More than through skin color, peculiar forms of political organization, or artistic manifestations," he argued, the Indian is defined by "his position as an oppressed class."[25]

Cárdenas's approach to the Indian question was echoed by numerous Mexican presentations to the Congress, which highlighted the importance of programs undertaken by the revolutionary state in changing the lives of indigenous peoples.[26] These presentations often privileged both the modernizing impulse and the role of the expert in ways that were quite similar to the US presentations, and thus had at their heart a paternalism that spoke of empowering Indians while nonetheless reserving for outsiders the most important forms of power. Yet they differed inasmuch as many were explicitly Marxist in their positioning of the Indian as a member of an oppressed class. Unlike in the United States, where romantic visions of Indian communism actually made the Indian seem even more of an "other" when compared to individualistic whites,[27] in Mexico the image of the commu-

nal Indian was linked to a nationalist ideology that called for certain (limited) forms of class struggle. Poor Mexicans (Indians included) were the
historical victims of both imperialism and exploitation at the hands of the
bosses/priests/landowners, and the country would reach its potential only
when this system of vast inequality was overthrown. The studies of schools,
roads, irrigation, social and health services the Mexicans presented at Pátzcuaro reinforced this view. They showed a nation where the revolutionary
state was actively bringing socialist modernity to the countryside, and they
paraded a host of recipients (actual delegates to the PCII) who not only
embraced these changes but demanded more.

We might call this the "official story" of Mexican indigenismo at the
PCII, though to do so would mask the fact that the Mexicans came to the
Congress with many different points of view on indigenous issues. Several
delegates in fact opposed the revolutionary nationalist perspective (the Indian as a member of an exploited class) and were instead attracted to the
Stalinist theory of oppressed nationalities, which posited that minorities
should be treated as nations within nations rather than as the objects of assimilation. This group included several prominent members of the Mexican
delegation, among them Alfonso Villa Rojas, Luis Álvarez Barret, Maurice Swadesh, Vicente Lombardo Toledano, and Luis Chávez Orozco (then
chief of the Departamento de Asuntos Indígenas). Even Moisés Sáenz, one
of the principal organizers of the conference, had grown increasingly uneasy with the Indian as super-exploited mestizo version of Cardenismo by
1940, and had come to embrace a vague notion of national integration.[28]

As with the presentations of the Americans, this was not the sort of pluralism that would characterize the radical turn in anthropology during the
1980s, when the very notion of expert authority was critiqued as a product
of western imperialism. Álvarez, like Villa Rojas and others, clearly saw an
important role for the state and the anthropologist in defining indigeneity,
in assigning it positive and negative attributes, and in transforming indigenous communities. Likewise, the BIA "guided" democratic practices in
tribal government, imposed the livestock reduction plan on the Navajo,
and was often reviled on the reservations, even under Collier. It is perhaps
notable though, that even if their pluralism reads like a form of paternalism
in retrospect, it was positively radical and hotly disputed in its day.

INDIAN RELIGIONS

The convergences in North American and Mexican pluralism evaporated
when the discussion turned to indigenous religions. For reasons that speak
volumes to the importance of local contexts in producing indigeneity, Mexican and American delegates seem to have had entirely different attitudes
toward the religions and by extension the religious rights of their indige-

nous peoples. In Mexico, where Liberal elites had been fiercely anticlerical for nearly a century, and where the most powerful challenges to the revolutionary state had come from a Catholic rebellion in the West,[29] few intellectuals considered religion, whether Catholic or indigenous, to be a right. Their state barely tolerated religiosity, and at times actively sought to stamp it out. The "degraded" and "pagan" Catholicism practiced by indigenous Mexicans only reinforced these views.[30]

A quite different sentiment prevailed in the United States. Indeed, the American delegates to Pátzcuaro formulated much of their sense of the right to self-determination through references to Indian religions, using the IRA as a critical reference point. Under the First Amendment all Americans could exercise freedom of religion, a right that had been fiercely debated within the BIA in the decades prior to the PCII. Before the 1930s the BIA and evangelical Protestant missionaries worked together to eradicate indigenous religions and promote allotment and Protestant Christianity, but by the 1920s a growing number of Americans had grown uneasy with this relationship. Indeed, John Collier made his name in the 1920s as a staunch defender of Indian dances and religions. Though his support of Indian dances and other rituals may have been rooted in the fact that many were clearly more non-Christian than the rituals Mexicans saw in their own indigenous communities, it was not merely the right to remain "pure" that Collier defended, but the right to exercise freedom in the choice of one's religious practices. It is thus not surprising that North American missionaries reacted with dismay when Collier was named commissioner of the BIA.[31] He was accused of being anti-Christian, of destroying generations of good work. At one point Collier was even accused of "Mexicanizing Indian education," an oblique suggestion that he was promoting godless Communism, paganism, or both.[32]

In part these battles played out at Pátzcuaro through American presentations that directly condemned generations of missionary work. It was however, Vincenzo Petrullo's presentation on peyote and the Native American Church that took the most novel approach. While seemingly esoteric in its subject matter, "Peyotism as an Emergent Indian Culture" spoke directly to the ways that the BIA was promoting indigenous self-determination. Petrullo's paper also spoke to broader efforts by Collier and his ilk to reshape the debate over peyote, which a decade earlier had been entirely dominated by the Prohibitionist sentiments of the missionaries. After over two decades of relentless attacks on peyotists, in which the cactus was (mis)labeled as an addictive narcotic, an orgy-producing aphrodisiac, and a danger to indigenous bodies and communities, Collier amassed a series of expert opinions that ran directly contrary to the missionaries' claims. Not to be deterred, his enemies pushed the debate to the floor of the US Senate in 1937 when a coalition of activists opposed to the IRA proposed a bill that would have enacted a federal ban on peyote.

Collier was prepared for this challenge, and he assembled a battery of experts to defend peyotism. Franz Boas described the proposed legislation as a bill that "exaggerates the evil influence of peyote beyond all bounds." He claimed that peyote had been in use in New Mexico for hundreds of years where "it has never had a detrimental effect upon the health of the people," and that it had actually facilitated the growth of Christianity. Dr. Richard Schultes of the Botanical Museum at Harvard University claimed that he could not find one case of habitual use, that peyote was only used as a religious sacrament and medicine, with no after-effects. He went further, claiming it was "not only not an aphrodisiac, but that it possesses anaph-rodisiac qualities." Users never lost consciousness, remained "rational," and though they had occasional hallucinations, the minor intoxicating qualities were passed in the urine the next day. "Many of the very old Indians who are apparently enjoying good health have used peyote steadily since child-hood [. . . with] no loss of moral or physical stamina." Dr. Weston La Barre, who had just completed a Yale dissertation on peyote, also testified that he had never seen anything to justify the claims against peyote. La Barre com-pared the effects of peyote to that of "several cups of strong coffee, followed by a pipe or a cigar." He too claimed it was not habit-forming and had no deleterious effects on the body. "I find I am more addicted to an after-dinner cigarette than I ever was to peyote in the field."[33]

MEXICAN PEYOTISTS

One thing that these defenses of peyotism shared was the fact that most of the speakers at the 1937 hearings (and indeed, Petrullo at the PCII) po-sitioned North American indigenous peyotism as both healthy (it did not hurt Indian bodies) and modern (it organized and disciplined those bodies, making them more capable of work). The fact that most peyote church-es invoked Jesus Christ and used Christian iconography strengthened this claim. They did not, however, describe Mexican indigenous peyotism in quite the same way. Marking a tradition in which Mexican peyotism would be rendered as similar in its health effects (Mexican peyotists had extremely healthy bodies) but profoundly different in its cultural practices (Mexican pcyotists wcrc stonc-age, communal, and backward looking, compared to individualistic and forward-looking American peyotists), the US experts who spoke at the 1937 hearings made a clear distinction between what they saw at home and what they saw south of the border.[34]

Mexican social scientists and government officials told yet another story about peyote, though truth be told, they often told no story at all. No Mex-ican papers at the PCII referenced peyote, in part because none of the significant research on indigenous peoples in Mexico undertaken by Mexicans during this era focused on Mexican peyotists. State-building in peyotist communities also lagged behind other regions characterized by significant indigenous populations, as the agencies of the revolutionary state made remarkably few inroads into the areas in which Mexico's principal peyotists lived.[35] In some sense, "peyotist" did not even really exist as a category in Mexico, where the veneration of peyote was assumed to be simply one of a number of archaic practices that characterized groups like the Huichols of the western sierra, and the Tarahumaras to the north.

Peyotism here was anything but a right. It was an archaic practice that impeded modernity, and those subjects who practiced peyotism existed outside of the very framework in which rights could be respected. Instead, they were profoundly primitive subjects in need of discipline and elevation. When the Huichols, Mexico's principal peyotists, appeared in the press during this period, their supposedly stone-age existence was not treated as a fascinating example of a pre-Colombian people (as was the tendency of the North Americans), but as a troublesome barrier to progress. Reporters commented on the "difficult work" and constant conflict that federal officials faced in their communities.[36] They were among the most recalcitrant and curious inhabitants of the nation, possessed of a "precortesian sadness," and an indomitable will to remain exactly as they were.[37] Government officials struggled, and mostly failed, in their efforts to get them to "change their archaic institutions, their archaic practices."[38]

One of the most detailed Mexican accounts of Huichol peyotism from this era comes in a short essay in Carlos Basauri's *La población indígena de México* (1940). The Huichols are described as very poor, with high rates of infant mortality, as a community that practiced no prenatal or postnatal care, as members of a generally backward culture.[39] Peyote is treated as a curiosity in the text, with effects similar to those of marijuana.[40] Drawing heavily on the work of Carl Lumholtz (but without the romanticism), the description of the peyote quest leaves them a profoundly backward people, trapped inside unchanging customs, in deep need of saving by the state.[41]

Though peyote receives only brief mention in the text, the larger descriptions of Huichol ritual life were tied to an intellectual tradition in which their mystical and backward sensibilities (peyotism, but other things too) acted as a critical challenge to the national project. Poverty, poor hygiene, and poor agricultural techniques were generally understood as rooted in two causes; the traditional exploitation of indigenous peoples and their isolation from the mainstream. The revolutionary state attempted to undo both of these historical tragedies through the reallocation of resources to indigenous peoples and a large-scale attempt to educate the countryside. Education would eradicate all forms of mental backwardness, from alcoholism, to Catholicism (fanaticism), to the "fuzzy" logic that clouded the primitive mind.

Peyote then, was essentially a stand-in for alcoholism. This might have aligned the Mexicans with American missionaries, but it was entirely out of step with the views of their counterparts in the BIA. This disconnect reminds us of the ways in which many of the convergences between US and Mexican indigenismos at Pátzcuaro were ephemeral, common discursive practices that masked deeper differences. In part this leads us to questions about how the state and national contexts "made" Indians differently in both societies. We see, for instance, that the BIA and the American anthropologists who studied American peyotism were principally concerned with religious rights and the physical health of individuals. Mexicans on the other hand were confronting demands for national integration and progress and the related fear that groups like the Huichols represented a drag on the nation. The image of Huichol mothers harming their children, of their resistance to the progressive imperatives of the state, and of the entrenched nature of Huichol beliefs and practices expressed, in the Mexican case, much larger anxieties about the capacity of Mexico to become a modern nation. Interestingly however, each of these fears also revealed a sense that the Huichols, however primitive they were, were in fact part of a national polity, and that their practices had a deleterious effect on the nation as a whole. When the state failed the Huichols (or vice versa), the nation was at stake.

TALKING PAST EACH OTHER

Contrasting US and Mexican views on this issue leads us to a series of larger questions about the different assumptions about the Indian problem that seem to have been at play during these years. Vague commitments to indigenous rights, limited forms of self-determination, applied or functionalist anthropology, and paternalistic social reform papered over the fact that these two groups spoke from within profoundly different national projects. In the United States, Indian alterity was assumed, and the Americans at the PCII seem to have been most concerned about developing indigenous communities within that alterity. In Mexico, it was the nation that was assumed, and most presenters seem to have been much more concerned with understanding how indigenous communities existed within the nation. Change was also presumed in both cases, though most Mexicans seem to have understood that change meant greater integration, while their northern counterparts did not. The Mexicans, in this sense, could easily be accused of practicing a form of racism without race, inasmuch as they continually insisted that that their goal was to make the peyotist a fully functioning citizen. They rejected any suggestion that this was impossible, insisting that integration or assimilation were simply a matter of finding the right tools, and that in the end, what truly distinguished them from their American counterparts was their unwillingness to relegate Indians to the slow death of the reservation.[42] Americans, who in defining the very category "Indian," relied on deeply racist measures (blood quotients and bloodlines), were more explicit in their racism, and easy targets for this criticism.

This may go to the heart of the difference in American and Mexican attitudes. It seems quite clear that no mainstream Mexican in this era would have held up the Huichols as an example of anything positive. Indigenistas celebrated Indians, just not groups like the Huichols, who were extreme outliers within the revolutionary project, in part because their customs were quite particular, and in part because they refused to cooperate with the state in any way. Few self-respecting Mexican intellectuals would have suggested that it was their racial alterity that doomed the revolutionary project in their communities. It was instead their extremely primitive culture. Tied to their ancestral ways, primitive in their hygiene and domestic habits, poor and vulnerable to disease and illness, the Huichols were anything but an example to follow. Peyotism was thus part of a larger package of primitive practices that would need to be eradicated to save the Huichols and the nation.

In the United States, peyotism was never understood as an existential threat to the nation. For some, peyote was a dangerous narcotic that destroyed indigenous bodies and undid the civilizing work of the missionaries. For others, it represented an opportunity for healthy and disciplined Indian bodies to break the chains of white rule. Unassimilable as their Indians might be, Collier and his ilk did not describe their peyotists as primitives, and framed peyotism north of the border within a series of modern corporeal concerns. They were not drug addicts. They were not causing their bodies to degenerate. Peyote was in fact helping them become productive individuals and good Christians. Peyotism allowed them to rescue their own lives from the ruin of alcoholism so that they could be sober workers. These observations made the claim that peyotism required First Amendment protection less controversial because it demonstrated that peyotism did not conflict with modern sensibilities. It was harmless, perhaps even beneficial. Peyotists themselves were modern subjects, if not truly citizens. After all, those bodies remained Indian bodies, never destined to disappear into the national mainstream in the way that Mexicans hoped that their Indians might.

This, of course, speaks to the impossibility of a transnational project in the 1940s, a time when nation-states retained profoundly different aspirations for their indigenous populations. For as long as a certain notion of citizenship retained its aspirational power—that is, a desire to create a state that could uplift the entire nation within a form of corporate citizenship articulated through *mexicanidad*—the claim that indigenous peoples represented distinct nations could gain no traction in Mexico. It was only thirty years later, when the failures of that state became patently obvious, that new models became possible.[43]

CHAPTER FIVE

NO PLACE IN THE COSMIC RACE?

THE FALSE PROMISES OF *MESTIZAJE* AND *INDIGENISMO* IN POSTREVOLUTIONARY MEXICO

Stephen E. Lewis

Postrevolutionary Mexico is widely known throughout the Americas for celebrating its mestizo majority, hailed as the "cosmic race" by José Vasconcelos in 1925,[1] and for developing a complicated set of policies and practices known as *indigenismo*. Practitioners of indigenismo, known as *indigenistas*, were typically not indigenous. They tended to celebrate an abstract notion of indigenous people and culture located securely in the past, but also called for the modernization and assimilation of living, breathing *indígenas* into the majority mestizo Mexican nation. Although the labels "mestizo" and "Indian" were originally rooted in biological or somatic difference, by the early twentieth century they were in fact relatively malleable and subjective social and cultural categories. On paper, at least, the relationship between *mestizaje* and indigenismo was complementary. Indigenismo seemed to promise complete acculturation and full inclusion to those who shed their indigeneity. But indigenismo's track record was spotty and controversial. Beginning in the late 1960s, critics argued that it was ineffective, patronizing, theoretically outdated, and incapable of addressing indigenous marginalization and poverty. Years later, the Mexican state gradually surrendered its long-standing, arguably quixotic attempt to forge a unified, homogenous national identity based on mestizaje.

This chapter traces the origins and development of both the cult of mestizaje (or "mestizophilia") and indigenismo in Mexico in the 1920s and 1930s. It then zeroes in on Mexican indigenismo as developed by the National Indigenist Institute (Instituto Nacional Indigenista, or INI). In 1951, the INI opened its pilot coordinating center in Chiapas, Mexico's southernmost (and arguably most marginal) state. There, in the highlands, indigenistas aimed to develop, modernize, and integrate Tseltal and Tsostil Maya communities into broader Mexican society. Many of Mexico's most renowned social scientists passed through this center, and the development programs that they charted and fine-tuned placed Mexico at the vanguard of hemispheric indigenista policy. But by 1970, indigenista policies in Chiapas and elsewhere had not integrated indigenous communities into the Mexican nation in a meaningful way. Tseltals and Tsotsils were still marginalized, exploited, and deeply impoverished, and full inclusion in the Mexican nation was effectively out of reach for them. The indigenista experience in Chiapas and Mexico at large highlights the contradictory attitudes of a mestizo-majority nation that reveres the historic contributions of past indigenous civilizations and recognizes a historical debt to contemporary indigenous people but also embraces a particular kind of mestizaje and a decidedly Europeanized notion of modernity and "progress."

FROM DENIGRATION TO CELEBRATION

Spanish explorers invented the term "Indian" and applied it to the hundreds of often mutually antagonistic ethnic groups that they encountered in the Americas. In effect, they lumped the indigenous together into one undifferentiated mass of tribute-payers. Although the Spaniards created a caste system that placed Indians near the bottom, this hierarchy allowed more social mobility than its name implied. Spanish colonialism imposed the Catholic faith and forced indigenous groups to participate in the market economy. Labor drafts had the unintended effect of forcing indigenous peoples to abandon ancestral lands. Assimilation was difficult, but it was not impossible, especially for indigenous elites. Despite attempts to keep Indians and Spaniards physically separate, on the eve of the wars for independence, few Mexicans were "pure" Indians in a biological sense. "'Indians' were seen to be darker, but 'Indians' were not defined solely or even primarily in somatic terms," writes Alan Knight. "A range of other characteristics determined 'racial'—or, we should properly say, *ethnic*—identification: language, dress, religion, social organization, culture and consciousness. Since these were social rather than innate biological attributes, they were capable of change."[2]

The first mestizos were the offspring of Spanish explorers and indigenous women; in fact, the term "mestizo" was synonymous with "bastard."[3] In time, "mestizo" also became a social category used to describe those who bore the marks of assimilation and had shed their indigeneity—they had become Catholics, spoke Spanish, changed their dress, and usually lived in market centers. Following independence from Spain, many of Mexico's leading thinkers—influenced by European racist thinking—disparaged miscegenation and the mestizo as well as indigenous peoples, whom they regarded as degenerate.[4] The denigration of both categories reached a climax during the second half of the nineteenth century. Paradoxically, the rehabilitation of both also began during this period. Writer Justo Sierra identified himself as a mestizo, recognized "the Indian roots of the Mexican 'mestizo family,'"[5] and called the mestizo "the dynamic factor in our history."[6] Andrés Molina Enríquez's widely influential *Los grandes problemas nacionales* (1909) equated mestizaje with *Mexicanidad* and argued that Mexico's future development and prosperity hinged on whether it could become ethnically homogenous. This text inaugurated the "golden age of mestizophilia."[7]

Many Mexican thinkers also came to believe that the country's indigenous populations could be redeemed. They had been influenced by neo-Lamarckian theories of evolution, named after the early nineteenth-century French naturalist, Jean Baptiste de Lamarck, who believed that environmentally induced changes to an adult organism could become part of that organism's genetic code. "Improvements" could then be passed on to future generations. Influential Mexicans believed that Indians could be improved through social and environmental interventions, such as public schooling, public health programs, and government programs to improve crop yields. This would facilitate their "incorporation" into the mestizo mainstream.[8]

Manuel Gamio's timely *Forjando patria* (1916) urged the need for a new nationalism that would "combine Mexico's disparate population in a solid patriotic union."[9] Gamio, Mexico's first professional anthropologist, was also its first mestizophilic indigenista. He proposed that anthropologists study territories and peoples in order to facilitate and even accelerate their "normal evolutionary development."[10] They would serve as "the enlightened arm of government . . . best equipped to deal with the management of population, with forging social harmony and promoting civilization," writes Claudio Lomnitz.[11]

Gamio got his chance to test his ideas in 1917, when he was named to head the Dirección de Antropología. His team of forty researchers studied the inhabitants of the Valley of Teotihuacán, just north of Mexico City. They collected information on consumption habits, living conditions, and social and cultural practices to assess whether the people of the valley were of "indigenous" civilization or whether they were "modern" and efficient. Gamio concluded that the "Indo-mestizo" population at Teotihuacán could be regenerated if conditions were improved. Gamio's work suggested a unilineal cultural evolutionism that plotted rural communities along a continuum ranging from degenerated and "primitive" to modern and "civilized."[12] This theoretical model, which emphasized culture over race, left its mark on both the "radical" Mexican indigenistas of the 1930s and the tamer, more institutional second-generation indigenistas that emerged in the 1950s.

FORGING *MESTIZAJE*

The popular upheaval of the Mexican Revolution (1910–1920) and its immediate aftermath presented an opportunity for intellectuals, politicians,
artists, educators, and social reformers to reject Porfirian paradigms and
forge a new nation based on new cultural ideals. This resulted in what some
scholars have called the "ethnicization" or "browning" of Mexican national identity.[13] Vasconcelos's most influential work, *La raza cósmica* (1925),
argued that mestizaje was "providential, progressive, and beneficial for
Mexico and Spanish America."[14] An unabashed Hispanist, he promoted a
Pan-Latin American identity inspired by Hispanic civilization (including
Catholicism). This "cosmic race," writes Karin Rosemblatt, "would combine the material successes of 'white' civilization with the artistic and spiritual merits of Latin America to create a worldwide racial fusion."[15]

Until recently, most histories described Mexico's postrevolutionary
cult of mestizaje as a relatively benign process of self-discovery. But Jason
Chang reminds us that "mestizo nationalism was never inevitable—it had
to be won."[16] Mexican mestizophilia inverted the previous racist thinking
that had denigrated both mestizos and indigenous peoples, but it was still
racist. Gamio's *Forjando patria* "excluded Asian and African peoples from
both his national imaginary and the benefits of the revolution,"[17] whereas
both Gamio and Vasconcelos "disavowed Asians and Africans from participating in mestizo racial progress" and "voiced yellow-peril racism in their
writings."[18] Mexican government officials crafted immigration policies that
aligned with the ideology of mestizaje. In 1927, the Ministry of Foreign
Relations excluded Chinese and Black immigration in order "to avoid the
mixing of races that have been scientifically proven to produce degenerate
offspring."[19]

Only Europeans (and fellow Latin Americans) would be invited to participate in Mexican mestizaje. But even here, Mexico played favorites; in
1929, the Department of Health recommended excluding certain Eastern
European populations "since such races are not desirable for our country
because they do not assimilate, constituting in most cases social parasites."[20]
In 1934, a confidential memo from the Ministry of the Interior (Gober-
nación) reaffirmed the previous bans and extended the prohibition to include Palestinians, Arabs, Turks, Bulgarians, Persians, Yugoslavs, Greeks,
Albanians, Algerians, Egyptians, and Moroccans. The memo included a
separate section that justified the prohibition of Jewish immigration because "more than any other race, it is undesirable due to its psychological
and moral characteristics."[21]

Chang argues that anti-Chinese sentiment helped define and determine
Mexico's cult of mestizaje. In the 1920s, anti-Chinese organizations had

cross-class appeal and were found throughout Mexico at a time when the postrevolutionary state was still in formation. They were especially prominent in the northern state of Sonora, home to the three men who would hold the presidency from 1920 to 1934: Adolfo de la Huerta, Álvaro Obregón, and Plutarco Elías Calles. As Chang notes, *anti-chinistas* "demanded an 'urgent' and 'genuine' nationalism to galvanize the people and drive the government to realize the radical potential of the revolution: not economic redistribution but the formation of a racial state." Their politics "affirmed the highest ideals of state power and a seemingly inexorable mestizo racial hegemony."[22] And they benefited from excellent timing. Anti-chinista organizations became building blocks for the emerging official party, the Party of the National Revolution (PNR), founded in 1929. During the Great Depression, anti-chinismo offered convenient scapegoats and led to mass expulsions in states like Sonora and Sinaloa.

FIRST-GENERATION *INDIGENISMO*

As the cult of mestizaje became the ideology of the postrevolutionary state, indigenismo emerged as its complement. Alexander Dawson writes that indigenistas "were united by their sympathy for the Indian and their desire to incorporate Indians into a reconstructed modern nation, in which living Indians were treated with respect and dignity."[23] Most indigenistas were not content simply to celebrate indigenous Mexicans, however; they also wanted to study, educate, incorporate, and otherwise "improve" them. If Mexican immigration policy limited the possibility of "improving the race" through immigration, indigenismo promised to acculturate the native people who had been living in Mexico all along.[24]

The high water mark of what might be called first-wave (or "radical") indigenismo came during the presidency of Lázaro Cárdenas (1934–1940). Indigenismo became part of the president's populist political project; his administration created the Department of Indigenous Affairs in 1936, redistributed tens of millions of acres of land to mestizo and indigenous peasants, built indigenous boarding schools, and hosted regional indigenous conferences.

Shortly before Cárdenas left office in 1940, Moisés Sáenz and US Commissioner of Indian Affairs John Collier hosted the Inter-American Conference on Indian Life in Cárdenas's home state of Michoacán, México. As told by Dawson in this volume, delegates from nineteen countries in the Americas presented their research, agreed to create national indigenist institutes in their home countries, and called for the creation of an Interamerican Indigenist Institute (Instituto Indigenista Interamericano).[25] Some delegates joined linguists and teachers in critiquing government attempts to "incorporate" indigenous groups into the national mainstream and made pluralist arguments in favor of protecting indigenous languages and cultures. This pluralist moment quickly passed, however, and after 1940, a gradualist, detached, and "scientific" indigenismo took root throughout the Americas. When the Interamerican Indigenist Institute was formally constituted in 1942, its director—Manuel Gamio—kept it studiously and intentionally apolitical.[26]

Recently, scholars have argued that during the 1940s—the gestational decade for Pan-American indigenista institutions—social scientists, pedagogues, and government officials still struggled to define the subject of their intervention. Laura Giraudo notes that this confusion complicated Pan-American efforts early in the decade to statistically categorize, quantify, and study indigenous populations. The US government considered an Indian to be anyone with more than one-fourth of what it called "Indian blood," but Latin American countries made no reference to a blood quantum. Rather, they considered a host of cultural, material, and economic factors that varied by country.[27] Paula López Caballero has argued that in Mexico, indigenista institutions were created before indigenistas proposed a clear-cut mestizo-Indian binary.[28] Gonzalo Aguirre Beltrán, Alfonso Caso, and others would later theorize these distinctions to "stabilize" the otherness of the Indian as a marginalized, rural person who lived in a "region of refuge," spoke a native language, and claimed to belong to an indigenous community.[29]

SECOND-WAVE *INDIGENISMO*: MEXICO'S NATIONAL INDIGENIST INSTITUTE AND ITS PILOT COORDINATING CENTER IN CHIAPAS

The law that created Mexico's INI in 1948 outlined a tame, paternalistic, and "scientific" agenda. The INI would research the "Indian problem," study and promote ways to "improve" indigenous populations, and coordinate the action of relevant government agencies. The INI insisted tirelessly that the "problem" was environmental and cultural, not racial. Like the Cardenistas, the INI's founders believed that indigenous people required material and technical assistance, although the INI greatly expanded this idea and sought to promote and manage cultural change related to agriculture, education, health care, and the like.[30]

The INI opened its first Indigenist Coordinating Center (CCI) in the Chiapas highlands, a remote, roadless area, home to the Tseltal and Tsotsil Maya. University of Chicago professor Sol Tax, his Mexican collaborator Alfonso Villa Rojas, and a team from Mexico's National School of Anthropology had conducted fieldwork there in the mid-1940s and commented extensively on the region's fierce ethnic divide, the grinding poverty, and the pervasive use of alcohol. According to the CCI's three-time director, Agustín Romano Delgado, the INI chose the Chiapas highlands precisely because it wanted "to put to the test, under the most difficult conditions," its methodologies and policies.[31]

One of the idiosyncracies of Chiapas was the existence of a third ethnic category—the *ladino*—that disrupted the Indian/mestizo binary found elsewhere in Mexico. In Chiapas, people who speak Spanish, irrespective of their phenotypical features, are labeled ladinos. Federal indigenistas— all of them born and raised outside of Chiapas—drew a sharp distinction between "modern" mestizos (like themselves) and "backward" ladinos who exploited indigenous peoples.

The linchpin of the INI's development program were the cultural promoters, indigenous men who literally promoted INI programs in their home communities. Shortly after the CCI opened its doors, the indigenistas gave crash courses for about fifty Tseltal and Tsotsil men who had some basic literacy skills in Spanish and agreed to promote INI programs. They built literacy centers and taught basic reading and writing in the mother tongue as a "bridge" to Spanish literacy. They also introduced improved seeds and agricultural techniques, supported the INI's health, hygiene, and road-building campaigns, and helped introduce piped water and consumer cooperatives.

The cultural promoters were the first to assimilate. In fact, in 1955, several male promoters began aspiring to ladina wives or felt embarrassed by their monolingual indigenous spouses. Two promoters had actually left their indigenous wives and married ladinas. For the CCI's director at the time, Agustín Romano, this pattern represented a "grave danger. If this process of 'passing' accelerates and only involves indigenous men and ladinas, the indigenous woman will remain in a state of cultural backwardness," jeopardizing the overall stability of indigenous society. Despite this, Romano found a silver lining, for it "represented a step forward in the process of incorporating the indigenous with the mestizo," citing a "'permeability' between the two groups that would have been unthinkable three years earlier."[32]

Between 1950 and 1955, and despite the INI's modest initial charge, its leading actors announced plans to dramatically restructure local economies in highland Chiapas, to the benefit of indigenous and nonindigenous alike. In one of his first reports to President Miguel Alemán, INI director Alfonso Caso noted that the INI's Council of Directors was considering a proposal to create an "industrial center" in the Maya highlands of Chiapas.[33] In 1953, the INI's most prolific ideologue, Gonzalo Aguirre Beltrán, boasted that the INI was elaborating an ambitious plan of regional, integral development in highland Chiapas that would improve indigenous standards of living, promote what he called "harmonious" acculturation, and create a mutually beneficial "economic interdependence" with the ladino population. This would be done "without creating grave situations of interethnic tension that impede the process of biological and cultural mestizaje." Aguirre was confident that this would result in "the final integration of the country into a great community that is sufficiently homogenous so that regional variations do not hinder the nation's progress."[34] Needless to say, this plan involved working directly with both indigenous and ladinos.

But the INI encountered fierce resistance from powerful ladino officials in Tuxtla Gutiérrez, the state capital of Chiapas, as well as in San Cristóbal de Las Casas, where the CCI was located. Local ladino ranchers, merchants, and alcohol vendors resented the intromission of a federal institute that sought to administer to and improve the lives of whom they considered to be *their* Indians. The indigenistas came to realize how lonely and isolated they were when they confronted the illegal statewide alcohol monopoly of ladino brothers Hernán and Moctezuma Pedrero.[35] Following a tense standoff in 1954 and 1955, the INI and the state government agreed to a series of compromises that, among other things, privatized some of the INI's operations and brought an end to the indigenistas' more utopian schemes to restructure the regional economy. The INI's wings were clipped at its pilot coordinating center, with profound implications for the indigenista project in the rest of Mexico.

After the INI was forced to abandon its plans to remake the Chiapas highlands, it turned its gaze inward to the only place where it would be allowed work—to the indigenous communities themselves. The indigenistas doubled down on their programs of cultural assimilation. Caso signaled as much when he pledged to address the "fundamentally *cultural* problems of the indigenous," such as the lack of communication with the outside world and the persistence of traditional farming and healing practices.[36] This renewed focus on cultural assimilation coincided with a fortuitous innovation in the CCI's Department of Visual Aids, a bilingual hand-puppet theater called the Teatro Petul. The CCI used the wildly popular puppets to promote all of its programs, particularly those related to education and public health and hygiene.[37]

By the late 1950s, the INI could claim modest victories in its education programs. More girls were attending INI schools, and in December 1959, nine students finished the sixth grade at the INI's boarding school, including the first three indigenous young women to ever finish primary school in the region.[38] They were well on their way to becoming *promotoras*. However, budget woes forced the INI to dismiss a teacher and send twenty-one aspiring cultural promoters to attend schools with ladinos in San Cristóbal. This established a dangerous precedent, as the INI began outsourcing the training of its most important assets. Most aspiring education promoters ended up at the Ministry of Public Education's Belisario Domínguez boarding school in San Cristóbal, where the pressure to assimilate could be summed up in the school's letterhead, which read: "Mexicanizar al indio y no indigenizar a México" (Mexicanize the Indian and don't "indigenize" Mexico). The students were encouraged to return to their home communities during vacations, but this was not enough contact to prevent what anthropologist Ulrich Köhler described as "certain disagreeable forms of 'ladinization.'" Even the barely literate students "felt superior to the elders and ridiculed their opinions." Köhler felt that a certain degree of ladinization was unavoidable, "and this is absolutely what the INI pursues, since these indigenous should act as mediators between both cultures." Too much ladinization, however, "could render such promoters as ineffective as those teachers that were born ladinos."[39] Indigenous individuals were assimilating, but they were leaving their communities behind.

Serious problems had emerged at the INI's pilot coordinating center, but Mexico was still considered to be at the cutting edge of hemispheric indigenista policy. Beginning in 1959, Mexico's National School of Anthropology and History began hosting a two-year program on the applied social sciences for the Organization of American States. As anthropologist Juan Comas wrote, "The fact that the project is based in Mexico . . . shows that our country can offer the rest of the continent's Indo-mestizo nations a valued experience using applied social anthropology to solve the problems of incorporation and integration of aboriginal groups and communities to their respective nationality."[40] In 1965, the Mexican government, the Pan-American Union, and the Organization of American States began training personnel to promote the modernization of indigenous communities. Students spent the first year at the INI's coordinating center in San Cristóbal and the second year at the INI's center in Peto, Yucatán; INI personnel provided the instruction. This program was open to students from all member states and offered instruction in applied anthropology, cultural assimilation, and the theory behind the CCIs.[41]

Unfortunately for the INI, its high profile international role did not translate into local support. During the presidential administration of the fiercely conservative Gustavo Díaz Ordaz (1964–1970), indigenistas throughout Mexico faced strong political headwinds, and the INI's budget woes became permanent. In Chiapas, many of the CCI's most creative collaborators resigned from their posts, and the INI struggled to attract high-caliber replacements. The CCI's agriculture and livestock programs remained necessarily modest. Shifting national priorities and local opposition took land and labor reform off the table, and the indigenistas struggled to provide Tseltal and Tsotsil farmers with the credit they needed. Late in the decade, the CCI's Department of Forestry suffered stinging defeats at the hands of ladino logging companies. Its medical programs, which had learned to function in a medically plural environment, gradually gave way to the federal Ministry of Health. The poorly funded indigenistas found themselves tending to the collateral damage of the federal government's hydroelectric projects.[42]

The CCI in highland Chiapas entered the 1970s as a badly weakened institution. But it was not yet irrelevant. The CCI director Maurilio Muñoz's concluding remark in his sober year-end report for 1969 shows that even after a long decade of decline, the CCI in Chiapas still drew an international audience. He noted with evident pride that researchers from dozens of world-renowned universities had visited the CCI that year, as had reporters from several countries, diplomats from the United Nations, France, Canada, and Great Britain, and development specialists from eighteen countries across Europe, Asia, and the Americas.[43] Still, it was clear that less than twenty years after its founding, the CCI in highland Chiapas was important more for what it had been than for what it had become.

THE ANTHROPOLOGICAL CRITIQUE

In 1970, five young, talented Mexican anthropologists declared open season on indigenista anthropology. Early that year they published a book that carried a derisive title—*De eso que llaman antropología mexicana* (What They Call Mexican Anthropology). The five contributors to this volume—Arturo Warman, Guillermo Bonfil Batalla, Margarita Nolasco Armas, Mercedes Olivera Bustamante, and Enrique Valencia—were part of a slightly larger group of anthropologists dubbed "the Siete Magníficos," the Magnificent Seven, by the national press.[44] Their book lambasted Mexican anthropology for placing itself at the service of the state, accused the state of internal colonialism, and eviscerated the INI's assimilationist project.

Guillermo Bonfil Batalla's chapter landed devastating blows to the indigenista project. "Stated brutally, it consists in disappearing Indians," he wrote. "Yes, there is talk of preserving indigenous values, without ever explaining clearly how this is to be achieved."[45] The indigenista's job, Bonfil concluded, was to introduce change in the communities "so that the goals of the dominant society are achieved with the least amount of conflict and tension. Stated less elegantly, the anthropologist is a specialist at manipulating Indians."[46]

In her chapter, Margarita Nolasco noted that Mexican indigenismo gave indigenous peoples only one unattractive option. "To survive, they need to change, but the class structure of global capitalism has them immobilized," she wrote. Once they shed their indigeneity, their only hope would be to "leave their region of refuge and become proletarianized, that is, they can trade colonial exploitation for class exploitation."[47] Bonfil also believed that the INI's goal of integration on an equal plane with other

Mexicans was an empty promise, since Mexican society was plagued with grave inequalities, and indigenous groups would almost certainly enter the mainstream at the bottom.[48]

In January 1971, Bonfil joined ten other high-profile Latin American social scientists at a symposium in Barbados to indict the allegedly colonial and classist nature of indigenista policies and accuse national states of direct or indirect responsibility for "many crimes of genocide and ethnocide." The Barbados Declaration I called for the creation of truly multiethnic states "where each ethnicity has the right to manage its own affairs" and where all indigenous populations have "the right to be and remain themselves."[49] For many, this emphatic statement represented a watershed marking the end of classic indigenismo.

Not only was INI theory stale and misguided, critics argued, but it had failed to deliver on its stated goal of assimilation. When he established the INI in 1948, Alfonso Caso predicted that the "indigenous problem" would disappear in twenty years. In 1968, however, there were more Indians in Mexico—based on the most common linguistic criteria—than there had been when the institute was founded. Just days before his death in 1970, Caso made another prediction—that if incoming president Echeverría dedicated sufficient funds, he was sure that "in not more than twenty-five years we could finish resolving the [indigenous] problem."[50] For the INI's critics, not only was Caso's goal of assimilation highly flawed, apparently it was also a moving target.

THE BALANCE SHEET IN HIGHLAND CHIAPAS

To what extent had two decades of INI projects developed, integrated, and assimilated Tseltals and Tsotsils into the Mexican mainstream? In the 1950s, indigenistas proclaimed that their projects would develop entire communities. In the Chiapas highlands, however, the evidence overwhelmingly suggests otherwise. Ulrich Köhler noted in 1963 that the INI's economic development programs were given less importance than the education and public health programs and "had barely passed the experimental phase."[51] In summer 1967, sixteen years after the CCI first opened its doors, the CCI's director had to ask Alfonso Caso for a loan in order to buy ten tons of corn each week to alleviate hunger in parts of Oxchuc, Chenalhó, and Pantelhó. Indigenous communities could not feed themselves, much less export to a regional or national market. That year, education subdirector Ignacio León Pacheco declared that hunger was still the single most important factor undermining the INI's education programs.[52]

Much has changed in the ensuing decades, but grinding poverty, malnutrition, and marginalization persist in the CCI's original zone of operations. In 2011, sixty years after the CCI opened its doors, Daniel Villafuerte published work showing that Chiapas was still Mexico's poorest state; 78.5 percent of Chiapanecos lived in moderate or extreme poverty. More to the point, the twelve indigenous municipalities in the CCI's original zone of operations ranked among the state's poorest.[53]

If the INI failed to lift entire communities and municipalities out of poverty and extreme poverty, how did indigenous individuals fare? The INI development programs tended to foster a small indigenous bourgeoisie, as some promoters and former promoters ended up controlling stores, transportation cooperatives, and even municipalities. These self-serving beneficiaries of Mexican indigenismo have attracted perhaps a disproportionate amount of scholarly attention in recent years. Often overlooked is the fact that indigenista policy also empowered thousands of indigenous people to work on behalf of their communities as cultural promoters and as teachers, nurses, mechanics, and agronomists. Other beneficiaries of INI programs include the tens of thousands of indigenous children and adults who were educated in INI schools, and countless others who benefited from the INI's infrastructure programs, its public health and hygiene campaigns, and its numerous modest innovations to stimulate local economic development.

The impact of the INI's much-maligned programs of cultural assimilation and integration are harder to assess because it is difficult to separate out the INI's efforts and results from the secular, modernizing trends that have influenced rural Mexico since the 1950s. In highland Chiapas, Tseltals and Tsotsils have taken on identities as Mexicans, but they have also become more conscious of their ethnic identities, not less, especially in the wake of the 1994 uprising of the Ejército Zapatista de Liberación Nacional.[54] Some municipalities have even undergone a process of "reindianization." In numerical terms, today there are more self-identifying Tseltals and Tsotsils than ever before in history. This rise in indigenous self-awareness is mirrored at the national level; in the 2010 census, 14.8 percent of the population identified as indigenous, up from just 6.2 percent in 2000.[55] Manuel Gamio, who plotted a unilinear progression from indigeneity to mestizaje, would be shocked by the sheer number and the cultural vitality of Tseltals and Tsotsils residing in the hamlets, towns, and cities of Chiapas today. So would Alfonso Caso, who often predicted the resolution and disappearance of the "Indian problem." Although the majority of indigenous people in highland Chiapas today are still poor and marginalized, many have doctorates or law degrees or are successful merchants, and all of them still consider themselves to be indigenous.

CLOSING OFF THE COSMIC RACE

From the 1920s to the 1970s, the cult of mestizaje and indigenismo in Mexico marched hand in hand. Mestizaje, in its biological and cultural forms, became official state dogma; indigenismo emerged as a discourse and a practice that would help the Mexican state create a unified, homogenous modern nation. But Mexican mestizophilia was more complicated than it appeared, and full inclusion in the Mexican nation was out of reach for most indigenous peoples. Claude Fell writes that José Vasconcelos's book celebrating the "cosmic race" was intended to be a rallying cry, a kind of spiritual compendium directed at the young, emerging Iberoamerican continent over which loomed the imperial United States. It was more a polemic than a blueprint for forging a new "race."[56] Rick López places even less stock in Vasconcelos's most influential work. "His writings make clear that he bemoaned Mexico's racial mixture and that he did not believe his own theory, which he admitted was merely a mythology meant to boost self-confidence," he writes.[57] And Marilyn Grace Miller notes that "almost immediately after the publication of *The Cosmic Race*, Vasconcelos began to backtrack and lose faith in the notion of Latin America as providentially mestizo."[58] In 1937, he dismissed his most influential publication as "a miserable little essay" and disparaged Latin America as a continent "inhabited by second-class races."[59] After a flirtation with Fascism in 1939 and 1940—he contributed pro-Axis and pro-Hitler editorials to an ephemeral journal in Mexico City—he declared that "the mixture of very distant types [of races], as in the case of Spaniards and American Indians, has questionable results."[60] Postrevolutionary Mexico's most prominent proponent of mestizaje had come full circle.

The next generation of Mexican intellectuals complicated the mestizophilic narrative and abandoned the racial determinism that undergirded the writings of Molina Enríquez and Vasconcelos. Perhaps Octavio Paz had the final word in 1950, when he famously suggested in *The Labyrinth of Solitude* that the Mexican mestizo is a violated orphan. "The Mexican does not want to be either an Indian or a Spaniard," Paz wrote. "Nor does he want to be descended from them. He denies them. And he does not affirm himself as a mixture. . . . He becomes the son of Nothingness."[61]

In the 1950s and 1960s, the INI was at the vanguard of Pan-American indigenismo, and yet it fell well short of its goals. At the INI's pilot coordinating center in highland Chiapas, the indigenistas' inability to overturn exploitative political and economic systems led to projects that attempted to induce cultural change in indigenous peoples themselves. These projects met with less opposition and were easier to implement.[62] Köhler observed, however, that "the INI certainly did not practice the kind of systematic cultural engineering that one might expect" from an institute that devoted itself to managed cultural change.[63] Indigenistas overestimated their ability to induce and manage change in the countryside and oversold their ability to resolve the so-called Indian problem.

Indigenismo's promise of full inclusion was empty, in part because post-revolutionary Mexico idealized and promoted a kind of mestizaje that was practically out of reach for indigenous people. During the 1920s and early 1930s, the heyday of mestizophilia, the Mexican state favored the modern, urban, industrial, and preferably light-skinned mestizo. This is made perfectly clear in the artwork that illustrated the official magazine of the Regional Confederation of Mexican Workers. True to the art deco and art nouveau styles that were current at the time, the artwork featured light-skinned men with European features who looked nothing like most Mexican factory workers and miners.[64] The Ministry of Public Education's celebrated school art programs and radio shows privileged urban (presumably mestizo) children over their rural, often indigenous peers.[65] Many Mexican eugenicists at the time believed that racial mixing would somehow result in the "whitening" of the population and the disappearance of the mestizo from the national landscape. One prominent Mexican eugenicist, Dr. Rafael Carrillo, told the Mexican Eugenics Society in 1932 that "if *mestizaje* continues indefinitely, it will disappear over time, given that the white race, being superior, will prevail over the inferior black and Indian."[66]

As Mexico's critical anthropologists noted decades later, even when the indigenous shed their indigineity, there was no place for them in Vasconcelos's disavowed "cosmic race." Despite the celebration of the mestizo and the quasi-indigenista lessons in the official education system, "aesthetic paradigms denigrate the great majority of the population," writes Agustín Basave.[67] Miller agrees. "The privileging of whiteness continued concurrently with the deployment of mestizaje as a national and regional doctrine." Official ideology "declared the worth and occasionally even the superiority of the non-white," but "sociopolitical circumstances continued to display the reality of prejudice."[68] Some scholars have argued recently that indigenismo may have inadvertently "hardened" ethnic distinctions in Mexico, and may have therefore worked at cross-purposes with its stated goal of acculturation and national unity. López Caballero ventures that the INI's institutionalization of indigenous alterity may have been its "most lasting legacy."[69]

During the administration of President José López Portillo (1976–1982), the INI officially disavowed its long-standing commitment to cultural assimilation. Its new director, Ignacio Ovalle Fernández, stated that indigenous communities had an "indisputable right" to preserve their ethnic identity. Ovalle pledged to end policies "that aimed at homogenization and cultural mestizaje, as well as paternalistic measures that supplanted the initiative of the communities themselves."[70] The INI—and the Mexican state—had officially surrendered its campaign to forge a unified mestizo national identity. This decision was confirmed in 1990, when a reform to

Article 4 of the Mexican Constitution read that "[t]he Mexican Nation has a multicultural composition, originally based on its indigenous peoples" and promised to "protect and promote the development of their languages, cultures, traditions, customs, resources, and specific forms of social organization."[71] In 2003, the INI disappeared and was replaced by the decentralized National Commission for the Development of Indigenous Peoples (*Comisión Nacional para el Desarrollo de los Pueblos Indígenas*, or CDI).

In late 2018, Mexican president-elect Andrés Manuel López Obrador—who directed an INI coordinating center as a young man in 1977—announced the disappearance of the ineffective CDI. In its place, his government created the *Instituto Nacional de los Pueblos Indígenas* and revived the coordinating centers, to be staffed by indigenous peoples themselves. Now that the long-held illusory dream of mestizo unity is dead and buried, time will tell whether this new institution can chart a new, more prosperous and inclusive course for Mexico's indigenous people.

CHAPTER SIX

CREATING FALSE ANALOGIES

RACE AND DRUG WARS, 1930S TO 1950S

Elaine Carey

On the US-Mexico border, whiteness has been constructed against the Mexican "other."[1] Historically, racialized narratives of northern European superiority served to limit Mexican Americans' access to land, jobs, economic resources, and political power in towns, cities, and states in the southwestern United States. Far from the periphery, policy makers, policing agents, and journalists associated the term Mexican—a national designation—with lawlessness, deviancy, and criminality. Beginning in the 1930s, Federal Bureau of Narcotics (FBN) director Harry J. Anslinger created an antidrug campaign based on alleged "Mexican" deviancy that included drug use, trafficking, and violence. His interpretation informed national and international drug policies that continue to the present. An example of the contemporary juxtaposition of Mexican deviancy emerged in the 2016 US presidential elections when then candidate Donald J. Trump proclaimed in June 2015: "When Mexico sends its people, they're not sending their best. . . . They're sending people with lots of problems, and they're bringing those problems with us. They're bringing drugs. They're bringing crime. They're rapists. And some, I assume are good people."[2]

Using critical race theory and intersectionality, I argue that policy makers embraced constructs of race on the US-Mexico border from the 1930s to the 1950s to obstruct social and economic inclusion and to mobilize political powers to criminalize Mexican Americans and Mexicans in the United States. Politicians and policing agents routinely crafted false narratives of deviance that defied medical professionals and ignored the increasing drug demand among whites in the United States to justify the use of tactics that violated laws and Mexican sovereignty. Most importantly, this analysis focuses on the drug wars of the 1930s to 1950s as forms of white supremacy that defied evidence regarding drug use and addiction to marginalize Mexican Americans on the border and in major cities across the United States while downplaying white Americans' agency in the drug trade.[3]

To interpret and problematize the historical continuities of race and vice as associated with Mexicans and Mexican Americans, I provide an overview of the tensions between the United States and Mexico over drug control beginning with the passage of the 1914 Harrison Narcotics Act. For American federal, state, and local police, Mexican leaders' alleged inability to secure ports and control the drug trade contributed to numerous hearings and studies in the US Congress as well as in state governments. In this chapter, I examine Senate hearings on illicit narcotics traffic that took place in 1955 in cities across the United States.[4] The hearings in Texas focused on the transnational flows of narcotics, specifically heroin, from Mexico to cities such as Austin, a city 380 kilometers from the border but part of the drug commodity chains. These hearings reflected historical arguments that Mexicans and Mexican Americans were responsible for intoxicating upstanding white Americans. Although the hearings focused on the drug trade, politicians questioned the citizenship of Mexican Americans and pondered how to respond to their savagery that undermined the public health and civic virtues of white America. Using the examples of Simona Cavazos and an Anglo informant Travis Schnautz, I explore the governing mentalities of gendered and racialized discourses regarding the drug trade in which Cacazos represented criminality and deviancy on multiple levels as a woman, as a Mexican, as working class, and as a potential foreigner in the United States.[5] Schnautz, though an addict, served as an informed victim who gained redemption through the hearings due to his knowledge of the drug trade in Texas.

Americans' anti-narcotics crusade emerged in the wake of the Spanish American War (1898) when Americans occupied the Philippines and debated issues of health, including what to do about opium use and trafficking. The US Philippine Commission, led by Maj. E. C. Carter, Dr. Jose Albert, and Rev. Charles H. Brent, issued a report that examined opium trafficking and use in East Asia. The members of the committee blamed Chinese traffickers for the widespread drug use in the Philippines and much of Asia. Moreover, they argued that non-Christian Filipinos like "Mohammedan Malays," were prone to opium use, and drug use in general, because of their weakness.[6] To the commission members, stronger men had to defend Filipinos from their purported vices.

Like their counterparts in the United States and Europe, Mexican officials judged addiction and drug peddling as social issues that undermined the health of its citizens who were needed to rebuild the nation after the Mexican Revolution. By 1920, Edmundo G. Aragón, the secretary-general of the Department of Health, implemented restrictions and limitations on the cultivation and distribution of products that "foment vice and that degenerate the people."[7] The Mexican federal government required that the

Department of Health grant permissions and maintain records of business-people and medical professionals who wished to import opium, morphine, heroin, or cocaine. Those products could be imported only for medicinal purposes issued by medical doctors and pharmacists. Previously, the United States and Canada had passed similar laws.[8] Mexican leaders, like their US counterparts, realized that the coastlines and the shared border were spaces of concern where illegal commodities and fugitives from the law flowed.

Sea and land ports of entry on the US coasts and those along the US-Canada and US-Mexico borders served as sites where the United States's constructs of deviance grew more rigid, particularly with regard to the southern border in the Prohibition era (1920–1933). Towns along the US-Mexico border created zones of tolerance that welcomed US travelers and tourists, offering both alcohol and sex tourism. In the 1920s, US-Mexico relations became fraught due to the bootlegging across the US-Mexico border, particularly with the passage of the Volstead Act, which established Prohibition. Along the southern border, concepts of race and criminality grew more pronounced due to Mexican leaders agreeing to abide by certain US restrictions, while *contrabandistas* defied these rules.[9] Whereas policy makers in the United States constructed narratives about Mexican deviancy, officials and medical professionals in Mexico recognized that certain people suffered from addiction, or engaged in criminal behavior due to drug use. As historian Isaac Campos has argued, Mexicans embraced a form of reefer madness. As medical doctors and scholars studied the impact of marijuana use, however, they concluded that it did not drive users insane.[10] Yet, their research was widely ignored by American leaders.

Borders became associated with crime and vice, much in the way that present-day El Paso, Texas, is characterized as a violent city even though its crime rates are very low. Cities such as San Diego-Tijuana, El Paso-Ciudad Juárez, and even Detroit-Windsor, Ontario, became associated with vice.[11] On both sides of the US-Mexico border, parents' organizations and women's groups challenged the zones of tolerance that flourished during Prohibition. Mexico as a site of production and transshipment remained a primary concern of the United States and that concern escalated over the 1920s and 1930s. The alleged Mexican defiance of US authorities contested narratives of success. That defiance was far more complicated because transnational organized crime networks engaged in smuggling of alcohol as well as drugs. The violence that engulfed US cities during Prohibition increased Anslinger's focus on immigrants while he was the assistant commissioner of the Bureau of Prohibition.[12] In that capacity, he had collected arrest records and seizure statistics of alcohol and marijuana from the US-Mexico border. Immigrants became suspected of violating the Volstead Act even though immigrants and citizens violated the law.[13] Many Americans saw Mexican immigrants as competition for jobs and a drain on early social welfare systems, which led to the creation of repatriation programs.[14]

Those fears were further exacerbated by elite Americans who embraced racist arguments during times of growing economic uncertainty. For example, in January of 1928, before the collapse of the economy, C. M. Goethe published "The Influx of Mexican Amerinds," in *Eugenics: A Journal of Race Betterment*. In his article, he decried the growing migration of poor and working-class Mexicans to California. He wrote, "It is doubtful whether ten percent of Mexico's say 15 million are free from Amerind blood. Eugenically as low-powered as the Negro, the peon is from a sanitation standpoint a menace. He not only does not understand health rules: being a superstitious savage, he resists them."[15] Mexicans, he evaluated, lowered wages for native-born workers. More significant, he asserted that they brought diseases and vice, and engaged in miscegenation. He added that Mexican women had more children than native white women. While he argued that Ellis Island may have closed, a back door along the US-Mexico border must close. A philanthropist who made his wealth in banking and real estate in California, Goethe's views and those of others, though extreme, found a growing audience in the United States during the 1920s and 1930s. Although he was an early environmentalist, he was also the founder of the Eugenic Society of Northern California.

In the 1920s, certain US public health professionals questioned eugenics proponents and considered whether Mexican drug addiction and deviance were more myth than reality. Charles Edward Terry differed in his analysis of Mexico and Mexican addicts compared to men such as Goethe. Terry finished medical school at the University of Maryland, after which he returned to his home state of Florida to practice medicine alongside his brother in Jacksonville.[16] There, he became the city's health officer. As a young doctor, he created a maintenance program for addicts in the city that lasted until the passage of the Harrison Act of 1914. Although he closed maintenance programs after that year, he wrote about his belief that the new legislation would not end addiction.[17] By the mid-1920s, he attained the position of the executive director of the Committee on Drug Addictions, which was funded by the Bureau of Social Hygiene founded by John D. Rockefeller.[18] In that capacity, he conducted the bureau's 1923–1924 study on narcotics use in six communities in the United States, including El Paso. There he argued that few Mexicans consulted medical doctors and few used narcotics. Instead, he wrote,

> The poverty of the patient and the disinclination of Mexican physicians to prescribe narcotics make for a very low Mexican legal per capita use. It is notice-

able that prescriptions including narcotics issued to Mexicans, were in the large majority of cases, written by American physicians. It was also noted that the number of prescriptions was considerably less in the Mexican drug stores in proportion to their other trade than in the American drug stores, and that ratio of narcotic prescriptions to the general file of prescriptions in the Mexican drug stores was about one-half that obtaining in the American drug stores, although both Americans and Mexicans patronized Mexican drug stores. This feature was so outstanding that it is believed the legal use of narcotics for Mexicans was practically negligible.[19]

In his analysis, Terry blamed American medical doctors for encouraging legalized addiction. Both in the past and today, US public health officials and narcotics policing agents ignored Mexico's historically low rates of drug use and addiction. Compared to those in the United States, the country's low addiction rates were not lost on Mexican officials, and some US medical professionals and government agencies provided evidence to support such data. Terry argued that Mexicans in El Paso turned to traditional methods to treat illnesses rather than seek out opiates. There may have been reasons for that. Terry's study took place in the midst of the 1924 Immigration Act that determined that Mexican workers who crossed the border were indeed illegal. Thus, white doctors in El Paso may not have been willing to treat Mexicans and Mexican Americans, or Mexicans distrusted white doctors in light of legal changes.

Even the US Internal Revenue Service noted that the lowest levels of drug use in the 1920s occurred in those southwestern American states that directly bordered Mexico. The two coasts harbored the largest number of addicts: California and Washington State in the West and Massachusetts, New York, New Jersey, Maryland, and Virginia in the East. States along the Mississippi River also had more addicts than those states that bordered Mexico.[20]

In Mexico, Dr. Leopoldo Salazar Viniegra studied the impact of drug use and addiction while serving as the director of the Hospital of Drug Addiction and Alcoholism in the La Castañeda mental asylum in the 1930s. Similar to medical doctors in the United States who saw addiction as a disease, Salazar considered an array of issues that contributed to drug addiction such as trauma or childhood abuse. Trained in psychiatry in Europe, Salazar worked closely with internal medicine doctors in efforts to understand addiction. Moreover, in his writings, he argued that addiction was an illness rather than a crime, and he continued to advocate for treatment. He attempted to collaborate with medical doctors researching drug addiction in the United States, but Anslinger ensured that Salazar could not visit the United States for such projects.[21]

With the formation of the FBN in 1930 under the Secretary of Treasury, Anslinger, a career diplomat, altered the approach to addiction and drug-related crimes that he had mastered while working for the Bureau of Prohibition.[22] He constructed a racist narrative that Chinese, Mexican, and African Americans, as drug traffickers, conspired against the health of the citizens of the United States who he represented and imagined as exclusively white. In the context of growing concerns regarding crime, drug use, and juvenile delinquency, Anslinger fostered an image of Mexicans as promoters of vice. He cast himself as the defender of white middle- and upper-middle-class women who were victims of foreign drug traffickers. As scholars Michael Omi and Howard Winant have argued, race and racism are manifested in historical moments.[23] Anslinger understood white Americans' fears of African Americans, Mexicans, and immigrants, and he used those fears to heighten tension and cast ethnic minorities as those solely responsible for drug use, addiction, and trafficking. His analysis never pursued questions of white demand for drugs but instead that drug abuse was an issue of supply, distribution, and selling. Having learned through Prohibition that he could not force Mexico and Canada to control smuggling, he altered his approach once director of the FBN. The bureau became the tool by which Anslinger manifested his racism to an international audience, demanding that all countries aggressively police drugs, expand drug enforcement, and adopt more punitive sentences.[24]

Anslinger became a primary vehicle for propaganda about race and drug use that defied the evidence of studies conducted by medical doctors such as Terry and Salazar. He elaborated "foreignness" to portray a country under attack by external forces. He argued that narcotics abuse was one of the four horsemen of the apocalypse, which included Communists, Orientals, Africans, and Central Americans. In his public talks, Anslinger dredged up twenty-year-old narratives of "reefer madness," which he claimed was afflicting Mexico. He highlighted the case of Victor Licata, a young, allegedly Mexican man who murdered his family while high on marijuana as evidence of his claims.[25] Newspaper reports and medicinal studies of the early 1900s argued that "Mexican" marijuana was a source of grave concerns. Ridiculous claims ensued. Some journalists wrote that the Empress Carlota had succumbed to insanity because of her penchant for marijuana.[26] Other reports argued that Mexico City's Belem Prison was full of marijuana addicts, that soldiers freely used the plant, and that miners who were intoxicated on it killed their American managers.[27]

The FBN, along with other federal agencies, monitored and controlled drugs and narcotics during World War II. Yet the United States also experienced a labor shortage during the conflict. Whereas the United States had repatriated Mexicans during the Depression, the US and Mexican governments signed an agreement in 1942 to create the Bracero Program, which brought Mexican agricultural laborers to the United States. The Bracero Program and the growing Mexican population in the Southwest added to renewed concerns about Mexicans and marijuana use and distribution. In 1944, New York City mayor Fiorella La Guardia's Committee on Marijuana further argued that Mexican workers, who naturally used marijuana in Mexico, continued to plant marijuana and made it available to "citizens."[28]

During World War II, the FBN sought to extradite Mexican drug traffickers and peddlers to the United States for violation of the Harrison Narcotics Act even when certain drug traffickers had never visited the country. Anslinger had successfully used this tactic against traditional organized crime figures such as those associated with the mafia. Although the FBN targeted the Italian mafia in the United States, it also placed special agents in Mexico without the knowledge or consent of the Mexican government. These agents collected intelligence that Mexican drug traffickers had contacts with Italian organized crime. These alliances emerged during Prohibition, and the networks have continued into the present.[29]

The FBN had some success in its attempts to deport, jail, or extradite organized crime drug traffickers. The most famous case was the deportation of Lucky Luciano. In Mexico, the FBN put pressure on the Mexican government, and on April 27, 1945, Mexican president Manuel Ávila Camacho issued a presidential decree that waived constitutional guarantees in the cases of narcotics trafficking, and permitted the immediate detention of peddlers and smugglers at the Federal Penitentiary at Tres Marías without trial in the Mexican courts.[30] Some drug traffickers were detained, but none were extradited to the United States.[31]

As Anslinger built a reputation as America's drug expert, he employed the media to become a celebrity expert on the decadence and decline of an America that was allegedly under attack by Black, Latino, and Asian hordes who brought their vices to the United States. Anslinger tended to associate marijuana, narcotics, and drug distribution and use with communities of color. He claimed that he originally became interested in narcotics control due to the overwhelming numbers of female addicts before the passage of the Harrison Act, and he remained gravely concerned about female drug use.[32] In his mind, drug use led white women to reject their families, to engage in miscegenation, and to prostitute themselves to support their addiction.

Women, too, fit into these constructs of deviance that Anslinger detailed in his books, articles, and speeches at public meetings and other venues. He argued that white women were more prone to addiction to narcotics such as heroin and laudanum. Thus, they needed more protection from disreputable doctors who overprescribed drugs. Although some female addicts could be rehabilitated to become proper women, others were deemed as incapable of doing so. In his speeches, he expressed an ongoing concern about Mexican women in the drug trade. His FBN staff sent reports to the Federal Bureau of Investigation director J. Edgar Hoover; they routinely reported about women who were leaders in the Mexican drug trade. Thus, they, as pushers, deviated from Anslinger's constructs of white femininity. Moreover, in Anslinger's writings, Mexican men were unable to control such women. Both scenarios further added to the nation's deviance and barbarism.[33] Anslinger's ability to shape the rhetoric of the early drug war seeped into government hearings whether at the state or national level. While he instilled this fear, addiction rates of Mexicans and Mexican Americans continued to be lower than those of the United States in general.

Across the United States, local, state, and national politicians embraced Anslinger's racialized arguments even when presented with evidence that contradicted many of these widely held falsehoods. A perfect example of these contradictions is evident in the 1955 Senate hearings on the Illicit Narcotics Traffic. In 1955, the US Senate Judiciary Committee created a subcommittee to undertake a study of drugs and the need to change the federal criminal code. Meetings were held in cities across the United States. In part, Price Daniel, the Democratic senator from Texas, held these public hearings to bolster legislative changes that ultimately influenced the passage of the 1956 Narcotics Control Act.[34] The hearings in the United States followed similar ones held in Canada in 1955 when the Canadian federal government formed the Special Committee on the Traffic in Narcotic Drugs.[35] Meetings were held in major Canadian cities in which medical professionals, social welfare agencies, police, and the American Anslinger, testified about drug trafficking and addiction.[36] In the United States, the Price Daniel hearings were held in different cities and states, including New York; Pennsylvania; Washington, DC; Texas; and California, with Anslinger testifying there as well.[37] The purpose of the hearings was to establish the extent of drug use and drug trafficking, with much of it associated with "Red China" and that country's attempts to poison Americans.[38]

Held in September, the hearings reflected clashes between the medical community and policing agencies over what to do about drug addiction. The New York hearings served as a platform to discuss efforts in the struggle against drug addiction; those held outside of Washington, DC, and New York had a regional focus with an emphasis on the growing drug problems in major cities and regions in the United States. In Chicago and Detroit, the hearings highlighted connections to Canada and the role of organized crime syndicates in drug trafficking and distribution in major Midwestern cities.

During the Texas and California hearings, Mexico emerged as the key supplier of heroin as well as a site of transshipment of European and Asian opiate derivatives. Anslinger also reported that Mexico accounted for 90 percent of the marijuana in the United States.[39] A close reading of what became commonly referred to as the Daniel Commission Report of 1955 on Illicit Narcotics Traffic challenges conclusions common in the drug literature published from the 1970s to the 1990s. Such hearings gave addicts, traffickers, police, and politicians numerous venues to discuss drug use, addiction, and crime as experts. The witnesses provided first-hand information about the drug trade in the 1950s. Yet, the racialized narrative constructed by Anslinger over twenty-five years remained evident. Frequently those in positions of power refused to hear their own experts' testimonies about addiction and trafficking. Instead, they steered questions or offered comments that constructed a narrative of vice associated with Mexicans. For example, when journalist Ruben Salazar testified about the drug trade in Ciudad Juárez, the World War II veteran had to prove his US citizenship to the members of the committee. Racism informed how white politicians portrayed drug use as a supply problem, and addiction as something that remained in urban cities and in Mexican American communities. Ever an astute bureaucrat, Anslinger framed his arguments and rhetoric from greater foreign policy to ensure the continuation of his bureau. The Texas and California hearings positioned Mexico as a historical site of marijuana and heroin supply, which was indeed true. Yet, addiction and drug use among whites in Texas and the Southwest was never considered to be key to the drug trade. Demand created the markets. Instead, white men and women in the drug trade were cast as victims of African American and Mexican drug pushers and criminals rather than active participants in all levels of the drug trade.[40]

In the Texas hearings, men and women appeared instrumental to the drug trade. Customs agents described how women crossed the international border with their husbands to smuggle marijuana for consumption in Texas. The border lured Americans to the area to engage in criminal behavior. Anslinger recognized that women "obeyed narcotics laws better than men in which men were arrested three times the rate of women."[41] Yet, white women from as far away as New York City smuggled marijuana across the US-Mexico border to sell it in Brooklyn and Manhattan and other cities. Women (and men) of all ethnicities used cars and planes, stuffed their clothing, and even used sanitary napkins to smuggle marijuana.[42] Yet white women were always portrayed as victims.

Even when witnesses challenged the racialized views of the drug trade that senators held, their testimony was met with wonder and astonishment. In the testimonies of Capt. R. B. Laws of the Criminal Investigation Division of the Austin Police Department and Lt. K. R. Herbert, the officer in charge, they outlined arrests of male and female addicts in Austin. In Laws's and Herbert's testimony, they presented evidence that more Anglo-Americans were addicts compared to Mexicans or African Americans.[43] Senator Daniel was shocked by this acknowledgement because it contradicted the meta-narrative of race, vice, and crime purported by men such as Anslinger. Daniel proclaimed:

> This is the first city in which we have held a hearing in which the Anglo Americans are more involved in arrests than the other races. The figures here are considerably higher than in the colored, for instance. In some cities it is unfortunately [a] thing, it may be the fault of the way we have taken care of certain races, but we find the arrests among [the] colored population to be high as 90 percent of the total arrests. Here, you have just the reverse, not that high a percentage, but there are twice as many Anglo Americans arrested during these years than you have colored.[44]

Captain Laws replied to Daniel's question with an affirmation that in Austin more Anglo-Americans were arrested. This striking exchange makes it appear that only in Texas, white Americans used drugs more than African Americans or Latinos. Yet, the evidence that had been gathered by Terry and others working with the Bureau of Social Hygiene as early as the 1920s in fact repeatedly demonstrated that whites remained the largest consumers of narcotics whether on the southern or northern borders. Moreover, Terry had found that whites in Washington State had higher addiction rates; in the Deep South in the 1920s African Americans had lower rates of narcotics use. What changed was that after Prohibition, organized crime targeted African American and Latino communities for drug distribution in major cities. Yet this caused little concern for US officials focused on a racialized view of drug trafficking and usage.

Although medical doctors and policing agents argued that Mexicans were not prone to addiction, during the Daniel hearings, Mexicans, like Chinese, were cast as the villains and responsible for the drug trade. One example emerged in the Austin hearings when police and addicts spoke of Mexican-born Simona Cavazos, a San Antonio-based dealer and trafficker. The focus on Cavazos and addicts who purchased drugs from her demonstrates how the politicians heard testimonies from witnesses but interpreted that information to support an ongoing narrative of Mexican vice and criminality.

One of the addicts who testified was Travis Schnautz, a twenty-three-year-old native of Austin, who described in detail Austin's drug culture to the senators. Schnautz explained that when he started working at a service station at the age of seventeen he was introduced to the drug trade. There, he observed boys from his school go to the gas station "to fix." One of those boys was Ben Curry who befriended Schnautz. Schnautz's mother testified that Curry, an Austin high school football star, addicted her son Travis, and Schnautz admitted to the senators that Curry gave him his "first shot of dope."[45]

In Schnautz's testimony, politicians asked about African Americans and Mexicans in the drug trade, but did not pursue questions regarding Curry. In his responses to the committee, Schnautz described that African Americans did not use heroin at the same level as whites, but they did smoke marijuana. The dealers who bought heroin purchased it from Mexican suppliers but in very small amounts. During the hearing, Schnautz, as the expert drug user, was asked about drug use in the African American community because he had accompanied a Mexican dealer to deliver heroin to an African American drug dealer. Schnautz had never used drugs purchased from African Americans, and he could not even name the alleged dealer. Yet, he was an expert who testified before the US Senate about African American drug use in Texas.[46]

Schnautz did, however, have more information regarding Mexicans in the drug trade because he insisted that much of the heroin and marijuana in Austin came from Cavazos. Cavazos had a complex past. The men on the committee portrayed her as someone who stumbled into being a heroin supplier who intoxicated more whites than other races. Yet in fact she was instrumental to facilitating the flow of heroin from Mexico to the Texas state capital, a city more than three hours away by car from Laredo-Nuevo Laredo.[47] Schnautz elaborated, "Simona had good connections. . . . I have seen her with 200 to 250 grams in her purse in one-gram packages. She was good to me. She would sell me on a credit."[48]

Lieutenant Herbert and R. C. Scott, an investigator with the Austin Police Department, worked with Thomas Bromley of the FBN. Scott described "a pattern that was handed to me that I had to conform to and I was introduced to these people by a special employee furnished by the Federal Bureau of Narcotics."[49] Scott told the committee about a sting operation in which the "special employee," Bromley, who was an FBN informant and former addict, had just been released from the Narcotics Farm, in Lexington, Kentucky.[50]

As part of the sting, Scott described visiting the Cavazos at a small bar in the "Latin American" district of San Antonio. Simona and her husband Alfonso ran and likely owned Al's Bar where Scott met them. After the initial meeting in the bar, the Cavazos couple invited him to their home that was across the street. In the course of their conversation, Simona stated that it was difficult to buy heroin by the ounce because Mexican vendors sold by *papelito* (a gram or less of heroin in a small paper). Thirty papers comprised approximately an ounce, and one paper cost $25 (approximately $240 in 2020).[51] In Scott's conversation, Simona explained that she ordered her drugs in Laredo, but she never crossed the border with the heroin herself. Instead, she arranged in Mexico to have it delivered to her in San Antonio.[52]

When Scott returned for the heroin, Simona told him she just received a shipment and could sell him two hundred grams for $5,000. Despite her misgivings about selling an ounce, she now offered to sell him a much larger amount. Narcotics officers in the 1950s would never have received $5,000 to front a drug buy.[53] Most likely, Simona offered this amount as a test. During that conversation, Scott also reported that Simona had mentioned the hearings. Scott stated: "She was under the impression you had passed a law that there was going to be a sentence of hanging for anyone who brought back from Mexico, and she was quite disturbed by that." Daniel followed up by asking Scott if he would recite one of her comments regarding the hearing. Scott did not want to say what she had said in mixed company. Daniel replied, "Well I'll ask you if she said this, if this is correct: 'I can't quit selling heroin as long as I can sit on my butt and make $400 to $500 a day.' Did she tell you that?" Scott replied that she indeed did.[54]

Because of Simona's deviance, her ethnic origin, and her posting of a $5,000 bail immediately upon her arrest, Daniel inquired if Simona was a US citizen. Scott assumed so because she and her husband Alfonso appeared to own the bar where he first met them. The question regarding her citizenship demonstrates that Daniel and others on the committee considered using extralegal methods such as deportation to remove Simona, her husband, and her organization.

As other people testified to Daniel, Simona and Alfonso's organization became more complex. Whereas some Mexicans trafficked and sold drugs for them, Schnautz's mother testified that she purchased from a white man named Raymond Murdock who worked for Simona. Others testified that Murdock worked with the Cavazos, perhaps as their lieutenant, whereas a report submitted by narcotics agents in San Antonio suggested that Murdock was Simona's lover and partner.[55] Whether Murdock and Simona were lovers or not, he worked closely with her and her extended family in buying and selling drugs and assisting in their operations of fronts to sell stolen goods.[56] More importantly, it was Murdock who sold Simona's heroin in Austin, a town with a far larger Anglo-American population than San Antonio. Texas and its cities such as San Antonio were nexus points between Mexican heroin and the lucrative US market. John Ben Sheppard, the attorney general for Texas, argued that heroin and marijuana moved through his state to neighboring states and further north.[57] The Cavazos and members of their organization realized that a Mexican distributor and dealer might be easily identified and detected in Austin. Thus, Murdock and Cavazos created a lucrative alliance.

Travis Schnautz's mother argued that her son's addiction led to her to seek out Cavazos. His mother described her role in enabling her son's addiction after he left a rehabilitation clinic in the early 1950s. She recalled that she helped her son buy heroin from Cavazos and Murdock. She also testified that they would deliver drugs to her house for a fee. Thus, Travis's mother explained that she was paying over $70 a week to maintain her son's addiction. Travis's addiction and legal problems caused the family to lose their property—a plight that many families surviving in the contemporary US opioid epidemic have experienced.[58] Although Mrs. Schnautz gave insight into her son's drug use, Cavazos remained the problem. Daniel and other senators never questioned Travis Schnautz or his mother's agency in the drug trade. They never asked him about his demand for drugs nor did they inquire about his mother's enabling of his addiction. Instead, they focused on Cavazos.

Daniel showed interest in Simona's citizenship, but he also followed up with investigator R. C. Scott about Cavazos's opinion of the committee and her comment that a law had been passed to sentence people to hanging for drug trafficking.

In an exchange, Senator Daniel asked: "Did she say that 'G.D. Senate committee recommended hanging?'"

Scott: "Yes sir."
Senator Daniel: "Well do you think hanging would be too severe for this traffic after having examined what she has done?"
Mr. Scott: "My personal opinion; it wouldn't."[59]

This exchange demonstrates the significance of time and place. Daniel was holding the hearing in Texas, a state that had a large and growing Mexican population that continued to grow due to the Bracero Program and the state's shared border with Mexico (and previous history as part of the country). The ethnic and class tensions between whites and Mexicans were over a century long.

Simona was a Mexican woman living in San Antonio, Texas, in 1955. She might have known people or heard stories about Mexican men and women being lynched with the assistance of policing agents such as the Texas Rangers.[60] Mexican women were lynched for forcefully rejecting white men's sexual overtures, speaking Spanish, or other crimes. Simona's thoughts about hanging and Daniel and Scott's exchange captures the history of violence against women who transgress proper gender roles. Simona not only had to fear male competitors who might rob and cheat her but she also contended with those in positions of power who questioned whether her crime deserved hanging rather than imprisonment.[61]

In the hearing, Daniel and Scott acknowledge that hanging was an appropriate punishment for a Mexican American woman drug trafficker.[62] Yet these ideas did not extend to white women who bought drugs and smuggled for their addicted adult children or who trafficked drugs to sell.[63] Those women who trafficked were pitied as fallen women who needed help. Moreover, harsh punishment also did not extend to white women who worked in the trade alongside their husbands, lovers, or other family members. These women too were considered victims of male vice and violence.

More intriguing, Daniel and other politicians never argued that someone such as Schnautz should be lynched. Instead, the committee treated him, a white addict, as an "expert" on the drug trade. Schnautz argued that he assisted Mexican dealers to deliver drugs to African American dealers, and yet the committee members never argued that he should be harmed for his involvement in the drug trade. The politicians craved Schnautz's insights and feared Cavazos because she trafficked and peddled drugs in Texas from a Mexican American working-class barrio. Working with a white man, Murdock and Cavazos sold to whites, and whites were the greatest consumers of heroin, on the basis of arrest records in Texas that most likely underreported their drug use compared to that of Mexicans, Asians, and African Americans.[64]

Anslinger's heightened rhetoric and the role of women in the drug trade demonstrates multiple historical continuities. In examining the Price Daniel Commission hearings, policing agents learned of the Cavazos operation from one of her customers. Cavazos's business was familial, complicated, and vast despite operating from an impoverished neighborhood in San Antonio. Simona did not addict Schnautz. He testified that his friend Curry, a white football star, gave him his first injections that greatly affected his life and that of his family. When Daniel interviewed his mother, he showed great sympathy for her even when she described buying heroin from Cavazos as well as in Mexico and smuggling it over the border for her addicted son.[65] Her demand for heroin was never presented or interpreted as a crime.

After the hearings, Cavazos disappeared from the historical record. For many drug traffickers, the loss of anonymity destroyed their businesses. These documentary silences in the historical records lead to speculation. Did Cavazos return to Mexico in fear for her life? Did she change her name and relocate to another location in the United States? Did she leave the drug trade and focus on her legal businesses?

Despite Schnautz's redemption in the hearings in which he was a cooperative witness and expert about the Texas drug market, his appearance before the committee did little to change his drug use. While employed in 1955, drug and criminal offenses marked his life in the following years. He died in 1976 at the age of forty-three when he was shot at his wife's massage parlor, causing speculation that he may have been killed because of his connection to Austin's Overton gang or his connection to a disbarred attorney John W. Flanagan who was a drug trafficker. At the time of Schnautz's murder, his former attorney Flanagan was a fugitive in Mexico escaping narcotics charges in Texas. Schnautz had been involved in the drug trade and with drug traffickers and dealers for his entire adult life. In the end, it was discovered that his wife had hired a hitman to kill him.[66] Like countless other white people in the drug trade, Schnautz's demand for drugs in the 1950s and 1960s remains mostly a documental and historical silence that surrounds his criminality.

Harry J. Anslinger's narrative of racialized vice has continued long after he retired. The exploration of Simona Cavazos and Travis Schnautz's involvement in the drug trade in the 1950s by US senators documents the gendered and racialized tensions within the policing of drugs. Schnautz and his mother were the victims of a working-class Mexican woman and her nation of origin. Even though she was not responsible for Schnautz's addiction, she and her native country became the villains of a complicated business. The perpetual hearings and multiple wars on drugs continue to undervalue white agency while elevating Mexican deviancy in the transnational drug trade.

CHAPTER SEVEN

BASEBALL AND THE CATEGORIZATION OF RACE IN VENEZUELA

David M. K. Sheinin

In 1945, Caracas sports promoters Luis Jesús Blanco Chataing and Bernardo Vizcaya organized a baseball round robin of three professional teams. "Las Estrellas Venezolanas" (The Venezuelan All-Stars) boasted members of Cervecería de Caracas of the newly organized Liga Venezolana de Béisbol Profesional (the Venezuelan Professional Baseball League or LVBP), with a few additional players from around Venezuela. There were two teams of "*importados*" (foreign athletes). "Las Estrellas del Caribe" (the Caribbean All-Stars), though, fielded mostly Venezuelans alongside two Americans and two Dominicans. The luminaries of the competition were the only team explicitly identified by race. "Las Estrellas Negras" (The Black All-Stars) were prominent African American players ineligible for segregated Major League Baseball (MLB) in the United States. They left a vital legacy on their tour. Stars of the Negro leagues in the United States, they were almost certainly the best baseball team ever to play in Venezuela, dominating the tournament, and sweeping other Venezuelan teams in a series of five games. Seven of the Americans stayed on after the visit for the 1946 LVBP season. This in itself was a landmark in that athletes from the Negro leagues had rarely played in Venezuela until then. Four went on to MLB in short order—Jackie Robinson (1947), Roy Campanella (1948), Sam Jethroe (1950), and Quince Trouppe (1952).[1] Forgotten by most Venezuelans, the Black All-Stars are remembered by some fans as a cultural and rights triumph—when Black American ball players were "integrated" into Venezuelan baseball on the eve of their incorporation into MLB.

That recollection may seem at odds with African Venezuelans having played professional baseball in Venezuela for decades (though they were rarely identified as "Black" in the media or by fans). Yet, there is no necessary contradiction. The 1945 visit of the Black All-Stars underscores a handful of key insights to Venezuelan baseball and categories of race. For more than two centuries, Venezuelans have built racial categories in relation to Blackness in a manner far more complex and nuanced than the severe post-Reconstruction Black-White binary in the United States and set in place by Plessy v. Ferguson (163 U.S. 537, 1896) and by dozens of other legal and extralegal violent norms. To be sure, constructions of race in the United States have also been more complex and nuanced than the omnipresent binary. However, as have other Latin Americans in the twentieth century, Venezuelans have at times constructed a distinct, parallel vision of US Blackness based on a binary US segregationism, with a range of cultural implications that include distinguishing a putatively less racist Venezuelan society (absent segregation and other violent US discriminatory forms) from the United States. That is evident in the 1945 characterization of the visiting Americans as "Black," even though had they been pressed, Venezuelans would likely have recognized that the other two round robin teams also included players of African descent.[2]

After 1960, baseball functioned as a unique cultural bridge between Venezuela and the United States. Just as the US players visiting in 1945 stuck around for the 1946 LBPV season, in an era before the intense, year-round training required of professional athletes in the United States today, dozens of US players finished their MLB seasons and headed for the LBPV "winter" league. In the decades following World War II, it was not uncommon for the nine players fielded by an LBPV team to be majority American, representing the full range of ethnic and racial diversity in MLB. As late as the 1980s, MLB spring training was still meant to "get players into shape," which for some, meant dropping their off-season beer bellies. Those most committed to working on their game and their conditioning often went to Venezuela in the MLB off-season. Baseball served as a cultural bridge between the United States and other countries, including Mexico, Cuba, and Panama. However, there was no equivalent elsewhere in regard to the quality and quantity of the US player presence in the LVBP—and the cultural impact on Venezuela of the movement of players, coaches, and managers from each country back and forth.[3]

The cultural bridge went far beyond the transnational movement of athletes. Venezuelan media and fans increasingly consumed and understood Venezuelan baseball through a US lens. They reported on and understood the successes and failures of teams and players in a context of US cultural constructions of baseball. Those Venezuelan approaches to the "American pastime" focused on moralities, work ethics, and a construction of race that went beyond the question of Blackness in the United States or Venezuela. The LVBP was Venezuela's number one sports attraction (and its most important leisure time diversion). It drew Venezuelan stars back from the United States. David Concepción played nineteen seasons in MLB from 1970 to 1988. A key player in what became known as "the Big Red Machine"—the 1970s Cincinnati Reds—Concepción helped the team to two consecutive World Series championships in 1975 and 1976. He was a nine-time MLB All-Star. But he also played twenty-three seasons in the Venezuelan league, from 1967 to 1990. That sort of back-and-forth was not unusual, even for a superstar World Series champion like Concepción.[4] Yet unlike the 1945 Black All-Stars, most US players who came to Venezuela in the 1960s and 1970s could not hold a candle to Concepción. They were often middling players, journeymen, athletes trying to break into MLB, or players trying to stave off retirement. That only enhanced the transnational link. They shared with most of their Venezuelan teammates a primary goal of breaking into (or staying in) MLB.

After 1950, for Venezuelans, as for many other Latin Americans, US Blackness referenced segregation and the violence of how race-based hierarchies were imposed in the United States. It also described racial and racist tropes in the US media, including criminality, urban unrest, and sports prowess. By contrast, Venezuelan Blackness was more ambiguous and varied. It was a racial category that could include a range of features and tropes that were marked by skin color and other aspects of physical appearance, place of origin in Venezuela, historical references to slavery and plantation labor, foreign origins (most specifically, migrants from the Atlantic coast of Colombia and from Trinidad), as well as purportedly "Black" pastimes or work, such as track and field athletics. At the same time, baseball became a forum in which people constructed a *Venezuelan* category that subsumed race to the larger, racially ambiguous *criollo* (Creole). In baseball, "*criollo*" referenced "Venezuelan male" without explicit regard to race or class boundaries but imbued with imagined characteristics aspired to by the best ball players (and perhaps, the best people) in both Venezuela and the United States—pluck, hard work, modesty, generosity, and high skill.[5]

Although this chapter argues that the construction of a Venezuelan, criollo baseball identity shaped race discourses, it does not reaffirm the long-standing argument among some historians that Venezuela presented "an exemplary case of mestizaje in Latin America"[6] or that life changed markedly for the better in the 1950s for African Venezuelans.[7] The idea of the criollo baseball player does, however, contribute to a literature on transnational race focusing on the intersections of racial constructions in the United States with those in various Latin American countries.[8] It also draws on aspects of a broader criollo identity in Venezuela and a transnational criollo identity in Latin America. As in the case of the case of northern Argentina examined by the historian Oscar Chamosa, the broader criollo identity in Venezuela underscored Spanish ancestry and subsumed indigenous (and in the Venezuelan case, African) identities to a larger national identity. Unlike Argentina, however, in Venezuela there was a less explicit process of "whitening" the nation tied to criollo identity formation.[9]

From the 1950s forward, baseball often reflected a happy cultural attachment to the United States. There were exceptions. Several non-Black Venezuelan players recalled having been discriminated against in the 1950s as Black. The Venezuelan Luis "Camaleón" García could never adapt to being refused entry to segregated restaurants along with his African American teammates and "Latinos who, like himself, had been burned by the sun," (i.e., Latinos of color).[10] But as early as the 1920s, many Venezuelans had measured their success in baseball as they had more broadly—against a US standard. Every fan knew that in the 1951 MLB All-Star Game, Alfonso Carrasquel had made three brilliant, rolling catches and that a decade later at Boston's Fenway Park, Luis Aparicio's sixth inning catch had saved the 1961 MLB All-Star Game for the American League side. By the 1970s, while long-standing LVBP rivalries between Caracas and Magallanes,[11] and between other clubs persisted, new standards cast Venezuelan baseball players in a US baseball frame of reference. The best players left, not on occasion or in exceptional cases only, but routinely.[12] Boasting such stars as David Concepción, Antonio Armas, Baudilio Díaz, Jesús Manuel Marcano Trillo, and Luis Salazar, by 1980 MLB had never had a richer array of Venezuelan talent.

STRUCTURING RACE

That more sharply bordered racial tropes distant from baseball featured prominently in media and popular culture made the racial blandness of Venezuelan baseball all the more exceptional. Racialized Venezuelan categories were often gendered. Reporting on the 1981 Miss Venezuela competition, for example, the journalist Zaidi Goussot noted the unusual number of contestants who were athletes. As had lesser beauty contests along the coasts of Venezuela and Colombia for decades, the Miss Venezuela competition had long emphasized whiteness and light skin color more generally as a virtue. In descriptions and in photographic images, Goussot focused on the Blackness of one contestant, Miurka Yánez, as unusually tall and dedicated to a sport many Venezuelans associated with African Venezuelans of British Caribbean origin, track and field. Her image and description were set against photos of white contestants that were so overexposed that their facial features were hard to make out. Yánez was the one contestant of color to "penetrate" (incursionar) the competition. "[Yánez is] from El Callao," Goussot gushed, "where calypso music is part of the identity of every inhabitant. . . . This girl of ebony is the first [Black woman] to take part in this sort of competition in Venezuela but hopes to do a good job of it all the same." Readers would have associated El Callao, a nineteenth-century mining town that had seen a significant wave of British Caribbean immigrants of African origin, with Blackness. By contrast, Pilin León, "Miss Aragua," was one of the most "elegant" contestants, whereas "Miss Federal District," Miriam Quintana, "is more sportswoman than Miss" (where "Miss" refers here to a constructed delicate, light-skinned beauty).[13]

On Venezuelan television, African Venezuelans were a rarity. As they did baseball players, the media often constructed television stars as Venezuelan criollos, without the baseball-related constructions of a moral good, and generally without racial signifiers. However, as in Zaidi Goussot's description of the Miss Venezuela contest, a racialized gendered Blackness sometimes emerged as crucial background—a way of directly or indirectly characterizing non-African Venezuelan performers and of outlining the contours of criollo categorization.[14] At times, the images were violent. In 1990, the satirical Caracas-based magazine *Indiscreta,* directed at women readers, included a mean-spirited tongue-in-cheek exposé on the former dancer and current television presenter Carmen Victoria Pérez. Across six pages, a storyboard sequence of fourteen photos featured nasty/humorous comic strip speech captions supposedly from the vedette, pointing (inaccurately) to her declining media presence. A running theme is Pérez's "failed" attempts at presenting herself as sexually available as she laid in wait for an assortment of men who might bring her fame and a revitalized television career.

At one point, a suitor warns her to be careful with her cigarette around Claudio Fermín. "He might put it out on his knee." The suitor continued, "por allí viene el negrito" ("here comes the black fellow now").[15] Meant as a funny and titillating allusion to sexual desire and racial humiliation, the story depended on the juxtaposition of the glamorous Pérez with a putative savage sexual Blackness of "El Negro" Fermín, mayor of Caracas and the most prominent African Venezuelan politician of his day. Pérez responds, laughing, in the next caption/photo, inviting what is projected as a lascivious, racialized sexual encounter: "I hope he comes and puts it out, so at least the media remember me and ask me for my views. I hope he puts it out for me to see if I matter any more, if only for that reason."[16]

Outside baseball, US media permeated Venezuelan society and helped entrench a range of generally ugly racial stereotypes. Cheaply produced, under-the-counter pornographic magazines directed at men were widely available in the 1970s and 1980s. Printed in Venezuela, Colombia, Spain, the United States, and elswhere, they were were largely undated, short-lived runs without publication information other than the issue number and the price on the cover in bolívares (and sometimes other currencies). Cartoons—many pilfered from American pornographic magazines at the newsstand—

evoked a style pioneered in *Playboy* magazine in the 1960s, exoticizing the degradation of American white women as stupid and sexually available. In a fetish evident in newsstand as well as under-the-counter men's magazines in the United States, African American women were frequently constructed in magazines that circulated in Venezuela as savage, with 1960s imagery that included Afro hairstyles. Most photographs in Venezuelan pornography exoticized what readers would have viewed as white American women in a style that reflected the early 1970s American magazines *Penthouse*, *Hustler*, and *Oui*, among others, that challenged what the historian Elizabeth Fraterrigo described as girl-next-door imagery in *Playboy* magazine. By contrast, women were now posed fully nude, exposed, and suggesting a passive availability and desire.[17] With no seeming reference to Venezuela, in one violent sequence of photographs in the Venezuelan magazine *Cuentos Prohibidos*, a female guard strips a white woman and shaves her head and body hair. A male guard rapes the prisoner before leading her to be executed in an electric chair, alongside the exclamation "Poof!"[18] Venezuela had abolished capital punishment in its 1863 constitution.

At the same time, *Hombre del Mundo* circulated widely among middle-class urban Venezuelan men. Registered in Panama, with a sales headquarters in Caracas, the magazine's editorial office was in Virginia Gardens, Florida, and its publicity base in New York. Modeled on American men's magazines (without the soft pornography), *Hombre del Mundo* also celebrated US constructions of whiteness. The April 1983 issue featured a stamp-sized image of Simón Bolívar on the cover referencing "Two Centuries of Glory, 1783–1982." A glossy tourism advertisement for the US Virgin Islands featured an athletic, young, white couple splashing about in the ocean while an advertisement for Ballantine's Scotch Whisky highlighted a staid, older white couple together on a sofa admiring a model wooden sailing vessel, surrounded by soft light and in the lap of luxury. By contrast, an article featured Ugandan dictator Idi Amin living an undeserved good life in Saudi Arabian exile. Amin was a recurring Venezuelan media theme, as were the "mysteries" of Haitian Vodou. Another piece racialized the "crisis" of the Japanese supercomputer invasion (though it was not clear when any supercomputers might reach Caracas). According to New York University professor Jacob T. Schwartz, "The Japanese might achieve a significant advantage in the building of advanced supercomputers. . . . Were that to happen, [US] laboratories working on nuclear weapons would have to buy supercomputers from the Japanese." The most elaborate racial construction in the issue came in an article on the "doctor-priests" of Tibet who practiced medicine as an ethereal, primitive puzzle for the ages. "They don't use instruments. They are guided only by their intuition and wisdom."[19]

The idea of the criollo baseball player was distinct from these and other Venezuelan media constructions of race. In the former, there was an absence of rigid nation-based racial identifiers (Venezuelan or otherwise), sharp definitions of whiteness, degrading linkages of race to female (or male) sexuality, sexuality tied to gender, and perhaps most important, negative moralities tied to identity. Even in the stories they told, when Venezuelan media juxtaposed the criollo baseball player with other ball players (by race or nation), the juxtaposed group was not portrayed negatively.

BASEBALL AND VENEZUELAN CONSTRUCTIONS OF RACIAL CATEGORIES

In 1961, a group that included former players, entrepreneurs, and two Catholic priests founded La Corporación Criollitos de Venezuela ("Los Criollitos," or little criollos). Based on the US Little League Baseball program, Criollitos produced MLB stars Bobby Abreu, Omar Vizquel, and Tony Armas (son of Antonio Armas), among many others. No version of the foundational Criollitos story assigns a stated meaning to the name "Criollitos." Even so, the term "Criollitos" played upon the criollo baseball player, referencing all children in what would quickly become Venezuela's predominant youth baseball organization. The word also underscored the moral qualities represented in the criollo baseball player, including hard work, courage, and high skill. By 2005, 90 percent of Venezuelans playing in MLB had come out of the Criollitos program. Modeled on a US moral ethos that charted Little League Baseball in the United States as a character-building organization, Criollitos went beyond simply organizing baseball leagues for children. Founded in 1938, Little League Baseball did not take off until the Cold War. The rise of organized youth baseball corresponded to revolutionary changes in community, neighborhood, and family structure for white middle-class, and to some extent, white working-class Americans. White flight from US cities led to growing numbers of traditional, nuclear families owning their own homes in newly built suburbs. As people drifted away from relatives and close-knit neighborhood communities in the cities, baseball kept families together, literally, at the ball field. Girls did not play until 1973, which meant that after having been disrupted during World War II, when many US women went to work outside the home, traditional gender roles were reinforced in Little League Baseball with a player's mother and sister in the stands watching the action.[20]

Little League Baseball addressed societal anxieties of juvenile delinquency; baseball could help keep kids out of trouble. Its organizers pitched it as wholesome recreation that might steer young people away from vandalism. Kids were meant to "learn how to win and to lose" while they could also find an outlet for energies that might otherwise go into sexual deviancy. Little League was meant to prepare boys for the rapidly changing post-World War II economy, away from the archetype of the small business economy and toward a more corporate work world of bureaucratic hierarchies. Baseball could teach children to learn to play by the rules.[21]

These Cold War era US moralities were on display in Criollitos, where organizers set out to build a category of national ethics that had the effect of diminishing race as an overt identifier. In 1984, a cloying report looking back argued that, "against all odds, dodging all obstacles in their way, Criollitos brought together thousands of kids from every part of the nation with a primary objective of unifying the children and young people of Venezuela."[22] In 2015, Universidad de Los Andes (in Mérida, Venezuela) communications professor Gustavo Villamizar Durán remembered the 1960s nostalgically as "years of armed insurrection [in South America], "*el mayo francés*" [the May 1968 protests in France], massive student unrest." But for adolescents in Venezuela, they were a time of "untamed passion for baseball. We played in the street, on outdoor fields, in the stadium and we learned to hit a curve ball playing stickball."[23] There was no *mayo francés* for diligent, cheerful Venezuelan baseball-playing youth.

As in the United States, through Criollitos and more generally, baseball in Venezuela became a moral antidote to violence and social change. Villamizar Durán recalled fondly playing in the newly formed Criollitos system in Táchira state, helping to train younger kids, and dreaming of playing professionally. His and other Venezuelan baseball ideals reference each of the stated Little League Baseball goals, in a Venezuelan context. Criollitos, he went on, was launched to promote baseball but also to help form morally sound future citizens. Sport was a fundamental part of the education of boys where "the weekend game functioned as a reward for hard work in school." Criollitos was not about stars or talented players. It was a place for friends to work together, get along in a collective enterprise, and have fun.

By the 1950s, through the media, Americans had come to think of baseball as emblematic of US society, far more so than other sports or pastimes. To some extent across regional, ethnic, and racial lines, through baseball Americans reaffirmed a mix of cultural values particularly in the face of rapid social and political change. Long before the Cold War era, baseball became a cultural space in which Americans routinely tied nostalgia to constructions of the "American Dream." Dream myths in baseball stories— fictional and nonfictional—brought together values that included social responsibility, social mobility, as well as collective and individual power."[24]

Venezuelans incorporated US mythologies in a manner that varied in one important aspect from the popular US culture equivalent. Michael L. Butterworth argues that US "baseball mythology is inherently conservative, and it idealizes not only a male, heterosexual norm but a White, Christian identity as well."[25] Butterworth might have added that the "white, Christian identity" in US baseball was not applicable around the globe but specifically American as a cultural, racial, and religious construction. As in the United States, the Venezuelan equivalent to a masculine, heterosexual norm in baseball was often unstated. In the United States, however, constructions of whiteness functioned as the basis for an exclusionary racism from the segregation of MLB to the reinforcement of racially segregated urban and suburban neighborhoods.

Venezuelan baseball never lionized whiteness in any context, but drawing on US baseball markers helped build a national, criollo Venezuelan category. Although not explicitly racial, it was at times tied to transnational ideas from the United States that identified the best players as "Latino."[26] When baseball players went north, in Venezuela they became "Latino." In baseball, that term was more complicated and less rigid as a racial qualifier than it was in broader US popular and political cultures. It included Latinx players as well as non-US Latin Americans whose racial identities did not fully align with US categories. In Venezuela, "Latino" disrupted notions of Venezuelan racial categories evident in popular Venezuelan media and in popular culture. The idea of the Latino ball player in Venezuela reflected how US media characterized Venezuelan players and other Latin American players, and in a manner that allowed Venezuelan fans to self-identify with non-Venezuelan "Latinos."

Latin American identities have always been a cultural construction. People throughout the hemisphere have not always thought of themselves as "Latin American" in the first instance (if at all), alongside indigenous, regional, national, and other identity markers. Large numbers of Chileans, for example, came to think of themselves as Latin American (or "more" Latin American) in the aftermath of the Cuban Revolution and during the Salvador Allende presidency. The progress of Venezuelan ball players in the United States and their media representation marked the first widespread, popular Venezuelan conception of the country's identity as Latin American. In October 1980, in one of many media examples where Venezuelans were described as Latino, the writer Mario Requena reported on the success of the Venezuelan Antonio Armas in the big leagues. He had joined a group of twelve "Latino" players who had batted more than thirty home runs and one hundred runs-batted-in since 1945, including Tony Oliva (Cuba), Rico Carty (Dominican Republic), Roberto Clemente (Puerto Rico), and Rod Carew (Panama).[27]

By the numbers, an apogee of US-Venezuelan baseball links came in 1981, reflecting a decade-long set of triumphs and a media construction of the Venezuelan ballplayer as an ideal Venezuelan citizen. David Concepción ("Dave" in US media) signed a five-year contract with the Cincinatti Reds for $4.75 million, placing him among the highest paid players in the history of baseball. The contract announcement capped a season in which the Venezuelans Luis Salazar and Baudilio Díaz both hit over .300, Jesús Manuel Marcano Trillo emerged among a handful of the best second basemen, Antonio Armas led the American League in home runs (with twenty-two in a strike-shortened season), and Luis Leal held a critical starting position in the Toronto Blue Jays pitching rotation. That same season, Concepción chased Luis Aparicio's record for most home runs by a Venezuelan in MLB—a feat rendered by the Venezuelan media all the more notable as juxtaposed against his teammate Pete Rose's hunt for Ty Cobb's hit record.[28]

In 1968, Jesús Manuel Marcano Trillo left Venezuela for the big leagues in the United States. For how Venezuelans perceived his skin tone and for how they interpreted the shape of his eyes, his nickname at the time was "El Indio." A decade and four MLB All-Star Game appearances later, "Manny" Trillo had become one of the best players in the world. His old nickname was irrelevant to how the media built his identity as an ideal Venezuelan in the image of Criollitos. He was lionized in the game's memory as a thoughtful, smart, disciplined boy from the small town of Caripito in Eastern Venezuela. He had learned to play at age five. On weekends, Trillo and his coach had made the eleven hundred kilometer (about 683 mile) round-trip trek to Caracas and back. Trillo recalled his coach obliging him to watch the weekend game intently. On the way home, Trillo would have to describe the game to his coach play by play. As an MLB star, he had a new nickname. "El Indio" had become "el Nureyeb de la segunda base," for his elegance of play and cold-blooded precision, widely reported on in the United States and then in Venezuela.[29] Nureyeb was a reference to Rudolf Nureyev, perhaps the greatest male classical ballet dancer of his generation. Trained in the Soviet Union, he defected to the West in 1961—the first defection of a Soviet performer after World War II.

Like Trillo, Luis Salazar's public story was of a Venezuelan criollo in keeping with Criollito/American baseball ideals and devoid of an explicit racial context. When he made his jump from the LVBP to MLB, he left a three-day-old baby behind in Venezuela. Salazar's professional dedication and seriousness of purpose meant that he would not return to live with his family until his son was seven. Able to play any position in the infield or outfield, like Trillo, Salazar was modest and tough minded. He understood the "rules of the game." Transferred from the minor league AAA Portland Beavers to the Hawaii Islanders, Salazar played Sunday night for Portland and the next night for Hawaii against his former team. Salazar had the hit that decided the latter game. When word came in Hawaii that he was to move up to San Diego in MLB, he boarded a plane, flew six hours, and played that night in a game that lasted twenty innings. Despite these demonstrations of high character and major league professionalism, and in a manner that reflected similarity to US baseball player Horatio Alger's stories, Salazar stayed "true" to his simple, boyhood roots. According to the journalist Zaidi Goussot, "Luis always remained in awe of how well ball players were treated [in the United States]—the best hotel in San Diego, the best food, and all sorts of other perks."[30]

In 1979, an unidentified American author published a piece about David Concepción in a Venezuelan magazine that underscored another feature of the criollo baseball star—surviving adversity as a child. The Cincinnati Reds' all-star first reached the United States in 1968 as a silent nineteen-year-old. He had grown up poor, the son of a chauffeur in Maracay (devoid, in the Venezuelan media, of racial markers). The Reds were initially skeptical about giving him a tryout. He was too skinny: "Steaks in the United States will fatten him up in no time," his manager in Venezuela, Wilfredo Calviño, is said to have advised the Reds. Venezuelans knew the winning story of Concepción's entry-level contract that paid him $450 a month, with the cost of a glove and spikes to be deducted from his first paycheck. Concepción always remained the kid from Maracay in the Venezuelan media. On arrival in the United States for the first time he was reported to have blurted out, "The United States is so big it scares me. They have people going to the moon. In my home town, people don't even travel to Caracas." Concepción triumphed over adversity. As a teenager in the United States, he anguished over why he was there. "I have no friends, I don't speak English. I'd never felt more alone. But I play baseball well," he told himself. "And what would I do if I went home? Drive a car for other people." Assigned to the Reds's minor league affiliate, the Tampa Tarpons, Concepción's manager George Scherger moved him to shortstop: "I can't leave an arm like yours on second."[31]

In 1970, the US media dubbed Concepción the shortstop of the future. His batting average dropped, though, in the next two seasons, and according to former player and Reds play-by-play announcer Pee Wee Reese, an old problem was resurfacing. Concepción was still too thin. But in the following seasons, strong coaching and the mentorship of his friend and traveling roommate Tony Pérez helped Concepción to star status. In 1973 he gained ten kilograms (about 22 pounds) and hit .287. When the Reds traded Pérez to the Montreal Expos in 1977, manager Sparky Anderson worried that Concepción's game would decline in the absence of his mentor. Anderson need not have feared. Concepción's reticence had given way to the traits of an on- and off-the-field team leader. Concepción took Pérez's place as a leader on the field and in the locker room, particularly among Latino players. Through the early 1980s, his personality—and the media trajectory of how he became the person he was—was that of an iconic American baseball star. For his teammate Pete Rose, there was an explanation for the change: "A .200 batter can't make noise. Now, at .280 he can."[32]

If Venezuelan players experienced personal crises that did not lead to redemption and triumph, those stories had no part in the 1970s baseball ideal. Moreover, Venezuelan media began to reconstruct the past in a way that sidestepped race while building a national identity by sometimes high-lighting a player's transition from a regional to a national identity, from modestly rambunctious behavior to a professional masculinity. In 1984, sports journalist Francisco Morales recalled that thirty-two years earlier legendary Cuban manager Martín Dihigo had been contracted to man-age Cervecería de Caracas, breaking a Venezuelan tradition of teams that were "*puros criollos*" (pure Creole, meaning no foreigners on the team). Also looking for a spot on the team that year was a player from Zulia state, Pompeyo Davalillo, who sported a mustache. Dihigo announced that, "Ese bigotico (that guy with the mustache) won't play a game for me as long as I'm manager of this team. I want men not dandies."[33]

As Dihigo was figuring out the final lineup for the season, Davalillo appeared, clean-shaven. Dihigo liked the Venezuelan's new "attitude" and put him on third base. What the manager may or may not have known was that Davalillo—according to legend—had gone off to the edge of the prac-tice field, found a broken bottle, and used it to cut off the mustache that he had once proudly displayed on Friday night outings at the Monumental, a large Caracas dance hall of the era. After the first game, in which Davalillo excelled, Dihigo said to him, "You see Shorty, without the mustache you're more a man and a better ball player." From that point forward, so the story went, Davalillo had a linear series of successes. He became a regular in a lineup that doubled as a "family" of criollos, Americans, and Cubans. Davalillo (the second shortest player in MLB history) went on to play for the Washington Senators, where fans called him "Yo-Yo," for his start-stop speed similar to the famous toy.[34]

Venezuelan stars returned from the United States as coaches to the LPBV. The often faulty assumption of club owners, fans, and the media was that having excelled in MLB, returning Venezuelans would have extraordi-nary coaching skills, but just as important, would have assumed a set of US personality and professional traits that might be imparted onto Venezuelan teams. Sometimes it worked. Near the start of his long career in MLB, the Panamanian American star Rod Carew managed the Tigres de Aragua of the LVBP, led by David Concepción, to the team's first championship in the 1971–1972 season. Having retired from MLB in 1973, Luis Aparicio managed four LVBP teams before taking on the floundering Navegantes de Magallanes in 1980.[35]

Aparicio arrived as a savior, somebody with an unusual knowledge of the US-Venezuelan cultural bridge. Players on the team from the United States seemed weak to fans. One journalist eagerly asked Aparicio, "Will you use your contacts in the north to bring in new pitchers?" Cast by the media in the image of Sparky Anderson and other US managers of the day who combined integrity, calm, high skill, and great knowledge, Aparicio came across as firm, controlled, and diplomatic. "I'll use my contacts with the White Sox, the Orioles, the Red Sox, and the Cubs to find the best available players." Using the English-language term, Aparicio lamented how difficult it had been in his first season with Magallanes to instill a sense of "team work" and discipline. In 1980, Aparicio coached the team to its worst record in history.[36]

BOXING AND THE END OF THE CRIOLLO BASEBALL NARRATIVE

Before the 2017 All-Star Game in Miami, MLB celebrated the contributions of Latin Americans to MLB. Media reports of the event used the terms "Latino" and "Latin American" interchangeably. Major League Baseball Commissioner Rob Manfred recognized Tony Pérez, Rod Carew, and Roberto Alomar, among others. Luis Aparicio had been invited. He declined. In a shocking departure from his cultural construction in the Venezuelan media as an apolitical, criollo player with all that implied of moralities and a hard work ethic, Aparicio surprised followers with a tweet in Spanish: "I can't celebrate while young people in my country are dying fighting for ideals of liberty."[37] It was a remarkable *anti-chavista*, "political" moment for a ball player who no one in the United States or Venezuela could ever remember having voiced a political opinion during his playing days. The highly moral player, above the base political fray was part of Americanized Venezuelan baseball. But that vision had begun to unravel long before Aparicio tweeted (gently and late) his concerns over *chavismo* (the political movement led until his death in 2013 by Venezuelan president Hugo Chávez) and the current Venezuelan government.

Jane Juffer sets the starting point for this transformation of Americanized Venezuelan baseball at roughly the time Aparicio was managing Magallanes's disastrous 1980 season. She argues that in the United States, with the arrival of cable in the 1980s, national television broadcasts helped globalize US baseball. In 1981, Fernando Valenzuela began pitching for the Los Angeles Dodgers. He was a sensation who self-identified as "Mexican" in a manner that shattered the blandness of "Latinos" in baseball. Unlike Latin American players in the past, he spoke to the media through an interpreter, gained a loud mass following among immigrants in the United States, developed an unprecedented Latin American following, and lunched with Ronald Reagan and José López Portillo, the presidents of the United States and Mexico, respectively. "Valenzuela's image was expressed in terms of national identity—a Mexican star refusing to kowtow to US biases about the national pastime."[38] Other "Latino" players emerged with larger-than-life skills and personalities. As in the case of Sammy Sosa, who routinely self-identified as both Domincan and Afro-Dominican, their Americanized-Latino identities no longer mattered as they had in a previous generation.

In this context and in a similarly globalized Venezuela, baseball remained an important sport but declined in relative significance to other sports, including soccer. The construction of criollo baseball fell by the wayside along with the decline of the idea of the Latino ball player. The Venezuela-US cultural bridge collapsed. Partly as a result of an early 1980s Venezuelan economic crisis, American MLB players and aspirants stopped heading for the LVBP in the winter. If criollo baseball had subsumed race as a relevant marker, after 2000 the rise of chavismo helped promote an inverse effect. Both supporters and opponents of Hugo Chávez began specifically investing Venezuelan identity with race, starting with Chávez himself who repeatedly self-identified as a mix of indigenous, African, and sometimes European heritage.[39] A baseball fan, Chávez recognized a key ingredient (and a key flaw) of criollo baseball as focused on Criollito moralities; on the baseball diamond and in life, the supposedly level playing field for all was a mirage. Many of his supporters saw stark constructions of race and racial hierarchies in Venezuela. According to Giles Harrison-Conwill, "denying recognition of the histories of exclusion and exploitation on which race and class privilege depend, middle-class notions of Venezuelan meritocracy conceal inequality. The resulting notions of justice naturalize class hierarchy. In so doing, political and social structures organized around a notion of equality—like those proposed by Chavista political rhetoric—constitute a threat to middle-class culture."[40] As distinct from the baseball criollo, chavismo social narratives explicitly linked race and class, setting aside notions of an "exemplary" Venezuelan *mestizaje.*

They also ended what was left of deracialized criollo baseball. Chapter 6 of the 1999 Venezuelan Constitution turned Venezuelan national identity on its head by describing the nation as pluricultural. The Constitution identifies "indigenous people, those of African descent, and popular urban and rural *criollo* cultures" as the constitutive cultures of the nation. More specifically, the cultural construction of a race- and ethnicity-based national identity during the Bolivarian Revolution was less concerned with hybridity processes than with a cultural obverse—regional variants on racial and ethnic identities that in their unique and lasting forms, constituted a national culture in their racial differences.[41]

The impact of chavismo on notions of race in sport is less evident in baseball than in boxing. In the 1960s and 1970s, when boxing was a popular sport in several Latin American countries, racial constructions of boxers were far sharper than in other sports. In Venezuela, however, racial touchstones in boxing were far less significant than in the United States, Colombia, Venezuela, Panama, or Argentina.[42] At times, Venezuelan boxing mirrored baseball *criollismo.* In November 1980, when Luis Primera took on Tommy Hearns for the welterweight world championship, the Venezuelan media characterized the former as *caraqueño* (from Caracas), criollo, and Venezuelan. As though speaking from the screen of a 1950s Hollywood boxing movie, the underdog Primera told reporters, "It seems impossible, but I'm going to win. I'm physically and mentally ready for the title shot and I'm not going to let this opportunity go by." (He lost.)[43] More commonly among Venezuela's best fighters, the media portrayal of boxing was less romanticized than the construction of Concepción or Salazar as morally superior and representative of an ideal Venezuelan criollo. Among Venezuelan fans, boxers were more human and more flawed versions of themselves and of the Venezuelan criollo—though still largely devoid of racial identifiers. By the first decade of the twenty-first century, however, as Venezuelan society grappled with what some considered long-obscured racial hierarchies, Venezuelan boxing quickly began to reflect the sort of racialized narratives that had been evident for decades elsewhere.[44]

The best Venezuelan boxer of the 1970s was Luis Estaba, born in 1938 in Macuro, Sucre—a place many Venezuelans associated with a significant Afro-Venezuelan population. Sports historians and journalists wrote repeatedly (and continue to write) that Estaba came by his nickname, "Lumumba," for his physical resemblance to the Congolese revolutionary Patrice Lumumba. If there is a similarity, it is not striking (though, of course, such opinions are subjective). The sports writer Simon Piña told me the story was nonsense: "They called him 'Lumumba' because he was black."[45] That, though, is where the racial component of the Estaba identity ended. At the time, as did Estaba, Colombian world champions Antonio "Kid Pambelé" Cervantes and his cousin Ricardo Cardona, both fought out of Caracas. All three were described in the media as unusually tall for their respective weight classes, with little bulk, long muscle structure, and unusual strength. This gave each a reach advantage when they fought, allowing them to land uncommonly powerful blows from a distance. However, whereas the Colombian media associated Cardona's body, and more particularly Pambelé's with a form of racialized Black purity linked to their town of origin, San Basilio de Palenque, in Venezuela there was no such association of body and race for Estaba. In fact, whereas race and Blackness were at the forefront of how Colombians understood Pambelé's many professional successes (and in the end, his drug- and alcohol-fueled downfall), race was absent from how Venezuelans constructed Estaba. For a racial identifier to function in boxing and beyond, it had to be applicable to a significant group of people supposedly of the same race. That never related to how the media or the public constructed Estaba's time as world champion.[46]

Age was the feature most commonly associated with Estaba's rise. Fans called him *"abuelito"* (grandpa) as often as they did "Lumumba." Almost impossibly, he did not turn professional until 1967 at the age of twenty-eight. He did not win the World Boxing Council championship until 1975. He had given up women, liquor, and cigarettes before the bout, reporting, "and I trained thinking of my children, my future, and Venezuela."[47] Estaba fought dirty. He made no secret of his tactics and the fans loved it. In December 1975, he defended his title against Takenobu Shimabukuro, winning by technical knockout. "Truth be told, the Asian was beating me," Estaba told reporters after the fight. "But thanks to my strength and what I call my 'box of tricks'—that is fists, bites, kicks, and foot stomping—I managed to eliminate him in the tenth."[48] Two months later he fought Leo Palacios. At one point, it seemed to fans that *abuelito* had run out of steam. But the champ found his way back into the fight with a flurry of hooks, upper cuts, elbows, head butts, and foot stomps. After another title defense in July 1976, Franco Udela claimed that Estaba had poked him the eye. Estaba was endearingly philosophical in response: "I played dirty, I put my glove thumb in his eye. These are things you learn in the school of life, observing other boxers, watching film of Sandy Saddler and Sugar [Ray] Robinson. But I also had my own school of self. The malice came from within me."[49] It helped that Estaba fought several of his title defences in Caracas where home advantage lessened the likelihood of sanctions for rules violations. After a November 1976 fight, Valentín *"Duende"* (Elf) Martínez complained of Estaba's head butts, forearm blows, elbows, and foot stomping. Officials and jubilant fans ignored him. With that victory, Estaba became the first Venezuelan boxing world champion to retain his title over six consecutive defenses. It had been less than a year since he had won the championship. In keeping with US baseball moralities, the construction of Venezuelan baseball players through the early 1980s never allowed a fan fondness for the dirty tricks employed by Estaba and other well-known boxers.[50]

Thirty years later, in 2006, the Mérida native Edwin "El Inca" Valero won the World Boxing Association Super Featherweight world title, followed by the World Boxing Council lightweight world championship three years later. In 2010, he committed suicide in jail after admitting to killing his wife, Jennifer Carolina Viera de Valero. El Inca—and his story—were the product of the post-1980 globalized Venezuelan culture that ended the criollo baseball ideal as well as the intimacy of local boxing in Venezuela where in the 1970s, Caracas fans could delight in a local, highly skilled world champion who defended his title with bites and head butts, as "one of us." Unlike Estaba, Valero is routinely ranked internationally among the best to have ever fought. His professional record was a terrifying 27–0, with nineteen fights won by knockout. There was no fooling around with poked eyes and foot stomping. Fans and the media cast Valero as a savage machine, in keeping with the racialized identity referenced by his nickname. The international media and the anti-Chávez media in Venezuela covered the femicide with the same racist animus that had made the violent, working-class, Black boxer an international trope, from Argentine world champion Carlos Monzón in the 1970s to US heavyweight champion Mike Tyson in the 1990s.[51]

Valero wore his politics literally on his chest in a tattoo featuring Hugo Chávez's face framed by the Venezuelan flag. Influenced by the revolutionary Cuban government that had banned professional boxing in the 1960s as exploitative and violent, Chávez fought with the World Boxing Association (which eventually transferred its headquarters from Venezuela to Panama). The Venezuelan government did not ban boxing but imposed bureaucratic impediments that made organizing fights difficult and sometimes impossible. Even so, Valero was a favorite of the president. He represented to Chávez, as he did to many Venezuelans, a racialized and class-based triumph of the "new" Venezuelan citizen, very different from the 1970s idea of a criollo baseball star.

When Valero died, all hell broke loose in the media and on social media in a reflection of profound political and social divisions in Venezuela. Opponents of the government underscored the boxer's violent nature and hammered away at rumors of drug and alcohol addiction. Supporters, including Hugo Chávez, remembered Valero as a great Venezuelan. Responding to the negative characterizations, including the view expressed by many that Valero had been a monster created by Hugo Chávez, the lawyer and social worker Martín Padrino described the attacks on Valero as a frontal assault on the Venezuelan state by an assortment of enemies that included Time Warner, the Walt Disney Corporation, and assorted Spanish media. The *chavista* political activist and journalist Cecilio Canelón called the attacks on Valero for what they were. The common accusation among many Venezuelans that Valero had killed his wife "debido a algo que lleva 'en la sangre,'" (for something "in his blood") and that the boxer was a "*gocho*" (pig), marked an all too common form of racism against Venezuelans of color.[52] By contrast, Luis Aparicio's 2017 anti-chavismo tweet seems a quaint and distant reminder of what ball players once meant to Venezuelans.

WEALTH AND THE NEW BASEBALL SUPERSTAR

As much as anything, another aspect of the American game changed Venezuelan baseball after 1980—money. Part of what made Luis Aparicio and

David Concepción relatable to Venezuelan fans and allowed for the construction of Criollito baseball was the illusion that athletes were "ordinary"
people. That idea came by way of Americanized Venezuelan baseball moralities, fueled by the cultural bridge created over decades by player movement
back and forth between the two countries and by the Venezuelan adoption
of Little League Baseball moralities through criollitos baseball – moralities
scorned in the rise of chavismo. As ordinary people, fans and the media
constructed their baseball heros as distinct from the sexualized, misogynist
racism evident in other areas of popular culture, and as morally dissimilar
from popular boxers. Concepción's eye-popping 1981 contract for $4.75
million might have been a harbinger of things to come, but it did not cut
into the myth of the criollo baseball everyman. At the end of the 1990s, the
signing of what Venezuelan media called "bonos millonarios" (millionaire
bonuses) ended the fantasy of local-player-makes-good.[53] It was not simply
that more Venezuelans were signing big contracts. It was that Concepción
and others of his era had won their contracts after years of excellent professional play. Now, sixteen-year-olds were receiving million-dollar signing
bonuses before they had played an inning in MLB or the LVBP. That was
the tip of a new organizational business iceberg. Swarms of MLB scouts,
recruiters, team representatives, and other employees, as well as independent operators hoping to make a buck, fanned out across Venezuela looking
for the next star. Fans understood that young players were now out on the
diamond performing for scouts and hoping for a big payday. The parents
of strong baseball prospects were adapting their lives and those of their
children to the lure of signing bonuses. Criollitos, which had almost ninety
thousand children in 1998, lost its ethical lustre as families, coaches, and
fans watched for the next million-dollar teenager.

When the Texas Rangers signed Ricardo Escoté Montilla to a bono
millonario in 1997, media reports were vapid and clinical, with no trace
of the criollo baseball professional. The Rangers's talent scout in Venezuela
"found" Escoté Montilla. The team's head scout for Latin America, Manny
Batista, flew to Venezuela to watch the eighteen-year-old, then sent him
to the Rangers's baseball academy in Maracaibo. The bonus came shortly
afterward.[54] Some began to see a grim side to globalization coming from the
United States. In 2001, the Caracas daily *El Nacional* reproduced a story
from the United States describing the signing of Latin American prospects
as a form of slavery where the development of a young player was similar to
the production and sale of an automobile. Those players groomed for glory
that never made it to MLB wound up selling mangos in the streets.[55]

In 1997, the sports writer Cristóbal Guerra summed up the disdain and
cynicism of many older sports enthusiasts in an article entitled "¿El béisbol?
¡Yo no leo deportes!" (Baseball? I don't read the sports pages!). Based on

his conversations with fans, he argued that the business of baseball had hived off Venezuelans from what the sport once was. "Baseball isn't for the political left or right, nor is it exclusively for rich or poor. When the Leones shut out the Navegantes . . . there are fireworks in the Country Club, and in Carapita [a poor Caracas neighborhood where stickball still thrived]. Doesn't matter where because the party is egalitarian." But now, Guerra continued, "rivers of dollars" had changed the behavior of parents heading off to watch their kids play Criollitos baseball on Sunday. "Behind the seemingly innocent refrain, 'I'm going to my kid's games to have something to share with him,' is the savage wolf of baseball avarice."[56] Baseball was likely never as egalitarian as Guerra imagined, just as racial hierarchies were never as flat as 1970s criollo baseball suggested and that Guerra now reproduced nostalgically. In the movement of Venezuelan players to MLB, after 2000, by two measures the US-Venezuelan baseball bridge had never been as strong. As a percentage of the total, there were more Venezuelans in MLB than ever before, and as a group, they were being paid far more than ever. Yet, in how Venezuelans consumed baseball, the cultural ties around identity had been broken. The criollo baseball identity as a defining feature of Venezuelan players in MLB and the LVBP was gone.[57]

CHAPTER EIGHT

MAKING THEIR OWN MAHATMA

SALVADOR'S FILHOS DE GANDHY AND THE LOCAL HISTORY OF A GLOBAL PHENOMENON

Marc Hertzman

In 1949, Black port workers in Salvador, Bahia, founded a Carnival association that would become one of the city's most iconic symbols of African-
descended culture. But rather than selecting from an available pantheon
of Black Brazilian figures, or from elsewhere in the diaspora, the all-male
Filhos de Gandhy (Sons of Gandhi) instead chose as their namesake the famous leader of India's struggle against British colonialism, slain by an assassin the previous year. Their choice suggests a tantalizing opening through
which to trace routes that may reorient our discussion of the transnational
shape and flow of racial identity and politics in Brazil and the Americas.
The selection of a South Asian icon in a country dominated by populations
of American, African, East Asian, and European descent serves to remind
that ideas and people do not always travel across borders in perfect tandem.
Ultimately, the Filhos de Gandhy also scramble scholarly common-sense expectations about the relationship between race and space by simultaneously
stretching our gaze far from Brazil even while rooting it ever more firmly
in the particular local and national context that gave rise to the group. In
short, the Filhos de Gandhy demonstrate the kind of geographic and racial
elasticity that is simultaneously at the heart of, and which also continues
to beguile, scholars of race and transnational history in Brazil, the rest of
Latin America, and beyond. This examination of the Filhos de Gandhy, the
first extended discussion of the group's origins, has two main objectives: to
understand the group's early years in local and national historical context,
and to place their interpretation and appropriation of Gandhi's likeness in
conversation with a larger set of global representations and ideas associated
with the Mahatma. Doing so shows that if the Bahian port workers did
not consider Gandhi himself to be Black, as Black men they understood
it to be possible, under the guise of Carnival, to inhabit his skin. They

could therefore "Play Indian" in a different way than the phrase is normally understood, thereby making a Gandhi who was at once an Orientalist construction and a radical symbol of resistance to white colonialism.[1]

BRAZIL'S "OTHER" ASIA

As a cultural icon in Salvador, a city often referred to as Brazil's "Black Rome," the Filhos de Gandhy are hyper-visible. But aside from the innovative work of Milton Araújo Moura there is hardly any historical research, and the small body of scholarship in other disciplines have left many questions unanswered.[2] A slim volume of recollections edited by the journalist Anísio Félix represents the most important source about the early history of Filhos de Gandhy.[3] The few scholars who have written recently about the group vary wildly in their conclusions. Pravina Shukla writes a scathing critique, suggesting that today's members of the Filhos de Gandhy "impersonate, distort, and trivialize" Gandhi, while also "manipulating" his image "to meet self-serving goals." She continues, "A close analysis of the group reveals that almost every aspect of their look and identity contradicts Gandhi—his morals, his persona, and his behavior."[4] Isis Costa McElroy provides a more thoughtful consideration, even while confessing "enchantment" with the group's "certain incongruent metaphors" and symbolism: terry-cloth turbans adorned with plastic stones; dark leather sandals; what Shukla describes as the "white toga-like sheet[s]" worn by members; plastic necklaces; visages of an elephant, snake, and a camel; a stuffed goat.[5] Although discordant, these symbols, McElroy suggests, are evidence of an original "process of a Hindu-Muslim-Bahian aesthetic enunciation" or "fantasty."[6] To understand what that means, and to also grasp why the Filhos de Gandhy can be so jarring to one scholar and so alluring to another, it is necessary to examine their origins and the historical context in which the group came into being. This is no easy task. While there is a great deal of literature about many aspects of Salvador and Brazil during the 1940s, there is very little material available about the group's early days, and the scholarship on South Asia and Brazil is exceedingly sparse.

One option, perhaps the natural choice for a transnational study, would be to find clues about possible Brazil-India connections. That, too, is a challenge. Though the vast majority of Brazilianist transnational work on race focuses on the African diaspora, there are significant bodies of literature that trace paths and relationships between Brazil and other areas of the world, notably Europe, the Middle East, and East Asia.[7] Whereas there is also a small but significant historiography on the Portuguese Empire in South Asia, with just one notable exception discussed below, next to nothing exists about connections between South Asia and Brazil after the nineteenth century.[8] Though indentured laborers from South Asia arrived en masse in the Caribbean, similar migration to Brazil was minimal. Although Brazilians alternately courted and rejected Chinese, European, Japanese, and Middle Eastern immigrants, those from South Asia have hardly registered in the written record.[9] Though the lack of secondary literature on South Asians in Brazil reflects a certain historical reality—migration, indentured or free, from the subcontinent was minimal—it is worth restating that transnational history is not simply about the movement of bodies but also commodities, culture, words, images, and ideas. Equally important, we will see, is how the history of the Filhos de Gandhy grounds our attention as much, perhaps much more, in the local than the transnational.

The most significant work on Brazil-India relations during the twentieth century is an article published in 2015 by Ananya Chakravarti, who frames her study within debates about subaltern and postcolonial studies in Latin America.[10] In the 1980s and 1990s, some Latin Americanists began to engage heavily with works in subaltern and postcolonial studies coming out of South Asia.[11] Not everyone approved of what followed. In 2006, José Moya cited the "diverging colonial experiences" of Latin America and the rest of the so-called third world as reason for caution when linking (or flattening out) disparate colonial and postcolonial societies.[12] As Moya points out, colonialism in most of Latin America happened earlier and lasted longer than in India. So, too, did most Latin American independence movements unfold along different timelines than South Asia's.

Chakravarti critically engages Moya's argument with a careful study of three prominent Brazilian intellectuals—the poet Cecília Meireles, the diplomat Ildefonso Falcão, and the writer-scholar Gilberto Freyre—each of whom "observed and engaged with India" during the mid-twentieth century.[13] Where Moya is dismissive of what he considers to be an uncritical application of "Indian-derived" postcolonial theory in America, Chakravarti envisions a fruitful opportunity for further inquiry, suggesting "the question worth exploring is why Latin Americans could be drawn to these Indian-derived postcolonial theories and whether these theories can be cross-fertilized by their very different (post)colonial histories."[14] To Chakravarti, the interest that Meireles, Freyre, and Falcão took in India was the product of a shared "sense of being consigned to the lower rungs of Western civilization, of being Western but peripherally so." That sense, she continues, could "occasionally allow rapprochement with the newly decolonized 'Third World,' despite their different (post)colonial trajectories."[15] But although Chakravarti is more hopeful than Moya about the potential for connectivity, her optimism comes with clear limits. Ultimately, "Brazilian self-identification with the West, and particularly its complex relationship with a heritage of European colonialism, prevented a truly commensurable experience, despite a sense of commonality with India based in their peripheral position in the global political structure."[16] The conclusion is convincing, at least from the vantage points accessible through the documents that Chakravarti analyzes. India's prominence in the Non-Aligned Movement did not correspond with Brazil's geopolitical compass, which generally pointed north during the Cold War.[17] As Chakravarti shows, the South-South ties forged at the 1955 Bandung Conference, and the larger Bandung Movement, did not gain traction among the Brazilian elite at least as they did elsewhere. But what did Brazilians who did not belong to the elite think about independent India? What lessons about the postcolonial condition, race, and transnationalism do the Filhos de Gandhy have to tell?

INSPIRATION IN HARD TIMES

When the Filhos de Gandhy formed in 1949, Brazil was four years into a democratic opening that stretched from the collapse of Getúlio Vargas's dictatorial Estado Novo (New State) in 1945 to the rise of a military dictatorship in 1964. Although 1945 signaled the end of the repressive Estado Novo, the respite was brief for Communists and the working class. In Salvador, rapid rural-to-urban migration swelled the city's population, which grew by more than 40 percent during the 1940s alone.[18] Workers' purchasing power declined dramatically, and strikes and work stoppages were frequent and widespread.[19] Nationally, the Brazilian Communist Party (Partido Comunista Brasileiro), which had been underground since a failed armed revolt in 1935, reconvened and then almost immediately was subject to repression, this time under the aegis of a democratic state and the beginning of the Cold War.[20] The existence of newly inclusive participatory politics alongside state-directed violence and intimidation created what Antonio Luigi Negro aptly calls a "difficult democracy."[21]

This all affected the Filhos de Gandhy, who for reasons explored below, feared police persecution. One of the group's founding members recalled, "The country was in a state of war and there was a lot of fear about being arrested."[22] Amid that fearful environment, the postwar years also saw, according to Scott Ickes, "the consolidation of the notion that 'Bahia' was synonymous with African-Bahian culture."[23] Even before that there was a dynamism, fraught to be sure, between Salvador's often overlapping leftist circles and Afro-Brazilian communities. The Black scholar Edison Carneiro, who later in his life would serve as an interlocutor for Nicomedes de Santa Cruz (see Introduction), was active in Communist networks, as was his good friend, the famous white author Jorge Amado. Carneiro was close to and wrote about the Afro-Brazilian religion Candomblé. Using typically colorful (and essentialist) language, writer Antonio Risério sums up Salvador's overlapping political and cultural-religious circles by describing the city as having "one foot in the Comintern, and one foot in Candomblé."[24]

The completion of a new highway to Rio de Janeiro and the four-hundredth anniversary of the founding of the city (both in 1949) along with a dramatic increase in domestic and foreign tourism to Bahia boosted Salvador's national and international visibility.[25]

This was the backdrop for the founding of the Filhos de Gandhy. During a work stoppage in 1949, a group of Black stevedores gathered in the shade of a large mango tree and resolved to create the group. There are different versions of the work stoppage. In some accounts, it was caused by a strike at English ports. One of the founding members recalled, "When we arrived at the docks in Salvador the stevedores, including my dad, didn't have work."[26] Others suggest that the Bahian workers refused to unload British ships when they arrived in Salvador out of solidarity with India's independence movement, though the timing would be difficult in this case as India had already gained independence in 1947.[27] A third narrative maintains that the Bahian laborers refused to unload ships in solidarity with striking British port workers. Yet others simply remember hard times marked by scarcity of work.[28] Whatever the cause, the international connections here are clear. Britain was indeed beset by massive port strikes at the time, but the multiple memories of the work stoppage in Salvador suggest an even broader set of possible connections and meanings: class- and perhaps race-based unity with port workers across the Atlantic, scarcity caused by events in England, and hard times at the hands of domestic political forces.[29] Even the chronologically incongruous notion that the Bahian men refused to work out of support for Indian independence is interesting. Though almost certainly untrue, the memory itself suggests the kind of international connections, real and imagined, that the Filhos de Gandhy have generated over time.

The group's inspiration and its collective knowledge and ideas about Gandhi were shaped especially by print media, film, and word-of-mouth depictions of India and "the Orient." Their costumes were comprised of a towel, worn as a turban and often decorated with beads, a sheet draped over the shoulder in the style of a toga, wooden sandals, and necklaces made of more beads. The turbans may have been inspired by Sikhs depicted in Hollywood movies and also perhaps by the headdresses worn by Black Bahian women (and also appropriated and restyled by Carmen Miranda).[30] It is unclear exactly how many men paraded the first year. One member places the number at 160, another at fifty, and another at closer to twenty.[31] The group steadily grew into the 1950s before a period of decline. During the 1970s, journalists and celebrities helped stimulate a revival that returned the Filhos de Gandhy to prominence. Today they boast some ten thousand members.

Over time, the Filhos de Gandhy incorporated different animals—an elephant, a goat, a camel, and a snake—as symbols. According to one account, "The camel represents strength, resistance. The elephant is positive energy. We had a cow, considered sacred, [and] a goat, which is also sacred for the people in India."[32] Other descriptions emphasize connections to Candomblé deities (*orixás*).[33] From the beginning, the men paraded first carrying a painted portrait of Gandhi, which they soon replaced (or sometimes supplemented) with a member dressed as Gandhi, who donned spectacles and shaved his head to become the Mahatma.

Economic necessity (the founders pooled money and chose the cheapest sandals they could find) and popular representations of Gandhi and South Asia shaped sartorial choices. Some of the founding members had recently seen the film *Gunga Din* (1939), which portrays a Hindu water bearer as a hero who helps thwart a would-be uprising against British forces. The actors' clothes inspired the Filhos de Gandhy's costumes, which, Moura points out, could just as easily have been interpreted as depicting Indian troops loyal to Great Britain as representations of Gandhi, an ambiguity that foreshadows others.[34] In general, the film had a formative impact. One member recalls "a documentary about Gandhi" showing at a local theater. Perhaps this was, in fact, *Gunga Din*, or maybe a newsreel about the Mahatma.[35] As one member put it, "The creation of the Filhos de Gandhi happened when [we] came back from the cinema."[36] *Gunga Din* also inspired wooden rifles and lances that some members carried at Carnival. Images of Gandhi and India also came via print media. One founding member recalled the circulation of "a magazine with a Hindu figure." "It was simple," he continued, explaining how they would emulate the picture with "a towel and a white sheet."[37]

Dressed vaguely as South Asians, the group paraded through the streets with a cord or string around them to distinguish and separate it from other revelers. Among Carnival groups, this was a common practice used by groups and known as *cordões* (the plural of *cordão*, "cord" in Portuguese). Although some called the group the Cordão Filhos de Gandhy, today it is universally known as an *afoxé*, a label that emphasizes its ties to Candomblé. Afoxé performances bring select elements of devotion into the streets, though an intricate process of selection ensures that the sacred is kept away from public consumption.[38] During the late nineteenth century, the two most famous afoxés were Embaixada Africana (African Embassy) and Pândegos da África (African Merrymakers), both of which gained limited acceptance during Carnival. Other, smaller Black groups did not, and between 1905 and 1914, the city banned Afrocentric Carnival groups altogether.[39] After 1914, new groups came on the scene, and by the 1930s the Bahian press, at least, had come to take a less judgmental approach to them than it previously had. There seems to have been a decrease in afoxé activity during World War II and then a revival in the late 1940s, just as the Filhos de Gandhy were created.[40]

For the Filhos de Gandhy, "afoxé" functoins as an important, if somewhat misleading label, cementing an association with Candomblé and
marking it as one of the city's premier symbols of Black culture and religion. That symbolism lies in tension with accounts of some of the group's
founders and oldest living members. Many insist that the group did not begin as an afoxé, and only later assumed a religious identity. Arnaldo Fagundes explained, "We admired Gandhi, a man who knew how to fight for the
independence of his country without violence." The Filhos de Gandhy, he
continued, "is completely linked to the stevedores because it was stevedores
who founded [it]." Only after three years did "people from Candomblé" become part of the group.[41] Fellow member Manoel José dos Santos describes
a similar chronology. "Filhos de Gandhi was created by the stevedores . . .
[and inspired by news] of the death of the great leader Mahatma Gandhi. . . .
Initially, [the group] did not have religious characteristics; the infiltration
of Candomblé came with the arrival of new members." Though he liked
"being part of Candomblé," Santos did not approve of the "infiltration"
because it represented a "complete departure" from the original, defining
inspiration: "a political leader from India."[42]

These recollections suggest how transnational and local histories can
get tangled up with and also erase one another. In this case, two important
histories of diasporic identity and invention, the afoxés and Candomblé,
have squeezed aside another, less visible one about Black labor mobilization
inspired in part by a South Asian leader. Though labeled and remembered
today as an afoxé, the memories of Fagundes and others emphasize another
aspect—Black stevedores united behind Gandhi. Though not mutually exclusive with the now more familiar afoxé and Candomblé labels, the worker
mobilization angle—and some members' emphatic differentiation between
the group's origins and the religious "infiltration" that came next—is an
important, underexamined aspect of the group's history.

To be sure, some of Filho de Gandhi's first members embraced Candomblé, even if the religion did not serve a central role as they founded the
group. The notion that Candomblé "infiltrated" an entirely secular project
is also misleading. Carnival was both a religious and a profane event. The
first portraits of Gandhi replaced the Babalôtim (or Babalotinho), a doll
often dressed in satin and representative of Candomblé *orixás* and carried
by earlier afoxés.[43] This could indicate a secular Gandhi replacing the religious symbols, or just as easily indicate an incorporation of Gandhi into a
larger spiritual pantheon. Africa and Afro-Brazilian religion were central to
the Filhos de Gandhy, and indeed in laying the groundwork for the group's
existence. At the same time, other influences and goals were clearly on the
minds of some of the founders, who self-consciously sought to differentiate
the group from other Black Carnival groups.

Fagundes described the Filhos de Gandhy as racially inclusive. "Black, white, yellow, blue, Chinese, German, French, whatever you've got, all go out. Everyone can parade with the Filhos de Gandhy." Though here he seemed to be speaking about the 1980s, he also had a message about the early days. Because the group abhorred racism, he explained, it "did not participate in Black movements. [But] the entire working class was included. We never had separatism. We had shoe shiners, carpenters, masons, typographers, etc. From the first year we went out eclectic. There's no reason to distinguish and separate. If the movement didn't originate among folk from the port, who were poor and modest, like Gandhi, we wouldn't have welcomed people from every caste. We're all brothers, sons of God, whether Catholic, syncretic, or from Candomblé."[44] In addition to the significance of his placing distance between the group and those that belonged to a race-based cultural and political movement, two words stand out. By explaining that the Filhos de Gandhy embraced people from any caste (*casta*), a word familiar to any follower of Gandhi, Fagundes seems to have made a conscious decision not to use the more common Brazilian term *classe* (class).[45] Fagundes's deployment of "syncretic" is also telling. Although he is specifically referencing religion here, it is clear that melding elements from multiple cultural traditions was also a priority for the group and one that lined up with long-standing practices involving Catholicism, Candomblé, and other religions in Brazil.

It is safe to say that among the early members, knowledge about Gandhi and South Asia varied significantly. Some recalled the Mahatma's specific importance as a leader, icon, architect of nonviolent resistance, advocate of national sovereignty, and adversary of imperialism. Fagundes insisted that the original inspiration did not come from *Gunga Din*, as some suggested, and instead from Gandhi himself. The film was important, though, "because it was about India and its fight against the English."[46] That battle clearly resonated with members, apparently on several levels: as a non-West, nonwhite struggle against white European colonizers, as a symbol of self-determination, and as a general example of resistance against oppressive authority. One man recalled, "There was a lot of persecution by the police, who didn't want us to be thinking about a man from India who held a hunger strike."[47]

Other members were less (or differently) invested in Gandhi's symbolic importance. One said, "When we paraded for the first time, we didn't know anything about Gandhi. We thought about Africa and began to beat a rhythm with a box of matches."[48] Matchboxes have long symbolized authenticity and "pure" Black music in Brazil. Whipped out of a pocket and spontaneously transformed into a musical instrument, here they also signal the importance of symbols that were read as representative of Africa and

Blackness, and highlight the multiplicity of ideas and influences that shaped the Filhos de Gandhy. The parade and the group itself offered an opportunity to unite and mobilize under the star of a South Asian icon (as workers, men, Black men, or some combination thereof) and for some the opportunity to channel or connect to Africa. Like any Carnival group, it is important to emphasize, a primary purpose was also to have fun and be seen.[49]

By parading as workers affiliated with Gandhi, the founding members also meant to send a signal about their own collective strength as well as solidarity with forces circulating the globe. Like Fagundes and Santos, other early members expressed reverence for Gandhi and what he symbolized to the hard-on-their-luck stevedores. One member felt it was important "to make [people] feel and understand what happened, who Gandhi was: a pacifist who fought without weapons. . . . When he returned to India [after studying in England], he found his nation in crisis. . . . The people wanted to revolt against the British," and he taught them how to do that.[50] Another described Gandhi as "a man who fought for peace," and Fagundes explained that the group's name was born of "the admiration that we had for the statesman, for the man who he was, a man who knew how to emancipate his people by sacrificing his own life. He gave his life for a cause!"[51] As a martyred pacifist, Gandhi represented a discursive double-edged sword. On one side, his nonviolent credo and distance from Brazil made him a heroic and powerful symbol. On the other, his radical ideas could draw unwanted attention. Summarizing a theme that appeared in many of the interviews, one member recalled, "Everything that came out of the port was seen by the authorities as something communist."[52] According to some, the group chose to spell Gandhi with a "y" in order to mask their intentions and confuse the police.[53] In 1981, Antonio Risério recounted stories told by "the old guys" (os velhos), who recalled that Bahian officials wanted to prevent the afoxé from parading because the name was "an offense to the United Kingdom."[54]

GLOBAL GANDHI, LOCAL GANDHI

The notion that Gandhi would represent a radical, dangerous figure is especially significant in light of the way he was seen elsewhere in the world.[55] Held up alongside Leninism and other icons of radical worker mobilizations of the early twentieth century, to many observers, Vijay Prashad writes, "Gandhi, by comparison, seemed serenely safe."[56] Ultimately, though, Gandhi occupied a complex, shifting, and often contradictory place in class- and race-based struggles and to national liberation movements across the world. Prashad notes that although "the captains of industry" might have preferred Gandhi to Lenin, his success nonetheless inspired radical groups and individuals around the globe.[57]

Gandhi's legacy in South Africa is especially complicated and also especially relevant to the case at hand. A recent forum on Ashwin Desai and Goolam Vahed's controversial book *The South African Gandhi: Stretcher-Bearer of Empire* provides two important insights to contextualize the Filhos de Gandhy.[58] First, *The South African Gandhi* and its critics highlight the long-standing tensions between depictions of a saintly Gandhi revered across the world and a more complex and even troubling figure. For decades, one critic of *The South African Gandhi* writes, observers have turned Gandhi's "ideas about non-violence into an anodyne prescription for world peace, and made of the Mahatma its patron saint."[59] *The South African Gandhi* provides a welcome rejoinder to that image. As Desai and Vahed show, Gandhi supported the British Empire during his time in South Africa and was, in the words of one of the forum contributors "as much an imperial as national thinker."[60] In South Africa, Gandhi also embraced race and caste hierarchies that would seem to run counter to the principles of unity and equality that became all but synonymous with his name.

There is no indication that members of the Filhos de Gandhy understood their namesake in anything other than in glowing and romantic terms. In that sense, they belong to a longer and broader global tradition of glorifying and flattening out Gandhi and his ideas. But a second conclusion from the book forum suggests an additional, more complex dynamic that must also be taken into account. Reflecting on Nelson Mandela's 1993 speech at the dedication of a statue commemorating Gandhi in Pietermaritzburg, South Africa, one forum contributor wonders why "Mandela and others, who knew at least the broad outlines of the South African Gandhi's views on empire and Africans, were nevertheless able to read him as an irreplaceable ancestor."[61] The answer lays in part in the 1940s, when Mandela and other "African political activists came to nationalist consciousness."[62] By then, Gandhi was an international symbol, and "India embodied self-determination beyond the West and its norms."[63] That symbolism is clearly what appealed to many original members of the Filhos de Gandhy. But did the South Asian Gandhi represent "an irreplaceable ancestor" for Black Brazilians as Mandela said it did for Black South Africans?

At least literally, the answer is yes. The Filhos de Gandhy called themselves Gandhi's sons and positioned themselves as Gandhi's heirs, a symbolic move that dialogues in fascinating ways with the more well-known debates and discussions about Gandhi elsewhere in the African diaspora. "In the 1920s and 1930s," Prashad writes, "as the Indian freedom struggle became synonymous with Gandhi, colonized and oppressed people in the darker nations took notice. From Jamaica, African America, and southern Africa, among other places, came the query, Where is our Black Gandhi? Will our Black Gandhi come?"[64] We do not know whether the founders of the Filhos de Gandhy or other Black Salvadorans openly pined for a "Black Gandhi," but a different question may be in order. Turning the query slightly, we may instead ask, "Was Gandhi the Bahian stevedores' Black Gandhi?" Two conundrums are embedded in the question. First, how many Brazilians saw Gandhi as the radical symbol that some of the Filhos de Gandhy recall, and how many instead considered him "serenely safe?" Second, how might the Brazilian stevedores have understood Gandhi in racial terms? Was he Indian? Could they have understood him to be Black, or something else entirely? Each question may only be addressed with attention to both Gandhi's biography and the particular social, cultural, and political milieus in which the Filhos de Gandhy were born.

One thing that seems certain is that Black communities in Brazil did not debate the viability of nonviolent Gandhism as a political strategy in the same way—or with the same visibility—as Blacks in the United States did. E. Franklin Frazier and W. E. B. DuBois both challenged the notion that "an American Gandhi" would be helpful or even possible, though by the 1960s, Martin Luther King Jr. all but assumed the mantle amid heated debates about the efficacy of nonviolent resistance.[65] In Brazil, discussions among Black activists and intellectuals turned on many axes—communism versus capitalism, the viability of real inclusion within local and national spheres, relationships with Africa and diasporic communities throughout the Americas, the place of culture—but violence versus nonviolence was not a central debate, at least not in the 1940s.[66]

If that difference is clear, other aspects are much fuzzier. Whereas some of the afoxé's founders feared that Gandhi would be seen as a subversive symbol, at least one was concerned about just the opposite, that the police would get things twisted and think that the group was criticizing Gandhi.[67] The differing memories line up not only with the contrasting opinions about Gandhi, then and now, but also the dramatic changes that he underwent over the course of his life. Prashad reminds, "Gandhi was not always Gandhi, and the Gandhi that we know only emerged because of his experience in the struggles for justice in southern Africa."[68] Gandhi came to South Africa as a twenty-four-year-old in 1893, leaving twenty-one years later. He eventually became involved in popular mobilizations there that would shape his identity, convictions, and the political strategies he embraced later. It is difficult to know how, if at all, the "South African Gandhi" figured into the ideas of the Filhos de Gandhy.[69] Although the group's members mentioned England and India, Africa does not appear in the interviews they gave during the 1980s. The absence is notable given the preponderance of (especially West and West Central) African connections and symbols that shaped life and culture—during Carnival and otherwise—in Salvador. Whether or not the Filhos de Gandhy saw their namesake as African, one wonders whether they understood him to be Black. Here, again, the written record is silent. But it is at least safe to suggest that some members understood Gandhi to share with them dark skin and a not-whiteness that could be inhabited or appropriated. By donning turbans, beads, and the larger collection of Orientalist accoutrements, the workers could become Gandhi, or at least channel his being, quite literally in the case of the individual designated each year to dress as the Mahatma.

ORIENTALISM AND MASCULINITY

To "become" Gandhi and to make their own Bahian version of the Mahatma, Salvador's port workers called upon a long history of Carnival Orientalism, which appropriated and projected racialized stereotypes of indigenous Brazilians as well as foreign "others," and a masculinist ethos that on the one hand channeled Gandhian discipline and on the other flaunted what at the time were the most well-known Gandhian gender ideals. What might appear to be eclectic and contradictory imagery and symbolism would be understood in much different terms during Carnival, when revelers dressed in any number of costumes and routinely transformed themselves, freely crossing not only racial and national boundaries but also gendered ones. The all-male Filhos de Gandhy projected (and still projects) a masculinist ideal that all but erases women, an ideal that dovetailed with other Brazilian representations of Gandhi and masculinity. In 1928, the famous modernist writer Mário de Andrade wrote a poem describing a peaceful walk through a garden. "What do I want" he asks rhetorically:

> A woman? No, I do not want a woman.
> If I could have at my side, walking there
> Let's suppose Lenin, Carlos Prestes, Gandhi, someone like that![70]

By linking Lenin, Gandhi, and Prestes, Andrade provides a glimpse at the racially and politically diverse (even contradictory) collection of international "great man" icons publicly celebrated alongside Gandhi in Brazil. (Luís) Carlos Prestes would later become the leader of the Brazilian Communist Party, and had just led a failed armed march (the Prestes Column), which intended to foment a Communist revolution. He would spend several years studying Marxism in Bolivia, Argentina, Uruguay, and finally the Soviet Union, returning to Brazil clandestinely to launch another failed uprising. Imprisoned during the Estado Novo, he was released and then became a congressman, just as the Filhos de Gandhy were coming into being.[71] Like Lenin, and unlike Gandhi, Prestes enthusiastically embraced violence as a means for revolution. What ties the three together for Andrade is a male cult of personality, embodied by Prestes as a "Knight of Hope," an image that Amado helped immortalize in a book of the same name.[72]

A year after Andrade published his poem, a newspaper in Rio counted Gandhi along with Benito Mussolini, Reza Shah (the shah of Iran), Tomáš Masaryk (the first president of Czechoslovakia), Saad Zaghloul (former prime minister of Egypt), and Mustafa Kemal Pasha (the first president of Turkey), among "great individuals that currently or in the past marked the world with their influence."[73] Once again, Gandhi found himself among an ungainly collection of powerful men, romanticized via the transnational transmission of news and reconfigured in Brazil. His visage belonged to a collection of lionized male figures who could be violent or nonviolent, and whose ethnicity and origins could come from almost anywhere, though not, perhaps, sub-Saharan Africa.

From an early moment, then, Gandhi represented a malleable, floating signifier, whose meaning could be interpreted and employed in different ways.[74] A newspaper in Rio contrasted Gandhi with the British-born US labor leader Samuel Gompers, calling Gandhi Gompers's "moral antithesis" and lauding the way he put his body and well-being on the line for the larger good but without resorting to violence. Gandhi was "poor," "truly humble," "sincere," and guided by "old oriental" spirits.[75] A paper in São Paulo presented two dueling pictures of Gandhi, first labeling him a Bolshevist, and then correcting itself at the urging of a reader "born in British India, and living among us for quite some time."[76] The reader rejected the idea that Gandhi or the nationalists were Bolsheviks—"No, never!" he told the paper, before painting a glowing portrait. Other papers presented Gandhi in less favorable terms, and some called him, unquestioningly, a "socialist."[77] Though on balance positive, the multiplicity of labels confirms Gandhi's presence in the Brazil imaginary at a relatively early moment and also the flexibility of his image.

As Andrade's poem suggests, Gandhi was often presented in masculinist terms that resonated with the all-male ethos of the Filhos de Gandhy. Explanations of why women are not allowed in the group always center on the idea that the founders prohibited women (and alcohol) to avoid trouble. One original member said, "Where there's alcohol and women, there necessarily are fights, and the cordão's motto was PEACE." Another said that the presence of "women among a lot of men creates fire," and a third suggested that the combination invariably created "volatile disagreements."[78] While banning women, the Filhos de Gandhy also often depended on them for supplying materials for their costumes and providing refreshments during the long hours parading in the streets. According to some, the men obtained the white sheets used as robes from prostitutes. Bráulio José de Bonfim borrowed a sheet from "a girl named Delza" and described how "lowly prostitutes" would follow closely behind the Filhos de Gandhy when they paraded, carrying "supplies" for the men "because all of us had our black girls."[79]Anísio Félix, the journalist who published interviews with the group, amplifies the paternalism and almost celebratory accounts of members with "girlfriends" on the side, some of whom they paid for sex. Félix describes one of the group's songs as a paean to the members' "wives, mothers, grandmothers, daughters, fiancées, and concubines."[80] The depictions of women as submissive, subservient, and providing readily available sexual adventure represent an obvious contrast to most images of Gandhi, who is famous for what Joseph S. Alter describes as "his desire to desexualize women by feminizing himself."[81] By barring women and alcohol, the group projected a disciplined, upright masculinity, however hypocritical. By contrast, the members' jovial, erotic memories starkly contrast with self-femininization, not to mention Gandhi's famous support for sexual abstinence.[82]

Carnival, an important space for the expression of Black and African cultural forms, and also a multiracial, sexualized site of ostentatious ethnic, national, and racial performance, is crucial for understanding this apparent paradox. Men regularly dressed as women, though the intention was rarely if ever to desexualize anything. In this milieu, to dress as Gandhi and to believe in him as a symbol of masculine discipline, nonwhite mobilization, and non-West autonomy while also orientalizing him and perpetuating chauvinist masculinity was less a paradox than an embrace of the kind of inversions and performances common among Carnival revelers across Brazil. Far from a defense of the Filhos de Gandhy, this contextualization suggests how and why they were able to, in a sense, "get away" with embracing Gandhi alongside symbols and practices that otherwise seem so incongruent.

As the Filhos de Gandhy appropriated and deployed an array of exotic, sometimes seemingly incongruent or anachronistic transnational and local symbols and images, they both built on and departed from earlier traditions. The particular emphasis on Gandhi and India was unique, though as we will see below, a smaller, heretofore unknown group did the same for at least a short time during the 1930s. But the costumes and the eclectic, Orientalist exoticizations were very much in line with other displays at Carnival, where revelers dressed up as indigenous people and also dressing in mock Turkish, Mexican, and other garb. The early afoxés that evoked Africa in their names and on the streets displayed a wide array of African symbols—for the most part, these were not flattened-out or generic references.[83] Some names also included places like Baghdad, even as they held themselves as conveyors of African culture.[84] This, Moura shows, is indicative of a broader Orientalist landscape that marked Bahian Carnival celebrations.[85] In the 1950s, Salvadoran oil workers named themselves the Merchants of Baghdad. The group represented an emerging Black middle class of workers employed in a new petroleum industry and also, Moura writes, a larger "oriental world" conveyed in films and during Carnival, and marked by a kind of "diffuse unity, that encompassed the worlds of caliphs, sheiks, and pashas . . . [and] their palaces, harems, and horses."[86] Salvador's Carnival, then, was filled with Orientalist symbols taken from a broad swath of Asia and the Middle East. The appropriation of those symbols was in turn tied to the development of distinct local Black identities.

A 1948 multipage spread in the Rio magazine *O Cruzeiro* further illustrates the way that "the Orient," broadly and vaguely conceived, pervaded Bahian Carnival. The article, which included photographs by the famous French transplant Pierre Verger, was an expose on what the author called Bahia's "barbaric" afoxé culture.[87] Printed a year before the founding of the Filhos de Gandhy, Verger's photos capture a broad spread that includes Black revelers carrying Babalotîm dolls, donning towering "Indian" (i.e., indigenous) headdresses, elaborate costumes meant to evoke Portuguese and African royalty, and, most notably, Black men wearing thick, "majestic Muslim turbans," described later in the article as "Arab."[88] Most likely meant to honor the city's rich Muslim history, highlighted by the famous 1835 revolt of Malê slaves, the displays also clearly prefigure the costumes that the Filhos de Gandhy would wear the next year.[89] Significantly, the afoxés of 1948 included a number of warrior figures as well as bow and arrows and other weapons. The wooden arms carried by the Filhos de Gandhy must be understood, then, not only as anachronistic, violent references drawn from *Gunga Din* but also as continuations of existent Carnival tropes.

Orientalist and primitivist performances at Carnival conveniently provided an anything-goes environment for an all-male group that was at once chaste and promiscuous. That mix bore interesting and multiple afterlives. In 1951, port workers in Rio formed their own Afoxé Filhos de Gandhi. In addition to the different spelling ("i" instead of "y"), this group differed from its Bahian inspiration in important ways. Unlike Salvador's Filhos de Gandhy, the version in Rio allowed women, who performed the role of "baianas," a feature of other Bahian afoxés and by that point also an obligatory feature of Carnival in Rio. In the 1930s, the government required Rio's samba schools participating in Carnival to have an *ala das baianas*, a group of women dressed up as Black women from Bahia. The costume included a head wrap, flowing dress, and often jewelry. Like other afoxés, Rio's Filhos de Gandhi also included in their repertoire of exotic representations members dressed as *índios*, Brazil's "other"—indigenous—Indians.[90]

The inversions here are almost too tangled to trace: in addition to the multiple, dramatically different representations of "Indian," "typical" Bahian womanhood is performed by so many different groups that its origins sccm to all but disappear. By including female members, Rio's Filhos de Gandhi differentiated themselves from their counterparts in Salvador while simultaneously carrying on a tradition of other Bahian afoxés and, in effect, asking their women to "play Bahian." Some of the women may have actually been from Bahia or of Bahian descent, so the degree of performance in Rio must have varied greatly. Further still, in 1979 a group of women in Salvador created the Afoxé Filhas de Gandhy, or Daughters of Gandhi. Fagundes explained that this afoxé was formed "because the women (wives), lovers, girlfriends, and daughters" of the male group "also wanted to celebrate in the same way." The women themselves suggest something more meaningful still. The group's Facebook page describes the afoxé as "an initiative of female empowerment," a powerful counterpoint to the all-male original.[91]

GANDHI AND POLITICS IN SALVADOR

The founders of the Filhos de Gandhy were also at the center of labor mobilizations. Though we still know relatively little about the relationships and interactions among Salvador's often overlapping spheres of Communists, workers, and Black cultural producers and community members, we do know that each group regularly drew inspiration from abroad. In addition to the Comintern, the United States, and multiple points in Africa, Bahian activists were also attuned to events elsewhere in Latin America.[92]

News and images of Gandhi and India flowed through the worlds inhabited by Salvador's stevedores, who identified and acted politically in ways that do not always map easily onto standard paradigms. Port workers founded a syndicate in 1912, which would eventually provide important institutional and legal support for the Filhos de Gandhy. The syndicate's composition and orientation are telling. On the one hand, its members were closely tied and also subordinate to a powerful Black port workers' syndicate in Rio de Janeiro, who until 1939 selected the president of the Salvador satellite.[93] The syndicate's inter-regional link underlines the dynamic contours of Brazil's many Black working-class groups and also the layers of differential power among them. The syndicate that would eventually back the Filhos de Gandhy also challenges easy equivalences between Communism and the working class. According to one member, once the Salvador syndicate secured the right to elect its own president, local members "never elected a white or a communist" to lead them.[94]

News about Gandhi and India circulated throughout Brazil, and Salvador was no exception. The diverse narratives, identities, and projects that news reports helped fuel are on full display in a handful of accounts that appeared in the Bahian newspaper *O Imparcial* in 1935, almost a decade and a half before the creation of the Filhos de Gandhy. In February, the paper lamented the fact that the Carnival group Cordão Emulos de Gandhi, "which conquered so many applauses last year," would not be participating in that year's revelry.[95] The group, which to my knowledge has not registered in previous studies, tantalizes as a possible prehistory, or alternate history, to the Filhos de Gandhy. *Emulos* has multiple meanings and may be translated here as "followers." Who were these followers of Gandhi? Did they share any relationship to the Filhos de Gandhy? At this point, it is impossible to answer the first question. For the second, one could reasonably surmise that the Cordão Emulos de Gandhi did not share a connection to the more famous Filhos de Gandhi, whose members do not mention a precursor in their published recollections. The Cordão nonetheless clearly indicates that Gandhi had currency not only in Bahia but in Bahian Carnival as early as the 1930s.

The meanings that Salvadorans pinned to Gandhi were manifold. Nelson de Souza Carneiro, Edison's brother and a leftist intellectual and politician who would go on to become the first Black president of the Brazilian Senate, mentioned Gandhi in a somewhat strange column addressed to an author and friend who had recently attempted to kill herself. Although for the most part tender, Carneiro closed the piece imploring the friend to stop writing fluffy poems and to be bolder. Punctuating the appeal, he challenged her not to continue "obstinately" in "Brazilian letters as Gandhi in Indian politics."[96] Carneiro's evocation, which amounts to a backhanded compliment, further illustrates the Mahatma's multidimensional presence in the Bahian imaginary. A more straightforward celebration came in an article by the white feminist writer Rachel Prado. In a short essay that criticized British rule in South Asia, Prado approvingly described Gandhi as "the apostle of non-violence" and a "pacifist without equal."[97] *O Imparcial* also reported on Gandhi's support for Ethiopia in its struggle against Italy, now also appropriately pitting him against Mussolini. "Gandhi," the paper wrote, "affirmed that India could not ignore the threat of Mussolini against the colored races."[98] If these references leave no doubt that Gandhi had an important presence in 1930s Salvador, a final example shows just how multifaceted that presence could be.

In February 1935, just two days after lamenting that the Cordão Emulos de Gandhi would not be participating in that year's Carnival, *O Imparcial* printed an article under the dramatic headline, "Will Febronio come to Bahia?"[99] Febrônio was "the famous degenerate" celebrity criminal Febrônio Índio do Brasil, who had fled authorities in Rio de Janeiro and was said to be headed to Bahia. He was charged with killing two young boys in Rio, crimes for which he confessed, though apparently under coercive force.[100] Identified by one author as *cafuzo* (mixed-race of African and indigenous descent), the dark-skinned Febrônio became the subject of fascination not only in the press but also among criminal anthropologists, psychiatrists, and others who wrote about him as a case study in degeneracy and deviance.[101]

Febrônio called himself Son of the Light, a phrase he tattooed across his chest and an indication to pundits of his esoteric spirituality and mysticism. In an interview reprinted in *O Imparcial*, Febrônio also spoke of a political project that received much less attention than his race, sexuality, and apparently abhorrent crimes. "Are you students?" he asked a group of journalists. "I also study. I just read a book by Gandhi. And what you see outside, on the streets, it's a disgrace. The police kill people. No one does anything." Suggesting that he had plans to change all that, he proclaimed, "I will be the Lenin of Brazil."[102]

That Febrônio would reference Gandhi and Lenin together is indicative of an expansive and sometimes confounding set of references. And yet, as we have seen in Mário de Andrade's poem, he was not alone. Like the Filhos de Gandhi, Febrônio drew inspiration from diverse and surprising places, though each indicative of the unruly transnational flow of international symbols of resistance. Each reminds us of how little we actually know about what the "revolutionary imagination" looked like during the first half of the twentieth century among nonwhite Brazilians, especially those who did not have access to Brazil's rich Black press.[103]

HISTORIES TO BE WRITTEN

Lenin, Gandhi, mysticism, police violence, voyeuristic and imaginative journalists, readers, and scholars. Each informed and shaped Febrônio, who nonetheless drew attention for a narrower set of reasons. Although Febrônio's life story deserves further study, here it may serve as a final example of the complex and sometimes perplexing swirl of influences and identities sweeping through Salvador in the 1930s and 1940s. That swirl included a multifaceted Gandhi and a larger political and cultural cosmos that the city's stevedores and other residents consumed and, in some cases, adopted as they traversed the threshold separating the authoritarian Estado Novo and the "difficult democracy" that followed. If, as Chakravarti suggests, Brazilian and Indian politics would eventually diverge in a way that prevented elites and power holders in both nations from forging lasting bonds, Febrônio, the Filhos de Gandhy, and the circulation of news of Gandhi himself suggest a quite different picture marked by more fluid and dynamic relationships and connections that at least sometimes crossed and linked seemingly disparate groups and places. Though Gilberto Freyre and Brazilian diplomats would eventually find more differences than similarities between Brazil and India, other historical actors seemed to have been more open to grander, more capacious visions. That these visions developed before

Bandung further suggests the need to more boldly reimagine chronologies, contours, connections, and fissures within the so-called Global South.[104]

The images, ideas, and people that shaped and were shaped by the Filhos de Gandhy also suggest coordinates for a map that extends far beyond and in directions rarely traveled by the ones commonly employed in works about Brazil and the rest of Latin America. The group's larger trajectory also raises crucial questions about sexism, misogyny, and cultural appropriation. The history of the Filhos de Gandhy, then, is not only one about the persistence and resistance of African-inspired religious forms and postcolonial solidarity, but also less celebratory matters. When the references from *O Imparcial* are added to the mix, the story that emerges becomes more complex still. In Rachel Prado's hands, Gandhi is a shining example of anticolonial pacifism. To Febrônio Índio do Brasil, he is something quite different: an inspiration akin to Lenin. Placed together, the pieces of evidence considered here suggest the outline of a still-incomplete puzzle, one that nonetheless already reveals an image that at once resembles and tugs at the borders of the literal and figurative maps employed by previous scholars.

The Black workers who created the Filhos de Gandhy found inspiration not only from across the South Atlantic but also from beyond the Pacific. The work shortage they faced was linked, at least in some way, to events in Great Britain, thus expanding our frame of reference not only west and east but also north. Although the Filhos de Gandhy also clearly suggest a need to further explore potential affinities and connections between Brazil and India, not to mention Brazil's all but invisible South Asian communities, the story here is not about finding new transnational connections or "discovering" a hidden group. To the contrary, the history of the Filhos de Gahndy demands further accounting for the local forces that shaped and helped give rise to it. This chapter, based mainly on printed oral histories and searchable digital archives, simply represents one small step in that process. In the "Muslim" turbans that afoxé members wore before the group was created, in the Cordão Emulos de Gandhi that also preceded it, and especially in the Filhas de Gandhy, who gained formal visibility well after their male counterparts, there is abundant evidence of important histories yet to be written.

CHAPTER NINE

READING THE CARIBBEAN AND UNITED STATES THROUGH PANAMANIAN *REGGAE EN ESPAÑOL*

Sonja Stephenson Watson

Research on Panama has primarily focused on the building of the canal (1904–1914) and the United States's relationship to the construction of the "eighth wonder of the modern world."[1] The canal, however, brought to Panama not only international recognition but also thousands of Black English-speaking laborers from Jamaica and Barbados. West Indian workers labored on the canal, made Panama their permanent home, and transformed the ethnic, racial, and linguistic composition of the nation. A century later, despite negligible recognition from the Panamanian nation-state, Black West Indian descendants in Panama continue to shape and influence the nation linguistically, culturally, and racially. One important cultural expression of that history is *reggae en español* (Spanish reggae).

Reggae en español is a hybrid cultural and musical art form that blends elements of Jamaican dancehall and reggae.[2] Reggae music rocked Jamaica in the 1960s. Comprising and influenced by a variety of musical styles from Jamaica (mento, ska, and rock steady[3]) and the United States (jazz and rhythm and blues), reggae emerged as a Jamaican musical sensation, one that catapulted to prominence and was commercialized by Bob Marley in the 1970s. The genre's impact spread beyond Jamaica to Panama where people from Jamaica, Barbados, and Trinidad had migrated to construct the railroad (1850–1855) and later the canal in the late nineteenth and early twentieth centuries. During the construction of the railroad, more than forty-five thousand Jamaicans came to Panama, along with workers from Grenada, England, Ireland, France, Germany, Austria, India, and China. The attempted construction of the failed French canal project from 1880 to 1889 would bring eighty-four thousand additional Jamaicans to Panama. After France's unsuccessful project, the United States intervened and imported 19,900 workers from Barbados and a small number of workers from Martinique, Guadeloupe, and Trinidad. The large population of West Indian immigrants (148,900) transformed the ethnic composition of the newly created Republic of Panama. The descendants of Panama's West Indian immigrant populations contributed to the creation and dissemination of reggae en español, though they were not the sole contributors.

Panamanian reggae en español emerged from transnational and transcultural networks of cultural exchange between the United States, the Caribbean, and Panama from the 1960s to the present.[4] In her discussion of Brazilian popular performance from 1888 to the 1950s, Lisa Shaw "considers how popular culture drew on transnational currents to construct new ideas about racial identity" in Brazil.[5] Specifically, she envisions the port city of Rio de Janeiro as a "nexus in transnational performance circuits" and discusses how notions of racial and national identity can be constructed through performance within circuits of transnational and transcultural exchange. Likewise, Lara Putnam argues that through circum-Caribbean transnational networks, Caribbean migrants "created sounds, steps, and social practices that were themselves then borrowed and reworked from site to site" in the 1920s and 1930s.[6] Putnam views circum-Caribbean networks during the Jazz Age as a product of migration and attendant cultural exchange and identity formations among British Caribbeans (from Jamaica, Barbados, Trinidad) who moved to Panama (Colón), Costa Rica (Port Limón), the United States (particularly New Orleans and Harlem), and Cuba.

In both studies, performance is a key element in the shaping of national identity politics, cultural transformation, and the construction of (trans) national identity. Whereas Shaw views the Brazilian port city of Rio de Janeiro as a site of cultural, racial, and linguistic exchange, Putnam analyzes Caribbean port cities as sites and recipients of cultural exchange resulting from the migration of people from Jamaica, Barbados, and Trinidad to the United States and Central America. These migrations were also influenced by international Black movements and the Black press. For example, by 1924, Marcus Garvey's United Negro Improvement Association had chapters throughout the Caribbean and South America, including forty-seven in Panama.[7] British Caribbean migrants also created an internationally linked Black press that connected local issues of Black disenfranchisement with related global problems.[8]

Building on Shaw and Putnam, I argue that transnational circuits of cultural, racial, and linguistic exchange fashioned Panamanian reggae en español. Forms of popular music such as reggae en español became hybridized and transculturated as they crossed national and cultural boundaries. More broadly, this analysis aims to further the discussion of race by viewing it through a transatlantic and transnational lens. Furthermore, the interplay of the Caribbean, US, and Panamanian cultures in fashioning reggae en español symbolizes how African diaspora communities transcend the boundaries of the nation-state through culture, race, language, and music. That interplay also shows how transnational networks of cultural exchange can be defined by migration, travel, and other aspects of globalization.[9] Reggae en español transcends national boundaries, and it yields a Black transnational discourse that influences the concept of race and nation in Panama by (re)defining, (re)imagining and (re)interpreting notions of *panameñidad*, or Panamanian cultural nationalism.

Reggae en español reflects a longer tradition of music in Panama that resulted from slavery and postcolonialism, as well as transnational migration. Reggae en español pulls from various geographic areas including Africa, the Caribbean, Panama, and the United States. However, music in Panama has traditionally originated from other migratory subjects and spaces. Traditional or "folklore" Panamanian music such as *tamborito*, *cumbia*, and *música típica* were all influenced by traditions outside of the nation. Tamborito dates to colonial Panama and is the product of African, indigenous, and Spanish influences. The tamborito dance is a romantic, couple's dance, often involving a small percussion ensemble. It is musically performed to the beat of drums, the stomping of feet, the clapping of hands, and the chanting of harmonic poems, called coplas, led vocally by a female singer. Tamborito is the national song and dance of Panama that symbolizes *panameñidad*, or Panamanian national identity. More broadly, panameñidad evokes Panamanian cultural nationalism that resulted from early twentieth-century nation-building rhetoric that favored Panamanian heritage over US influence during the building of the Panama Canal (1904–1914). Cultural nationalists viewed the nation as a common culture with a shared sense of community, identity, and "peoplehood."[10] Panameñidad emphasized cultural, national, and patriotic affiliation with Panama and dismissed the need for any emphasis on race. Because panameñidad was understood in terms of the customs, habits, religion, and language that Panamanians shared, there was no need to acknowledge racial differences. The tamborito is emblematic of Panamanian cultural nationalism. Panama's most famous tamborito, "Al tambor de la alegría" ("At the pinnacle of happiness") (1918), is referenced in the lyrics of contemporary Panamanian *reggaeseros*. Cumbia, also an amalgam of African, indigenous, and Spanish influences, originated in Colombia and became a part of Panamanian culture while Panama was a department of Colombia from 1821 to 1903.[11] In addition, Colombian vallenato and cumbia influenced Panama's traditional folklore music known as música típica.[12] Panamanian música típica is a violin or accordion-based dance music genre, derived from the country's folkloric musical traditions, such as the mejorana[13] and tamborito.[14]

Twentieth-century Panamanian music also drew from outside influences. Between 1900 and 1930, Panamanians often listened to music imported from Cuban radio stations, due to the lack of radio stations in Panama.[15] Thus, cultural hybridity and the intermingling of musical influences has characterized Panamanian musical art forms from the colonial period to the present; reggae en español is no exception.

Transculturation and hybridity fashioned Panamanian reggae en español. Transculturation characterizes cultures comprised of "two or more ethnic identities, two or more aesthetic codes and historical experiences."[16] Cuban musician and anthropologist Fernando Ortiz (1881–1969) utilized the term to explain the transformation of Cuban culture, one altered by centuries of race mixing since the European encounter with the indigenous populations during the colonial period.[17] Ortiz preferred "transculturation" over "acculturation" because, for him, the former involves a combination of cultures that persisted—albeit in a transformed way—whereas the latter evokes a loss of the initial culture(s). Transculturation explains cultural phenomena that emerged in Cuba and elsewhere in Latin America and the Caribbean where there was also cultural, racial, and linguistic, racial mixing. Reggae en español as a musical genre can be defined by transculturation. Rooted in the Jamaican rhythms of dancehall music and reggae, this music came to be performed with Spanish lyrics.

As a musical art form typified by hybridity and transculturation, reggae en español borrows from myriad cultures to forge a unique genre in Panama. Transculturation not only defines reggae en español but explains the development of other musical genres in Latin America and the Caribbean. In Panama as elsewhere, Caribbean migration and the US hip-hop movement played a large part in reggae en español. El General and Nando Boom's movement between Panama and the United States explored below also played a major role in crafting the musical form as did Panamanian reggae artists' experiences growing up in the US-Panama Canal Zone, their ability to speak English, and the overwhelming cultural impact of the United States elsewhere in the Americas. Black cultural identity and performance in Panama is essential to the development of reggae en español.

Black identity in Panama informs the lyrics of Panamanian reggae artists. Black populations in Panama largely fall into two groups. The first group includes Spanish-speaking Blacks (Afro-Hispanics) who are direct descendants of enslaved Africans in Panama and who overwhelming identify with their Panamanian national heritage rather than their Blackness. The second group includes the descendants of English-speaking West Indians. As immigrants from Jamaica, Barbados, and Trinidad, Black West Indians vehemently challenge the racial (Hispanic), linguistic (Spanish), and religious (Catholic) components of Panamanian nation-building rhetoric. In Panama, nineteenth-century *mestizaje* (race-mixing) discourse encouraged cultural uniformity and in turn fashioned a national anti-Black sentiment. Mestizaje discourse and anti-Black sentiment continues to affect Black West Indians and reggae artists in Panama who are primarily of Anglophone Caribbean ancestry.

West Indian immigration to Panama fueled Panamanian nationalism during the period of 1880–1920. The short story "El Orejano" (1882) and the letter "Carta a un amigo" (Letter to a Friend,1904) by essayist, writer, and later President Belisario Porras defined Panamanian nationality in opposition to the Panamanian port cities such as Colón and the parts of the country heavily populated with Black West Indians and Americans. Porras defined Panama based on its indigenous roots grounded in the interior. In part as an attempt to counter the perception of other Latin American intellectuals and politicians that the US-dominated Panama was a territory devoid of its Hispanic heritage, the country attempted to reaffirm its *hispanidad* by utilizing neocolonial architecture, constructing a monument of Miguel de Cervantes, and by naming its currency the *balboa*, in honor of the Panamanian conquistador, Vasco Núñez de Balboa (1475–1519).[18] Hispanidad became a major tenet of Panamanian nationalism of the period, which also held a desire to "whiten" Panamanian culture.[19] Panamanian *criollos* (peoples of European or Spanish descent born in Panama) appropriated the discourse of mestizaje to reinforce hispanidad and the nation's racial, cultural, and linguistic homogeneity against US imperialism. In short, to counter demographic changes, many Panamanian intellectuals ignored the African majority while propagating ideals of an independent republic based on hispanidad as they also vehemently rejected North American and West Indian influences.

Panamanian writers demonized the West Indian population in hopes of impeding North American imperialism and to encourage the new immigrants to return to their native homelands. *El peligro antillano en la América Central* (West Indian Danger in Central America), for example, articulated anti-West Indian sentiment and the perceived differences between Afro-Hispanics (Spanish) and West Indians (Black) in Panama. "It is evident that there is a large difference between the Black West Indian and the man of color raised in the Indo-American civilization, not only because of his status in the neighboring English colonies where his economic situation is depressing and his wages unfair, but also because of the respectable environment that our colored races enjoy, considerations that have been accorded because of their noble character and assimilation to our most moral virtues."[20] These assertions reflect nationalistic opposition to Black West Indians. The message is clear: unlike Afro-Hispanics, West Indians were culturally and linguistically different from other Panamanians and did not

reflect hispanidad. Anti-West Indianism contributed to several laws directed against those who did not fit this vision of Panamanian nationality. In
1926, Law 13 prohibited non-Spanish-speaking Blacks from entering the
country. In 1941, President Arnulfo Arias made it a requirement to speak
Spanish in order to become a citizen. Ultimately, West Indians were encouraged to give up their own culture and adopt that of Panama or leave.[21]
As a result, many West Indians decided to repatriate to their native homelands. Anti-West Indian sentiment in Panama in the early twentieth century contributed to feelings of antipathy, hurt, and despair by West Indian
immigrants and their descendants. Reggae en español artists are a product
of anti-West Indian sentiment and Panamanian national identity politics.
Thus, it is not a surprise that reggae artists in Panama faced discrimination
by the Panamanian nation-state in the early 1980s for their style and dress.
Artists such as El General, for example, sported dreadlocks and faced harassment from the police for his display of Black culture.[22] Yet El General's
subsequent rise to fame became one way that that historic discrimination
was contested.

The descendants of 1890s Anglophone Caribbean migrants to Panama
gave birth to reggae en español in the late 1970s in the predominately urban
West Indian barrios of Río Abajo and Parque Lefevre in Panama City. Reggae's arrival in Panama and influence on Panamanian musicians is in itself
a product of multiple migratory paths. Panamanian poet and sociology professor Gerardo Maloney, for example, frequently visited Jamaica, brought
reggae records back to Panama, and played them for aspiring Spanish reggae artists such as El General (Edgardo Franco), the primary subject of
this study. Panamanian reggae artists encountered Caribbean music (Haiti,
Trinidad and Tobago, and Jamaica) through records, radio, and traveling
performers.[23] Artists such as El General, Renato, Nando Boom, El Maleante, and Chicho Man either sang over the recordings in Spanish or created their own lyrics using the same beat.[24]

While Spanish reggae developed in Panama, it emerged on a parallel
course in the United States spurred by West Indian migration from Panama
after 1950. The Remón-Eisenhower Treaty (1955) allowed Panama to tax
thousands of non-US citizens in the Panama Canal Zone. Consequently,
thousands of Panamanian West Indians lost their jobs.[25] Economic conditions and poor racial and political dynamics in the Canal Zone led numerous West Indians to migrate to New York City. From 1960 to 1969, 8,168
West Indians migrated to the United States for education and economic ad-
vancement, yet maintained ties with Panama.[26] The 1964 flag riots further
contributed to anxiety among West Indians and their mass exodus from the
Canal Zone to the United States and to areas outside of the Canal Zone,
including Panama City.[27] The 1964 riots led to the renegotiation of the

1903 Hay-Bunau-Varilla Treaty to improve US-Panamanian relations.[28] The renegotiation of the Hay-Bunau-Varilla Treaty resulted in the 1977 Carter-Torrijos Treaties, which would grant Panama complete control over the Canal in 1999. The Carter-Torrijos Treaties prompted a second major migration of Panamanian West Indians to New York in the 1970s.

Black West Indian migration from Panama to New York City, and above all Brooklyn, is key to the transnational development of reggae en español.[29] Brooklyn has also become a "central geographic point in the transnational network of reggae (non-Panamanian) music production" and is a site of cultural exchange for the production of reggae and Panamanian reggae en español.[30] In the 1970s, Jamaicans migrated to Brooklyn and brought with them reggae records to be sold in local record stores. They also brought sound systems that enabled them to have reggae battles that maintained diasporic interest and cultivation of the genre in New York City. The sound system is a key element in the dissemination of reggae music in Brooklyn and its impact on the broader West Indian diaspora and Brooklyn community at large. Sound systems are comprised of disc jockeys, engineers, and MCs playing reggae music. The broad reach of a sound system is an important part of these social dynamics because "the decibels expelled from sound system speakers can resonate for miles."[31]

As Sabia McCoy Torres argues, the "transnationalization of reggae . . . transformed Brooklyn into a transmigratory space for reggae music recording."[32] Radio stations in New York that catered to reggae music also forged cultural ties to Jamaica. Jamaican Philip Smart started a reggae radio show on WNYU[33] called "Get Smart" in the mid-1970s followed by the opening of HC&F Studios in Freeport, Long Island, in 1982. HC&F Studios cultivated the genre in New York City and became the premier studio for producing reggae hits in the 1980s and 1990s that included artists who had recently migrated from Jamaica and its diaspora in Panama, such as El General and Nando Boom.[34] HC&F Studios served as a "gathering place for emerging Jamaican reggae/dancehall acts based in New York and those visiting from the island."[35]

The transnationalization of reggae had an impact on music in the United States, the Caribbean, Panama, and beyond. The West Indian diaspora was essential to this transformation due to contact between migratory subjects from the Anglophone and Hispanophone Caribbean as well as Panama. The connection between West Indian immigrants from Jamaica and Panamanian West Indians in the circum-migratory space of Brooklyn and the broader New York City area was key to fashioning reggae en español. Soon after Jamaican reggae emerged in the 1960s, it circulated throughout the (Panamanian) West Indian community in both Panama and New York in the late 1970s and 1980s.

El General's experience as a reggae en español artist in both Panama and New York elevated his influence on the development of the genre. El General moved to New York in 1985 and attended the Erasmus Hall Academy of Art and Music in Brooklyn, where he excelled as president of the Latino Club. Shortly after, El General met Panamanian music producer Michael F. Ellis through a mutual friend, Tony Rodríguez. Ellis had recently (in 1987) established his own record label called New Creation Enterprises.[36] Ellis produced El General's groundbreaking dance hits "Te Ves Buena" ("You Look Good") and "Son Bow," and is considered to be one of the pioneers in producing reggae en español artists in the United States.

El General was not the only Panamanian reggae artist to cultivate the genre in New York. Nando Boom (Fernando Brown) also joined the Panamanian West Indian expatriate community in New York to record reggae en español records. Brown left Panama circa 1988 during the military dictatorship of Gen. Manuel Noriega. Noriega was hostile to reggae music because of its anti-national, pro-Black sentiment and sexist and misogynistic lyrics. The Panamanian government's censorship board often censored lyrics and performances by Panamanian reggae artists for the genre's sexually suggestive and explicate lyrics and dance. Panamanian music producer Fabio Matos noted that reggae en español was considered to be "ghetto music" by white and mixed-raced Panamanians.[37] Brown was reprimanded for grinding his hips at a concert, and El General's 1991 "El Caramelo" was censored because it referred to oral sex. Brown launched his first hit, "Mi mujer que habla así" ("My Woman Talks Like This") in 1984, which was followed by the launch of his self-titled album (*Nando Boom*) in 1988.

Brown's reggae career catapulted to fame in Panama City in the 1980s when he met burgeoning reggae producer Ramón "Pucho" Bustamante. An industrial engineer, Bustamante disseminated Panamanian reggae music in mobile discoteques (Guerreros de la Música [Musical Warriors], Triple S, and Sound Power Disco), which served as mobile sound systems that blasted music throughout the city. Bustamante met Brown when the latter was performing at his first major concert at the local Gimnasio Nuevo Panamá in 1988,[38] and they soon collaborated. In fact, Bustamante followed Brown to New York due to the harsh governmental censorship in Panama. Like El General, Brown began recording Spanish reggae in Brooklyn that was heavily infused with a Jamaican dembow beat used in dancehall. He recorded "Ellos Benia," a Spanish-language version of "Dem Bow." His producer, Bustamante, collaborated with Jamaican producers and artists such as Dennis "the Menace" Thompson to assist with the creation of the unique-sounding reggae en español songs infused with Jamaican dancehall beats with a Latin flavor in New York. Brown released a collection of pioneering reggae en español lyrics on the appropriately titled album *Reggae es-*

pañol in 1991, a collection of signature records that compiled Spanish translations of popular Jamaican dancehall hits. The album catapulted the artist
to fame and helped define the new genre that was an amalgam of reggae
and dancehall with a Latin sound. Produced by Bustamente in collaboration with HC&F records, "Ellos Benia" was a vocal collaboration between
Jamaican and Panamanian artists. Thus, the song was a cross-cultural collaboration that incorporated Latin style music with Jamaican dancehall.
The Latin style flavor provided the songs with a unique sound that distinguished them from the Jamaican dancehall dembow.

EDGARDO FRANCO A.K.A. "EL GENERAL"

El General is a founder of Panamanian reggae. He was born as Edgardo
Franco in Panama City in 1969 to a Trinidadian/Jamaican mother and a
Panamanian/Colombian father. Franco's professional persona as El General
is as fascinating as his renowned Panamanian reggae songs in Spanish that
eventually launched his solo career in the United States in the early 1990s.
Franco began singing and composing music at the age of twelve and soon
joined and began performing with the group "Renato y las 4 Estrellas"
(Renato and the 4 Stars). Along with Renato, he listened to reggae music
that Gerardo Maloney brought from Jamaica. Franco began recording records primarily in Jamaican patois but then translated the lyrics to Spanish
because the Panamanian audience could not understand him. Renato y las
4 Estrellas gained notoriety by distributing their records on Panamanian
buses.[39] The group began performing at local clubs and *quinceañeras* (celebration of a girl's fifteenth birthday), gaining notoriety and honing their
skills. However, Franco's musical career in Panama stopped in 1985 when
he moved to New York to live with his mother to attend high school and
pursue a degree in business administration. Three years later, still in New
York, Franco met Michael Ellis and began recording as a solo artist.[40]

Franco's first solo hit in the United States as El General was called "Tu
Pum Pum" (Your Pum Pum, 1990), a dancehall song in Spanish performed
to the beat box and baseline rhythms that characterize US rap. "Tu Pum
Pum" derives its name from the Jamaican term for the female sexual organ.
It reached number five on American radio stations. The hit song enabled El
General to continue recording tracks such as "Te Ves Buena" (You Look
Good, 1991), "Muévelo" (Move it, 1991), "El Caramelo" (Caramel, 1991),
"Las Chicas" (The Girls, 1995), and "Robi-Rob's Boriqua Anthem" (Robi-
Rob's Puerto Rican Anthem, 1994).[41] In addition, in the 1990s, El General
toured and performed with the rap group, the Cold Crush Brothers, and
the hip-hop music sensation, C & C Music Factory. The success of these
hits earned him coveted awards such as MTV Award for Best Latin Video
in 1992 and the Lo Nuestro Rap Awards Artist of the Year in 1993. El

General's music points to the genre's hybrid nature and the interplay of the US hip-hop movement and Jamaican dancehall and reggae in its fruition. The artist's trajectory from Panama to New York explains how the genre was simultaneously nurtured by Jamaican dancehall rhythms and reggae as well as the burgeoning 1980s hip-hop movement in the United States.[42] Between 1990 and 2004, El General recorded over seventeen albums before retiring in 2004 from the music industry due to the cancellation of his visa.

Performing throughout the United States and Latin America, El General dressed in full military uniform imitating General Oar Torrijos, a seminal figure in national and Black politics in Panama from 1968 to 1981. El General's imitation of Omar Torrijos is no surprise given that Torrijos "openly recruited political support among West Indian Panamanians and supported racially defined Black mobilization."[43] Racial mobilization increased during the Torrijos era, and several organizations mobilized to combat racism and discrimination of Black Panamanians residing in Panama and abroad.

Although his political platform continued to equate Spanish heritage with Panamanian nationality thereby reinforcing the mestizaje rhetoric, the Torrijos regime attempted to attenuate discriminatory practices."[44] Torrijos established the Partido Revolucionario Democrático (Revolutionary Democratic Party) in 1979. Because Torrijos represented the masses and not the *rabiblancos* (the white minority of elites whom the government represented prior to Torrijos assuming power), he excluded the traditional elites from political power and secured support from the rural provinces of Panama. His unexpected death from a mysterious plane crash in 1981 led many to believe that he was assassinated because of his progressive reforms for underrepresented sectors of the population. Before Torrijos's short presidency, the environment for Blacks in Panama was dismal. In the 1970s, the police frequently cut Black people's afros in Panama and especially those who had traveled from the United States.[45] However, the Torrijos regime provided an environment for Blacks in Panama to reopen discussions on class, race, and ethnicity and to claim a place for Blackness in the national body. Assuming the persona of General Omar Torrijos, El General dressed in concerts in a military uniform. When he performed a concert in Chile, Augusto Pinochet, who during that time was commander-in-chief of the Chilean Army, refused to allow him to dress as El General. Franco recalls the 1992 experience as follows:

> Then I get to Chile and this crazy situation happens. Pinochet didn't want me to come into the country, or that I call myself El General, or that I wear the uniform. He was saying he was the only general. That no other general can go there. So when we get to the airport in Chile, we had to stay like for three

hours. They inspected our bags, then closed them, then inspected them again. They confiscated all of El General's uniforms. Everything having to do with El General they confiscated. And they made me sign a document saying that if I sang I couldn't say I was El General. I had to say I was Edgardo Franco.[46]

Dressing as El General, Franco's reference to Torrijos inserted himself, and by extension, Blackness into the national Panamanian polity. Blackness, which was not a part of Panamanian national identity politics, moved to the center through reggae en español.

Reggae en español embodies Blackness and brings together a multiplicity of voices and genres rooted in the African diaspora. The 1991 lyric "Son Bow" is the Spanish-language cover of Jamaican dancehall musician Shabba Ranks's "Dem Bow" and utilizes the same musical track. The success of Ranks led other artists in Panama, New York, and San Juan to rerecord the song. Thematically, "Dem Bow" commences "as an anti-gay, anti-colonial anthem, implicitly interpolating its audience along the lines of race and nation . . . but ultimately finds itself defused and diffused . . . into a mere symbol of seduction, describing a distinctive, sexy, transnational and utterly marketable beat."[47] Similar to "Dem Bow," "Son Bow" conflates "sexual deviancy and colonialism" and "resistance and nationalism."[48] Most importantly, the song nods to Jamaica and Brooklyn as proprietors of "Son Bow" or dancehall.

> Son bow
> Son bow, son bow, son bow
> Easy Jamaican, you know you nuh bow
> Calma Panamá, tú no eres un bow
> Easy Canadian, you know who bow
> Calma Puerto Rico, tú no eres un bow
> Easy Brooklyn, man you know you nuh bow
> Calma Colombia, tú no eres un bow
>
> Son bow
> Son bow, son bow, son bow
> Easy Jamaican, you know you know bow
> Stay calm Panama, you are not a bow
> Easy Canadian, you know who bow
> Stay calm Puerto Rico, you are not a bow
> Easy Brooklyn, man you know you know bow
> Stay calm Colombia, you are not a bow

"Son Bow" is the product of transnational and transcultural exchange between Jamaica, the United States, and Panama. Ironically, "Son Bow" was recorded in the United States and not Panama or the Caribbean, illustrating the boundless nature of music and the transnational communities that they represent, reference, and reflect. It is a product of cultural hybridity and transnational/transcultural networks that originated in the Caribbean and that were transformed in the United States and shaped by a Panamanian artist. The reinterpretation of "Dem Bow" as "Son Bow" points to the transnational aspect of reggae en español and how it transcends national, racial, cultural, and linguistic boundaries and borders.

"Son Bow" is important because of its hybrid beat but also because it helped fashion the international phenomenon of *reggaetón*, a genre whose origins are linked to Panamanian Spanish reggae. Reggaetón is a Puerto Rican musical genre that is often confused with reggae en español because of the similarities of their sound and their connection to Panama. The dembow sound defines reggaetón. The dembow beat is an interplay of a steady kick drum and a syncopated snare. The kick drum emphasized a 4/4 beat, while the snare comes on the "and" of the third eighth note and right on the fourth eighth note. This makes the powerful "boom-ch-boom-chick" sound used in reggaetón lyrics. El General's cover of the Spanish-language version of "Dem Bow" provides one example of why artists often equate reggaetón with reggae en español. Reggaetón is associated with the success of white Puerto Rican artists such as Daddy Yankee who helped commercialize reggaetón in the United States with his crossover hit "Gasolina" (2005). By contrast, reggae en español is a less commercialized musical genre whose artists are primarily Black singers. The two genres remain linked because the origins of reggaetón commence with the Panamanian isthmus. For many, reggaetón commenced in Panama, was developed in Puerto Rico, and was commercialized in the United States, while others insist that the genre has its roots in 1990s' Puerto Rican underground music.[49] Puerto Rican *reggaeseros* DJ Nelson and DJ Goldy hold that reggaetón came "straight outta Puerto Rico."[50] Proprietorship of reggaetón's origins has as much to do with bragging rights as to subtle stylistic differences between the two genres. While reggae en español is characterized by dancehall and Jamaican reggae, reggaetón is infused with hip-hop, rap, and above all, the renowned *dembow riddim* or percussion/drum pattern. For some, the distinctions are clear, yet for others the differentiations remain murky precisely because the two are interconnected, intertwined, and in some instances interchangeable. In a 2015 interview, Renato noted that the differences between the two are unfounded and that basically "it's the same thing" by noting that reggaetón derived from reggae en español.[51] However, in an interview five years earlier, Renato attempted to tease out the differences by noting that reggae en español is more romantic and less gangsta than reggaetón.[52]

Nevertheless, reggaetón's trajectory is linked to Panama and follows a lineage initiated by the pioneers of reggae en español. For example, *reggaesera* Ivy Queen and rapper Vico C, both from Puerto Rico, frequently visited Panama during the 1990s, the height of Panamanian reggae, and brought those very same rhythms and beats back to the island.[53] Without a doubt, the line between reggaetón and reggae en español has always been fluid, blurring distinctions between the two genres. As various artists from the 2004 documentary *Chosen Few: El Documental* noted, "Reggaetón . . . es el nombre internacional de reggae en español" (Reggaetón . . . is the international name of reggae in Spanish) or, more simply put, "Reggaetón es reggae en español" (Reggaetón is reggae in Spanish). By contrast, most Panamanian artists view reggae en español as a distinct genre that gave rise to the international phenomenon of reggaetón. For them, reggae en español and reggaetón's genesis is linked to the West Indian communities of the Canal Zone, Colón, Panama City, and the United States. Although it is beyond the focus of this study to discuss reggaetón, like reggae en español, it has also been influenced by the processes of transculturation and cultural hybridization. The Panamanian reggae artists I explore below capture these processes by fusing multiple genres, cultures, and transnational communities.

Panamanian reggae artists Chicho Man and Pepito Casanova bring together the United States, the Caribbean, and Panama in "Muévela" ("Move it," 1989).[54] "Muévela" evokes a geographic and cultural multiplicity and points to the impact of transculturation and transnationalism.

> Oh Lord have Mercy Mercy Mercy
> Chicho Man está en el baile baile baile
> Oh Lord have Mercy Mercy Mercy
> Casanova está en el baile baile baile
> Chicho Man y Casanova llegaron a Nueva York
> Toman un nuevo ritmo somos la sensación
> Chicho Man y Casanova llegaron a Nueva York
> Toman un nuevo ritmo somos la sensación
> Un nuevo ritmo traemos ya desde América a Nueva York
> Un nuevo ritmo traemos ya para que lo gocen en Panamá
> Un nuevo ritmo traemos ya desde mi Panamá a Nueva York
>
> Oh Lord have Mercy Mercy Mercy
> Chicho Man is dancing, dancing, dancing
> Oh Lord have Mercy Mercy Mercy
> Casanova is dancing, dancing, dancing
> Chicho Man and Casanova arrived in New York

They play a new rhythm we are a sensation
Chicho Man and Casanova arrived in New York
They play a new rhythm we are a sensation
A new rhythm we already brought from America to New York
A new rhythm we already brought for you to enjoy in Panama
A new rhythm we already brought from my Panama to New York

The artists invite the listener to evoke this new rhythm brought from Latin America and from Panama to New York. The verses, "Un nuevo ritmo traemos ya desde América a Nueva York/Un nuevo ritmo traemos ya para que lo gocen en Panamá/Un nuevo ritmo traemos ya desde mi Panamá a Nueva York" point to the constant movement of knowledge, language, and culture between Latin/Central America, New York, and Panama. The first verse of the song is in English, "Oh Lord have Mercy Mercy Mercy" and evokes the religious phrase, "Oh Lord have mercy on me." However, the artists reconfigure the verse in a nonreligious setting to encourage mercy on the dance floor and perhaps when viewing a woman's gyrating hips. The lyrics are a fun-loving dance song meant to inspire female gyrating hips that "llevan [the artists] al tambor de la alegría" (take the artists to the pinnacle of happiness). In addition, the refrain "tambor de la alegría" originates from the Panamanian national folklore song and dance, "El tambor de la alegría" that commences, "Panameño, panameño/panameño vida mía. . . . Yo quiero que tú me lleves/al tambor de la alegría (Panamanian, Panamanian/Panamanian my love. . . . I want you to take me to the pinnacle of happiness.").[55] Thus, Chicho Man and Pepito Casanova insert reggae en español into a Panamanian national music tradition vis-à-vis the *tamborito*, a popular musical genre that dates to the colonial period and reflects the fusion of African, Hispanic, and indigenous culture in Panama. "Muévela" reflects a hybridized culture symbolized by geographic, linguistic, and cultural differences that the artists bring together through reggae en español.

Songs by Leonardo "Renato" Aulder also possess local color and represent a creolized version of reggae en español, by incorporating *panameñismos* as well as Jamaican riddims. Like El General, Renato is one of the pioneers of the movement and is known for his romantic verses that express love, desire, and sexuality. Renato's personal story as a young Jamaican and Barbadian descendant growing up in the Canal Zone as "American" contrasts with his shocking discovery that he was indeed Panamanian after his family relocated to Río Abajo in 1978. His cultural and ideological transformation from North American to Panamanian reflects the transatlantic and trans-Caribbean experience that complicates yet enriches Panamanian identity. Renato's comfortable "American" childhood growing up in the Canal Zone watching US football and Major League Baseball contrasted with his experiences as a teenager in Río Abajo. In Río Abajo, his family relocated to 13th Street, a neighborhood Renato describes as a "ghetto."[56] These differences would plague his consciousness as both a teenager and future reggaesero. Ironically, he had to teach himself Spanish in order to sing reggae en español after he formed Renato y las 4 Estrellas.

Renato's music as well as his personal style reflect cultural and racial hybridity and is influenced by both the United States and Panama. For example, he purchases all of his clothes in the United States and has appropriated the style and dress of hip-hop artists there. In a June 2015 interview with Renato, I noted the influence of US hip-hop culture. He wore a yellow New York Yankee baseball cap, gold chain, gold watch, and gold-rimmed sunglasses. On the one hand, style and dress are important to all artists and musicians. However, Renato's choice to emulate the style of US hip-hop artists points to the obvious effect of US culture and Renato's own upbringing in the US Canal Zone where he felt more American than Panamanian and spoke English before he learned Spanish as a teenager. This hybridity is reflected in his music where he frequently incorporates English verses into his Spanish songs. It is also reflected in his personal style and attitude. He claims in several of his songs, "Por Abajo" and "Respeta otra vez," that he is the "King of reggae" in Panama. For example, "Respeta otra vez" ("Respect again" 1993) reminds other artists to respect the origins and the pioneers of Panamanian reggae. Renato commands, "Les voy a educar/El rey del regué mami esté en Panamá" (I'm going to educate you/The King of reggae mami is in Panama). Much like US hip-hop artists who demand respect from newer generations of artists who follow, Renato demands the same from other artists who followed his artistic path.

Songs in Renato's repertoire reflect a hybridized United States/Caribbean/Panamanian culture. Songs such as "La chica de los ojos café" (The Brown-eyed Girl), "El huracán" (Hurricane), "Isla del amor" (Island of Love), "Devórame" (Devour me), "Magnate" (Magnet), "El animal" (The Animal), "Acid," "El más sensual" (The Most Sensual), "Cinturita" (Little Belt), "Por abajo" (Down Below), and "Baby," to name a few, all evoke sex and sexuality and the romantic themes that catapulted Renato to fame. For example, Renato's most popular hit, "El más sensual" commences:

Ay ya ya
Soy tu papi el más sensual
Ay el más sensual
Y cuando estoy contigo me siento original
Y dice
Dámelo mami, Dámelo mami, Dame, Dame, Dame 2X

¿Y si te beso en el cuello?
¿What?
¿Y si te beso en la boca?
¿What?
¿Y si te beso en la espalda?
¿What?
¿Y si te beso de nuevo?
¿What?
Badam Badam
Dáme tu corazón
No sé que está pasando
Los hombres te ven se están desmayando
Eres mi esperanza y mi felicidad
Al final encontré un amor de verdad
Dámelo mami, Dámelo mami, Dáme, Dáme, Dáme 2X

Ay ya ya
I am your most sensual papi
Ay the most sensual
And when I am with you I feel original
And say
Give it to me mami, Give it to me mami, Give me, Give me, and Give me 2 X

¿And if I kiss you on your neck?
¿What?
¿And if I kiss your mouth?
¿What?
¿And if I kiss you on your back?
¿What?
¿And if I kiss you again?
¿What?
Badam Badam
Give me your heart
I don't know what is happening
The men that see you faint
You are my hope and my happiness
In the end I found my true love
Give it to me mami, Give it to me mami, Give me, Give me, and Give me 2 X

"El más sensual" resembles many of Renato's bilingual songs. It is worth noting the call and response that is a "widespread feature of African music."[57] Call and response has a long history in African American speech acts and is often employed by orators, African American preachers, and the like.[58] This technique is most evident in the following verses: "Y si te beso en el cuello? /What? /Y si te beso en la boca? /What?". Although it is a rhetorical question and thus does not require a response, the repetition of the sign "what?" after the interrogatives commands the participation and engagement of the listener. It also makes light of kissing a girl on her neck, mouth, and back without permission. By making use of call and response, Renato's song in Spanish transcends geographic, national, and cultural boundaries and speaks beyond (Afro) Latin American and African American communities.

Renato's bilingual song "América" (1987) reinterprets the United States's narrow vision of the Americas and is a prime example of transnationalism.[59] Sung utilizing the same beat and rhythm of the popular US patriotic song, "America, the Beautiful," Renato inserts Central and South America into the geopolitical concept of America.

> America is number one
> América es número uno
> Oh-Oh America, America
> Say God shed His grace on thee
> And crown thy good with brotherhood from sea to shining sea
> Oye señores, esto es para ti[60] . . .
> Yo soy centroamericano, oye mi amigo,
> El saludo para todos los latinos
> Los suramericanos no se quedan atrás
> Y hasta Chile yo voy a viajar . . .
> Sisters and brothers let's get together
> Love and peace we want it forever
> New York City, California, Washington D.C.
> This is Renato y esto es para ti

Renato's inclusion of Spanish-speaking countries reinforces America's geographic, cultural, and linguistic plurality. He rewrites "American" history by including all of the Americas. "América" is both transnational and transcultural, encompassing various geographic areas and a manifold of cultures that transcend the Isthmus of Panamanian. Renato reinterprets the Anglo-Saxon vision of America and illustrates Panamanian, Central American, and South American unity. The music video, for example, showcases Latin American adults and youth of various racial and ethnic hues and provides a visual image to the cultural hybridity that the song foregrounds.[61] Renato also "speaks" to his Black brethren in the United States by utilizing the Black vernacular "Sisters and brothers let's get together." Renato's pioneering reggae en español lyrics catapulted him to fame in the mid-1980s. The song pulls from various genres and discourses across the border, signaling that reggae en español is a transnational discourse rooted in hybridity, diversity, and difference.

TRANSNATIONAL NETWORKS OF CULTURAL EXCHANGE

Reggae en español is a product of transmigratory patterns of circuitous exchange between Jamaica, Panama, and the United States. Panamanian reggae artists utilize reggae en español to create transnational networks of cultural exchange. The genre inserts the Black Panamanian experience into a broader dialogue of race and migration. The genre illustrates that culture, language, and race transcend national boundaries, borders, and barriers. The interplay of the United States, the Caribbean, and Panama in the genesis and fruition of reggae en español alters the nation's cultural, national, and racial foundation and necessitates the incorporation of the African diaspora into its identity formation. Cultural hybridization, transculturation, and transnationalism explicate the phenomenon of Panamanian reggae en español, a genre that pulls from various geographic, linguistic, and racial discourses to fashion a unique type of music inherent in Panamanian culture. The identity of the nation transcends national, racial, cultural, and linguistic boundaries that permit a new transcultural identity impacted by "contact zones."[62] These zones of contact color Panamanian history and are essential to the interplay of race, culture, language, and geography in Panamanian reggae en español.

CHAPTER TEN

THE TORTUOUS ROAD TOWARD THE BUILDING OF A MOSQUE IN BUENOS AIRES

OVERCOMING RACIAL STEREOTYPES UNDER POPULIST GOVERNMENTS

Raanan Rein

The wish of Argentine president Carlos Saúl Menem did not materialize. The son of Syrian immigrants, he hoped to inaugurate the largest mosque in Latin America before his presidency ended. In December 1995, following a state visit to Saudi Arabia and in a move that provoked heated debate, Menem's government donated a large tract of municipal land in the upscale Buenos Aires neighborhood of Palermo to the embassy of Saudi Arabia, so it could build a mosque and Islamic center there.[1] The mosque, named after King Fahd, was indeed built but was inaugurated only in September 2000. By then, Menem was no longer president and served only as the unofficial host of the ceremony.

This is not to say that Argentine Muslims were invisible before the inauguration of the grand mosque or not considered an integral part of the nation. In fact, the establishment of this temple was the culmination of a long process that started with a wave of immigration of Middle Easterners in the late nineteenth century. This process was accompanied by the efforts of the immigrants and their descendants to overcome negative stereotypes and whiten themselves so that they could fit the idealized concept of a white, European-oriented society. A milestone in this process of social integration was marked during the Peronist decade of 1946 to 1955.

There was a great difference between the statist policies of Populist president Juan Domingo Perón in the 1940s and 1950s, and the neoliberal policies of neo-Populist president Carlos Menem in the 1990s.[2] However, the two leaders did have several traits in common, including, among others, their efforts to better integrate various ethnic communities, especially

Jews and Arabs, into Argentine society. This chapter traces the attempts to establish a mosque in the Argentine capital from the mid-1940s, during Juan Perón's first presidency, and up to the revival and grandiose materialization of the project during the so-called *Menemato* (1989–1999). Over this half century, the image of Arab Argentines changed dramatically, from unwelcome immigrants, stereotyped as *mercachifles* (ambulatory peddlers) or as mendicants, but later seen as successful businessmen who were well integrated into Argentine society. Over the course of the twentieth century, doubts about their whiteness largely disappeared.[3] More importantly, Perón's use of Spain's Muslim past to justify the presence of this ethnic group in Argentina contributed to their claims of belonging to the Argentine people.

By focusing on a group that is not of African descent, indigenous, or mestizo, this chapter complicates discussions about race in Argentina. The binary categories of Blackness and whiteness seem somewhat blurred when used in discussing the experiences of Arab, Jewish, or Asian Argentines, which some might consider, at least for the first generation of immigrants, as in-between groups. The mosque is a case study that points to a group whose members had felt targeted by racialized stereotypes but managed to have their concerns heard and addressed.

AN INCLUSIVE POPULIST MOVEMENT

Following the election of Donald Trump as president of the United States and the rise of extreme right-wing movements in Europe, much has been published on Populism in both the media and scholarly works, claiming that Populism is a global and transnational phenomenon and its discussion should not be reduced to a particular country or region. Statements such as "Populism is as American as it is Argentine" tend, however, to blur several important differences among distinct Populist movements and leaderships.[4] Thus, while most Western European Populist movements in the early twenty-first century and Donald Trump in the United States have been distinguished by xenophobia and anti-immigrant rhetoric, Latin American Populism has been characterized by an inclusive approach. At the same time, whereas post–World War II Western European Populism has frequently been backward looking and reactionary, Latin American Populism has often looked forward, with more Progressive traits. The prime example of this trait of Latin American Populism is the Peronist movement.[5]

Space does not allow us to discuss in detail the main characteristics of Latin American Populism or the nature of Peronism. It is worth emphasizing, however, that solving the "social problem" by politically and socially integrating the masses lay at the core of Perón's *Justicialista* movement (from the Spanish word for justice). Peronism offered nonviolent solutions to some of the main problems of contemporary Argentine society. It rejected the oligarchy, on the one hand, and the socialist revolution, on the other, proposing a reformist middle way that stressed statist values, namely, the control of social and economic affairs in order to avoid distortions and ensure progress, yet without challenging the principle of capitalist private property.

At the same time, Peronism promised social solidarity in order to counter the alienation engendered by workers under modern industrial capitalism and by rural people as the result of traditional exploitation of landowners. Peronist leaders praised work and workers, recognized labor trade unions and encouraged their expansion. No less important, they strove to rehabilitate various aspects of popular culture and folklore that had previously been viewed with contempt by European-oriented elites. Thus, a new symbolic hierarchy of society was established. After all, the figurative expressions of social integration and political incorporation were no less important than their concrete expressions.[6]

Although it certainly had several authoritarian characteristics, Populism also advanced democratization in a situation of social and economic inequality. The efforts to include previously excluded groups went beyond the working class and also targeted women, children, indigenous peoples, and immigrant groups. Most studies have focused on the principal beneficiaries newly integrated into the national polity, that is the working class. My own research highlights that immigrant groups, including Jews, Arabs, and Japanese, also made important gains.

The Peronist decade was a time of shifting meanings and frontiers of citizenship in Argentina.[7] The country went through profound changes, and government actions contributed to a debate on the understanding and conceptualization of citizenship. Argentina in those years experienced transformations in political representation, and simultaneously moved toward a model of participatory democracy and what would today be considered a multicultural society. Ethnic identities became less of a threat to the concept of *argentinidad*. Instead of the traditional melting pot, Perón's government supported hyphenated identities and emphasized the wide variety of cultural sources on which Argentine society was based. Authorities offered unprecedented recognition of cultural and ethnic difference. President Menem would take this process to a certain peak, which was very symbolic, by authorizing the building of a major mosque in the Argentine capital.

Perón clearly manifested an older vision of Argentina as an essentially Catholic country while he was a key figure in the military dictatorship of 1943–1945, during his presidential campaign of late 1945 and early 1946, as well as in the initial stages of his presidency. When they first came to power, Peronists considered non-Catholics as not "good Argentines." The government transformed into law the December 1943 military decree instituting compulsory Catholic education in all state schools.[8] On one occasion Perón declared: "I think that in our country it is impossible to speak of an Argentine home that is not a Christian home. Under the cross we formed our ideas. Under the cross we recited our ABCs. . . . Everything distinctive in our habits is Christian and Catholic."[9] According to Perón in the early 1940s, national belonging excluded non-Catholics. Early Peronist immigration policies also reflected "an ethnic concern" and an endeavor to assure as much as possible ethnic and cultural homogeneity in the country's population.[10]

And indeed, in the early years of Peronism, both Jews and Arabs had to confront various obstacles on their immigration to Argentina. Curiously enough, the anti-Semitic Santiago M. Peralta, director of the Oficina de Etnografía (Ethnography Office) during the years 1943–1945 and Director General of Immigration between November 1945 and July 1947, had a positive view of Arab immigrants and their contribution to Argentina's development. Peralta adopted very strict immigration criteria, and Jews, unlike Syrian-Lebanese immigrants, were among the main victims of this policy.[11] In his 1946 book *Influencia del pueblo árabe en la Argentina*, Peralta praised the capacity of Middle Eastern immigrants to integrate themselves into Argentine society.[12]

In 1947, however, Peralta had to leave his position due to accusations in Argentina and abroad about arbitrary and discriminatory policies, specifically about his radical anti-Semitism. His successor was Pablo Diana, but he did not last more than a year. Diana was accused by the Peronist senator Alejando M. Hoyos of discriminating against the Arab community. In his travel to Europe, Hoyos heard complaints from various Argentine consuls about the country's migration policies. At the end of the same year, Carlos Brunel, of the Argentine consulate in Istanbul, also had to resign his position following accusations in Lebanon about his attitude toward Lebanese immigrants.[13]

Many scholars have studied the Peronist regime as static, paying little attention to dynamics and changes occurring during these years. Historian Eduardo Elena claims that "the regime's ideologues highlighted the nation's white, Catholic, and Hispanic character in the design of propaganda, tourism material, and school texts."[14] This was true for the initial phase as we have seen. By the early 1950s, however, the Argentine Populist movement had adopted a more inclusive approach where respect for all religions became a crucial feature of Peronism. The Peronist ambition of protecting the rights of minorities and weak, marginal groups from the encroachments of the privileged now extended to the ethnic and religious spheres. Peronism was presented as a conglomerate with a room for every Argentine who supported the *Justicialista* project.

Perón incorporated anti-discriminatory language into the national constitution. A Peronist-dominated constitutional convention in 1949 approved the inclusion of a clause that forbade discrimination on the basis of racial or religious differences. In 1994, another constitutional convention would approve several amendments, promoted by Carlos Menem, which included removing the requirement that the president be a Roman Catholic.[15] Certainly, both the working class and Arab Argentines have generally showed a great deal of enduring loyalty to Peronism, attributed to the combination of both material improvements in their lives as well as the fostering of a strong sense of symbolic dignity and belonging, of being an important and inseparable part of the Argentine nation, without denying their transnational ties.[16]

GAINING "ASSIMILATIVE POWER"

The number of Arab immigrants and their descendants in twentieth century Argentina is a matter of an ongoing debate. Lack of precise information resulted as many left their homeland illegally during the late Ottoman Empire, and their origins were recorded unsystematically in Argentina (sometimes they were registered as Turks, Ottomans, Syrians, Syrian-Lebanese, etc.). Immigrants who entered Argentina by land from neighboring countries often did not appear in any statistic. Common estimates oscillate between one hundred and one hundred fifty thousand migrants from the Middle East by the end of World War I. During the first quarter of the twentieth century, Arabs represented the fourth largest group of immigrants to Argentina. These migrants were a heterogeneous group, fragmented by origins, social class, and religious affiliation. The first wave of Arab migrants, until 1910, had a Maronite Catholic majority, with a smaller number of Muslims and Jews. The Muslims were divided between Sunni, Shiite, Alawite, Druze, and Ismaelite immigrants.

A common perception in pre-Peronist Argentina was the identification of Arabic-speaking immigrants as peddlers who contributed little to Argentine economy and only competed unfairly with local business owners.[17] For the "Semitic race," according to the intellectual and statesman Domingo Faustino Sarmiento (a former president of Argentina, 1868–1874), Argentina was "an article of negotiable old clothing and material for industry."[18] They were often viewed in racial terms, just as Jewish immigrants, and described as people unable to adapt and fully integrate into the host society. In the same vein, as shown by Benjamin Bryce, the contemporary Argentine press warned against a possible stream of Japanese immigration.[19] Thus, the prestigious daily *La Prensa* asserted that Europeanization was the "supreme ideal of the Latin American world. . . . We are not the enemies of the yellow race, whose abilities the prosperous and strong Japan has plainly shown:

we only want to note that because of the form of its civilization, it is not suitable to meld with the nationalities of the Americas."[20]

In this framework of racial hierarchies, it is no wonder that in 1902 the Buenos Aires weekly *Caras y Carretas* lashed out against these "irritant" immigrants who offered a bad example to Argentine workers: "'A plague' of Turkish peddlers has appeared, worse than if they were locusts. The police must prevent them from continuing to commit such abuse."[21] In his recent study, Steven Hyland Jr. points to the fact that in the post–World War I period the criminal arrest rates of Syrian immigrants in the province of Tucumán were significantly higher than the provincial average, reflecting in part the labeling of this group as a source of aberrant behavior and essentializing their characteristics.[22] These Semitic immigrants had to confront changing degrees of discrimination, exclusion, and violence in the early twentieth century.

The large number of Arabic speakers incarcerated in Tucumán during the 1910s and 1920s was to some extent a result of the many intersections between race, familism, ethnicity, and culture, as well as the delicate balance between empirical facts, cultural imagination, and competing visions of the social order. This attitude should be understood in the context of a kind of binary scheme imposed on many discussions about race and color in Argentina since the mid-nineteenth century. *Facundo or Civilization and Barbarism*, a book published by Sarmiento in 1845, had a major impact on how Argentines have viewed themselves.[23] In this seminal book, Sarmiento distinguished between the "barbaric" gauchos of the provinces, who usually were people of color, and the "civilized" inhabitants of European descent in the major urban centers.

Similar to Sandra McGee Deutsch's study of the ambiguous racial status of Jews in Argentina, many descriptions of Arabs by Argentine public figures and media in the late nineteenth century and first half of the twentieth century pointed to the unruly nature of Arab immigrants, their animal-like behavior, and their supposed inability to assimilate and be absorbed by Argentine society.[24] Thus, Arab Argentines were at times put in the barbaric, that is, nonwhite, category.

As they achieved wealth and upward mobility, however, the racial stereotypes about Arabs—which generally focused on cultural rather than biological markers—partially disappeared. These stereotypes were largely not essentialist in nature but were more based on social class. Once middle-class Arab Argentines replaced the poor Arab immigrants, the language of race changed and became less overt. Unlike Jewish Argentines, a large number of Arab Argentines lived in the provinces, alongside populations of mixed indigenous descent, and in these circumstances, it made it somewhat easier for them to be considered as "white," thus highlighting the fluidity and inconsistency of racial categories in Argentina. Furthermore, at certain points of time, when "threatened" by "more exotic" immigrants from Asia, the Europeanness of people from the Ottoman empire was less questioned by Argentine elites. As Benjamin Bryce writes, "In response to new South Asian immigration, officials at the General Directorate of Immigration bent over backward to assert that Ottoman subjects were European. In its 1912 annual report, for example, the General Directorate included all Ottomans who arrived that year in the category of 'Europeans' but the Persian, Indian, Chinese, and Japanese arrivals in the category of 'Asians.'"[25]

Arab Argentines had engaged with the national authorities since the 1910s, following the election of Hipólito Yrigoyen to the presidency. However, in most cases this was limited to expressing support for the contemporary administration. Juan Perón, on the other hand, was the first president to publicly show, time and again, his support for the Arab community as an integral part of Argentine society. The president emphasized how well Arabic-speaking immigrants had integrated into the host society and how loyal they had been to Argentina.

Perón valued the integrative power of the Arabs, without denying their ethnic identity: "Here in our land, the assimilative power of the Arabs is widely known. Assimilative power is perhaps the most extraordinary feature of men of action. In general, it is that unquenchable action of the effort that assimilates and attaches to the land. Arabs in our homeland have set an example by being, perhaps, those who most rapidly assimilated into our land and to our customs, our glories, and our traditions."[26] In fact, when Perón highlighted "assimilative power," he was referring to the ability to adopt Argentine customs and culture without denying their compatibility with those brought over from their countries of origin. Eva Perón supported her husband's opinion, stressing, too, Arabs' integrative capacity: "These Arab people, who have proven to be honest and hard-working men, who have assimilated in our homeland and who have felt proud to live under the blue and white flag."[27] Generally speaking, both Juan and Eva Perón rejected the alienation of Arab Argentines and emphasized their loyalty to Argentina, while trying to incorporate them as an integral part of the Argentine people. This is reflected in the speech given by Perón to Argentine parliamentarians with Lebanese roots, in which he said: "Now that you have reached this [presidential] House, I do not consider only that the Lebanese community has arrived [here]; I believe a sector of my countrymen has arrived."[28]

This discourse was directed not only toward Arab Argentines but toward other ethnic groups as well, such as the Jews or the much smaller Japanese community.[29] Regarding the first, at the dedication of the building of the Organización Israelita Argentina (the Jewish section of the Peronist party) in 1948, the president underscored his joy in taking part in the event and in expressing the "infinite honor of being the President of all Argentines."[30] As in the speech addressing Arab Argentines, by including this ethnic group in Argentine citizenry, Perón made it clear that Jews were an integral part of the Argentine people. In the case of the Japanese, the Populist president also considered it necessary to clarify that they were part of the totality of Argentine society, emphasizing, "when we say 'for all the Argentine people,' we have the immense satisfaction of including all the Japanese who live with us as full constituents of the Argentine people for whom we strive and work."[31]

During the second half of the twentieth century, the role of Arab Argentines in politics became significant at the municipal and provincial level, as well as the national level. Perón's presidency represented, however, a milestone. One of the Arab Argentine periodicals, *Azzam: La Época. Órgano Libanés*, proudly announced a new era in the political involvement of this ethnic group. The newspaper informed its readers on the front page that the February 1946 elections resulted in one vice governor of Arab origins (in the province of Córdoba), one national senator (representing the province of Catamarca) and five national congressmen. Two years later, following the 1948 midterm elections, out of two hundred Peronist congressmen, twenty-five were descendants of Arab immigrants.[32]

When Carlos Menem was elected president in 1989, Arab Argentines reached the high point of political inclusion. During the ten years of Menem's administration, Arab Argentines exerted remarkable influence on the Argentine political system. Like Menem himself, who started and ended his political career in the province of La Rioja, many of them initiated their participation in politics in the provinces of the interior and through the Peronist or neo-Peronist movements. This was the case of Vicente Leónidas Saadi, the son of Lebanese immigrants who arrived in the province of Catamarca in the early twentieth century. As members of the Peronist movement, the Saadi family controlled local politics for nearly fifty years. A similar case is that of Felipe Sapag, from the province of Neuquén. His family ruled there for decades, from the time it was upgraded from the status of National Territory to a Province in 1955, well into the twenty-first century via the neo-Peronist political party they founded, the Movimiento Popular Neuquino. A third emblematic case of a provincial chieftain of Arab heritage is that of the governor of the province of Corrientes, Julio Romero, whose family came from the Lebanese town of Baalbek. Romero was considered one of Perón's right-hand men. And his family carried on his legacy in the province and supported Menem's administration.[33]

COMMUNITY INITIATIVES, TRANSNATIONAL SUPPORT, AND STATE SPONSORSHIP

Carlos Menem personally pushed for giving away a plot of land in the city of Buenos Aires, valued at $20 million, on which to build the largest mosque in the world outside an Arab country.[34] This decision was motivated by the "historical debt" owed by Peronism to Muslims, by Menem's desire to improve his ambiguous image in the Muslim world, as well as a Populist reflex, which sought to provide a space for the various communities that inhabited Argentina. Strictly speaking, this was not the only space given away to the Arab world. Menem also assigned a building for the headquarters of the Federación de Entidades Árabes Argentinas, as well as one for the diplomatic mission of the Palestinian National Authority. But given its size, value, and public repercussion, this plot—33,726 square meters (363,023 square feet) between Libertador and Bullrich Avenues—on which the Centro Cultural Islámico Custodio de las Dos Sagradas Mezquitas Rey Fahd is located, was without a doubt the largest donation.[35]

The Centro Islámico de Buenos Aires houses a mosque in which twelve hundred men and four hundred women can pray toward Mecca, separately. It also includes a cultural center, art galleries, a library for ten thousand books, and a coffee shop open to the general public. On the premises there is also a kindergarten, two school buildings for boys and two for girls, dorms for 120 students from the rest of the country, underground parking, and two minarets that are forty-eight meters (about 157 feet) tall.[36]

Community lore tells of the hardship faced by Sunni Muslims in the early twentieth century who lived in the tenement house at Charcas 400 (bordering on the Turkish Quarter), while looking for a place in which to pray. They had to walk with their carpets to Plaza San Martin, which became "the great open-air mosque" so as not to disturb their neighbors in the tenement house. The praying Muslims were nicknamed "sun worshippers."[37]

The history of the current Islamic Center starts in the late 1940s. At the time, Argentine Muslims were making their first attempts to take advantage of the new political climate in order to build a mosque and a cultural center, and thus underscore their presence in Buenos Aires.[38] This was at a time when Maronite Catholics, Greek Orthodox Christians, and Sephardic Jews, all with roots in the Middle East, already had religious temples and cultural centers of their own.

In early 1950, the Egyptian Minister Plenipotentiary in Buenos Aires, Muhammad al-Said, managed to unify an important Muslim sector in the capital city and promised to use his contacts with Perón and financial support by King Farouk to build a mosque. Arriving in Buenos Aires in 1947, al-Said was an experienced diplomat, stationed previously in a large number of cities, including New York, Jerusalem, Athens, Istanbul, Bagdad, and Teheran. He also managed to obtain funds from al-Azhar University, Egypt's Ministry of Religious Affairs, and the Syrian Lebanese Bank in Cairo. In addition, Prince Muhammad Ali—Farouk's uncle—also contributed.

Although the majority of Arab Argentines were of Lebanese or Syrian extraction, with a small number of Palestinian, Egyptian, or Moroccan background, Egypt's prominent position in the Muslim world at the time was hardly disputed. More or less at the same time, the Egyptian ambassador to Washington, DC, Kamil Abdul Rahim, led the efforts to build a mosque in the American capital. The mosque was completed in 1954 and dedicated by President Dwight Eisenhower in June 1957. This initiative by al-Said thus highlighted the importance of the diasporic ties between Argentines with Arab roots and the region—broadly defined—from which they came.

The promoters of this initiative harbored hopes that the new mosque might help unite Middle Eastern immigrants of all denominations and ensure that both the Argentine State and society acknowledged the contribution of these immigrants to Argentina and their belonging in that society.[39] The cornerstone-laying ceremony took place in May 1950 in the Caballito neighborhood, at the corner of Avenida Rivadavia and Cucha Cucha (now Félix Lora). At the ceremony the Argentine national anthem was sung and a chapter of the Qur'an read. Several speakers followed—Arab diplomats, national and municipal authorities, as well as Arab Argentine leaders.

The year 1950, which marked one hundred years since the death of General José de San Martín, was declared the Año del Libertador (year of the liberator) in Argentina, and the government did its best to surround the events glorifying the national hero with as much fanfare as possible. In this context, Ibrahim Hallar, secretary of the mosque committee, compared General San Martín in his struggle for liberation to Faisal I bin Hussein bin Ali al-Hashemi, King of the Arab Kingdom of Syria in 1920 and then King of Iraq (1921–1933), who promoted Pan-Arab nationalism. He stated, "Liberty is not conquered, said the American Liberator. The same sentence was pronounced by his namesake, the Arab Faisal. Both fought with the unbreakable faith of their peoples, convinced that they fought for a just and sovereign cause." Hallar ended his intervention, explaining that the Muslims "offer to this Republic, to this just and sovereign New Argentina, the sentiment of gratitude that all Arabs and their descendants have for it."[40]

Of Muslim Lebanese descent, Hallar (1915–1973) devoted his life to highlight the deep roots of Arabs in Argentina, and published books, such as *Descubrimiento de América por los árabes* (1959) and *El gaucho. Su originalidad arábiga* (1962).[41] These books bring us back to the issue of foundational claims and the myth of origins of Arab/Jewish/Japanese presence in Argentina or Brazil before the arrival of mass migration in the late nineteenth century and the discourse that ethnic groups have elaborated in order to establish their place among other ethnic groups in the highest possible positions.[42] Jewish Argentines had their Jewish gaucho myth, immortalized by Alberto Gerchunoff in 1910. Arab Argentines needed to have theirs as well. Facing doubts as to their whiteness, this was part of their struggle for belonging and acceptance in the Argentine nation.

Arab Argentine intellectuals like Ibrahim Hallar and Juan Yasser offered a narrative that highlighted the relationship between the Hispanic and the Arab Worlds in Al-Andalus, thus creating the Spanish-Arab connection in Argentina. They portrayed the gaucho's codes of conduct as influenced by Spain's Muslim past, emphasizing in this way that the ties between Arabs and Argentina preceded the immigration waves from Europe of the late nineteenth and early twentieth centuries.[43] Juan Perón adopted this narrative, using Spain's Muslim past to justify the presence of this ethnic group in Argentina and their belonging in Argentine society.

When he was presented the Order of Umayaad by the Syrian government in September 1950 the Argentine leader stated, "I am thankful and deeply moved by this high honor bestowed by His Excellency the President of Syria, from the old dynasty that this medal represents, abiding by the mandate of the civilization and culture of Muhammad, linked with our own blood in Muslim Spain and confirmed, with no exception, by the noble Syrians who have come to our land to bring about, together with us, the greatness of this new homeland."[44]

At the 1950 event, Hallar emphasized the support of Argentina's Muslims for the Peronist project. The ceremony was reported in all mass media, not just those of the Arab community.[45] The initiative was unanimously commended by them and, in some cases, Buenos Aires was compared with London and Paris, where supposedly all monotheistic communities coexisted in a brotherly manner. The integrative nature of Peronist Populism was clearly evident.

However, the Caballito mosque, which was supposed to be a site of interfaith dialogue and larger than the contemporary mosques of London or Paris, was never built. The leaders backing the initiative lost interest or were involved in various scandals; the Muslim community was fragmented, and many within it were rather indifferent to the project, in part due to the waning involvement of many in an ethno-religious community. In addition, the Egyptian diplomat who sponsored the initiative, Muhammad al-Said, returned to Cairo. In a way, the deposing of King Farouk—not an Argentine event—also marked the end of this initiative. Another property was acquired in 1957, a more modest one on Avenida Rivadavia, with space for prayers and teaching Arabic as well as the tenets of the Muslim faith.[46]

CARLOS MENEM STANDS BY JUAN PERÓN'S PROMISE TO MUSLIM ARGENTINES

A son of immigrants hailing from Yabrud, a town near Damascus, Carlos Menem was born into the Muslim faith. According to his ex-wife, Zulema

Fatimah Yoma, Menem converted to Roman Catholicism, the official religion of Argentina, in 1966, the year the couple got married in a Muslim religious ceremony. According to Yoma, Menem was motivated by his political ambitions to become a presidential candidate, at a time when the constitution still prevented non-Catholics from holding such a position.[47]

Menem's government included more officials of Arab descent than any previous administration in Argentina. Menem was, in some regards, a faithful follower of Perón. This was certainly true where it concerned the social integration of the descendants of Semitic immigrants. In May 1992, when Menem visited the Kingdom of Saudi Arabia, he personally promised King Fahd a site in Argentina on which to build a mosque for all the Muslims living in Argentina—the third largest such community in the Americas, after the United States and Brazil.[48] Only three months later, Buenos Aires mayor Carlos Grosso—a Menem appointee—declared a lot belonging to the railway company and located in Palermo, one of the most expensive neighborhoods in Argentina, as "not needed for government action." This was required for Congress to authorize, in December 1995, its handing over to the Saudi embassy. Interestingly enough, this is precisely the neighborhood in which the former consul general of the Ottoman Empire, Emir Emin Arslan (who had arrived in Buenos Aires in 1910) envisioned creating an Islamic cultural center.[49]

Paradoxically, the only senator who voted against the initiative was Fernando de la Rúa.[50] In the end, he would be among those who laid the cornerstone and was in charge of implementing the donation. For this he received a gift from King Fahd, the "Abdul Aziz" necklace, made of gold and sapphires and valued at $700,000.[51] Despite opposition by both the Radicals and the Frepaso—the other major political party during the mid-1990s—the Peronist majority in Parliament passed Law 24,619 on December 20, 1995. Six days later, Menem enacted Decrees 1004/95 and later 840/96, enabling the assigning of the land to the embassy of Saudi Arabia.[52] In the ensuing controversy provoked by the decision to build a mosque, one argument raised included the lack of freedom of worship in Saudi Arabia, and that as the Arab country with the highest income, it could certainly manage without such generous gifts.[53]

Crown Prince Abdullah bin Abdul Aziz Al Saud, half-brother of King Fahd, traveled to Argentina in August 1996 to lay, together with Menem himself and with Fernando de la Rúa (then mayor of Buenos Aires), the cornerstone of the future mosque, which would also include an Islamic complex. According to the Saudi authorities, their budget for the building was $40 million, although the final price for construction of the 20,000-square-meter (about 215,278 square feet) building was estimated at $14 million.[54] It was run by the firm of prestigious architect Mario Roberto Álvarez, following a design by Saudi architect Zuhair Faiz. The construction company was Riva, linked to public works for various Argentine governments, but all the carpets were imported from Arab countries. Trees from these countries were planted, and a group of Moroccan artisans came especially to sculpt verses of the Qur'an on the wall.[55]

Thus, on September 25, 2000, then president de la Rúa presided over the opening ceremony. However, the largest ovation from the six hundred present was for former president Menem. He arrived with his daughter, Zulema. Wearing a veil, she turned to prayer during the ceremony. The event, secured by three hundred police officers and gendarmes, was attended by the crown prince of Saudi Arabia, the vice president of the Council of Ministers and chief of the National Guard of the Kingdom, Abdullah Ben Abdul Aziz Al Saud, who was awarded the *Orden del Libertador* (the highest decoration given by the Argentine president to foreign dignitaries) by de la Rúa, and the keys to the city of Buenos Aires by then mayor Aníbal Ibarra. Also in attendance was a retinue of some two hundred and fifty members of the Royal House and the Royal Cabinet, and among those invited was the chief rabbi of Buenos Aires, Shlomó Benhamú, in order to emphasize the importance of an interreligious dialogue. De la Rúa stated that "as of today, the city integrates into its landscape and its cultural and spiritual pulse an Islamic cultural center, dedicated to projecting an ancient traditional culture." He added that "in Argentina, we are proud that religious and ethnic origins are not cause for discrimination but rather for a unifying exchange."[56]

PERONISM AND THE QUEST FOR A MULTICULTURAL SOCIETY

This chapter is part of a larger attempt at highlighting the relationship between two charismatic leaders, Juan Perón and Carlos Menem, and a specific ethnic group: Arab Argentines. Within this relationship, a dynamic was established that brought about a redefinition of the concepts of citizenship and nationality promoted by Peronism from its early days, as well as their intersection with ethnicity. Peronism struggled for the inclusion of various social sectors previously excluded from Argentine politics, such as the working class, women, the inhabitants of the national territories, and non-Latin ethnic groups, among them Jewish and Arab immigrants. The two Populist leaders accepted the ethnic identity of these immigrant groups as an integral part of Argentine nationality and encouraged transnational links to countries of origin or imagined homelands.

In the pre-Perón era, Arabs and Jews were often considered as unassimilated groups and therefore were looked at as "savages," lacking cultural refinement. They supposedly threatened the Argentine "civilized" way of life and were less fit for citizenship. Social prejudices, however, not racial ones, strictly speaking, were dominant, although it was often difficult to distinguish one from the other. At any rate, at least some forms of marking difference such as religion, culture, language, or geographic origins gradually lost their influence in Peronist Argentina. To use Eduardo Elena's words, "Peronist authorities muted the exclusionary features of whiteness by insisting on national unity."[57]

Peronism encouraged a sense of partisan solidarity among its supporters, regardless of their diverse origins or physical appearance. In this context, the boundaries of membership in the political community were expanded and the concept of citizenship in Argentina was re-elaborated. This generated a new understanding of the nature of Argentine collective identities within the framework of which Arab Argentines as well as other non-Latin ethnicities managed to renegotiate between their ethnic identity and their nationality.

Menem ruled Argentina between 1989 and 1999, promoted important changes, and was the Arab Argentine of Syrian descent who rose to the highest in the country's political hierarchy.[58] A Muslim converted to Catholicism, he claimed to represent all Arabs and even promoted a Mosque as a symbol of Arab Argentines. This is indeed how the move was interpreted in Argentine society. Setting aside both the approval and criticism to which his administration was subjected, there was also backlash against his ethnic heritage by Argentine society. His ascent and the large Arab presence around him brought on what Christina Civantos called a "second wave" of anti-Arabism in Argentina. Much of society's reaction was characterized by an "Orientalist" outlook, melding long-standing prejudices with new, romanticized images. This proves the elasticity and persistence of older notions of difference in the face of changing social and political realities.

In the late nineteenth and early twentieth centuries, according to historian Carl Solberg, Jews, Arabs, and East Asians were all considered as inferior races, unproductive and parasitic, who might corrupt Argentines physically and morally.[59] In the 1930s, Argentina was characterized again by growing anti-immigration views, a result of the disappointment of the ruling classes with the newcomers. In that context, characterized by xenophobia and cultural nationalism, Jews and Arabs were singled out as the most undesirable elements among immigrants, incapable of assimilating into the nation, and their whiteness was again called into question. Thus, from the outset, the terms "Russians" and "Turks" used to refer to them were clearly demeaning. Immigrants of Arab descent were called "Turks," because most came from the Ottoman Empire. Despite the fact that most were Christians, they were at times associated with Islam. That was the first wave of anti-Arab feeling, framed by anti-Semitism broadly aimed at Jews and Arabs. The second anti-Arab wave started in the late 1980s, in response to Carlos Saúl Menem becoming president. Within that social imaginary, he would become the "Turk" par excellence.

The project of building a mosque in Buenos Aires, which took decades to materialize, highlighted the multilayered relationship of minority group members with other minorities, with majority culture and the state, and with the diasporic homeland (real or imagined). These complex and dynamic relations at the national and transnational levels are at the core of the new ethnic studies that I and others have tried to promote in recent years. We seek to understand the changing meanings of belonging and otherness in Latin America.

CHAPTER ELEVEN

BURIED

RACE, PHOTOGRAPHY, AND MEMORY IN *DAMIANA KRYYGI*

Kevin Coleman with Julia Irion Martins

The viewer is looking up into the canopy of a forest. Leaves rustle, crickets chirp. In a lilting *porteño* accent, the narrator reads: "On September 25th 1896, a settler from Sandoa found the remains of one of his horses on his estate." A caption designates the source of these words: "*Anales del Museo de La Plata*, Charles de la Hitte, 1897."[1] The camera pans down and into a vanishing point of dense foliage. "The horse," the narrator continues, "had undoubtedly been killed and torn apart by the Guayakis."

The camera—and with it, the viewer—begins walking through the understory. Leaves slap against the lens. The ground passes below, placing the audience in the position of the colonist. The narrator continues reading from the 1897 document: "On the 26th, the settler, accompanied by his three sons, searched the bush to no avail. The Guayakis' arbitrary tracks disappeared in all directions."

A brief pause to look at the ground, and then the camera seems to find a path. "On the 27th, at daybreak, a light column of smoke revealed the location of the Indian camp. With the heavy rain absorbing the sound of their footsteps, these men dragged themselves through the bushes." Despite the words, it is not raining. Hence this is not a historical reenactment of events recorded by the French anthropologist more than a century ago. It is, rather, something of an imaginative walking-in-the-shoes of a past stalker of indigenous people.

The thwacking of leaves against the screen subsides. The camera pans up to find smoke rising through the trees. "In this way they reached the place without being discovered, up to 20 footsteps from the Indians, there were 17 or 18, gathered around the fire under a shelter made from palm leaves." Following the smoke down to its source, the viewer discovers a thatched refuge. "They were peacefully attending to their food, they could be heard talking cheerfully, even noisily." Now, layered within the sounds of the forest, the audience can make out faint voices. "From time to time they suddenly became silent." The camera continues to track the smoke through the uppermost trees and back down to an encampment. A long shot takes in an indigenous community in the viewer's present. A boy holds a plastic thermos. A girl in an orange t-shirt stands with her back to the camera. The narrator continues reading from the *Anales del Museo de La Plata:* "Then the Indians would beat the ground together and return to the conversation. Two rifle shots, like lightning bolts, spread panic as the first victim fell."

CAPTURED AND ARCHIVED

This is an early sequence in the documentary film *Damiana Kryygi* (2015), directed by Alejandro Fernández Mouján. The film uses a photograph as a site for the historical reconstruction of racialist science and examines how the Ache, a group referred to by de la Hitte and others of his era as the "Guayaki" of Paraguay, used that same image to remember a series of catastrophic acts of violence suffered by their community.

Back to the forest, picking up at the point when the two rifle shots spread terror, the screen is filled with a group of Ache children talking with each other, as if the camera is not there. Fernández Mouján continues to read from de la Hitte's report from 1897: "Unable to use their bows and arrows or to put up a fight, the Guayakis dispersed in disorder, abandoning their weapons and tools." The kids pass a water jug around and drink from a large conical plant. The camera shifts to a close-up of an old woman. She's smiling, is toothless, and wears a black fleece cap. The spoken words from a historical account are intercalated with footage from the present, creating an explicitly mediated collision between violent rupture and quiet continuity: "Another Indian fell with the second shot, and a woman was wounded. Her assailants fell on her and finished her off with machetes and knives."

The audience is invited to imagine murder and to link past and present. "We can add that the settlers guided us to the place of this bloody slaughter, in which they took part." Early in this scene, the camera's movement situated viewers as embodied observers, jostling through thick brush to find a gathering of indigenous people. But with these words, spectators realize that they have imaginatively retraced two paths, that of the settlers who killed and the anthropologists who collected. "They even helped us to dissect the corpse in situ of the murdered woman," Mouján reads from de la Hitte's scholarly article. On screen, a partial view of another woman, obstructed by the moving heads of children in the foreground. "Little Damiana, abandoned in this massacre, was nonetheless saved and taken to Sandoa where today she is brought up by the murderers of her family."

More than a century later, members of the contemporary Ache community worked with Argentine anthropologists to wrest her remains from two

FIGURE 11.1. Charles de la Hitte and Herman ten Kate on the trip in which they visited the house of the settlers to measure and photograph Damiana Kryygi. *Credit: Museo de La Plata.*

powerful institutions, one in La Plata and the other in Berlin, and to bury those remains some two hundred kilometers (about 124 miles) from where she was captured in 1896. The circuitous route from Damiana's ancestral home to the archives of the museum and hospital that held her bones in their collections can be explained through an examination of the settler colonialism of the late nineteenth and early twentieth centuries, the early history of anthropology as an academic discipline, and recent efforts to reckon with past wrongs by reappropriating artifacts that were violently acquired in previous eras. My contribution to this volume's discussion of the relation of race to transnationalism is to explain the intense impact of this film, *Damiana Kryygi.* I do so by considering the peculiar features of photography and the way the medium enables us to add new layers of meaning onto even the most objectifying images. Along the way, I consider the tensions and shifting meanings of these racializing photographs in several national contexts.

From the American Southwest to Paris, from Buenos Aires to Berlin, the anthropological archives of the early twentieth century contain tens of thousands of racial-type photos.[2] Across different colonial and postcolonial settings, the making of these photographs reflected larger social structures. Scientists teamed up with locals who had state, religious, or economic authority that enabled them to coerce indigenous peoples into having their bodies measured and photographed.

To get a sense of the scale of this global photographic archive of colonial anthropology, consider just two examples. The National Archives of the United States holds the Records of the Bureau of Insular Affairs, "Photographs of the Philippine Islands, 1898–1935"; it is a truly massive collection, containing 12,059 photographic prints, 171 photographic negatives, 852 lantern slides, and one poster.[3] By way of a second example, let us take the racial type photographs from Oaxaca, a region that was subjected to a classifying gaze as early as the 1860s by French photographers who worked under the direction of Emperor Maximiliano and, much more extensively, by the Porfirian state that created identification photos of "prisoners, prostitutes, shoe shine boys, *cargadores* [porters], and water carriers" from the 1890s to around 1940, as anthropologist Deborah Poole has described. Poole argues that photography made it "possible to conceive of the Indian as at once distant and inferior, degenerate and noble, viscerally 'other' and sentimentally 'ours.'" She suggests that photographic realism contributed to the "popular understanding of race as an empirically measurable, materially tangible, and, above all, visible reality," while simultaneously reinforcing "the ambiguity or imprecision inherent in the concept of race."[4]

Considered together, these archives were formed through processes of "visual primitive accumulation," a term that theorist Jens Andermann developed to account for the way that late nineteenth-century Brazil and Argentina conquered their indigenous populations on the frontiers and registered that conquest in the visual terms demanded by emerging capitalist nation-states.[5] Territorialized global capitalism generates archives through imperial, racialized, and gendered encounters that are often registered photographically. Such photographs tend to naturalize and legitimize the very moments of conquest and appropriation. Yet the meanings of photographs are inherently unstable, and thus the amassing of photos from the late nineteenth century to the present might be understood as an anxious, and ultimately futile, attempt to counteract that very instability.

But what are scholars to do with these collections? Does the use of such photos inevitably involve repeating initial acts of violent objectification? Or could these photos be used to create historical understandings of the mechanisms of dispossession that have been disavowed in official narratives of the nation-state and science? How might the communities that were subjected to this photographic treatment repurpose these images to foster memory?

At age twenty, Robert Lehmann-Nitsche began studying medicine and natural science at the Ludwig-Maximilians-Universität of Munich, where he was a student of Johannes Ranke, the first university chair of anthropology in Germany. In 1894, Lehmann-Nitsche earned a PhD in anthropology and another in medicine three years later. His doctoral dissertation was a study of the long bones from burial sites in southern Bavaria.[6] Awarded a prize by the Société d'Anthropologie of Paris, Lehmann-Nitsche's doctoral thesis became a standard reference in physical anthropology.[7] Over the course of his life, he would author some 375 scholarly titles, signing all but one as "Robert Lehmann-Nitsche." (Under the pseudonym of "Victor Borde," he published the comprehensive, and by turns titillating, *Textos eróticos del Río de La Plata* [Leipzig, 1923] in a series that listed Franz Boas and Sigmund Freud among its editors.)

The German scholarly community of the late nineteenth century invited Lehmann-Nitsche to take a scientific approach to studying human difference. As historian Andrew Zimmerman has argued, German historicists understood human history as one of progress, the highest forms of which could be found in Europe, and thus could be known and narrated by going back to the texts produced in ancient Greece and Rome. These humanists considered those outside of European civilizations to be "natural" peoples, without history and unworthy of consideration. In response to this humanist tradition, German anthropologists developed an antihistoricist method, one that regarded "natural" peoples as unchanged by culture, and they sought to discover universal features of humanity through the comparative study of physical characteristics. They too would exalt Europe, but they would do so by comparing Europeans with their racial others, purporting to discover laws that were outside of time and narrative.[8] Their leading proponent was Rudolf Virchow, a staunch anti-Darwinist who argued against the idea that changes in populations came about through adaptions inherited via natural selection and, instead, insisted that static human types were punctuated only by aberrant, individual pathologies.

One seemingly objective basis on which to ground claims of racial difference was in the systematic measurement of human features, particularly skulls. If standardized procedures were applied to measuring skulls, stripped of the distorting effects of facial tissue, then physical anthropologists might be able to mathematically calculate the dimensions of the typical skull for any given population.[9] But calculating averages could not be done with a single skull. They needed a data set. The German Anthropological Society had the capacity to secure samples in the quantities necessary. But these scientists also needed to agree upon the methods of craniometry. With a couple of competing schema on offer, in 1883 Johannes Ranke challenged Virchow to "expound a craniometric methodology."[10] In what came to be known as "the Frankfurt Agreement," German anthropologists agreed that the primary measure would be "the cephalic index, the ratio of the length of the skull to its breadth."[11]

After finishing his thesis, Lehmann-Nitsche accepted a position as director of the Anthropological Section of the Museo de Ciencias Naturales de La Plata in Argentina. His mentor Rudolf Martin recommended him to Herman ten Kate,[12] the man Lehmann-Nitsche would replace as director at the museum. The mission of the Museo de La Plata was well suited to Lehmann-Nitsche's expertise in physical anthropology and put him at South America's premier institute for natural history and comparative anatomical and ethnological research. Containing bones and pottery shards as evidence of Argentina's prehistoric past and boldly announcing in neoclassical design its civilizational future, the Museo de La Plata would serve as an interpretive base for Lehmann-Nitsche's data-collecting expeditions to Patagonia (1902), Northwest Argentina (1906), and the Argentine Chaco (1926).[13]

And there were other reasons to take the job. In a letter dated February 1, 1897, ten Kate wrote to Lehmann-Nitsche, describing the advantages of the position at the Museo de la Plata: "After consultation with the [musuem] director I could work on what I wanted, in each of the three divisions of my section. One almost always works for the publications of the museum (*Revista* and *Anales*), which is very convenient. Of course, one receives no royalties for that but your works, richly illustrated, are sent to most institutes and [scientific] societies in the world, without you having to spend a penny."[14] Such publishing opportunities were indeed available. Under the auspices of the museum and only weeks before writing this letter, ten Kate had accompanied Charles de la Hitte on a voyage into the tropical forests of Paraguay to collect data on the Ache. Less than a month after returning from their expedition of December 1896 to January 1897, the *Anales del Museo de La Plata* published their coauthored paper describing the massacre of Damiana's family and the discovery of a young girl in the house of settlers in Sandoa.

Eleven years later, in a 1908 article published in the *Revista del Museo de La Plata*, Lehmann-Nitsche would cite that same paper by de la Hitte and ten Kate. "Some readers of these lines will recall that the inhabitants of a community known as Sandoa . . . carried out an assault against a group of Guayaquí indians, killing three and carrying with them an unharmed girl they called 'Damiana,' in honour of the day of the saint on which the massacre took place."[15] Lehmann-Nitsche cites the 1897 work of his predecessors to provide context for the anthropometric and "anthroposcopic" measurements that he himself made of a pubescent Damiana. He then adds a detail that was not in their earlier paper: "Doctor ten Kate took advantage of the opportunity to photograph young Damiana (see the reproduction of the photo. *Anales*, pl. II, n° 4) and to make some anthropological observations which we will examine at the proper time."[16] The picture that he refers to is more like a studio portrait of a young child than a racial type photo. It is this photograph that ten Kate took of a two-to-four-year-old girl that

Figure 11.2. Contemporary anthropologists and the Ache repurposed the photograph taken by Herman ten Kate in his 1896–1897 trek. *Credit: Still from* Damiana Kryygi, *directed by Alejandro Fernández Mouján, minute 20:42.*

would be held, a century later, by a filmmaker and the contemporary Ache to mourn and to generate a historical memory of that which their community had collectively suffered but which the current generation had not experienced directly.

"At the end of 1898, the little Indian girl was taken from Villa Encarnación to San Vicente, in the province of Buenos Aires," Lehmann-Nitsche wrote, "to the house of the mother of Dr. Alejandro Korn, director of the Melchor Romero Hospital; in San Vicente she worked as a maidservant and developed normally."[17] As the girl is moved further from her community in the forests of Paraguay and closer to the seats of science in Buenos Aires and Germany, the anthropologist becomes less interested in the ways that she is exploited. In the house of Dr. Korn's mother, Damiana served as unpaid domestic labor. Scientific racism was here predicated on the racialized expropriation of various forms of unfree labor. Then, in a bizarre passage in which he seems to both blame the victim and project his own fantasies onto the adolescent girl, Lehmann-Nitsche produces the very sexualized subject that he studies. As recounted in the film:

> With regard to her life, there is nothing special to mention until she entered puberty and the situation changed. The sexual *libido* manifested itself in such an alarming way that all education and reprimands by the family were ineffective. She frequently left the house, for up to three days at a time, in the company of a gallant and even poisoned a dog that slept in the room, to enable the man to enter. She considered sexual acts as the most natural thing in the world and she satisfied her desires with the instinctive spontaneity of a naive being.[18]

FIGURE 11.3. Photograph taken by Robert Lehmann-Nitsche of Damiana Kryygi in the Hospital Melchor Romero. [Cropped by the author.] *Credit: Ibero-Amerikanisches Institut.*

Damiana's purportedly uncontrollable desire is the reason given for taking her out of servitude in the house of Dr. Korn's mother and to place her into the mental hospital that Korn himself supervised.

Lehmann-Nitsche used the earlier measurements taken by ten Kate as a benchmark against which he could compare the ones that he made of the same girl ten years later, enabling something of a longitudinal study. He observes, "The cephalic index, therefore, has decreased from 86.3 to 81.3; Dr. Ten Kate believed at that time that Damiana's high brachycephaly was due to her half-rickety, half-scrofulous state, but from the recent investigations of [Carl] Roese and others, we know that a very marked brachycephaly is characteristic for the years of childhood and that such brachycephaly decreases proportionally with the years of growth."[19] The racial science of early twentieth-century Germany was the key point of reference in Lehmann-Nitsche's study of this young indigenous girl from Paraguay: "We reproduce to facilitate the comparison, a table created by Roese showing the average measurements of 20,947 Germanic girls and to which we add the respective figures of Damiana."[20] The unit of measurement (the cephalic index), the citations, the comparison to German girls: all were a paradigmatically colonial discourse of Europe and its others. Yet while his list of references was replete with German sources, the fallacious notion that intelligence could be inferred from skull size was by no means unique to Germany or Argentina. This was a transnational enterprise that cloaked prejudices in science to justify brutal, even genocidal, policies that exacerbated existing hierarchies based on race, sex, and class.[21] This was also an academic pursuit that shaped the lives of real, living people, and two and a half months after he photographed and measured her, Damiana died of "a galloping tuberculosis."

One hundred years later, it was not the numbers that Lehmann-Nitsche meticulously gathered, but the photographs that he took of an adolescent Ache girl standing naked against a wall that became central to the documentary film, *Damiana Kryygi*. Height: 144.5 cm. Mouth: 20 mm high, 43 mm wide. Nose: 49 mm long, 39 mm wide at the base, 36 mm wide at the flanks. A detailed description of her breasts. Yet in an article that fragmented and measured this girl's body in at least forty-seven different ways, Lehmann-Nitsche remarked: "I photographed her twice and both times I found her reserved, elusive, distrusting; this is also seen in the curious expression of her gaze (see my photograph)." In these reflections, Lehmann-Nitsche drops the pretence to detached observation.

To make these photographs, the white, fully clothed European man was up close with the unclothed indigenous girl that he was observing. The sexualized affection subtending the images makes them all the more exploitative. The soft lighting and his comments on the impression she made on him betray a certain tenderness, a feeling that the scientist had for his subject.

A couple months after being photographed, Damiana Kryygi died of tuberculosis. Lehmann-Nitsche placed her head, with the brains still inside the cranium and facial tissue undisturbed, into a jar with a mixture of nine parts alcohol and one part formalin.[22] "The head of the little Indian, with her brains, was sent to Professor Virchow, of Berlin, to study the facial musculature, the brain."

Referring to a public lecture and published work in three separate volumes of the *Zeitschrift für Ethnologie* (*Journal of Ethnology*), Virchow celebrated: "It is a special occasion to be able to present the head of a Guajaki Indian in Europe." Just as the Argentine and Paraguayan states understood the Ache to be on the verge of extinction, so too did Virchow. "It's a remarkable tribe whose members, although they are not living far from settlements or even cities of white people in the jungle, live a shy and hidden existence, disappear by every attempt of contact and still have the culture of the Stone Age," he noted. Virchow understood the receipt of Damiana's head to be a gift, one that came from a place that persisted outside of historical time. By preserving and dissecting "heads with soft tissue," science might "gradually answer the question of how far racial characteristics are located in the bones and how far in the different soft tissues."[23]

Virchow was also committed to photographic documentation. He notes: "I am also able to present two excellent photographs which show the front view and side view of the face." Here again disinterested scientific inquiry mingled with lay networks of nonspecialists. He acknowledged,

Diese ungewöhnliche und dabei sehr schwierige Art der Zerlegung
des Kopfes wurde mir erst verständlich, als ich durch den Brief des
Hrn. Lehmann-Nitsche erfuhr, dass das Mädchen in der letzten Zeit
seines Lebens als Wärterin in einer Irrenanstalt beschäftigt gewesen war,
wo dasselbe an Phthise verstarb. Es war offenbar darauf Bedacht ge-
nommen, das Gehirn in sorgfältigster Weise in seiner Form zu erhalten.
Und dieser Zweck ist auch bis auf einige kleine Verletzungen erreicht
worden. Für meine speziellen Absichten jedoch, d. h. die Untersuchung
der Weichteile des Gesichtes, ist eine nicht unbedenkliche Beeinträchti-
gung entstanden.

Fig. 1.

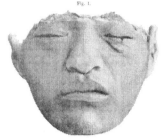

Kopf eines Guajaki-Mädchens (von vorn).

Hierzu kommt ein zweites, nämlich die Einwirkung der Formalin-
Lösung auf das Präparat. Für die Konservierung des Gehirnes bietet
bekanntlich dieses Mittel ausserordentliche Vorteile, und es ist durch
dasselbe möglich geworden, Gehirne in einem Zustande zu versenden, wie
es vordem nicht der Fall war. Auch die übrigen Weichteile werden in
der Form vorzüglich erhalten und so sind a. B. an unserem Kopf die
Muskeln und Drüsen zwischen Unterkiefer und Zungenbein in einem
hervorragend guten Zustande. Jedoch ist durch die Lösung der Blut-
farbstoff und der Farbstoff der Muskeln gänzlich ausgezogen, und dieser
Übelstand ist zwar bei den grösseren gut abgegrenzten Muskeln nicht
störend, jedoch bei den Gesichtsmuskeln, deren flache Bündel sich z. T.
verflechten, z. T isoliert im Bindegewebe analaufen, wird es, wie ich
fürchte, kaum möglich sein, eine völlig zuverlässige Präparation durch-
zuführen. Es kommt dazu, dass das Bindegewebe hart und undurchsichtig

FIGURE 11.4. "Head of a Guayaki Girl (from the Front)," caption by Hans Virchow, "Der Kopf Eines Guajaki-Mädchens," in *Zeitschrift Für Ethnologie*, vol. 40, 1908.

"I owe those [photographs] to the charity of Mrs. G. Greiszen the owner of the local photo studio whose daughter is studying medicine at the local university at the moment." These metropolitan women lent their energies to the scientific extraction of knowledge from the body of a brown woman on the periphery.

Although he made his career in Argentina, Lehmann-Nitsche was edu-cated in Germany and remained connected to German scientific networks. He maintained regular correspondence with colleagues in Berlin, Munich, and Frankfurt, continued to publish in German, and occasionally returned to participate in academic meetings. In this new age of imperialism and internal territorial conquests, Lehmann-Nitsche's work brought prestige both to Germany's scientific community and to the new provincial capital, with its evolutionary museum that interwove natural history with national history, geomorphology with art. After thirty-three years at the Museo de La Plata, he retired, spending the last four years of his life as an independent lecturer at the Friedrich-Wilhelms-Universität in Berlin, where he died in 1938.[24] Meanwhile, Damiana's bones were stored in a basement in the Mu-seo de La Plata, while her brains were held at the Charité Hospital in Berlin.

Nonscientific commentary by the scientist-photographer on his human subjects is rare. Of the estimated 1,458 anthropological photos taken by Lehmann-Nitsche, 932 were of indigenous people.[25] Guided by the leading methods of early twentieth century physical anthropology, Lehmann-Nitsche abstracted out the individuality of his subjects in search of their general, average type.

The routinely expropriative nature of these encounters can be seen in Lehmann-Nitsche's photographs of the indigenous workers in the sugar mills of Jujuy. In 1906, he went on an expedition to the extreme northwest of Argentina with Carlos Bruch, a German colleague who ran the printing department of the Museo de La Plata. The result of their trip was the publication of *Estudios antropológicos sobre los chiriguanos, chorotes, matacos y togas (Chaco occidental). Resultados generales de la expedición á Jujuy realizado por los profesores Doctor Robert Lehmann-Nitsche y Señor Carlos Bruch. Con 50 laminas segue fotografías tomadas por Carlos Bruch* (1908).

The owners of the mills, Roger and Walter Leach, were two English brothers who converted the old haciendas of the region into highly capitalized sugar plantations. By the turn of the century, two of the mills employed "more than 5,000 indigenous people from the Chaco: Wichí, Toba, Chorote, Pilagá, and Nivaclé."[26] Lehmann-Nitsche referred to them as "cheap arms that constitute a body of workers that is extremely cheap and without pretensions."[27] The Leach family facilitated the work of the German duo from the Museo de La Plata. The owners assigned them bedrooms on the grounds of their plantations. Walter Leach was personally responsible for sending Lehmann-Nitsche his objects of study.[28] "As a background, we took advantage of the wall of the house that Mr. Walter Leach ordered prepared for this purpose," Lehmann-Nitsche wrote.[29]

In some of these objectifying images, Lehmann-Nitsche himself happens to be captured in the frame. In one, the German anthropologist stands in a formal suit a few feet behind an indigenous worker who has been made to pose completely unclothed, in profile ("Chiriguanos, No. 36, Mariano, 35 á 40 años, de Machareté, Bolivia. Cabello cortado"). Lehmann-Nitsche holds his right hand above his brow to block the sun; the indigenous man has been told to keep his arms at his side, a pose repeated throughout this corpus of images. Caught in the same frame, the physical anthropologist appears here as a fully embodied observer; objective distance is accidentally figured as the result of careful stagecraft. Such feigning of objectivity was given its clearest and most fallacious expression in the cephalic index and in the hundreds of photographs of indigenous men and woman captured at a standardized medium distance in full frontal nudity, from the rear, and in profile. So even though the bulk of nineteenth- and early twentieth-century anthropology was done at a distance, an "epistolary ethnography" in George Stocking's phrase, this photograph inadvertently discloses a truth about Lehmann-Nitsche's anthropological practice. He not only relied upon priests, military officers, and businessmen who worked in remote regions of Paraguay, Bolivia, and Argentina, he also worked in the field.[30]

For early twentieth-century social scientists, the promise of photography was that it seemed to provide an objective record. A photograph was mechanically produced evidence. The black box with an aperture, the chemicals that reacted when exposed to light, the laws of nature that governed both the physics and chemistry of the process: each seemed to control for the wonton effects of a human observer. The value that anthropologists assigned to these images was their capacity to abstract out the individual. The photographed subject became a specimen, a representative of a general type, one that helped to reveal evolutionary laws. Meanwhile, the photographing observer stood outside the frame, using mathematics to help nature reveal herself. But even those ideals were, in practice, recognized as conflicting with the ego of the scientist driven to narrate the stories of his discoveries. The book of nature required an interpreter. Writing on the captive labor force that he photographed and measured on the sugarcane plantations of Jujuy, Lehmann-Nitsche acknowledges this other valence of the pictures that he and Bruch made: "So as not to tire out the gaze, we have alternated mathematical disclosures [photographs] with others of a more artistic nature."[31]

EXHUMED AND BURIED

Immediately after dramatizing the capture of a young indigenous girl who would come to be known as "Damiana," the film cuts to a park with ordered trees. Slowly, cultivated nature gives way to institution. Through the leaves, one word: "Museo." The viewer now faces bright white monumental columns. The camera zooms in on the museum's keeper, a stone jaguar. Nature here is quite literally petrified, rendered a symbolic guard of an official national repository.

Built between 1884 and 1888, the Museo de La Plata was the first purpose-built natural history museum in South America.[32] Fernández Mouján presents the museum and its archival catacombs as contradictory spaces, at once beautiful in their symmetry and suffocating. Inside, natural light streams in from above, and sweeping views are accompanied by a classical track of bassoon, oboe, and violin. Within this institution that stands, at least in part, for a country's place in an international community of modern, scientifically documented civilization, the mood is eerie and melancholic.

Shifting from panoramas of the Museo de La Plata, the viewer suddenly finds herself being shuttled through a tight corridor, lit only by a few fluorescent tube lights. The camera/viewer advances toward a large, grey filing

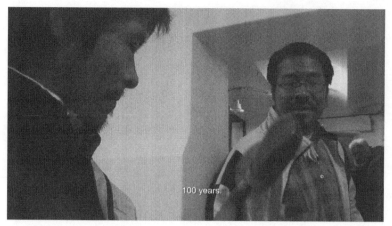

FIGURE 11.5. Emiliano and Ismael examine Ache artifacts held by the Museo de La Plata. *Credit: Still from* Damiana Kryygi, *directed by Alejandro Fernández Mouján, minute 13:54.*

cabinet. Hurdled along toward the order of numbered drawers, the viewer is forced through a labyrinth. A turn to the right and more filing cabinets from floor to ceiling, each with dozens of drawers containing objects that serve as the empirical basis of the museum's claim to authority.

Emerging from the cramped passageways, the movie cuts to a close-up of rubber-gloved hands unwrapping an object. "June 2010, Museo de La Plata," a caption informs. The last of the cellophane wrapping removed, two white archivists expose a woven basket and a gourd. From there, the frame is filled with bare, brown-skinned hands examining a stone ax. "100 years," the man holding the ax says in rough Spanish as he passes it to his companion. As these two representatives sent by the Ache community handle the stone ax, their mere presence in this space subtly subverts the museum's founding premise. The Museo de La Plata anticipated the extinction of their people, and for that very reason it acquired these artifacts, evidence of a race destined for demise.

"It feels sad to be in this place," one says. "I hope the museum returns all these objects that were the result of a massacre." On this day, the museum gives back the bones (minus the skull) of Damiana Kryygi and the cranium of another Ache youth.

With his camera, Fernández Mouján joins these two men, Emiliano and Ismael, as they return to their community. In accompanying the Ache from the bowels of the museum to the forests of Paraguay, the filmmaker is both witness, historian, and protagonist. The repatriation of Damiana Kryygi's remains is an historical event, one in which a new memory of all that led up to it is being forged. With the camera-as-witness, Fernández Mouján invites viewers of the film to become witnesses themselves.[33] *Da-*

miana Kryygi enables viewers to watch a community grapple with a trauma that most of its members had probably not known much about. What this young girl experienced was similar to what the Ache had collectively, in many different ways, suffered. This film is, thus, both historical and a history of the present: *Damiana Kryygi* is about a young girl, settlers, and scientists in the early twentieth century; it is also about the current generation of Ache generating a new memory of their loss in alliance with activist anthropologists trying to right the wrongs of their disciplinary forebears.

As an activist filmmaker from Buenos Aires, Alejandro Fernández Mouján is part of a tradition of politicized cinematic work that emerged out of the Peronist labor movement, was radicalized in the post-1968 civil uprisings, faced brutal repression and censorship under the dictatorship of 1976–1983, and finally resurfaced in the transition to democracy. These are, roughly, the three phases of political filmmaking on the Argentine Left that historian Jessica Stites Mor describes.[34] Stites Mor charts how film became a key site through which traumatic and fragmented collective memories were processed, incorporating previously marginalized voices into public debate. When Fernández Mouján takes his camera into the Museo de La Plata to film the restitution of bones taken from the Ache more than a century before by Charles de la Hitte, Herman ten Kate, and Robert Lehmann-Nitsche, he extends this tradition of filmmaking.

As both a self-reflexive cineaste and a radicalized film activist, Fernández Mouján should be located within what I might suggest is a fourth phase of political filmmaking in Argentina, one that is characterized by an attempt to intervene in politics as well as a commitment to artistic form. By making the archive itself the explicit subject of his film, he not only situates viewers in the past, he also asks how we know the past, revealing the ways that our knowledge—and the contents of the museum—are premised on acts of violence that have been sublimated and painstakingly preserved. *Damiana Kryygi* figures this archival violence as ongoing yet interruptible. In documenting the ceremonious repatriation of ill-gotten human remains to the Ache, Fernández Mouján intercedes in what are usually rather discontinuous communities of memory: one in Argentina, another in Paraguay, still another among the Ache of Paraguay, and a fourth in Germany. In each of these contexts, the film extends moments of grappling with historical wrongs committed, and traumas suffered.

While clearly part of a tradition of Argentine filmmaking that took shape in and through the transition from dictatorship to democracy, *Damiana Kryygi* is predicated on non-cinematic background conditions that enabled it to come into being. The first of these is the political climate that led the Argentine Congress in 2001 to pass Law 25,517, which mandated that "the mortal remains of aboriginal peoples, regardless of their ethnicity, that are part of museums and/or public or private collections, should be put at the disposition of the indigenous communities to whom they belonged."[35] This "Indigenous Peoples Decree" made it possible for radical anthropologists in Buenos Aires to work with members of the Ache community to begin reassembling the remains of Damiana, to remove them from the Museo de La Plata, and for the Ache to rename her "Kryygi," to cry for her, and eventually to bury her in their ancestral lands.

That law and the repatriation of her remains are also part of a broader shift that took place from roughly 1980 to 2000 throughout Latin America. That shift was characterized by a racially inflected transformation of political discourse. It was a move away from categories of social class, with workers and peasants (*campesinos*) as crucial agents of historical change, and toward various forms of identity politics. That is, *mestizaje*, with its gestures of harmonious racial mixing, was the hegemonic racial discourse in much of early twentieth-century Latin America. But after the Cold War, there was a broad move toward racial democracy, as citizens increasingly self identified as Black, indigenous, evangelical, or queer, and mobilized to have these differences recognized. In our era, deploying socially constructed identities became politically useful for making public claims and for occasionally slowing down the ravages of the capitalist machine.

The second condition of possibility for the making of this film was finding the photographs of Damiana and her physical remains. In 2007, Fernando Pepe, coordinator of the GUIAS collective (Grupo Universitario de Investigación en Antropología Social) in La Plata, found her skeleton in a box below the display cases in the exhibit of Biological Anthropology.[36]

A third condition was that the Ache community formally requested the restitution of her remains. Through the intervention of Patricia Arenas of the Universidad Nacional de Tucumán, GUIAS contacted the Federación Nativa Aché del Paraguay and shepherded the process of reclamation that culminated in the June 2010 restitution of her remains by the Museo de Ciencias Naturales de La Plata.[37]

Yet a fourth factor was that of financing and securing the equipment and expertise to produce the film. Cine Argentino, the Instituto Nacional de Cine y Artes Audiovisuales, Océano Films, Gema Films, and Alta Definición Argentina each provided material support, indicating something of the anticipated circulation, exhibition, and reception of the film. In these four preconditions to the making of the movie, the agency of Argentines and of Argentine institutions was crucial.

It is thus no surprise that noted cultural critic Osvaldo Bayer saw the effort to return the skeletal remains of Damiana Kryygi as an attempt to *"reparar el daño moral"* (repair the moral damage) of Argentina. When the

Museo de La Plata returned her bones to the Ache, Bayer concluded that "this indicates once again that in the end ethics finally triumph." His story exalted the role of Argentines, "the Argentine representatives knew to apologize for what had been done with Damiana."[38] In Bayer's account, the German authorities come out looking base. Rather than returning Damiana Kryygi's cranium directly to the Ache, the government of Germany instead insisted on returning it to the government of Paraguay, noting that it had to deal horizontally with another sovereign government, which, by implication, the Ache were not. Then, when the Ache insisted that they be able to speak for themselves, Bayer wonders how this indigenous community could stand in the way of Argentine scientists and students who seek to perform "positive gestures" of "self-criticism and the reparation of the nefarious crime with that girl."[39] In other words, Bayer is frustrated precisely because the contemporary Ache would not allow Argentine intellectuals to use them as balm for their guilty consciences.

But in striving to make art, Fernández Mouján examines the contamination of Argentina's claims to knowledge while also transcending the sort of expiatory gestures that Bayer seeks. The result is that the film, in its form and content, reveals the structures that make every document of civilization a trace of expropriative barbarism. Fernández Mouján tacitly gives visual and narrative form to this Benjaminian notion of debased progress. In other ways, too, the film explains how the museum, a paradigmatic institution that exhibits enlightenment practices of evidence-based reasoning, implicates viewers in acts of violence that are preserved within their galleries and collections. I have already noted how Lehmann-Nitsche saw in Damiana both an object of study and an alluring beauty. As a film, *Damiana Kryygi* keeps that disturbing tension in play, as Fernández Mouján attempts to create a document of restitution, a catalyst for remembrance in at least three different national contexts, and a way to ethically respond to Damiana Kryygi's gaze in and through her photographs.

The Dirty War and the public battles over history and memory that followed in its wake are, undoubtedly, part of the larger context out of which this film emerges.[40] But as a work of art, the film should not be reduced to its historical, social, and political moment. To do so would flatten it and the intentions of its director. When I asked Fernández Mouján about locating his film within this landscape of post-dictatorship political filmmaking in Argentina, he responded: "I could have begun by saying: among the genocides committed against the first peoples of Latin America we have the genocide of the Ache and in this the history of Damiana is inscribed. But then I would not need to research anything, I'd only have to denounce wrongdoing and the violence of the ruling classes, with their museums and scientists."[41]

The seamless integration of a political and historical drive with a commitment to making art is generally not a profit-making combination. This was a point made by Roger Koza in a retrospective on films released in 2015: "But what does it matter if *Damiana Kryygi,* the movie by Alejandro Fernández Mouján, reaches 10,000 viewers! If political work on the sensibility of spectators still has validity, then its existence is self-justifying."[42] But in arguing that the impact of the film on the conscience of viewers is "infinitely superior to that of all the trivial demands made by aboriginal communities," Koza manages both to ignore the ongoing voicing of grievances that made this film possible and to subscribe to a top-down notion of aesthetics, which is to say politics, that makes the vanguard artist the key agent of change. The intentions of the artist, in this case Fernández Mouján, are crucial here but so too is the agency of the Ache and the anthropologists who seek to right a historical wrong and remember historical acts of violence.

Screened throughout the Americas, across Europe, and in places further still, the film has won a number of prizes. *Damiana Kryygi* won Best Picture at the Society for Visual Anthropology's Film and Media Festival in the United States; the Audience Choice Award at the Festival Internacional de Cine de Paraguay (2015); Honourable Mention at the Festival Biarritz Amérique Latine in France (2016); Honourable Mention at the LASA Film Festival, Peru (2017); Premio Especial del Jurado, Mostra Ecofalante de Cinema Ambiental, Brazil (2017); and was a finalist for the international Social Impact Media Award (2017). The recognition that this film received at these festivals indicates the extent to which it has brought its representations of the past to international audiences that most historians rarely reach.

Since at least the 1980s, documentary filmmakers have foregrounded their own positions vis-a-vis the subject of their work, a formal move that parallels the broader post–Cold War political shift away from structural analysis and organizing toward more situated, identity-based reflexivity and claims-making. By portraying himself as a foreign character entering the Ache community, Fernández Mouján invites viewers to compare him to Charles de la Hitte, Herman F. C. ten Kate, and Robert Lehmann-Nitsche. Via testimony from Ache who have been kidnapped and raised abroad, the film suggests that the abuse of the Ache people is not yet history. The film conjures ghosts and crystallizes memories, showing how deforestation and today's mass cultivation of soy are structurally linked to the late nineteenth-century expansion of frontiers.

The room was packed during the ceremony in which the Museo de La Plata handed over the bones of Damiana Kryygi to Emiliano and Ismael. As the two men carry a wooden box containing the girl's remains and the picture of her as a toddler, they walk past the nineteenth-century paintings of Argentina's vast, seemingly unpopulated landscapes.

In Paraguay, the first stop was a brief ceremony at the Museo de las Memorias, housed in a building that the Stroessner dictatorship had once used to torture political prisoners. Candles flickered in front of the boxes of bones. The photograph of Damiana that Herman ten Kate took of her is enlarged and afixed onto one of the boxes. A small plaque captions the otherwise anonymous wooden boxes: "*Kryygi, 14 años, Pueblo Aché, Falleció en 1907, en Argentina.*" Journalists with cameras and microphones obtrusively record this event of public mourning. With tears streaming down his cheeks, an Ache man addresses those gathered: "When we look at the history of our people, pain is always in our hearts. No one can fix that. All the massacres, the murders, the dictatorship that abused our people, and kicked us down. All of that is in our hearts and minds. Today we honor Kryygi Damiana, a young girl from the Aché people, who died 114 years ago and has finally returned to her country, to her people, to her community."

After the event at the Museo de las Memorias, they travel to the remaining ancestral territory of the Ache for a private burial ceremony.[43] "On the journey from Asunción to Ypetimí," Fernández Mouján narrates, "Where the final ceremony will be held, we pass through nearly 300 kilometres [186 miles] of uninterrupted farmland dedicated to the so-called mechanized agriculture." His camera bounces along the road, capturing monocrop fields to the horizon with billowing cumulus clouds above. Taken alone, the visual might lull viewers into waxing eloquent about the sublimity of nature. But the voiceover checks that impulse: "The forests that once covered Paraguay are now just patches, little islands in this green desert."

Their arrival in Ypetemí is marked by Ache men with their faces painted and feathered, thrusting spears toward a procession of women bearing the boxes containing Damiana Kryygi's bones. Inside, people weep and comfort each other. Men hold up transparent plastic bags containing the whitish pieces of her disaggregated skeleton. A couple of tall, white men—some of them anthropologists from the United States and France—look on, embodying an ongoing ethnographic fascination with the Ache. Women tenderly place their hands on the photograph of Damiana Kryygi as a toddler.

The following day, the Ache bury her in the Caazapá National Park. "The exact burial site," Fernández Mouján tells us, "is kept secret by the elders." But in this case, the outsider documentarian is in on this secret.

After the Charité – Universitätsmedizin Hospital in Berlin restituted the cranium in April 2012 to the government of Paraguay, which, in turn, gave it to the Ache, the community conducted a second interment ceremo-

FIGURE 11.6. Members of the Ache community film the burial ceremony of Damania Kryygi's restituted skull, which is inside the box affixed with a cropped photograph by Robert Lehmann-Nitsche. *Credit: Still from* Damiana Kryygi, *directed by Alejandro Fernández Mouján, minute 1:23:58.*

FIGURE 11.7. Photo taken by Robert Lehmann-Nitsche in 1907. Cropped by Alejandro Fernández Mouján. *Credit: Still from* Damiana Kryygi, *directed by Alejandro Fernández Mouján, minute 1:17:26.*

ny. This time, the photograph that Robert Lehmann-Nitsche had taken of her was cropped just below the shoulders and affixed to a small box containing her skull. On other occasions, the Ache held the full, voyeuristic image in their hands as they used it to talk about what happened to her years before they were born. But in this funeral ceremony, the partial photograph is used. They had resignified an image that had been made under the most exploitative conditions. The photo now stood both for what happened to her at the hands of settlers and scientists and for her inherent worth as a de-

With this floor, this texture.

FIGURE 11.8. Alejandro Fernández Mouján and Enrique Pérez Balcedo reconstruct how Lehmann-Nitsche made this photograph. *Credit: Still from* Damiana Kryygi, *directed by Alejandro Fernández Mouján, minute 1:17:58.*

parted member of their community. This time, the Ache themselves wield cameras. Members of the community sing in the forest, forming a circle around red soil beside a deep hole, near the box with the skull and Damiana Kryygi's picture. Before burying the bones, an old man carefully removes the racial-type-photo-cum-portrait of the one they mourn.

RECONSTRUCTED AND REMEMBERED

In a crucial scene toward the end of the film, Fernández Mouján narrates how the photograph was taken. The screen is filled with a black and white picture of Damiana Kryygi in profile against a marbled wall. The filmmaker has cropped out everything below her bare shoulders. Sunlight rakes her face and reflects off her upper chest.

As a film still, the image is both a representation and a physical trace of the encounter between Lehmann-Nitsche and Damiana Kryygi in 1907. It is a fraction of a second from 1907 unhurriedly stretched. It is, quite literally, history on film.

But moments later, Fernández Mouján holds the uncropped photograph. As a print in his hand, the image is used as evidence to reconstruct the past. With these multiple uses of the same photograph, the film discloses and displaces the racialized gaze that produced the picture. In the process, the filmmaker enacts a method of historical research, one that imagines the past through the reconstruction of a photographic event.

Cut to a close up of a wall. The camera itself is fixed, but tiny filaments of lichen move in the breeze, revealing that this still life is really time-lapsed. Fernández Mouján problematizes the relationship between cinema and photography in the precise moment in which he is reconstructing, on video, the making of a photograph.[44]

The director and a companion stand in the courtyard of the Melchor Romero Hospital in La Plata, which was opened in 1884. In May of that year, the general hospital admitted its first patients. By June, a new wing was ready for "the alienated," the term used at the time to describe patients in the psychiatric ward.[45] This hospital was Damiana Kryygi's terminus on the road from her place of birth, indicating something of the broader spatial dynamics of the region. The Río de la Plata was a transnational space. Buenos Aires was a hub and Paraguay a hinterland, at least for Germans like Robert Lehmann-Nitsche, who mainly hung out in Buenos Aires.[46] Eleven years after the Melchor Romero was inaugurated, Lehmann-Nitsche would subject this adolescent girl to the glare of his camera.

"It looks like it, doesn't it?" Fernández Moují́án asks. "Because of the column, it does," his companion replies. They hold a folder with notes and one of Lehmann-Nitsche's photographs. The camera quickly captures the photograph of Damiana Kryygi standing naked against a wall. Fernández Moují́án gestures across the image, "with that floor, this texture," he says.

Then a cut to an enlarged detail from the photograph: Damiana's bare legs, her dirty feet planted on a tiled floor. In the old black and white picture, the viewer sees the same marbled wall with the same bevelled edge as the actual wall with lichen. The filmmaker invites viewers to contemplate the verisimilitude between the pictured wall and the wall in front of which Fernández Moují́án and his companion now stand. "Clearly, the photo was taken here at the Melchor Romero."

Unlike a filmic reenactment whose perfection might be measured by its indistinguishability from the original, Fernández Moují́án leaves viewers in no doubt that they are thinking about the past from a vantage point in the present. "It was at that time and in the month of May 1907 when thanks to the gallantry of doctor Korn, I was able to take the photograph that accompanies these lines, and to make anthropological observations," he reads from Lehmann-Nitsche's published article. On the grounds of the hospital, the filmmaker uses the primary source document to imaginatively reconstruct the moment in which the racial type photo was made: "She was clearly taken outdoors, they made her strip." From a medium distance, the camera captures both men in their present looking at the wall. One says to the other, "So Damiana was there and I get the feeling that she almost left her mark, you can see a color in the wall almost at her height."

In the photographic event that they unpack on screen, the needs of art and science took priority over the young woman's privacy. The anthropologist needed a "good" photo of her and with the technology of the day, that meant they needed a lot of natural light, which was most easily found outdoors. But they also needed a standard image, one that would enable them to measure her body against those sampled from other racial and ethnic groups.

This photo becomes the site from which the past is joined with reflection about how historical knowledge is generated. But that hermeneutic movement is not so much the result of a choice made by the filmmaker as one that was compelled by this particular kind of document—a photograph—that he uses to reconstruct a life and the larger forces that abused it. The filmmaker made a series of political and artistic choices that led him to a set of objects: dehumanizing photographs, articles published in scientific journals, bones, a mask made from horse hide, a stone ax, a cranium stored in a box. In a sense, each of these objects is material evidence of Damiana Kryygi and her people, and one could potentially trace the itinerary of each one, from the forest to the museum, to explain instances of the violent appropriation by science. Yet understanding a photograph requires particular movements of mind that are generated by its very ontology. Whatever else it is, a photo is also an irreducible trace of a past encounter between a camera and what it captured. That is what makes this photograph and the film that uses it so powerful.

The same picture serves both as the point of departure for reconstructing what happened to its subject and for creating new memories of her. During the course of the movie, the viewer comes to understand that this photograph, diachronically embedded within other primary source documents and material remains, documents the violence exercised by the settler colonists who captured this girl as well as the scientists and the dominant anthropological paradigms of the era. In the present, a new generation of anthropologists, the Ache community, and the filmmaker convert that image into an object of remembrance. By repeatedly circling from encounters with contemporary Ache back to a photograph taken in 1907 by Lehmann-Nitsche, *Damiana Kryygi* traces the capture, archival exhumation, and eventual reclamation of that image and, through it, the girl who can now be mourned.

OVERCOMING THE NATIONAL

Benjamin Bryce and David M. K. Sheinin

Ideas and experiences of race and racialization have transcended national borders in the Americas. Yet much of what we know about race and history in the region has been framed with a national focus. As in the United States, scholars in Brazil, Cuba, Peru, and elsewhere have frequently sought to understand the formation of the nation-state and the construction of national cultures in a context of race. This is largely because nation-states are often the authors of laws that codify racial categories, and people often define themselves and mark difference based on perceptions of the so-called other. Yet transnational forces have fundamentally shaped visions of racial difference and ideas of race and national belonging throughout the Americas.

In 2011, the literary critic Henry Louis Gates Jr. wrote and produced the four-part documentary series *Black in Latin America* in a manner that confirmed these cultural solitudes on race. Gates structured his approach on the premise that US Americans had no idea that people of African descent had also shaped nations elsewhere in the Americas. "When I was growing up," Gates told an interviewer, "I thought to talk about the slave trade was to talk about our ancestors here in the United States. But it turns out the real 'African-American experience' . . . unfolded south of our borders." He continued, "The average American—and even the average academic and the average journalist—has no idea of the huge number of Black people who landed south of the United States."[1] As naïve and US-centric as those statements are, they are a telling example of the dominance of the national scale. Gates of course would have saved himself some trouble had he read more widely on the history of race in Latin America, including the writings of some of those in this collection. He might also have reflected on the argument that for a host of reasons and in many ways, the boundaries between the United States and Latin America are fluid.

Gates's journey of discovery in the Americas reflects the manner in which many in the United States and elsewhere have tended to limit themselves to national contexts. In so doing, some have applied flawed and discriminatory thinking in their construction of race. In 2002, Argentine-born María Magdalena Lamadrid arrived at Buenos Aires Ezeiza Airport to catch a flight to Panama. A border agent reviewing her passport told her it was a fake because it was not possible that she was both "Black" and Argentine. A descendant of African Argentines, Lamadrid denounced the border agency to the National Institute Against Discrimination, Xenophobia, and Racism.[2] There are two layers to the Lamadrid story. The first highlights the long-standing Argentine myth of a "white" republic that includes fantasies of the eradication of indigenous peoples during the 1879 Conquest of the Desert and the consignment of African Argentines to a murky distant past. This was likely the backdrop to the border agent's befuddlement. The second is framed by the appearance of the story on the front page of the Buenos Aires daily newspaper *Clarín*. The story was important news both because Lamadrid was a sympathetic, wronged victim of discrimination and because many readers knew that they might well have made the same false assumption as the border official.

Flawed racial narratives framed by national or regional borders can have a transnational component. In 2002, the Chilean writer Sergio Gómez published an explosive finding in the Argentine daily newspaper *Página/12*. The story generated outrage in Chile and death threats toward Gómez. The article concerned Matilde Urrutia, the wife and muse of Chilean Nobel laureate Pablo Neruda who, as his widow, had jealously and rigorously guarded Neruda's public memory as that of a literary giant and hero of the Chilean left. Urrutia had a hidden side. In the mid-1940s, she had trafficked "young girls" from Chile in the Peruvian sex trade. According to Gómez, the girls were "without an unhappy indigenous mix, as the Peruvians preferred them: Pure Chileans, white and young."[3]

Here the layering of national and transnational racial (and racist) tropes was far more complex than the case of María Magdalena Lamadrid. Gómez was never able to make a compelling empirical case for his argument. It shocked some in Argentina that *Página/12* would reproduce Gómez's discriminatory language, unfiltered, on "pure" Chileans and indigenous Peruvians. In addition, Gómez trafficked in two historical constructions of race in Chile, that of the "white" Chilean versus that of the "indigenous" Peruvian across the border. What made the article explosive for many Chilean readers was the explicit accusation that Urrutia was defiling white Chilean girlhood and, as such, Neruda's legacy. The episode underscores the ease with which people can quickly invoke national borders in "defense" of racial myths.

Gates himself sometimes fell into this trap in the making of his series. He noted as a problem that in much of Latin America, race is no longer recorded in the census. "If because of historical reasons, the people who are disproportionately discriminated against happen to be that group of people with dark skin, kinky hair and thick lips, how do you count them if you don't have a census category?"[4] Gates's approach to counting reflects a narrow American experience with race, counting, and the census, where robust census numbers have at times been an effective tool to win access to federal government services for urban African Americans. Historically, the US census has also been adamant about slotting people into racial categories.[5]

Stephen E. Lewis's chapter in this volume, "No Place in the Cosmic Race? The False Promises of *Mestizaje* and *Indigenismo* in Postrevolutionary Mexico," effectively demonstrates that the process of counting (or not counting) people by racial category cannot be reasonably reduced to a census. David M. K. Sheinin's chapter, "Baseball and the Categorization of Race in Venezuela," makes clear that the US racial binary set in place by Plessy v. Ferguson (163 U.S. 537, 1896) that allows for the sort of clarity Gates assumes possible in a federal census, simply cannot be applied as easily in other parts of the region. Moreover, the 2020 census count initiatives in Flint, Michigan, and dozens of other US cities to make certain that people are counted in the next census underscore the long-standing failure of the federal census to accurately count people of African heritage in the United States.[6]

Some of today's most pressing international social crises are concerned with race, transnationalism, and the growing porousness of borders. One example is the vast movement of Colombian refugees across national borders in South America over the past five decades. There has been massive migration from the Atlantic coast of Colombia to Caracas and other Venezuelan cities since the 1950s. The administration of Venezuelan president Hugo Chávez (1999–2013) recognized this migrant community and its political clout by accelerating the path to citizenship for many, thereby enfranchising tens of thousands of working-class (and potentially *chavista*) voters. Chávez's discourse on a racially mixed Venezuelan identity resonated with Colombian Venezuelans, many of whom self identified as Black or mestizo. The administration of President Cristina Fernández de Kirchner in Argentina followed Chávez's example by encouraging an equally speedy path from migrant to citizen for Paraguayan, Peruvian, and Bolivian immigrants. There has long been a racialized and discriminatory narrative on Blackness in Venezuela about Colombian Venezuelans, evident in the vicious attacks on Nicolás Maduro after he won the presidency in 2013, as a purported Colombian interloper. Some Argentines have likewise expressed similar discriminatory sentiments toward immigrants from neighboring countries.

In her chapter "Creating False Analogies: Race and Drug Wars 1930s to 1950s," Elaine Carey argues that "policy makers embraced constructs of race on the US-Mexico border from the 1930s to the 1960s to obstruct social and economic inclusion and to mobilize political powers to criminalize Mexican Americans." That same argument on what Carey calls "false narratives of deviance" might also be applied to another case of current Colombian migrant communities, this time in Ecuador. As in the case of Venezuela, large numbers of Colombians began to move to Ecuador in the 1950s. By the 1970s, there were some fifty thousand undocumented Colombians in Ecuador, 80 percent of whom worked in agriculture. After 1990, many Colombians in Ecuador were there to escape civil war. The brutal mistreatment of Colombian migrant women by Ecuadorean police in the recent past has not only depended on identity factors that might include race but it has also revealed that the intersection of race with class, gender, and other factors are at play as police view migrant women as criminals.[7]

Constructions of whiteness are at the core of Benjamin Bryce's chapter on East and South Asian exclusion in Argentina at the turn of the twentieth century. He reasons that the rationale for the exclusion of Asians in early twentieth-century Argentina depended on a defense of the idea that Argentina was a white republic. A similar defense of whiteness informs US president Donald Trump's politics on Latin American immigration. Yet as several chapters in this book show, notions of racial identities morph when people move into other national contexts. In the United States, Latin American or Latinx can become a racial identity or label applied to others, but such transformations are far more malleable than people often realize.

In stark contrast to how he imagines his own immigrant past, Trump expends great energy on the Mara Salvatrucha gang, also known as MS-13, as a grotesque stand-in for Latin American, nonwhite migrants. This coincided with and followed his June 2015 presidential campaign launch when he famously announced that Mexico was sending rapists and drug traffickers to the United States.[8] The choice draws in part on an alarmist linkage of a criminal gang with the politics of criminalizing undocumented migrants. It reflects the ugly intersection of race, immigration policy, and ideas of national belonging in recent Republican Party positions. Trump's focus on the US-Mexico border is part of this same process. Building a border wall and ramping up "security" stand in for a broader concern about the racial implications of Latin American immigration to what right-wing nationalists see as a white republic.

In the 1970s, Salvadoran immigrants (many of them undocumented) first organized MS-13 in response to threats from existing gangs in Los Angeles. With as many as twelve thousand members in the United States today and fifty thousand around the world, MS-13 has thrived in drug trafficking, extortion, and armed robbery. In the past forty years, the multimillion dollar gang has built a reputation for extreme violence. In the 1980s many MS-13 members were teenaged migrants or the children of migrants from war-torn El Salvador. Hundreds had fled a civil war in that country created in part by US counter-insurgency warfare in the region that desta-bilized democratic rule and directly fostered the rise of violent, right-wing paramilitary groups during the final stages of the Cold War. In the 1990s, the US government began deporting convicted MS-13 gang members to El Salvador. On their return, many worked to transplant gang culture and or-ganized crime activity to that country and to Honduras, unleashing a level of frenetic violence there unseen since the early 1980s.[9]

In early 2019, the journalist Dara Lind described MS-13 as "the face of the Trump administration's favorite trope: the idea that people from other countries are sneaking into America and importing violence and crime."[10] Before the COVID-19 pandemic, MS-13 emerged as an important com-ponent in the president's 2020 political strategy that brought together how many Americans had come to understand national identity, transnational problems of race, and immigration. The 2020 election, argued journalist Thomas B. Edsall in August 2019, "will be fought over the current loss of certainty—the absolute lack of consensus—on the issue of 'race.'"[11]

Trump and his supporters' concerns about a fading white republic in the United States run deeper. He draws on his own past in the New York City borough of Queens, where he grew up in an upper-middle-class white residential enclave. After the First World War, European immigrants and their children began to move from Brooklyn to what were then suburban communities in Queens. Trump's father, Fred Trump, developed some of the middle-class housing blocks newly occupied by Brooklyn expats in a borough perceived as distant from the rest of the city not only because of its poorly serviced public transportation network but also because of a relative absence of African Americans (unlike the rapidly diversifying neighbor-hoods of Brooklyn). After the Second World War, a wave of New Yorkers took part in a new exodus from Brooklyn and Queens further east to Long Island. Like Americans of European origins in St. Louis, Detroit, and oth-er cities at the same time, they left in part to escape a growing influx of African Americans in an increasingly segregated urban landscape in the Midwest and along the Eastern Seaboard. For years, Long Island bedroom communities of middle-class Americans bore a cultural resentment against people of color—many of whom were from Latin America and the Carib-bean—that had "taken over" the old European immigrant neighborhoods in New York City. Donald Trump's personal trajectory and politics of race reflect that cultural anxiety.[12]

People and ideas crisscross over borders, and meanings ascribed to skin color and how skin color is perceived change as the result of that movement. An indigenous person in Chile becomes mestizo in Peru, a white Venezuelan becomes Latino in the United States, and a Japanese immigrant is member of a desired group in Brazil but a problem in Argentina. Yet that person's social class and legal status affects the racial labels applied to him or her in another national context, making even this list of slippage more slippery still. As the chapters of this book have shown, the transnational and local scales intersect and overlap, and they complicate and are complicated by evolving notions of race in the Americas.

NOTES

INTRODUCTION. TOWARD NEW COORDINATES?

The author would like to thank Benjamin Bryce and David Sheinin for the invitation to contribute to this volume, and for their helpful feedback along the way. I am also grateful to Keila Grinberg, Dalia Muller, Lara Putnam, and Camilo Trumper for their very helpful insights and suggestions.

1. Lara Putnam, "The Transnational and the Text-Searchable: Digitized Sources and the Shadows They Cast," *American Historical Review* 121, no. 2 (April 2016): 401.

2. Laura Briggs, Gladys McCormick, and J. T. Way, "Transnationalism: A Category of Analysis," *American Quarterly* 60, no. 3 (September 2008): 625–48.

3. José Luís Bendicho Beired, "Comparación e historia transnacional: ¿Cuál es su pertinencia para el estudio del Hispanismo en Latinoamérica?" (paper, Fourth Discussion Workshop "Las Derechas en el Cono Sur, siglo XX," Universidad Nacional de General Sarmiento, Los Polvorines, May 31, 2012), 7.

4. David Sartorius and Micol Seigel, "Introduction: Dislocation across the Americas," *Social Text* 28, no. 3 (Fall 2010): 1–10.

5. Pamela Voekel and Elliott Young, "The Tepoztlán Institute for the Transnational History of the Americas," *Social Text* 25, no. 3 (Fall 2007): 12.

6. Frank Tannenbaum, *Slave and Citizen: The Classic Comparative Study of Race Relations in the Americas* (Boston: Beacon, 1992).

7. Gonzalo Aguirre Beltrán, *La población negra de México: Estudio etnohistórico* (Mexico City: Fonde Cultura Económica, 1972); Melville J. Herskovits, *The Myth of the Negro Past* (New York: Harper & Brothers, 1941); Fernando Ortiz, *Los negros brujos*, 2nd ed. (Havana: Editorial de Ciencias Sociales, 2007); Raymundo Nina Rodrigues, *Os africanos no Brasil*, 7th ed. (Brasília: Editora Nacional, 1988).

8. See Briggs, McCormick, and Way, "Transnationalism"; Diego Galeano, *Criminosos viajantes: circulações transnacionais entre Rio de Janeiro e Buenos Aires, 1890–1930* (Rio de Janeiro: Ministério da Justiça, Arquivo Nacional, 2016), 13–25; Evelyn Hu-Dehart and Kathleen López, "Asian Diasporas in Latin America and the Caribbean: An Historical Overview," *Afro-Hispanic Review* 27, no. 1 (Spring 2008): 9–21; Lara Putnam, "Transnational Frames of Afro-Latin Expe-

rience: Evolving Spaces and Means of Connection, 1600–2000," in *Afro-Latin American Studies: An Introduction*, ed. Alejandro de la Fuente and George Reid Andrews (Cambridge: Cambridge University Press, 2018), 537–68; Heidi Tinsman and Sandhya Shukla, "Introduction: Across the Americas," in *Imagining Our Americas: Toward a Transnational Frame*, ed. Heidi Tinsman and Sandhya Shukla (Durham, NC: Duke University Press, 2007).

9. Voekel and Young, "Tepoztlán Institute," 11.

10. Lisa Lowe, *The Intimacies of Four Continents* (Durham, NC: Duke University Press, 2015), 1; C. L. R. James, *The Black Jacobins: Toussaint L'Ouverture and the San Domingo Revolution* (New York: Random House, 1963); Fernando Ortiz, *Cuban Counterpoint: Tobacco and Sugar* (Durham, NC: Duke University Press, 1995).

11. Prasenjit Duara, *Rescuing History from the Nation: Questioning Narratives of Modern China* (Chicago: University of Chicago Press, 1997); Gilbert M. Joseph, Catherine C. LeGrand, and Ricardo D. Salvatore, eds., *Close Encounters of Empire: Writing the Cultural History of U.S.–Latin American Relations* (Durham, NC: Duke University Press, 1998); Tinsman and Shukla, "Introduction."

12. Paul Gilroy, *The Black Atlantic: Modernity and Double-Consciousness* (Cambridge, MA: Harvard University Press, 1993).

13. Florencia E. Mallon, "Introduction: Decolonizing Knowledge, Language, and Narrative," in *Decolonizing Native Histories: Collaboration, Knowledge, and Language in the Americas*, ed. Florencia E. Mallon (Durham, NC: Duke University Press, 2012), 16.

14. Heidi Feldman, *Black Rhythms of Peru: Reviving African Musical Heritage in the Black Pacific* (Middletown, CT: Wesleyan University Press, 2006). See also Tamara J. Walker, *Exquisite Slaves: Race, Clothing, and Status in Colonial Lima* (Cambridge: Cambridge University Press, 2017).

15. Feldman, *Black Rhythms*, 100–104.

16. On lundu and its possible origins, see Carlos Sandroni, *Feitiço decente: transformações do samba no Rio de Janeiro, 1917–1933* (Rio de Janeiro: Jorge Zahar, 2001), 39–61; James H. Sweet, "The Evolution of Ritual in the African Diaspora: Central African Kilundu in Brazil, St. Domingue, and the United States, Seventeenth-Nineteenth Centuries," in *Diasporic Africa: A Reader*, ed. Michael A. Gomez (New York: New York University Press, 2006), 64–80.

17. Anne Eller, *We Dream Together: Dominican Independence, Haiti, and the Fight for Caribbean Freedom* (Durham, NC: Duke University Press, 2016); Ada Ferrer, *Freedom's Mirror: Cuba and Haiti in the Age of Revolution* (New York: Cambridge University Press, 2014). See also Ernesto Bassi, *An Aqueous Territory: Sailor Geographies and New Granada's Transimperial Greater Caribbean World* (Durham, NC: Duke University Press, 2017).

18. Lara Putnam, *Radical Moves: Caribbean Migrants and the Politics of Race in the Jazz Age* (Chapel Hill: University of North Carolina Press, 2013). See also Jesse Hoffnung-Garskof, *A Tale of Two Cities: Santo Domingo and New York after 1950*

(Princeton, NJ: Princeton University Press, 2010); Carlos Agudelo, "Génesis de redes transnacionales: movimientos afrolatinoamericanos en América Central," in *Política e Identidad: Afrodescendientes en México y América Central*, ed. Odile Hoffmann (Mexico City: Centro de Estudios Mexicanos y Centroamericanos, 2010).

19. Tatiana Seijas, *Asian Slaves in Colonial Mexico: From Chinos to Indians* (Cambridge: Cambridge University Press, 2014).

20. See Hu-Dehart and López, "Asian Diasporas in Latin America"; Kathleen López, *Chinese Cubans: A Transnational History* (Chapel Hill: University of North Carolina Press, 2013); Watt Stewart, *Chinese Bondage in Peru: A History of the Chinese Coolie in Peru, 1849–1874* (Durham, NC: Duke University Press, 1951); Lisa Yun, *The Coolie Speaks: Chinese Indentured Laborers and African Slaves in Cuba*, Asian American History and Culture (Philadelphia: Temple University Press, 2008).

21. Gaiutra Bahadur, *Coolie Woman: The Odyssey of Indenture* (Chicago: University of Chicago Press, 2013), xx–xxi; Benjamin Nicolas Narvaez, "Chinese Coolies in Cuba and Peru: Race, Labor, and Immigration, 1839–1886" (PhD diss., University of Texas at Austin, 2010), 37–39.

22. Rebecca Earle, *The Return of the Native: Indians and Myth-Making in Spanish America, 1810–1930* (Durham, NC: Duke University Press, 2007).

23. José Carlos de la Puente Luna, *Andean Cosmopolitans: Seeking Justice and Reward at the Spanish Royal Court* (Austin: University of Texas Press, 2018); Nancy E. van Deusen, *Global Indios: The Indigenous Struggle for Justice in Sixteenth-Century Spain* (Durham, NC: Duke University Press, 2015); Jace Weaver, *The Red Atlantic: American Indigenes and the Making of the Modern World, 1000–1927* (Chapel Hill: University of North Carolina Press, 2014); Coll Thrush, *Indigenous London: Native Travelers at the Heart of Empire*, (New Haven, CT: Yale University Press, 2016).

24. James E. Sanders, *The Vanguard of the Atlantic World: Creating Modernity, Nation, and Democracy in Nineteenth-Century Latin America* (Durham, NC: Duke University Press, 2014); Mark Thurner, *History's Peru: The Poetics of Colonial and Postcolonial Historiography* (Gainesville: University Press of Florida, 2012).

25. Jeff Lesser, *Immigration, Ethnicity, and National Identity in Brazil, 1808 to the Present* (Cambridge: Cambridge University Press, 2013); Jeffrey Lesser, *Negotiating National Identity: Immigrants, Minorities, and the Struggle for Ethnicity in Brazil* (Durham, NC: Duke University Press, 1999); Jeffrey Lesser, *Welcoming the Undesirables* (Berkeley: University of California Press, 1995); Raanan Rein, *Fútbol, Jews, and the Making of Argentina* (Stanford, CA: Stanford University Press, 2014).

26. Andre Kobayashi Deckrow, "'Friendship Between Antipodes': Pre–World War II Japanese Colonial Emigration to Brazil" (PhD diss., Columbia University, 2019).

27. Benjamin Bryce, "Asian Migration, Racial Hierarchies, and Exclusion in Argentina, 1890–1920," in this volume, 21.

28. Heidi Tinsman, *Buying into the Regime: Grapes and Consumption in Cold War Chile and the United States* (Durham, NC: Duke University Press, 2014), ix; Tinsman and Shukla, "Introduction," 1.

29. Alec Dawson, "Crossing the Border at the Primer Congreso Indigenista Interamericano, 1940" in this volume, 77.

30. Waskar Ari-Chachaki, "Intersections, Barriers, and Borders in Gregorio Titiriku's Republic of Qullasuyu," in this volume.

31. Putnam, "Transnational Frames," 554.

32. Putnam, *Radical Moves.* Similar dynamics characterize recent work on the Oito Batutas, a mixed-race Brazilian band often glossed as Black and that traveled to Argentina and Paris, where their success helped eventually pave the way for samba to ascend as Brazil's putatively national music. Rafael José de Menezes Bastos, "Brazil in France, 1922: An Anthropological Study of the Congenital International Nexus of Popular Music," *Latin American Music Review* 29, no. 1 (Spring/Summer 2008): 1–28; Luís Fernando Hering Coelho, "Os musicos transeuntes: de palavras e coisas em torno de uns batutas" (Universidade Federal de Santa Catarina, 2009); Luís Fernando Hering Coelho, "Palcos, enterros e gravações: os Oito Batutas na Argentina (1922–1923)," *ArtCultura* 13, no. 23 (July 2011): 65–83; Marc A. Hertzman, "Brincando de Índio . . . e muito mais: atravessando espaço (e tempo) com os Oito Batutas, dentro e fora da cidade," in *Negros nas cidades brasileiras (1890–1950)*, ed. Ana Barone and Flávia Rios (São Paulo: Intermeios, 2019); Luiza Mara Braga Martins, "Racismo e música popular: a experiência dos Oito Batutas no atlântico negro na década de 1920," in *Histórias do pós-abolição no mundo atlântico, vol. 3: cultura, relações raciais e cidadania*, ed. Martha Abreu (Niterói: Editora da UFF, 2013); Micol Seigel, *Uneven Encounters: Making Race and Nation in Brazil and the United States* (Durham, NC: Duke University Press, 2009).

33. Petrônio Domingues and Flávio dos Santos Gomes, "'Este samba selvagem': O charleston na arena transatlântica," in *Da nitidez e invisibilidade: legados do pós-emancipação no Brasil*, ed. Flávio dos Santos Gomes and Petrônio Domingues (Belo Horizonte: Fino Traço, 2013), 177–202.

34. Domingues and Gomes, 199; Pierre Bourdieu and Loïc Wacquant, "On the Cunning of Imperialist Reason," *Theory, Culture & Society* 16, no. 1 (1999): 41–58; Barbara Weinstein, "Prefácio," in *Da nitidez e invisibilidade*, 7–11. For an earlier refutation, see John D. French, "The Missteps of Anti-Imperialist Reason: Bourdieu, Wacquant and Hanchard's Orpheus and Power," *Theory, Culture & Society* 17, no. 1 (2000): 107–28.

35. Galeano, *Criminosos viajantes*; Ricardo Donato Salvatore, ed., *Los lugares del saber: contextos locales y redes transnacionales en la formación del conocimiento moderno* (Rosario, Argentina: Beatriz Viterbo Editora, 2007); Catherine Vézina, *Diplomacia migratoria: una historia transnacional del programa bracero, 1947–1952* (México: Secretaría de Relaciones Exteriores, Acervo Histórico Diplomático, 2017). Also of note is the work by scholars at Mexico's Instituto Mora and the Universidad Autóno-

ma de Yucatán who for years have studied, if not by name then in practice, transnational relationships between Mexico and the Caribbean. Seminario Relaciones de México con el Caribe, Instituto Mora, https://www.institutomora.edu.mx/Semi narios/remexcar/SitePages/Inicio.aspx; "Estudios sobre el Caribe: perspectivas transdisciplinarias," Cuerpo Académico Estudios Literarios, Universidad Autónoma de Yucatan, http://www.antropologia.uady.mx/ca/ca_literatura/seminarioPermanente .php. Europe-based Latin Americanists have also discussed and debated the meanings and worthiness of transnationalism. See Darina Martykánová and Florencia Peyrou, eds., "Dosier: la historia transnacional," *Ayer* 94, no. 2 (2014).

36. Vézina, *Diplomacia migratoria*, 14. In a similar vein, see Carolina Ortega, "De Guanajuato to Green Bay: A Generational Story of Labor, Place and Community, 1926–2010" (PhD diss., University of Illinois, Urbana-Champaign, 2020). Within Latin America, transnationalism and US transnational scholarship seem to carry more salience in Brazil, which may be due in part to the outsized role that comparison (especially with the United States) has shaped and in some cases limited the historiography on race. In that context, transnationalism can offer a welcome departure from the past. See Cristián Castro, "The Transnational Imagined Community of the Black Press of São Paulo and Chicago, 1900–1940s," *Estudos Históricos* 30, no. 60 (January–April 2017): 71–92; Maria Ligia Coelho Prado, "América Latina: historia comparada, historias conectadas, historia transnacional," *Escuela de Historia* 24, no. 3 (2012): 9–22; João Júlio Gomes dos Santos Júnior, "A história política na hora da virada transnacional: novas posibilidades de pesquisa," *Esboços* 26, no. 41 (2019): 67–83. Much of the transnational Brazilian(ist) work overlaps with, builds from, and is otherwise in dialogue with scholarship on the colonial era. This is especially so for the nineteenth century, a period full of rich and complex histories of exchange between Angola and Brazil, which scholars have shown to have flowed in both directions across the Atlantic. Mariana P. Candido, *An African Slaving Port and the Atlantic World: Benguela and its Hinterland* (New York: Cambridge University Press, 2013); Mariana P. Candido, "South Atlantic Exchanges: The Role of Brazilian-Born Agents in Benguela, 1650–1850," *Luso-Brazilian Review* 50, no. 1 (2013): 53–82; Roquinaldo Ferreira, *Cross-Cultural Exchange in the Atlantic World: Angola and Brazil during the Era of the Slave Trade*, repr. ed. (Cambridge: Cambridge University Press, 2012); Pierre Verger, *Flux et Reflux de la Traite des Nègres entre le Golfe de Bénin et Bahia de Todos os Santos: du XVIIe au XIXe Siècle* (Paris: Mouton, 1968).

37. Voekel and Young, "Tepoztlán Institute," 13.

38. Barbara Weinstein, "Pensando a história fora da nação: a historiografia da américa latina e o viés transnacional," *Revista Eletrônica da ANPHLAC*, no. 14 (June 2013): 11.

39. Philip J. Deloria, "American Indians, American Studies, and the ASA," *American Quarterly* 55, no. 4 (December 2003): 669–80.

40. Galeano, *Criminosos viajantes*, 22.

41. Silmei de Sant'Ana Petiz, *Buscando a liberdade: as fugas de escravos da província de São Pedro para o além-fronteira, 1815–1851* (Passo Fundo: Universidade de Passo Fundo Editora, 2006); Keila Grinberg, "Illegal Enslavement, International Relations, and International Law on the Southern Border of Brazil," *Law and History Review* 35, no. 1 (February 2017): 33. In addition to Petiz, Grinberg also builds on Flávio Gomes's work on the colonial period in northern Brazil. Flávio dos Santos Gomes, "A 'Safe Haven': Runaway Slaves, Mocambos, and Borders in Colonial Amazonia, Brazil," *Hispanic American Historical Review* 82, no. 3 (August 2002): 469–98.

42. Grinberg, "Illegal Enslavement," 44; Keila Grinberg, "The Two Enslavements of Rufina: Slavery and International Relations on the Southern Border of Nineteenth-Century Brazil," *Hispanic American Historical Review* 96, no. 2 (May 2016): 259–90.

43. Grinberg, "Illegal Enslavement," 32.

44. For related work on the larger Río de la Plata region with emphasis on the Spanish-American side, see Alex Borucki, *Esclavitud y trabajo: un estudio sobre los afrodescendientes en la frontera uruguaya (1835–1855)* (Montevideo: Pulmón Ediciones, 2004); Alex Borucki, *From Shipmates to Soldiers: Emerging Black Identities in the Río de la Plata* (Albuquerque: University of New Mexico Press, 2015).

45. "Special Issue: ReCapricorning the Atlantic," *Luso-Brazilian Review* 45, no. 1 (2008). See also João José Reis, Flávio dos Santos Gomes, and Marcus J. M. Carvalho, *The Story of Rufino: Slavery, Freedom, and Islam in the Black Atlantic* (Oxford: Oxford University Press, 2020); James H. Sweet, *Domingos Álvares, African Healing, and the Intellectual History of the Atlantic World* (Chapel Hill: University of North Carolina Press, 2011).

46. J. Lorand Matory, *Black Atlantic Religion: Tradition, Transnationalism, and Matriarchy in the Afro-Brazilian Candomblé* (Princeton, NJ: Princeton University Press, 2005), 16. In dialogue with Matory, Luis Nicolau Parés and Stefania Capone examine how and why specific kinds of Africanness became, as Parés puts it "the most privileged" in Brazil. Stefania Capone, *Searching for Africa in Brazil: Power and Tradition in Candomblé*, trans. Lucy Lyall Grant (Durham, NC: Duke University Press, 2010); Luis Nicolau Parés, *The Formation of Candomblé: Vodun History and Ritual in Brazil*, trans. Richard Vernon (Chapel Hill: University of North Carolina Press, 2013), 121.

47. See also Marc A. Hertzman, "A Brazilian Counterweight: Music, Intellectual Property and the African Diaspora in Rio de Janeiro (1910s–1930s)," *Journal of Latin American Studies* 41, no. 4 (2009): 695–722; Tiffany Ruby Patterson and Robin D. G. Kelley, "Unfinished Migrations: Reflections on the African Diaspora and the Making of the Modern World," *African Studies Review* 43, no. 1, Special Issue on the Diaspora (2000): 11–45.

48. Lauren Derby, "Imperial Idols: French and United States Revenants in Haitian Vodou," *History of Religions* 54, no. 4 (May 2015): 421–22.

49. For a hemispheric overview, see Paulina L. Alberto and Jesse Hoffnung-Garskof, "'Racial Democracy' and Racial Inclusion: Hemispheric Histories," in *Afro-Latin American Studies: An Introduction*, ed. Alejandro de la Fuente and George Reid Andrews (Cambridge: Cambridge University Press, 2018), 264–318.

50. David M. K. Sheinin, "Baseball and the Categorization of Race in Venezuela," in this volume, 122.

51. Two important exceptions are Putnam, *Radical Moves*; Tinsman, *Buying into the Regime*. For a recent example of transnational labor history that also pays close attention to race, see Elizabeth Esch, *The Color Line and the Assembly Line: Managing Race in the Ford Empire* (Berkeley: University of California Press, 2018).

52. Flávio dos Santos Gomes, Petrônio Domingues, and Anamaria Fagundes, "'Idiossincrasias cromáticas': projetos e propostas de 'imigração negra' no Brasil republicano," in *Da nitidez e invisibilidade*, 208.

53. Marc Becker, *Indians and Leftists in the Making of Ecuador's Modern Indigenous Movements* (Durham, NC: Duke University Press, 2008), 35.

54. Jaymie Heilman, *Before the Shining Path: Politics in Rural Ayacucho, 1895–1980* (Stanford, CA: Stanford University Press, 2010).

55. Hervé Do Alto, "'Cuando el nacionalismo se pone el poncho': una mirada retrospectiva a la etnicidad y la case en el movimiento popular boliviano (1952–2007)," in *Bolivia: memoria, insurgencia y movimientos sociales*, ed. Maristella Svampa and Pablo Stefanoni (Buenos Aires: CLACSO Libros, 2007).

56. Do Alto, 48.

57. Alberto, *Terms of Inclusion*, 139–40.

58. Jessica Graham, *Shifting the Meaning of Democracy: Race, Politics, and Culture in the United States and Brazil* (Berkeley: University of California Press, 2019).

59. Aruã Silva de Lima, "Comunismo contra o racismo: autodeterminação e vieses de integração de classe no Brasil e nos Estados Unidos (1919–1939)" (PhD diss., Universidade de São Paulo, 2015).

60. Kim D. Butler, *Freedoms Given, Freedoms Won: Afro-Brazilians in Post-Abolition São Paolo and Salvador* (New Brunswick, NJ: Rutgers University Press, 1998), esp. 121–23; Graham, *Shifting the Meaning of Democracy*.

61. Ari-Chachaki, "Intersections, Barriers, and Borders," in this volume, 39.

62. Ari-Chachaki, in this volume, 55.

63. Putnam, "Race and Political Rights," in this volume, 73.

64. Dawson, "Crossing the Border," in this volume, 77.

65. Rein, "The Tortuous Road," in this volume, 178.

CHAPTER ONE. ASIAN MIGRATION, RACIAL HIERARCHIES, AND EXCLUSION IN ARGENTINA, 1890–1920

I wish to acknowledge financial support from the Social Sciences and Humanities Research Council of Canada and from the Office of Research at the University of Northern British Columbia. Lily Balloffet, Steven Hyland, Jeffrey Lesser, Julia Sarreal, and David Sheinin as well as members of the BC Latin American History

Group and the Toronto Latin American Research Group all provided excellent comments on previous versions of this manuscript. Martín Marimón helped me track down some documents that were difficult to access in Buenos Aires, and Ryan McKenney was a huge help at the National Archives of Japan. Thank you!

Epigraph: Letter from Reginald Tower to Foreign Office, February 23, 1912, FO 369/439—1912, The National Archives of the United Kingdom, Kew (hereafter TNA).

1. Letter from Silvestre de Marchi to Doctor Don V. de la Plaza, March 22, 1910, Caja 1180, División Europa y Asia, Dinamarca–Japón, Año 1910, Archivo del Ministerio de Relaciones Exteriores y Culto, Buenos Aires (hereafter AMREC).

2. "South America Society of Japan," *Japan Times* (Tokyo), February 11, 1910, in "Records of the Department of State Relating to Internal Affairs of Argentina, 1910–29," reel 30, 835.50 Economic Matters, 835.55 Immigration, 835.56 Emigration.

3. "South America Society."

4. "La emigración japonesa," *La Prensa*, February 14, 1910, in "Records of the Department of State Relating to Internal Affairs of Argentina, 1910–29," reel 30, 835.50 Economic Matters, 835.55 Immigration, 835.56 Emigration.

5. "La inmigración japonesa," *La Prensa*, February 17, 1910, in Caja 1180, División Europa y Asia. Dinamarca–Japón, Año 1910, AMREC.

6. "La inmigración japonesa."

7. "La inmigración japonesa."

8. On Asian immigration, see the vast body of literature on immigration on the period before 1945 to notice the relative absence of research on Asian migrants and the handful of studies on Asian immigrants who came later. See, for example, Chisu Teresa Ko, "Between Foreigners and Heroes: Asian-Argentines in a Multicultural Nation," in *Rethinking Race in Modern Argentina*, ed. Paulina Alberto and Eduardo Elena (Cambridge: Cambridge University Press, 2016), 268–88; and Debbie Lee-DiStefano and Zelideth María Rivas, ed., *Imagining Asia in the Americas* (New Brunswick, NJ: Rutgers University Press, 2016). On the topic of race-based exclusion in the Americas and the absence of Argentina, see for example, David Scott FitzGerald and David Cook-Martín, *Culling the Masses: The Democratic Origins of Racist Immigration Policy in the Americas* (Cambridge, MA: Harvard University Press, 2014), 299; Diego Acosta, *The National versus the Foreigner in South America: 200 Years of Migration and Citizenship Law* (Cambridge: Cambridge University Press, 2018); Erika Lee, "The 'Yellow Peril' and Asian Exclusion in the Americas," *Pacific Historical Review* 76, no. 4 (2007): 537–62.

9. Benjamin Bryce, "Undesirable Britons: South Asian Migration and the Making of a White Argentina," *Hispanic American Historical Review* 99, no. 2 (2019): 248.

10. Manuel Ugarte, *El porvenir de la América Española* (Valencia: Prometeo, Sociedad Editorial, 1920), 96.

11. Carlos Octavio Bunge, *Nuestra América* (Barcelona: Imprenta de Henrich y Cía., editores, 1903), 32.

12. Bunge, 33.

13. Gastón Gordillo, "The Savage Outside of White Argentina," in *Rethinking Race in Modern Argentina*, ed. Paulina Alberto and Eduardo Elena (Cambridge: Cambridge University Press, 2016), 243.

14. *Memoria de la Dirección General de Inmigración, correspondiente al año 1913* (Buenos Aires: Talleres Gráficos del Ministerio de Agricultura, 1915), 54.

15. *Resumen estadístico del movimiento migratorio en la República Argentina, años 1857–1924* (Buenos Aires: Talleres gráficos del Ministerio de Agricultura de la Nación, 1925), 3; José C. Moya, *Cousins and Strangers: Spanish Immigrants in Buenos Aires, 1850-1930* (Berkeley: University of California Press, 1998), 56. In these same five decades, 2.6 million people left the country, but not all those who left were immigrants.

16. *Segundo Censo de la República Argentina, tomo II, Población* (Buenos Aires: Taller Tipográfico de la Penitenciaría Nacional, 1898), xviii; *Tercer censo nacional, tomo I, antecedentes y comentarios* (Buenos Aires: Talleres Gráficos de L. J. Rosso y Cía, 1916), 65. I first discussed these data in Benjamin Bryce, *To Belong in Buenos Aires: Germans, Argentines, and the Rise of a Pluralist Society* (Stanford, CA: Stanford University Press, 2018), 15.

17. Marilyn Lake and Henry Reynolds, *Drawing the Global Colour Line: White Men's Countries and the Question of Racial Equality* (Cambridge: Cambridge University Press, 2008).

18. Adam McKeown, *Melancholy Order: Asian Migration and the Globalization of Borders* (New York: Columbia University Press, 2008); Seema Sohi, *Echoes of Mutiny: Race, Surveillance and Indian Anticolonialism in North America* (Oxford: Oxford University Press, 2014); David C. Atkinson, *The Burden of White Supremacy: Containing Asian Migration in the British Empire and the United States* (Chapel Hill: University of North Carolina Press, 2017).

19. David Atkinson similarly charts out the global reverberations of the 1921 Emergency Quota Act and the 1924 National Origins Act passed by the United States Congress in "The International Consequences of American National Origins Quotas: The Australian Case," *Journal of American Studies* 50 (2016): 377–96.

20. Preexisting treaties and diplomatic concerns bound American and Canadian officials to seek this diplomatic solution, and Japan was eager to collaborate because Japanese officials worried that emigrant laborers' likely exclusion would harm the country's aspirations to join the nascent international order of civilized and industrialized nations. Atkinson, *Burden of White Supremacy*, 110; McKeown, *Melancholy Order*, 203; Eiichiro Azuma, *Between Two Empires: Race, History, and Transnationalism in Japanese America* (New York: Oxford University Press, 2005); Frederick Dickinson, "Toward a Global Perspective of the Great War: Japan and the Foundations of a Twentieth-Century World," *American Historical Review* 119

(2014): 1154–83; Sho Konishi, "The Emergence of an International Humanitarian Organization in Japan: The Tokugawa Origins of the Japanese Red Cross," *American Historical Review* 119 (2014): 1129–53.

21. Atkinson, *Burden of White Supremacy*, 134–41; Sarah Isabel Wallace, *Not Fit to Stay: Public Health Panics and South Asian Exclusion* (Vancouver: University of British Columbia Press, 2017), 12, 138.

22. Lee, "'Yellow Peril,'" 559. The US Commissioner General of Immigration Daniel Keefe stated that beginning in 1909, it was "the general policy of the Immigration Service to exclude Hindus." Quoted in Seema Sohi, "Race, Surveillance, and Indian Anticolonialism in the Transnational Western U.S.-Canadian Borderlands," *Journal of American History* 98 (2011), 426. In 1909, the United States excluded 331 Indian migrants and allowed entry to only 337. In 1911, only 517 of the 1,379 Indians to arrive at the country's border gained entry, and over the subsequent five years, fewer than six hundred Indians were admitted to the United States. Sohi, "Race, Surveillance, and Indian Anticolonialism," 426.

23. *Memoria de la Dirección General de Inmigración correspondiente al año 1913* (Buenos Aires: Talleres Gráficos del Ministerio de Agricultura, 1915), 54.

24. Jeffrey Lesser, *A Discontented Diaspora: Japanese Brazilians and the Meanings of Ethnic Militancy, 1960–1980* (Durham, NC: Duke University Press, 2007), 7. That initial shift from North America to Brazil was only the beginning, and 176,775 Japanese entered the main Brazilian port of Santos between 1908 and 1936. Jeffrey Lesser, *Immigration, Ethnicity, and National Identity in Brazil, 1808 to the Present* (New York: Cambridge University Press, 2013), 73.

25. Ayumi Takenaka, "The Japanese in Peru: History of Immigration, Settlement, and Racialization," *Latin American Perspectives* 31 (2004), 82. Unlike Brazil, Peru had a longer history of recruiting Japanese and Chinese contract laborers. Japanese laborers had begun migrating to Peru in the 1870s, and by 1918 there were, according to the Peruvian census, 9,891 Japanese in the country. Takenaka, "Japanese in Peru," 81; Toraji Irie and William Himel, "History of Japanese Migration to Peru, Part III [Conclusion]," *Hispanic American Historical Review* 32, no. 1 (1952): 73.

26. Daniel Masterson with Sayaka Funada-Classen, *The Japanese in Latin America* (Urbana: University of Illinois Press, 2004), 16.

27. McKeown, *Melancholy Order*, 202.

28. Bryce, *To Belong in Buenos Aires*; Sebastian Conrad, *Globalisation and the Nation in Imperial Germany* (Cambridge: Cambridge University Press, 2010); Lee, "'Yellow Peril.'"

29. W. L. R. Goetsch to Auswärtiges Amt, Berlin, February 18, 1908, R 901 30422, "Die Überwachung der Auswanderer aus Deutschland nach Argentinien, 1908," Bundesarchiv, Berlin.

30. Grace Peña Delgado, "Sexual Self: Morals Policing and the Expansion of the U.S. Immigration Bureau at America's Early Twentieth-Century Borders," in *Entangling Migration History: Borderlands and Transnationalism in the United States*

and Canada, ed. Benjamin Bryce and Alexander Freund (Gainesville: University Press of Florida, 2015), 100–119; Julia Rodriguez, "Inoculating against Barbarism? State Medicine and Immigrant Policy in Turn-of-the-Century Argentina," *Science in Context* 19 (2006): 357–80; Alexandra Minna Stern, "Buildings, Boundaries, and Blood: Medicalization and Nation-Building on the U.S.-Mexico Border," *Hispanic American Historical Review* 79 (1999): 41–81; Tobias Brinkmann, "'Travelling with Ballin': The Impact of American Immigration Policies on Jewish Transmigration within Central Europe, 1880–1914," *International Instituut voor Sociale Geschiedenis* 53 (2008): 459–84; Krista Maglen, "'In This Miserable Spot Called Quarantine': The Healthy and Unhealthy in Nineteenth Century Australian and Pacific Quarantine Stations," *Science in Context* 19 (2006): 317–36.

31. Carl Solberg, *Immigration and Nationalism: Argentina and Chile, 1890–1914* (Austin: University of Texas Press, 1970), 136.

32. Juan A. Alsina, *Memoria del Departamento General de Inmigración. Correspondiente al año 1893*, in Caja 831, Sección Asuntos Comerciales, Países Bajos–Mexico–Japón–Monaco, AMREC.

33. Alsina.

34. Letter from Juan Alsina to Ministerio de Relaciones Exteriores, November 26, 1903, Caja 831, Sección Asuntos Comerciales, Países Bajos–Mexico–Japón–Monaco, AMREC.

35. Letter from Juan Alsina.

36. Juan Alsina, *La inmigración en el primer siglo de la independencia* (Buenos Aires: Felipe S. Alsina, 1910), 203.

37. Alsina, 205–6.

38. Juan B. Alberdi, *Bases y puntos de partida para la organización política de la República Argentina* (Buenos Aires: "La Cultura Argentina," 1915), 15.

39. Alberdi, 89–96.

40. Alfredo Elías, "Restricciones para el inmigrado," *La Nación*, April 1, 1912, 7.

41. "Movimiento inmigratorio: Rechazo de los ceilaneses," *La Prensa*, August 23, 1912, 9.

42. "Movimiento inmigratorio."

43. "Die Einwanderung," *Argentinisches Tageblatt*, August 23, 1912, 2.

44. Newspaper clipping from *La Nación*, July 4, 1910, in 3.8.2 189, Document 3, National Archives of Japan, Tokyo (hereafter NAJ).

45. Newspaper clipping from *La Nación*, July 4, 1910.

46. *Memoria de la Dirección General de Inmigración, correspondiente al año 1913*, 54; *Memoria de la Dirección General de Inmigración, correspondiente a los años 1914–15 y resúmenes de los últimos diez años 1906–1915* (Buenos Aires: Talleres Gráficos del Ministerio de Agricultura, 1916), 49.

47. Letter from N. Okoshi, sub-director de la Sociedad Japonesa de la América Latina, to Señor Consul de la República Argnetina, Don Fieravanti-Chimenz, in

Tokio, October 16, 1913, Caja 1421, División Europa y Asia, Japón–Rumania–Santa Sede–Turquía, Año 1913, AMREC; see also Letter from Ferotake Hiroatto, Transoceanic Emigration Company, to Don Baldomero García Sagastume, August 16, 1905, Caja 904, Japón–México–Nicaragua–Noruega–Panamá–Países Bajos, Año 1905, AMREC.

48. Letter from Herbert Shepherd, Consul of H.I.M. of Japan in the Argentine Republic, to Legation of Japan, Rio de Janeiro, December 30, 1906, 3.8.2 189, Document 1, NAJ.

49. Letter from Alfonso de Laferrere, Cónsul General, Yokohama, to Señor Ministro de Relaciones Exteriores, August 25, 1903, Caja 831, Sección Asuntos Comerciales, Países Bajos–México–Japón–Monaco, 1903, AMREC.

50. Letter from Alfonso de Laferrere.

51. Letter from Juan Alsina to Ministerio de Relaciones Exteriores, November 26, 1903, Caja 831, Sección Asuntos Comerciales, Países Bajos–México–Japón–Monaco, 1903, AMREC.

52. Letter from Juan Alsina to Ministerio de Relaciones Exteriores.

53. Letter from Juan Alsina to Ministerio de Relaciones Exteriores.

54. Letter from Vice-Consul á Yokohama, Sosisanode Vincensiy [*sic*], to Estanislao S. Zeballos, August 1907, Caja 980, Sección Asuntos Comerciales, Japón–Persia–Dinamarca, Año 1907, AMREC.

55. Letter from Vice-Consul á Yokohama.

56. Bryce, "Undesirable Britons," 259–61.

57. Letter from Reginald Tower to Right Hon. Edward Grey Bart, June 27, 1912, "Gypsies,"

FO 369/440, TNA.

58. In all, 15,720 had come between 1857 and 1903. "Immigrants to Argentina from 1857 to 1913," Records of the Department of State Relating to Internal Affairs of Argentina, 1910–1929, reel 30, 835.50 Economic Matters, 835.55 Immigration, 835.56 Emigration. After the United States, Argentina was the second most common destination in the Americas for Ottoman subjects before the First World War. *Fourteenth Census of the United States Taken in the Year 1920, vol. II. Population* (Washington, DC: Government Printing Office, 1922), 693. Between 1894 and 1913, 53,127 "Turks" and "Syrians" entered Brazil, 87 percent of whom came after 1904. Lesser, *Immigration, Ethnicity, and National Identity in Brazil*, 124.

59. The Ottoman consul general in Buenos Aires estimated in 1912 that 80 percent of the Ottoman subjects in the city were Christians, 15 percent were Muslims, and 5 percent were Jews. Steven Hyland, *More Argentine than You: Arabic-Speaking Immigrants in Argentina* (Albuquerque, New Mexico: University of New Mexico Press, 2017), 44; According to the annual report of the Dirección General de Inmigración, 78 percent of the "Syrian" immigrants to enter Argentina between 1876 and 1909 were "Catholic." The state was most likely referring to all Ottoman

subjects and those who were of some Christian denomination. Juan Alsina, *Inmigración en el año 1909* (Buenos Aires, 1910). Alongside Maronites, there was a noticeable Armenian contingent. Between 1900 and 1923, 2,221 Armenians arrived in Argentina. Ignacio Klich and Jeffrey Lesser, "Introduction: 'Turco' Immigrants in Latin America," *Americas* 53 (1996): 4.

60. Letter from Reginald Tower to Argentine Ministro Ernesto Bosch, January 30, 1912, FO 369/439—1912, TNA.

61. Bryce, "Undesirable Britons," 248.

62. "Noticias Diplomáticas: Inmigración hindú," *La Nación*, February 2, 1912, 10.

63. Alsina, *La inmigración en el primer siglo*, 167–69.

64. Reginald Tower, "The Sikhs," *Standard*, July 25, 1912, 13.

65. Letter from Reginald Toward to Sir Edward Grey Bart, July 4, 1912, FO 369/439—1912, TNA.

66. Letter from Reginald Tower to Sir Edward Grey Bart, June 25, 1912, FO 369/439—1912, TNA.

67. Bryce, "Undesirable Britons," 257.

68. "La inmigración asiática. Juicios desfavorables a su respecto. Circular de la dirección de inmigración," *La Nación*, June 24, 1912, 9.

69. "La inmigración asiática."

70. "La selección de los inmigrantes. Actitud de la Dirección de Inmigración," *La Prensa*, June 24, 1912, 7.

71. "La inmigración asiática," *La Nación*, June 25, 1912, 9.

72. *Resumen estadístico, 1857–1924*, 82.

73. Ronald Newton, *German Buenos Aires, 1900–1933: Social Change and Cultural* (Austin: University of Texas Press, 1977), 15; D. C. M. Platt, "Canada and Argentina: The first preference of the British investor, 1904–14," *Journal of Imperial and Commonwealth History* 13, no. 3 (1985): 77–92; Jeremy Adelman, *Frontier Development: Land, Labour, and Capital on the Wheatlands of Argentina and Canada, 1890–1914* (Oxford: Clarendon Press, 1994), 4; David Rock, *The British in Argentina: Commerce, Settlers and Power, 1800-2000* (Cham, Switzerland: Palgrave Macmillan, 2019).

74. "Emigration of Indians (Sikhs from the Punjab) to the Argentine Republic," Bengal Proceedings, India Office Records, P/8924, no. 6213-56, August 15, 1912, 3.

75. Letter from Reginald Tower to Right Hon. Edward Grey Bart, June 27, 1912, "Gypsies,"

FO 369/440, TNA.

76. "La inmigración gitana: Sus antecedentes: Nota de la dirección de inmigración," *La Prensa*, July 22, 1912, 9.

77. "La inmigración gitana."

78. "Die Zigeunereinwanderung," *Argentinisches Tageblatt*, July 23, 1912, 2.

79. *Censo general de población, edificación, comercio é industrias de la ciudad de Buenos Aires, capital federal de la República Argentina, tomo I* (Buenos Aires: Compañía sud-americana de billetes de banco, 1910), 17.

80. Dirección General de Inmigración, Ministerio de Agricultura, *Inmigración en el año 1912* (Buenos Aires), 1–2.

81. "Residencia de extranjeros. Proyecto de ley," August 28, 1916, *Diario de sesiones de la Cámara de Diputados. Tomo II, 1916* (Buenos Aires: Talleres Gráficos de L. J. Rosso y Cía, 1916), 1650.

82. Bryce, *To Belong in Buenos Aires*, 18–19, 80.

83. "Indian Immigration," *Standard*, January 31, 1912, 6.

84. The meaning of the term "Nap" is unclear, but it may refer to Southern Italians and apply the label of Neapolitan (*napolitano* or *napoletano* in Spanish and Italian) to the whole group.

85. "Indian Immigration," *Standard*, January 31, 1912, 6.

86. "Indian Immigration."

87. Letter from R. Ritchie, Under Secretary of State, Foreign Office, to the India Office, June 22, 1912, FO 369/439—1912, TNA; Letter from Reginald Tower to Sir Edward Grey Bart, June 13, 1912, FO 369/439—1912, TNA.

88. M. A. Farias, "Indian Immigration in Argentina," *Buenos Aires Herald*, April 9, 1912, 7.

89. "Hindoo Immigrants," *Standard*, June 26, 1912, 3.

90. "Hindoo Immigrants."

91. "Our 'Poor Indians,'" *Buenos Aires Herald*, June 25, 1912, 4.

92. Letter from Reginald Tower to Sir Edward Grey Bart, February 3, 1912, FO 369/439—1912, TNA.

93. "TOWER, Sir Reginald (Thomas)," *Who Was Who*, A & C Black, an imprint of Bloomsbury Publishing, 1920–2016; online ed., Oxford University Press, April 2014, accessed June 21, 2017, http://www.ukwhoswho.com/view/article/oupww/whowaswho/U218253.

94. "Indo-Germanic" is a synonym for "Indo-European" although it has largely fallen out of use in English.

95. "Indian Immigration," *Standard*, February 3, 1912, 10.

96. "Editor's Table: Hindoo Immigrants," *Standard*, June 25, 1912, 3.

97. Matthew Frye Jacobson, *Whiteness of a Different Color: European Immigrants and the Alchemy of Race* (Cambridge, MA: Harvard University Press, 1998), 2.

98. People in Canada at the turn of the twentieth century made similar climactic arguments to talk about the racial unsuitability of both South Asian and African American or Afro-Caribbean migrants. See Wallace, *Not Fit to Stay*, 70; Robin Winks, *The Blacks in Canada* (Montreal: McGill-Queen's University Press, 1997), 296, 312.

99. "Hindoo Immigrants," *Standard*, June 26, 1912, 3.

100. "Hindoo Immigrants."

101. "Editor's Table: Hindu Immigrants," *Standard*, July 6, 1912, 3.

102. "Editor's Table: Hindu Immigrants."

103. "Editor's Table: Hindu Immigrants."

104. Bryce, "Undesirable Britons," 248, 269.

105. Rodriguez, "Inoculating against Barbarism?"; Stern, "Buildings, Boundaries, and Blood"; Peña Delgado, "Sexual Self"; Brinkmann, "'Travelling with Ballin'"; Maglen, "'In This Miserable Spot.'"

CHAPTER TWO. INTERSECTIONS, BARRIERS, AND BORDERS IN GREGORIO TITIRIKU'S REPUBLIC OF QULLASUYU

1. "Mariano Qhispi, Estación de la Policía, La Paz, August 1925," Folio 1, 3, Fondo Melitón Gallardo (FPMG).

2. "Mariano Qhispi."

3. Waskar Ari, "Dos repúblicas: Las plazas de Ambana y Achacachi," 7, Archivo Amuyasiñataki.

4. Eugenio Gómez, *Bautista Saavedra* (La Paz: Biblioteca del Sesquicentenario, 1975), 240.

5. Alcides Arguedas, *Pueblo Enfermo* (Santiago de Chile: Ercilla, 1937), 55.

6. Arguedas, 55–155.

7. Silvia Rivera Cusicanqui, *Oprimidos pero no vencidos, luchas del campesinado Aymara y Qhechwa de Bolivia 1900–1980* (La Paz: Hisbol, 1984), 3–20; THOA, *El indio Santos MarkaT'ula: Cacique principal de los Ayllus de Qallapa y Apoderado General de las comunidades originarias de la República* (La Paz: Aruwiri, 1984), 13–25.

8. Diane M. Nelson, *A Finger in the Wound: Body Politics in Quincentennial Guatemala* (Durham, NC: Duke University Press, 1999), 249.

9. "Gregorio Titiriku, Marzo 14, 1945," Fondo 1, 45 Archivo Andrés Jachakollo y Matilde Colque (APAJMC); see also Benedict Anderson, *Imagined Communities* (London: Verso, 1991).

10. Andrés Jach'aqulu,"El Kollasuyu y Gregorio Titiriku," (Memoir, 1977), Oruro APAJMAC, 2, 7/8.

11. Gregorio Titiriku's petition to the Minister of Education, February 27, 1937, Folio 1, 3, Fondo Gregorio Titiriku y Rosa Ramos (FPGTRR).

12. Fernando Huanacuni, *Filosofía, políticas, estrategias y experiencias regionales* (La Paz, 2010), 37–95.

13. Jach'aqulu, "El Kollasuyu y Gregorio Titiriku," 7/9. See also Honorable Alcaldía Municipal de La Paz (HAM), *Cuarto Centenario* (La Paz: HAM, 1948), 480–620.

14. Ezequiel Carmona, "El tiempo de Peñaranda, (Memoir, 1975)," Fondo 3, 3–5, Archivo Privado de Historia Oral de Nabil Saavedra (APHONS).

15. "Expediente de demanda del Ayllu Condo y comunidad Palqa contra la hacienda Luwichutu, 1926–1934," Fondo 1920–1945, 3–17, Fondo Privado de Agapito Ponce.

16. Rosa Ramos, "Así le he ayudado," (Memoir, 1979) 11–12, APHOMI.

17. Maria Titiriku, "Gregorio Titiriku," (Memoir, 1979), 9–12.

18. Andrés Jach'aqullu, "Sobre Gregorio Titiriku," Fondo 2, 3–6, APAJMC.

19. *El hombre libre*, February 23, 1926, 3–4; Rosa Ramos, "Asi le he ayudado" (Memoir, 1979), Folio 1, 12, APHOA.

20. Silvia Rivera Cusicanqui and Zulema Lehm Ardaya, *Los artesanos libertarios y la ética del trabajo* (La Paz: Ediciones del THOA, 1988), 51–63; *El hombre libre*, February 23, 1926, 3–4.

21. Jach'aqulu, "El Kollasuyu y Gregorio Titiriku," 80–120.

22. Juan Arias, "Memorias de Florencia Burgoa," Fondo 5, 6–8, APHOA.

23. Sinclair Thomson, "La cuestión India en Bolivia a comienzos del siglo: El caso de Manuel Rigoberto Paredes," *Autodeterminación* 4 (1988): 83–116.

24. Silvia Rivera Cusicanqui, *Oprimidos pero no vencidos, luchas del campesina-do Aymara y Qhechwa de Bolivia 1900–1980* (La Paz: Hisbol, 1984), 3–20; THOA, *El indio Santos MarkaT'ula*, 13–25.

25. Gómez, *Bautista Saavedra*, 240.

26. *El Diario*, 5, February 11, 1924; *El Diario*, 7, September 23, 1925. See also Rivera Cusicanqui and Lehm Ardaya, *Artesanos libertarios*, 72–173.

27. Rivera Cusicanqui and Lehm Ardaya, *Artesanos libertarios*, 153–198.

28. Rosa Ramos, "Así le he ayudado," (Memoir, 1979), Folio 1, 9, APHOA.

29. Arguedas, *Pueblo Enfermo*, 55–65.

30. Rossana Barragan, "Entre polleras, lliqllas y ñañacas: Los mestizos y la emergencia de la tercera república," in *Etnicidad economía y simbolismo en los Andes*, ed. Silvia Arze, Rossana Barragán, Laura Escobari, and Ximena Medinaceli (La Paz: Hisbol-IFEA, 1992) 85–127.

31. Fernando Olmos, "Oruro y el progreso," *La Trinchera*, February 18, 1938, 5–6, folio 3, APAJMC.

32. Arguedas, *Pueblo Enfermo*, 55.

33. "Demanda por violación y calumnias de José Mamani contra Carlos Rein-aga, 1927–1935," Folio 3, 37–41, Archivo Judicial de la Provincia Dalence.

34. "Declaración de Antonio García en la Estación de Policía Camacho," Folio 3, 2, Fondo Privado de los Hermanos Espirituales (FPHE).

35. "Demanda por violación y calumnias."

36. See Richard Graham, *The Idea of Race in Latin America 1870–1945* (Aus-tin: University of Texas Press, 1990); Marisol De la Cadena, *Indigenous Mestizos: The Politics of Race and Culture in Cuzco 1921–1991* (Durham, NC: Duke Univer-sity Press, 2000); Laura Gotkowitz, *Histories of Race and Racism: The Andes and Mesoamerica from Colonial Times to the Present* (Durham, NC: Duke University Press, 2011).

37. "Interesante petición de Indígenas," *La República*, October 25, 1925, 3.

38. René Danilo Arze, *Guerras y conflictos sociales. El caso rural boliviano duran-te la campaña del Chaco* (La Paz: Ceres, 1987), 15–45. See also Forrest Hylton, "El

Federalismo Insurgente: Una aproximación a Juan Lero, los comunarios y la guerra federal," *T'inkasos* 7, no. 16 (2004): 99–118.

39. Herbert Klein, *Bolivia: The Evolution of a Multiethnic Society* (New York: Oxford University Press, 1992).

40. Carlos Medinaceli, *La Chaskañawi* (La Paz: Fundación Patiño, 1947), 15–98.

41. Rivera Cusicanqui and Lehm Ardaya, *Artesanos libertarios*, 5–75. Leandro Condori Chura y Esteban Ticona Alejo, *El escribano de los Caciques apoderados-kasikinakan purirarunakan qillqiripa* (La Paz: Hisbol/THOA, 1992), 22–55. Carlos Mamani, *Taraqu*, Masacre, Guerra y Renovacion en la biografia de Eduardo nina Quispi (La Paz: Aruwiyiri, 1991), 43–45 and 127–134.

42. Melitón Gallardo, "*Chutas y Cholos*, (Memoir, 1972), 20–23, APHONS; Waskar Ari, *Apuntes para una perspectiva comparativa de los ch'utas en La Paz y Sucre* (La Paz: APHOA, 1997), 3–8.

43. Guillermo Lora, *Formación de la clase obrera boliviana* (La Paz: Masas, 1980), 15–55.

44. Rivera Cusicanqui and Lehm Ardaya, *Artesanos libertarios*, 21–113.

45. Michael Aronna, *"Pueblos Enfermos": The Discourse of Illness in the Turn of the Century Spanish and Latin America Essay* (Chapel Hill: University of North Carolina Press, 1999): 15–108.

46. Arguedas, *Pueblo Enfermo*, 58; Josefa Salmón *El espejo indigenista en Bolivia: 1900—1956* (La Paz: Plural, 1997), 63–73.

47. Franz Tamayo, *Obras escogidas* (Caracas: Biblioteca Ayacucho, 1979), 3–105.

48. "Acta de buena conducta entre Gregorio Titiriku y Jacinto Díaz Quispe y Pedro Conde Iturri, 1934," Fondo 1, 3–5, FPGTRR.

49. "Acta de buena conducta."

50. Titiriku, "Gregorio Titiriku," 5–7.

51. Porfirio Díaz Machicao, *Historia de Bolivia: Saavedra, 1920–1925* (La Paz: Don Bosco, 1954), 56–80.

52. Machicao, 45–190.

53. "Carta de Gregorio Titiriku a Honorato Rocha, Enero 14, 1928," Fondo 2, Archivo Privado de Ezequiel Orieta (APEO).

54. Titiriku, "Gregorio Titiriku," 5–7.

55. Jach'aqullu, "El Kollasuyu," APAJMC 4–8; Roberto Choque and Esteban Ticona, *Jesús de Machaqa: Sublevación y Masacre de 1921* (La Paz: CIPCA, CEDOIN, 1996), 21–35.

56. Julian Ugarte, "Los antiguos caminantes," (Memoir, 1979), Folio 2, 5, APHOMI.

57. Juan Iquiapaza, "Titiriku y su camino," (testimony, 1969), 5; Folio 3, Fondo Privado de la Familia Quyu.

58. Iquiapaza, 3.

59. Xavier Albo, "Suma Qamanha, el buen convivir," *Revista Obets* no. 4 (2009): 25–40.

60. "Acta de posesión del Alcalde Particular Carlos Condori, Septiembre 12, 1936," Fondo 1, 1, FPHE.

61. Julio Salles,"El sufrimiento de los Alcaldes Particulares" (Testimony, 1964), Fondo Privado de Francisco Rivera (FPFR), 3–6.

62. "Gregorio Titiriku a Felix Choque, Mayo 22, 1937," Fondo 2, APPM.

63. "Gregorio Titiriku a Andrés Jachakollo, Marzo 21, 1941," Fondo 1, 2, Fondo Privado de Tomás Quevedo (FPTQ).

64. "Acta de detención de Mariano Qhispi, Estación de la Policía, La Paz, August 1925," 1, 3, FPMG.

65. "Denuncia de la propietaria de la hacienda Churumatas," December 15, 1939, Folio 3, FPFR.

66. "Informe del Corregidor Don Pedro Molle, Noviembre 1947," Folio 1, 3, Fondo Privado de Lucas Marka.

67. "Informe del Corregidor Don Pedro Molle," 2.

68. Julian Ugarte, Los Antiguos caminantes,"(Memoir, 1979), Folio2, APHOMI.

69. Informe del Corregidor, Febrero 15, 1944, Folio 7, 13, Archivo Judicial de Ambaná.

70. Titiriku, "Gregorio Titiriku," 8–9.

71. "Sumario informativo contra Carlos Rivera y Timoteo Sotomayor por abusos denunciados," folio 3, 2–3, Fondo Privado de Hilarión Cuellar.

72. "Sumario informativo," 4.

73. "Sumario informativo," 1–2.

74. "Sumario informativo," 5.

75. "Sumario informativo."

76. "Sumario informativo," 6.

77. "Declaración de Antonio García en la Estación de Policía Camacho," 3, 2, FPHE.

78. "Declaración de Antonio García," 2–3.

79. Lorenzo Titiriku, *Historia de la llegada de la Iglesia Evangélica Metodista en Bolivia: El caso del altiplano* (Ancoraimes, La Paz: IEMB, 1984), 3–9; Titiriku, "Gregorio Titiriku," 5–13.

80. "Carta de Gregorio Titiriku a Lorenzo Titiriku, Julio 1, 1935," Fondo 1, 3, FPTQ.

81. Brooke Larsen, "Warisata: A Historical Footnote," *ReVista: Harvard Review of Latin America* 11, no. 1 (2011), 65–67.

82. Elizardo Perez, *Warisata, la escuela Ayllu* (Buenos Aires: Burillo, 1962), 50–120.

83. "Carta de Gregorio Titiriku a Mateo Apaza, Febrero 25, 1938," 33, Fondo 4, APTQ; Adolfo Velasco, *La escuela indígenal de Warisata* (México: Departamento de *Asuntos indígenas*, 1940), 1–69.

84. Velasco, *La escuela indígenal*, 10–45.

85. Perez, *Warisata*, 334–401.

86. "Carta de Gregorio Titiriku a Isidro Mullisaca, Abril 14, 1939," Fondo 1, 1, APEO.

87. "Carta y listas de Alcaldes, de Gregorio Titiriku a Manuel Iquiapaza, Junio 6, 1944," Fondo 1, 7, APEO.

88. "Carta de Gregorio Titiriku a Andrés Jachaqullu, Enero, 3, 1941," Fondo 1, 2, APEO.

89. "Carta de Gregorio Titiriku a Toribio Miranda, Septiembre 1, 1936," Fondo 2, 12, APTQ.

90. Velasco, *La escuela indígenal*, 25–67; Pérez, *Warisata*, 21–220.

91. Roberto Choque, Vitaliano Soria, Humberto Mamani, Esteban Ticona, and Ramón Conde. *Educación indígena: Ciudadanía ó colonización* (La Paz: HISBOL, 1992), 23–75.

92. "Carta de Toribio Miranda a Lucas Marka, Marzo 6, 1937," Fondo 2, 13–15, APAJMC.

93. "Carta de Toribio Miranda," 3.

94. "Carta de Toribio Miranda," 1.

95. Nabil Saavedra, "Lista de Alcaldes Mayores Particulares," 10–35, FPMG.

CHAPTER THREE. RACE AND POLITICAL RIGHTS

This chapter is a revised and abbreviated version of Lara Putnam, "Citizenship from the Margins: Vernacular Theories of Rights and the State from the Interwar Caribbean," *Journal of British Studies* 53, no. 1 (2014): 162–91. Reprinted with permission.

1. Lara Putnam, *Radical Moves: Caribbean Migrants and the Politics of Race in the Jazz Age* (Chapel Hill: University of North Carolina Press, 2013), ch. 4; Lara Putnam, "Circum-Atlantic Print Circuits and Internationalism from the Peripheries in the Interwar Era," in *Print Culture Histories beyond the Metropolis*, ed. James Connolly (Toronto: University of Toronto Press, 2016).

2. On the subsequent struggle within the United Kingdom by the men and women of this generation of migrants to claim full political belonging, see Kennetta Hammond Perry, *London is the Place for Me: Black Britons, Citizenship and the Politics of Race* (New York: Oxford University Press, 2015). Over a half century later, a new wave of anti-immigrant politicking would generate tragedies and scandal. From 2013 to 2018 some surviving members of this generation—born British subjects within British colonies—were deprived of legal benefits, or even wrongly deported from the United Kingdom, due to difficulty presenting now-requisite documentation, some of which, including landing cards, had been recently destroyed by the Home Office itself. See Amelia Gentleman, *The Windrush Betrayal: Exposing the Hostile Environment* (London: Guardian Books, 2019).

3. The *Central American Express* (Bocas del Toro) reported a circulation of 1,700 in 1917; the *West Indian* (St. George's, Grenada) 1,600 in 1922; the *Panama Tribune* 3,500 in 1932; Marcus Garvey's *Blackman* (Kingston, Jamaica) 2,000 in 1930.

4. Putnam, *Radical Moves*, 128–29; Lara Putnam, "Provincializing Harlem: The 'Negro Metropolis' as Northern Frontier of an Interconnected Greater Caribbean," *Modernism/modernity* 20, no. 3 (September 2013): 469–84.

5. This map reports foreign-born British West Indians based on census data. Numbers for multigenerational community size reflect census data where available and contemporary estimates where it is not. For sources, see Putnam, "Citizenship from the Margins," 169, fn 20.

6. The United States and Cuba were the two partial exceptions to the pattern of explicit anti-Black bans: in each case, draconian action against Black immigrants was carried out under new restrictive legislation that did not mention the Black race in particular. See Putnam, *Radical Moves*, 88–104; Lara Putnam, "The Making and Unmaking of the Circum-Caribbean Migratory Sphere: Mobility, Sex across Boundaries, and Collective Destinies, 1840–1940," in *Migrants and Migration in Modern North America: Cross-Border Lives, Labor Markets, and Politics in Canada, the Caribbean, Mexico, and the United States*, ed. Dirk Hoerder and Nora Faires (Durham, NC: Duke University Press, 2011), 99–128.

7. See Daniel Gorman, *Imperial Citizenship: Empire and the Question of Belonging* (Manchester, UK: Manchester University Press, 2006), 19–24.

8. *Minutes of Proceedings of the Imperial Conference, 1911* (London, 1911), 256, accessed October 31, 2013, http://www.archive.org/details/1911minutesof pro00impeuoft.

9. "Lord Plunket, sometime Governor of New Zealand," in *British Citizenship: A discussion initiated by E. B. Sargant*, and reprinted by permission from the *Journal of the Royal Colonial Institute* ("United Empire") (New York, Bombay, and Calcutta, 1912), 11, accessed October 31, 2013, http://www.archive.org/stream/ britishcitizensh00sarguoft. See discussion in Gorman, *Imperial Citizenship*, 19–24.

10. "Walter Hely-Hutchinson, sometime Governor of Windward Islands, Natal, and Cape Colony," in *British Citizenship*, 18–19.

11. E. B. Sargant, *British Citizenship*, 44.

12. For example, "Scenes and Sights in Metropolis by Night," *Daily Gleaner* (Kingston, Jamaica), September 22, 1922, 3; "Round the Town," *Weekly Guardian* (Port of Spain), March 27, 1920, 1.

13. Letter to Editors from "The Lagoon," *Central American Express*, September 29, 1917, n.p.

14. "Estrada," *Searchlight* (Limón, Costa Rica), April 12, 1930, 1.

15. Andreas Fahrmier, *Citizenship: The Rise and Fall of a Modern Concept* (New Haven, CT: Yale University Press, 2008); Andreas Wimmer and Nina Glick Schiller, "Methodological Nationalism and Beyond: Nation-state Building, Migration and the Social Sciences," *Global Networks* 2, no. 4 (2002): 301–34.

16. Letter from J. A. Phillips, Balboa Heights, CZ to Mallet, January 28, 1919, TNA, Foreign Office Series 288/200.

17. "Emigration of Jamaicans to U.S. Stopped," *Daily Gleaner*, June 14, 1924, 1. See Lara Putnam, "Unspoken Exclusions: Race, Nation, and Empire in the Immigration Restrictions of the 1920s in North America and the Greater Caribbean," in *Workers across the Americas: The Transnational Turn in Labor History*, ed. Leon Fink (New York: Oxford University Press, 2011), 267–93.

18. United States, Bureau of Immigration, *Annual Report of the Commissioner General of Immigration to the Secretary of Labor for the fiscal year ended . . . June 30, 1925* (Washington, DC, 1925) 62, 151. See Lara Putnam, "The Ties Allowed to Bind: Kinship Legalities and Migration Restriction in the Interwar Americas," *International Labor and Working-Class History* 83 (Spring 2013): 191–209.

19. See Lara Putnam, "'Nothing Matters but Color': Transnational Circuits, the Interwar Caribbean, and the Black International," in *From Toussaint to Tupac: The Black International since the Age of Revolution*, ed. Michael O. West, William G. Martin, and Fanon Che Wilkins (Chapel Hill: University of North Carolina Press, 2009), 107–29; Lara Putnam, "Sidney Adolphus Young," in *Dictionary of Caribbean and Afro-Latin American Biography*, ed. Franklin W. Knight and Henry Louis Gates Jr. (Oxford: Oxford University Press, 2016); Putnam, *Radical Moves*, 135, 142–45, 200–202.

20. Despatch from Crosby, Panama, November 28, 1932, TNA, CO 318/408/3. See Lara Putnam, "Eventually Alien: The Multigenerational Saga of British West Indians in Central America and Beyond, 1880–1940," in *Blacks and Blackness in Central America: Between Race and Place*, ed. Lowell Gudmundson and Justin Wolfe (Durham, NC: Duke University Press, 2010), 288–96.

21. Editorial, "The Future of the Boy Scouts," *Panama Tribune*, October 30,1932, 8.

22. Clifford Bolt, "Making Good Citizens," *Panama Tribune*, October 16, 1932, 15. For more on scouting in interwar Panama, see Lara Putnam, "To Study the Fragments/Whole: Microhistory and the Atlantic World," *Journal of Social History* 39, no. 3 (Spring 2006): 615–30.

23. "Why such animosity?", *Searchlight*, August 22, 1931, 1.

24. See Diana Senior Angulo, "La incorporación social en Costa Rica de la población afrocostarricense durante el siglo XX, 1927–1963" (tesis de maestría, Universidad de Costa Rica, 2007); Putnam, "Eventually Alien," 296–99.

25. "Unjust discrimination at Siquirres," *Searchlight*, June 28, 1930, 1.

26. See Senior Angulo, "Incorporación social." Dual citizenship would not be legally recognized in Costa Rica until the 1990s.

27. For instance, none of the participants in the 1912 debate over British citizenship, cited above, disputed this. See also discussion in Putnam, *Radical Moves*, 41–42, 147.

28. Editorial, "Their Point of View," *Daily Gleaner*, October 20, 1921, 6.

29. "James Graham handed to Cuban Police and British Protection," *Searchlight*, August 9, 1930, 3.

30. "British Protection," *Searchlight*, February 1, 1930, 2.

31. "James Graham handed to Cuban Police and British Protection," *Searchlight*, August 9, 1930, 3.

32. "West Indian Labourers in the Republics: A Practical Issue," *Daily Gleaner*, September 5, 1924, 3.

33. Letter to the Editor, "Correspondence: The Question of Loyalty and Patriotism," *Panama American*, January 9, 1927, West Indian page.

34. F. A. Hoyos, "Inniss and Wickham," in *Our Common Heritage* (Bridgetown, Barbados, 1953), 142–47; Keith Hunte, "The Struggle for Political Democracy: Charles Duncan O'Neal and the Democratic League," in *The Empowering Impulse: The Nationalist Tradition of Barbados*, ed. Glenford Howe and Don Marshall (Mona, Jamaica: University Press of the West Indies, 2001), 133–48.

35. "The Democratic League, Its Policy and Creed," *Weekly Herald* (Bridgetown, Barbados), March 28, 1925, 4.

36. Letter to Editor, "Some Phases in Our Politics," *Weekly Herald*, May 30, 1925, 3.

37. "The Bell Has Struck in Barbados," *West Indian*, February 9, 1930, 4.

38. See also Clennell Wickham, "The Problem of the Distribution of the World's Peoples," *Weekly Herald*, March 14, 1925, 4.

39. "Trinidad Protests against Venezuela Ban on West Indians," *Daily Gleaner*, October 14, 1930, 10. See Putnam, *Radical Moves*, 206–7.

40. Sahadeo Basdeo, "Indian Participation in Labour Politics in Trinidad, 1919–1939," *Caribbean Quarterly* 32, no. 3/4, (1986): 50–65; Kelvin Singh, "Conflict and Collaboration: Tradition and Modernizing Indo-Trinidadian Elites (1917–1956)," *New West Indian Guide* 70, no. 3/4 (1996): 229–53.

41. Petition enclosed in letter from Governor, Trinidad, to Ormsby-Gore, May 15, 1937, TNA, CO 318/425/15.

42. Prefatory note by editors of "United Empire" in *British Citizenship*, 8.

43. "Trinidad protests Against Venezuela Ban on West Indians," *Daily Gleaner*, October 14,1930, 10.

44. "West Indian Students Protest Color Bar," *Panama Tribune*, December 29, 1929, 5.

45. Harold Moody, "Communications," *Journal of Negro History* 18 (1933): 92–99, quotes 97, 98. See David Killingray, "'A Good West Indian, a Good African, and, in Short, a Good Britisher': Black and British in a Colour-Conscious Empire, 1760–1950," *Journal of Imperial and Commonwealth History* 36, no. 3 (2008): 372.

46. "Color Prejudice in London Again Bitterly Denounced," *Panama Tribune*, December 4,1932, 3.

47. Harvey Neptune, *Caliban and the Yankees: Trinidad and the United States Occupation* (Chapel Hill: University of North Carolina Press, 2007).

48. Malcolm J. Proudfoot, *Population Movements in the Caribbean* (Port of Spain, 1950), 17; Cindy Hahamovitch, *No Man's Land: Jamaican Guestworkers in America and the Global History of Deportable Labor* (Princeton, NJ: Princeton University Press, 2011), 22–85.

49. Sonya Rose, *Which People's War? National Identity and Citizenship in Britain, 1939-1945* (Oxford: Oxford University Press, 2003), 245.

50. Hahamovitch, *No Man's Land*, 86–109.

51. T. H. Marshall, "Citizenship and Social Class," in *Sociology at the Crossroads and Other Essays* (Chicago: University of Chicago Press, 1963), 67–127.

52. Randall Hansen, *Citizenship and Immigration in Post-War Britain: The Institutional Origins of a Multicultural Nation* (Oxford: Oxford University Press, 2000), quotes 53; see also 17, 35. See Paul Foot, *Immigration and Race in British Politics* (New York: Penguin, 1965); Kathleen Paul, *Whitewashing Britain: Race and Citizenship in the Postwar Era* (Ithaca, NY: Cornell University Press, 1997), 9–24; Rieko Karatani, *Defining British Citizenship: Empire, Commonwealth and Modern Britain* (London: Routledge, 2003), 106–43.

53. For example, "The Reception," *Daily Gleaner*, June 24, 1948, 8; "So This Is England? High Cost of Living Shocks W. I. Job-Seekers," *Daily Gleaner*, June 29, 1948, 1; "Disillusionment," *Daily Gleaner*, July 28, 1948, 8.

54. Carole Boyce Davies, *Left of Karl Marx: The Political Life of Black Communist Claudia Jones* (Durham, NC: Duke University Press, 2008).

55. Salisbury (Conservative Leader of House of Lords), 1954, as quoted in Hansen, *Citizenship and Immigration*, 70; see also 67.

56. Hannah Arendt, "We Refugees," *Menorah Journal* 31 (1943), reprinted in *Altogether Elsewhere: Writers on Exile*, ed. Marc Robinson (Boston: Harvest Books, 1996), 118–19.

57. Hannah Arendt, *The Burden of Our Time* (London: Kecker & Warburg, 1951), 290.

58. On Arendt and race, see Norma Claire Moruzzi, *Speaking through the Mask: Hannah Arendt and the Politics of Social Identity* (Ithaca, NY: Cornell University Press, 2000), 86–113; Kathryn Gines, "Race-Thinking and Racism in Hannah Arendt's *The Origins of Totalitarianism*," in *Hannah Arendt and the Uses of History: Imperialism, Nation, Race, and Genocide*, ed. Richard H. King and Dan Stone (Oxford: Berghahn Books, 2007), 38–53.

59. Claudia Jones, "The Caribbean Community in Britain," in *Black Society in the New World*, ed. Richard Frucht (New York, 1971), 238, orig. pub. *Freedomways Magazine* 4, no. 3 (1964); Foot, *Immigration and Race*.

60. Paul, *Whitewashing Britain*, 181–85; Karatani, *Defining British Citizenship*, 128–33; R. A. Huttenback, "The British Empire as a 'White Man's Country': Racial Attitudes and Immigration Legislation in the Colonies of White Settlement,"

Journal of British Studies 13, no. 1 (1973): 108-37; Radhika Mongia, "Race, Nationality, Mobility: History of the Passport," *Public Culture* 11, no. 3 (1999): 527-55; Marilyn Lake and Henry Reynolds, *Drawing the Global Colour Line: White Men's Countries and the International Challenge of Racial Equality* (Cambridge: Cambridge Univeristy Press, 2008).

61. *British Citizenship*, 44.

62. Rose, *Which People's War*, 14–15.

CHAPTER FOUR: CROSSING THE BORDER AT THE PRIMER CONGRESO INDIGENISTA INTERAMERICANO, 1940

1. See Alexandra Minna Stern, "Buildings, Boundaries, and Blood: Medicalization and Nation-Building on the U.S.-Mexico Border, 1910–1930," *Hispanic American Historical Review* 79, no. 1 (February 1999): 41–81; Grace Peña Delgado, "Morals Policing and the Expansion of the U.S. Immigration Bureau at America's Early Twentieth-Century Borders," in *Entangling Migration History: Borderlands and Transnationalism in the United States and Canada*, ed. Benjamin Bryce and Alexander Freund (Gainesville: University of Florida Press, 2015), 100–119.

2. See José Vasconcelos, *The Cosmic Race: A Bilingual Edition*, trans. Didier T. Jaén (Baltimore: John Hopkins University Press, 1979); Alexander Dawson, "From Models for the Nation to Model Citizens: Indigenismo and the 'Revindication' of the Mexican Indian, 1920–40," *Journal of Latin American Studies* 30, no. 2 (May 1998): 279–308; Alan Knight, "Racism, Revolution, and Indigenismo: Mexico, 1910–1940," in *The Idea of Race in Latin America*, ed. Richard Graham (Austin: University of Texas Press, 1990), 71–113; Henri Favre, *El Indigenismo* (Mexico City: FCE, 1998); Eva Sanz Jara, *Los indios de la nación. Los Indígenas en los escritos de intelectuales y políticos del México independiente* (Mexico City: Iberoamericana, 2011).

3. The term "indigenismo" speaks to a series of national and Pan-American movements of government bureaucrats, educators, social scientists, artists, and others who advocated policies and practices that advanced the interests of indigenous peoples. These movements were mostly paternalistic and not made up of individuals who identified as indigenous. These movements also tended to be nationalist inasmuch as they generally embraced the incorporation of indigenous peoples into the nation rather than self-determination. See Alexander Dawson, *Indian and Nation in Revolutionary Mexico* (Tucson: University of Arizona Press, 2004).

4. See Alexander S. Dawson, "'Wild Indians,' 'Mexican Gentlemen,' and the Lessons Learned in the Casa del Estudiante Indígena, 1926–1932," *Americas* 57, no. 3 (January 2001): 329–61; Engracia Loyo, "Los centros de educación indígena y su papel en el medio rural (1930–1940)," *Educación rural e indígena en Iberoamérica*, ed. Pilar Gonzalbo Aizpuru (Mexico City: El Colegio de México, 1996), 139–59; Engracia Loyo, "La empresa redentora. La Casa del Estudiante Indígena," *Historia Mexicana* XLVI, no. 1 (1996): 99–130; Gonzalo Aguirre Beltrán, *Teoría y práctica de la educación indígena* (Mexico City: Fondo de Cultura Económica, 1992 [1973]);

David Wallace Adams, *Education for Extinction: American Indians and the Boarding School Experience* (Lawrence: University of Kansas Press, 1995); Brenda Child, *Boarding School Seasons: American Indian Families, 1900–1940* (Lincoln: University of Nebraska Press, 2000); Ward Churchill, *Kill the Indian, Save the Man: The Genocidal Impact of American Residential Schools* (San Francisco: City Lights, 2004); K. Tsianina Lomawaima, *They Called It Prairie Light: The Story of Chilocco Indian School* (Lincoln: University of Nebraska Press, 1994); Carmen Martínez Novo, *Who Defines Indigenous: Identities, Development, Intellectuals, and the State in Northern Mexico* (New Brunswick, NJ: Rutgers University Press, 2006). I wrote about the larger comparison in "Histories and Memories of the Indian Boarding Schools in Mexico, Canada, and the United States," *Latin American Perspectives* 39, no. 5 (September 2012): 80–99.

5. The following quotations are all taken from Vincenzo Petrullo, "Peyotism as an Emergent Indian Culture," presented at the PCII, April 1940, National Archives and Records Administration (hereafter NARA), 75 (178), Box 15.

6. Laura Giraudo, "Un campo indigenista transnacional y casi profesional: la apertura en Pátzcuaro (1940) de un espacio por y para los indigenistas," in *La ambivalente historia del indigenismo: campo interamericano y trayectorias nacionales, 1940–1970*, ed. Laura Giraudo and Juan-Martin Sánchez (Lima: Instituto de Estudios Peruanos, 2011), 1–98; Anne Marie McGee et al, "Forjando un México nuevo: revolución, nación y cultura en el México posrevolucionario," *Anuario de Estudios Americanos* 67, no. 2 (2010): 415–24; Laura Giraudo, "El Instituto Indigenista Interamericano y la participación indígena (1940–1998)," *América Indígena* 62, no. 3 (July–September 2006): 6–34; Laura Giraudo, "No hay propiamente todavía Instituto: los inicios del Instituto Indigenista Interamericano (abril 1940–marzo 1942)," *América Indígena* 62, no. 2 (April–June 2006): 6–32.

7. For a good overview of the Congress, see Guillermo de la Peña, "Social and Cultural Policies Toward Indigenous Peoples: Perspectives from Latin America," *Annual Review of Anthropology* 34 (2005): 717–39.

8. See for example, Daniel Rubín de la Borbolla and Ralph L. Beals, "The Tarasca Project: a Cooperative Enterprise of the Mexican bureau of Indian Affairs, and the University of California, National Polytechnic Institute-Instituto Politécnico Nacional," *American Anthropologist* 42 (1940): 708–12.

9. On the Congress more generally, see Laura Giraudo, "Un campo indigenista transnacional," 1–98; Alexander Dawson, "El peyote y la autodeterminación a lo largo de la frontera entre Estados Unidos y México, desde Pátzcuaro hasta Avándaro," in *La ambivalente historia del indigenismo: campo interamericano y trayectorias nacionales, 1940–1970*, ed. Laura Giraudo and Juan-Martin Sánchez (Lima, Peru: Instituto de Estudios Peruanos, 2011), 159–90.

10. The Mexicans were led by Luis Chávez Orozco, president of the PCII, and Moisés Sáenz, general secretary. Mexico's president Cárdenas even expressed his opposition to such a path at his address to the Congress. Lázaro Cárdenas, "Dis-

curso al Primer Congreso," *Primer Congreso Indigenista Interamericano* (hereafter PCII), Biblioteca Nacional de Antropología e Historia (hereafter BNAH), Mexico City.

11. Several Mexican delegates gave papers that advocated limited forms of pluralism; see Dawson, *Indian and Nation*, 78–87. See also "Sección Jurídica" and "Educación Indígena," PCII, BNAH.

12. See Borbolla and Beals, "The Tarasca Project," 708–12.

13. See Karin Rosemblatt, *The Science and Politics of Race in Mexico and the United States, 1910–1950* (Chapel Hill: University of North Carolina Press, 2018). On the larger history of these interactions, see Ruben Flores, *Backroads Pragmatists: Mexico's Melting Pot and Civil Rights in the United States* (Philadelphia: University of Pennsylvania Press, 2014). For an interesting evaluation of the IRA, see Lawrence Kelly, "The Indian Reorganization Act: The Dream and the Reality," *Pacific Historical Review* 44, no. 3 (1975): 291–312. These issues are still debated in the United States. See E. A. Schwartz, "Red Atlantis Revisited: Community and Culture in the Writings of John Collier," *American Indian Quarterly* 18, no. 4 (1994): 507–31; Stephen J. Kunitz, "The Social Philosophy of John Collier," *Ethnohistory* 18, no. 3 (1971): 213–29; Donald Parman, *The Navajos and the New Deal* (New Haven, CT: Yale University Press, 1976); Daniel L. Boxberger, "Individualism or Tribalism?: The 'Dialectic' of Indian Policy," *American Indian Quarterly* 15, no. 1 (Winter 1991): 29–31; Thomas Biolsi, "'Indian Self-Government' as a Technique of Domination," *American Indian Quarterly* 15, no.1 (1991): 23–28. More ambiguous renderings can be found in Graham Taylor, *The New Deal and American Indian Tribalism: The Administration of the Indian Reorganization Act, 1934–45* (Lincoln: University of Nebraska Press, 1980); Elmer R. Rusco, "John Collier: Architect of Sovereignty or Assimilation?", *American Indian Quarterly* 15, no.1 (1991): 49–54; Wilcomb E. Washburn, "A Fifty-Year Perspective on the Indian Reorganization Act," *American Anthropologist* 86, no. 2 (1984): 279–89; Kenneth R. Philp, *Termination Revisited: American Indians on the Trail to Self-Determination, 1933–1953* (Lincoln: University of Nebraska Press, 1999); Vine Deloria Jr. and Clifford Lytle, *The Nations Within* (Austin: University of Texas Press, 1988).

14. The Dawes Act, also known as The General Allotment Act, sought to eliminate tribal government and Indian reservations by granting individual allotments to members of Indian tribes. On the critique of its effects, see Lewis Meriam, *Problem of Indian Administration: Report of a Survey made at the Request of the Honorable Hubert Work, Secretary of the Interior, and Submitted to Him February 21, 1928* (Baltimore: Johns Hopkins University Press, 1928).

15. "Indian" is obviously a loaded term. I use it in this chapter to reflect the nomenclature of the day and to avoid describing individuals and communities in an anachronistic fashion. It was not intended as a derogatory term in the way "indio" might signal inferiority. It instead reflected membership in communities whose history predated the European conquest.

16. See Alexander Dawson, *The Peyote Effect: From the Inquisition to the War on Drugs* (Berkeley: University of California Press, 2018). See also, among others, Omer Stewart, *Peyote Religion: A History* (Norman: University of Oklahoma Press, 1993).

17. See Dawson, *Indian and Nation*; Alan Knight, "Cardenismo: Juggernaut or Jalopy?", *Journal of Latin American Studies* 26, no. 1 (February 1994): 73–107; Stephen Lewis, *The Ambivalent Revolution: Forging State and Nation in Chiapas, 1910–1945* (Albuquerque: University of New Mexico Press, 2005); Arnoldo Córdova, *La política de masas del cardenismo* (Mexico City: Era, 1974); Adolfo Gilly, *El cardenismo. Una utopia Mexicana* (Mexico City, Cal y Arena, 1994).

18. Alan Harper, "The Indian and the Land," in *Indians and the Land. Contributions of the Delegation of the United States, First Inter-American Conference on Indian Life, Pátzcuaro, Mexico, April 1940* (Washington, DC: Library of Congress, 1940).

19. Alida C. Bowler, "Credit for Indian Landholders in Mexico and the United States," in *Indians and the Land*. Ruben Flores discusses Mexican influences on American reformers in *Backroads Pragmatists*.

20. H. H. Bennett, "Conservation of Social and Water in the Americas," in *Indians and the Land*.

21. Harper, "The Indian and the Land."

22. For a good discussion of the project see Lawrence C. Kelly, "Anthropology in the Soil Conservation Service," *Agricultural History* 59, no. 2 (1985): 143–47.

23. See "La política de irrigación en beneficio del indio," PCII, BNAH.

24. See for example, Rebecca Earle, *The Return of the Native: Indians and Mythmaking in Spanish America, 1810–1930* (Durham, NC: Duke University Press, 2008).

25. Cárdenas, "Discurso al Primer Congreso Indigenista Interamericano," BNAH.

26. See Dawson, *Indian and Nation*, 83–87.

27. Kunitz, "The Social Philosophy of John Collier," 213–29.

28. See Moisés Sáenz, *México Integro* (Lima, Perú: Impr. Torres Aguirre, 1939). See also Dawson, *Indian and Nation*, 83–86; Mauricio Swadesh, "Proyecto de Plan de Educación Indígena en Lengua Nativa Tarasca," *Boletín Bibliográfico de Antropología Americana* 3 (1939): 222–27; Borbolla and Beals, "The Tarasca Project."

29. Jean Meyer, *The Cristero Rebellion: The Mexican People Between Church and State, 1926–1929* (Cambridge: Cambridge University Press, 1976); Jennie Purnell, *Popular Movements and State Formation in Revolutionary Mexico: The Agraristas and Cristeros of Michoacán* (Durham, NC: Duke University Press, 1999).

30. Manuel Gamio used these terms to describe folk Catholicism in his epic three-volume study of the Valley of Teotihuacán, *La Población del Valle de Teotihuacán* (Mexico City: Secretaría de Educación Pública, Dirección de Talleres Gráficos, 1922).

31. David Daily, *Battle for the BIA: G. E. E. Lindquist and the Missionary Crusade against John Collier* (Tucson: University of Arizona Press, 2004).

32. *Christian Century*, October 11, 1934, NARA, 75 (178), Box 18. This was the era of *Educación Socialista* in Mexico. See also "Does Uncle Sam Foster Paganism?", *Christian Century*, August 8, 1934, NARA, 75 (178), Box 18. See also Lawrence C. Kelly, *The Assault on Assimilation: John Collier and the Origins of Indian Policy Reform* (Albuquerque: University of New Mexico Press, 1983); Daily, *Battle for the BIA*.

33. Dr. John P. Harrington, of the Bureau of American Ethnology at the Smithsonian, Dr. M. R. Harrington, curator of the Southwest Museum, A. L. Kroeber, and Petrullo, who also spoke at these hearings, made similar claims about peyote's salubriousness. All comments from the Senate Hearing are found in NARA, 75, Box 1.

34. This includes Ales Hrdlicka and Kroeber at the 1937 hearings and would be repeated by Weston LaBarre, Omer Stewart, and others over time.

35. See Nathaniel Morris, "'Civilising the Savage': State-Building, Education and Huichol Autonomy in Revolutionary Mexico, 1920–40," *Journal of Latin American Studies* 49, no. 4 (November 2017): 739–39. Mexicans did not begin to do any significant research on either until the 1960s.

36. "Las tribus Huicholes en un constante antagonismo," *El Nacional*, June 11, 1936.

37. "Las tribus Huicholes"; "Los Huicholes," *El Maestro Rural* 6, no. 5 (March 1, 1937). See also Alberto Morales Jimenez, "Jesús López, Huichol, Habla de su intimidades," *El Nacional*, March 4, 1944; "La Vida Social y espiritual de la raza de Huicholes," *El Nacional*, June 11, 1943.

38. "Los Huicholes," *El Maestro Rural*.

39. Carlos Basauri, *La población indígena de Mexico* III Vol., (Mexico City: Secretaría de Educación Pública, 1940): 64.

40. Basauri, 43.

41. Basauri, 67.

42. See José Vasconcelos, "The Race Problem in Latin America," in *Aspects of Mexican Civilization: Lectures of the Harris Foundation* (Chicago: University of Chicago Press, 1926), 77–79. Similar sentiments were expressed by Manuel Gamio in "Incorporating the Indian in the Mexican Population," in *Aspects of Mexican Civilization: Lectures of the Harris Foundation* (Chicago: University of Chicago Press, 1926), 105–28; and José Manuel Puig Casauranc, *La Casa del Estudiante Indígena. 16 meses de labor en un experimento psicológico con indios, febrero de 1926-junio de 1927* (Mexico City: Secretaría de Educación Pública, 1927). See also Emiko Saldívar, "'It's Not Race, It's Culture': Untangling Racial Politics in Mexico," *Latin American and Caribbean Ethnic Studies* 9, no. 1 (2014): 89–108; Emiko Saldívar, *Prácticas Cotidianas del Estado: Una Etnografía del Indigenismo* (Mexico City: Universidad Iberoamericana/Plaza y Valdes, 2008).

43. See for example, Ricardo Pozas, *La antropología y la burocracia indigenista* (Mexico City: Editorial Tlacuilco [Cuaderno para trabajadores, 1], 1976); Arturo Warman, Margarita Nolasco, Guillermo Bonfil, Mercedes Olivera, and Enrique Valencia, *De eso que llaman la antropología Mexicana* (Mexico City: Editorial Nuestro Tiempo, 1970).

CHAPTER FIVE: NO PLACE IN THE COSMIC RACE?

1. José Vasconcelos, *La raza cósmica: Misión de la raza iberoamericana* (París: Agencia Mundial de Librería, 1925).

2. Alan Knight, "Racism, Revolution, and *Indigenismo*: Mexico, 1910–1940" in *The Idea of Race in Latin America*, ed. Richard Graham (Austin: University of Texas Press, 1990), 73.

3. Agustín F. Basave Benítez, *México mestizo: Análisis del nacionalismo mexicano en torno a la mestizofilia de Andrés Molina Enríquez* (México, DF: Fondo de Cultura Económica, 1993 [1992]), 18.

4. Alexander Dawson, *Indian and Nation in Revolutionary Mexico* (Tucson: University of Arizona Press, 2004), 4–5; Knight, "Racism, Revolution, and *Indigenismo*," 78; Tomás Pérez Vejo, "Raza y construcción nacional. México, 1810–1910," in *Raza y política en Hispanoamérica*, ed. Tomás Pérez Vejo and Pablo Yankelevich, (Madrid y Ciudad de México: Iberoamericana/Bonilla Artigas Editores/El Colegio de México, 2018), 74–76, 84–85.

5. Charles A. Hale, *The Transformation of Liberalism in Late Nineteenth-Century Mexico* (Princeton, NJ: Princeton University Press, 1989), 234.

6. Basave, *México mestizo*, 33–35.

7. Basave, 13, 121, 123.

8. Karin Alejandra Rosemblatt, *The Science and Politics of Race in Mexico and the United States, 1910–1950* (Chapel Hill: University of North Carolina Press, 2018), 22–23, 26; Alexandra Minna Stern, "From Mestizophilia to Biotypology: Racialization and Science in Mexico, 1920–1960," in *Race and Nation in Modern Latin America,* ed. Nancy P. Appelbaum, Anne S. Macpherson, and Karin Alejandra Rosemblatt (Chapel Hill: University of North Carolina Press, 2003), 190.

9. Dawson, *Indian and Nation*, 6–7; Knight, "Racism, Revolution, and *Indigenismo*," 84–85.

10. Manuel Gamio, "Heterogeneidad de la población," in Instituto Nacional Indigenista, *INI, 30 años después: revisión crítica* (Mexico City: Instituto Nacional Indigenista, 1978), 27–28; see also Guillermo de la Peña, "Nacionales y extranjeros en la historia de la antropología mexicana," in *La historia de la antropología en México: Fuentes y transmisión,* ed. Mechthild Rutsch (Mexico City: Plaza y Valdés/Universidad Iberoamericana/Instituto Nacional Indigenista, 1996), 62.

11. Claudio Lomnitz, "Bordering on Anthropology: Dialects of a National Tradition in Mexico," in *Empires, Nations, and Natives: Anthropology and State-Making,* ed. Benoît de L'Estoile, Federico Neiburg, and Lygia Sigaud (Durham,

NC: Duke University Press, 2005), 184–85; see also Manuel Gamio, *Forjando patria* (Mexico City: Editorial Porrúa, 1960 [1916]).

12. Rosemblatt, *Science and Politics,* 24, 138, 167–68.

13. Rick A. López, *Crafting Mexico: Intellectuals, Artisans, and the State after the Revolution* (Durham, NC: Duke University Press, 2010), 7, 9.

14. Marilyn Grace Miller, *Rise and Fall of the Cosmic Race: The Culture of Mestizaje in Latin America* (Austin: University of Texas Press, 2004), 28.

15. Rosemblatt, *Science and Politics,* 48.

16. Jason Oliver Chang, *Chino: Anti-Chinese Racism in Mexico, 1880–1940* (Chicago: University of Illinois Press, 2017), 125.

17. Chang, *Chino: Anti-Chinese Racism,* 129.

18. Chang, 130.

19. Pablo Yankelevich, "Nuestra raza y las otras. A propósito de la inmigración en el México revolucionario," in *Raza y política en Hispanoamérica,* ed. Tomás Pérez Vejo and Pablo Yankelevich (Madrid y Ciudad de México: Iberoamericana/Bonilla Artigas/El Colegio de México, 2018), 330.

20. Yankelevich, "Nuestra raza," 330.

21. Yankelevich, 331. Well more than half of the foreigners who were awarded Mexican citizenship between 1900 and 1950 were either Spanish or Guatemalan, "Indolatinos" who were considered "assimilable" and therefore "desirable"; see Daniela Gleizer, "Los límites de la nación. Naturalización y exclusión en el México posrevolucionario," in *Nación y alteridad: Mestizos, indígenas y extranjeros en el proceso de formación nacional,* ed. Daniela Gleizer and Paula López Caballero (Mexico City: Universidad Autónoma Metropolitana, 2015), 109–62.

22. Chang, *Chino: Anti-Chinese Racism,* 132, 184; see also Gerardo Rénique, "Sonora's Anti-Chinese Racism and Mexico's Postrevolutionary Nationalism, 1920s-1930s," in *Race and Nation in Modern Latin America,* ed. Nancy P. Appelbaum, Anne S. Macpherson, and Karin Alejandra Rosemblatt (Chapel Hill: University of North Carolina Press, 2003), 211–36.

23. Dawson, *Indian and Nation,* xiv–xv.

24. Indigenous people in the United States were not invited. When Seminoles living in the United States met with President Cárdenas in 1937 to request the right to colonize a region in the northern state in Coahuila, Gamio wrote to the president to advise against it, suggesting that they would not assimilate.

25. See Dawson in this volume; also Laura Giraudo, "Neither 'Scientific' nor 'Colonialist': The Ambiguous Course of Inter-American Indigenismo in the 1940s," *Latin American Perspectives* 39, no. 5 (September 2012), 13; Departamento de Asuntos Indígenas, *Primer Congreso Indigenista Interamericano* (Mexico City: Departamento de Asuntos Indígenas, 1940).

26. Manuel Gamio, *Antología* (Mexico City: Universidad Nacional Autónoma de México, 1993 [1975]), 28–29; Laura Giraudo, "Un campo indigenista transna-

cional y 'casi profesional': La apertura en Pátzcuaro (1940) de un espacio por y para los indigenistas," in *La ambivalente historia del indigenismo: Campo interamericano y trayectorias nacionales, 1940–1970*, ed. Laura Giraudo and Juan-Martín Sánchez (Lima: Instituto de Estudios Peruanos, 2011), 82–87.

27. Laura Giraudo, "Entre 'atraso estadístico' e 'indigenismo científico': Uniformar los censos y definir a los indígenas en las Américas," in *La novedad estadística: Cuantificar, cualificar y transformar las poblaciones en Europa y América Latina, siglos XIX y XX*, ed. Jesús Bustamante, Laura Giraudo, and Leticia Mayer (Madrid: Ediciones Polifemo, 2014), 143–62.

28. Paula López Caballero, "Las políticas indigenistas y la 'fábrica' de su sujecto de intervención en la creación del primer Centro Coordinador del Instituto Nacional Indigenista (1948–1952)," in *Nación y alteridad: Mestizos, indígenas y extranjeros en el proceso de formación nacional*, ed. Daniela Gleizer and Paula López Caballero (Mexico City: Universidad Metropolitana, 2015), 71, 80–86, 98–100.

29. Aguirre Beltrán's first major theoretical work, *Formas de gobierno indígena*, was published in 1953, two years after he opened the INI's pilot coordinating center in San Cristóbal. This book, which presented his ideas on acculturation, modernity, and Mexican citizenship, drew heavily on his experience as director of the coordinating center in 1951.

30. See various issues of the INI's official periodical, *Acción Indigenista*, in 1953; Alfonso Caso, "Definición del indio y lo indio," in *Homenaje a Alfonso Caso: Obras escogidas* (Mexico City: Patronato para el Fomento de Actividades Culturales y de Asistencia Social a las Comunidades Indígenas, 1996), 338.

31. Agustín Romano Delgado, "Veinticinco años del Centro Coordinador Indigenista Tzeltal-Tzotzil," in *El indigenismo en acción: XXV aniversario del Centro Coordinador Indigenista Tzeltal-Tzotzil, Chiapas* ed. Gonzalo Aguirre Beltrán, Alfonso Villa Rojas, Agustín Romano Delgado, et al. (Mexico City: Instituto Nacional Indigenista/Secretaría de Educación Pública, 1976), 44–45.

32. Comisión Nacional para el Desarrollo de los Pueblos Indígenas (hereafter CDI), Biblioteca Juan Rulfo (hereafter BJR), Agustín Romano Delgado, "Problemas fundamentales del Centro Tzeltal Tzotzil," unpublished manuscript, 1955.

33. CDI, BJR, Alfonso Caso, "Informe de Actividades presentado por el Dir. Gen. Dr. Alfonso Caso, 1949–1970," from Caso to Presidente, January 10, 1950.

34. Gonzalo Aguirre Beltrán, *Formas de gobierno indígena* (Mexico City: Imprenta Universitaria, 1953), 143.

35. *Monopolio de aguardiente y alcoholismo en los Altos de Chiapas: Un estudio "incómodo" de Julio de la Fuente*, ed. Stephen E. Lewis and Margarita Sosa Suárez (Mexico City: Comisión Nacional para el Desarrollo de los Pueblos Indígenas, 2009).

36. Juan Comas, ed., *La antropología social aplicada en México: Trayectoria y antología* (Mexico City: Instituto Indigenista Interamericano, 1964), 76; see also "Conclusiones sobre indigenismo," *Acción Indigenista*, 29 (November 1955).

37. Stephen E. Lewis, "Modernizing Message, Mystical Messenger: The Teatro Petul in the Chiapas Highlands, 1954–1974," *The Americas* 67, no. 3 (February 2011), 375–97.

38. CDI, BJR, Informe del Centro Coordinador Indigenista Tzeltal-Tzotzil (hereafter ICCITT), 1959, from Alfonso Villa Rojas, February 1959; "9 jóvenes terminan los cursos de educación en el internado del INI," *Acción Indigenista* 81 (March 1960).

39. Ülrich Köhler, *Cambio cultural dirigido en los Altos de Chiapas: Un estudio sobre la antropología social aplicada* (Mexico City: Instituto Nacional Indigenista/ Secretaría de Educación Pública, 1975 [1969]), 240; CDI, BJR, ICCITT, 1960, "Informe de marzo de 1960," from Alfonso Villa Rojas.

40. Comas, *La antropología social aplicada*, 63.

41. Archivo Histórico del Centro Coordinador Indigenista Tzeltal-Tzotzil (hereafter AHCCITT), 1966/2, Dir., "Convenio entre el gobierno de los Estados Unidos Mexicanos y la Unión Panamericana, Secretaría General de la Organización de los Estados Americanos, para el Establecimiento del proyecto 208, Programa interamericano de adiestramiento de personal en Desarrollo de Comunidades Indígenas del programa de cooperación técnica en los Estados Unidos Mexicanos"; Guillermo de la Peña, "The End of Revolutionary Anthropology? Notes on Indigenismo," in *Dictablanda: Politics, Work, and Culture in Mexico, 1938–1968*, ed. Paul Gillingham and Benjamin T. Smith (Durham, NC: Duke University Press, 2014), 293.

42. For more information on the decline of the CCI's programs in the long 1960s, see Stephen E. Lewis, *Rethinking Mexican Indigenismo: The INI's Coordinating Center in Highland Chiapas and the Fate of a Utopian Project* (Albuquerque: University of New Mexico Press, 2018).

43. AHCCITT, 1969/5, "Informe annual, 1969."

44. Ángel Palerm and Rodolfo Stavenhagen rounded out the Magnificent Seven but did not contribute chapters to *De eso que llaman antropología mexicana*.

45. Guillermo Bonfil Batalla, "Del indigenismo de la revolución a la antropología crítica," in *De eso que llaman antropología mexicana*, ed. Arturo Warman, Margarita Nolaso Armas, Guillermo Bonfil Batalla, Merecedes Olivera Bustamante, and Enrique Valencia (Mexico City: Editorial Nuestro Tiempo, 1970), 43.

46. Bonfil, 55, 59.

47. Margarita Nolasco Armas, "La antropología aplicada y su destino final, el indigenismo," in *De eso que llaman antropología mexicana*, 81.

48. Bonfil, "Del indigenismo de la revolución," 43.

49. "Declaración de Barbados I (1971)," in *Documentos fundamentales del indigenismo en México* ed. José del Val and Carlos Zolla, (Mexico City: UNAM, 2014), 611–19.

50. Demetrio Sodi M., "Algunas ideas de Alfonso Caso," in *INI, 30 años después*, 198.

51. Köhler, *Cambio cultural dirigido*, 309.

52. AHCCITT, 1967/3, Dir., to Prof. Alberto Jiménez Rodríguez from Subdirector Técnico de Educación Ignacio León Pacheco, August 31, 1967.

53. The next poorest state is strife-ridden Guerrero, with 67.4 percent of the population living in moderate or extreme poverty, followed by Oaxaca with 67.2 percent; see Daniel Villafuerte Solís, "La catástrofe neoliberal en Chiapas: Pobreza, precarización laboral y migraciones," in *Viejas y nuevas migraciones forzadas en el sur de México, Centroamérica y el Caribe*, ed. Enrique Baltar Rodríguez, María da Gloria Marroni, and Daniel Villafuerte Solís (Mexico City: Universidad de Quintana Roo, 2013), 316–19.

54. The Zapatistas, which included insurgents from the four largest ethnic groups in Chiapas, negotiated with the federal government for more cultural autonomy; see several chapters in *Mayan Lives, Mayan Utopias: The Indigenous People of Chiapas and the Zapatista Rebellion*, ed. Jan Rus, Rosalva Aída Hernández Castillo, and Shannan L. Mattiace (Boulder, CO: Rowman and Littlefield Publishers, 2003).

55. Edward Telles and the Project on Ethnicity and Race in Latin America (PERLA), *Pigmentocracies* (Chapel Hill: University of North Carolina Press, 2014), 47.

56. Claude Fell, *José Vasconcelos: Los años de águila (1920–1925)* (Mexico City: UNAM, 1989), 654–55.

57. López, *Crafting Mexico*, 134.

58. Miller, *Rise and Fall*, 41.

59. Basave, *México mestizo*, 133–34.

60. Miller, *Rise and Fall*, 41–42.

61. Miller, 150.

62. Jan Rus, "Rereading Tzotzil Ethnography: Recent Scholarship from Chiapas, Mexico," in *Pluralizing Ethnography: Comparison and Representation in Maya Cultures, Histories, and Identities*, ed. John M. Watanabe and Edward F. Fischer (Santa Fe: School of American Research Press, 2004), 203–4.

63. Köhler, *Cambio cultural dirigido*, 173–74.

64. John Lear, *Picturing the Proletariat: Artists and Labor in Revolutionary Mexico, 1908–1940* (Austin: University of Texas Press, 2017), 113–32.

65. Elena Jackson Albarrán, *Seen and Heard in Mexico: Children and Revolutionary Cultural Nationalism* (Lincoln: University of Nebraska Press, 2015), 75–174.

66. Cited in Stern, "From Mestizophilia," 192–93.

67. Basave, *México mestizo*, 142.

68. Miller, *Rise and Fall*, 4.

69. López Caballero, "Las políticas indigenistas," 71, 80–85.

70. Ignacio Ovalle Fernández, "Bases programáticas de la política indigenista," in *INI, 30 años después: revisión crítica*, 12, 20.

71. Shannan L. Mattiace, *To See with Two Eyes: Peasant Activism and Indian Autonomy in Chiapas, Mexico* (Albuquerque: University of New Mexico Press, 2003), 94.

CHAPTER SIX: CREATING FALSE ANALOGIES

1. Gloria Anzaldúa, *Borderlands/Frontera: The New Mestiza* (San Francisco: Aunt Lute, 2007); Lee Bebout, *Whiteness on the Border: Mapping the U.S. Racial Imagination in Brown and White* (New York: New York University Press, 2016); Laura Gómez, *Manifest Destinies: The Making of the Mexican America Race* (New York: New York University Press, 2007).

2. Washington Post Staff, "Full text: Donald Trump announces a presidential bid," June 16, 2015, https://www.washingtonpost.com/news/post-politics/wp/2015/06/16/full-text-donald-trump-announces-a-presidential-bid.

3. Karyn McKinney, *Being White: Stories of Race and Racism* (New York: Routledge, 2005); Steve Martinot, *The Machinery of Whiteness: Studies in the Structure of Racialization* (Philadelphia: Temple University Press 2010).

4. Hearing Before the Subcommittee on Improvements in the Federal Code of the Committee on the Judiciary, United States Senate, 84th Congress. Illicit Narcotics Traffic (Austin, Dallas, Forth Worth, Houston, and San Antonio, Texas (Washington, DC: Government Printing Office, 1956).

5. Nancy D. Campbell, *Using Women: Gender, Drug Policy, and Social Justice* (New York: Routledge, 2000). See also Nancy D. Campbell and David Herzberg, "Gender and Critical Drug Studies: An Introduction and Invitation," *Contemporary Drug Problems* 44 no. 4 (2017): 251–64.

6. United States, Philippine Commission, "Report of the Committee Appointed by the Philippine Commission to Investigate the Use of Opium and Traffic" (Washington, DC: Government Printing Office, 1905). See also Warwick Anderson, *Colonial Pathologies: American Tropic Medicine, Race, and Hygiene in the Philippines* (Durham, NC: Duke University Press, 2006).

7. *El Diario Oficial* (March 20, 1920). See also Ricardo Pérez Monfort, *Tolerancia y prohibición: Aproximaciones a la historia social y cultural de las drogas en México 1940–1840* (México: Penguin Random House Grupo Editorial México, 2016).

8. Beginning in the early 1900s, the United States embarked on a war that would continue into the twenty-first century. The modern drug war began with legal changes in in 1906 with the passage of the Pure Food and Drug Act and evolved with the 1914 Harrison Narcotics Tax Act, the 1922 Narcotic Drugs Import and Export Act, and the 1924 Heroin Act; however, actual drug enforcement was meager. The Pure Food and Drug Act dismantled the patent remedies industry in the United States, in which consumers easily found opiates and cocaine in everything from gripe water (treatment for colic in children and toddlers) to love potions and asthma treatments. These American initiatives as well as the increasing number of medical studies on narcotics use helped determine the legislative agenda in Mexico after 1920. Druggists and doctors on both sides of the border did not welcome many of these legislative restrictions, and they vigorously fought them, questioning whether politicians should legislate how doctors treated their patients.

Patients feared that the laws would render their accustomed relief-giving prescriptions illegal.

9. George Diaz, *Border Contraband: A History of Smuggling Across the Rio Grande* (Austin: University of Texas Press, 2015).

10. Isaac Campos, *Home Grown: Marijuana and the Origins of Mexico's War on Drugs* (Chapel Hill: University of North Carolina Press, 2014).

11. Holly M. Karibo, *Sin City North: Sex, Drugs, and Citizenship in the De-troit-Windsor Borderland* (Chapel Hill: University of North Carolina Press, 2015).

12. Alexandra Chasin, *Assassin of Youth: A Kaleidoscopic History of Harry J. Anslinger's War on Drugs* (Chicago: University of Chicago Press, 2016), 190–98.

13. For example, see the US Senate, Administration of Federal Food and Drugs Act, Hearings before the Committee on Agriculture and Forestry, February 12 to June 30, 1930 (Washington, DC: Government Printing Office, 1930).

14. Francisco Balderrama and Raymond Rodríguez, *Decade of Betrayal: Mexican Repatriation in the 1930s* (Albuquerque: University of New Mexico Press, 2006).

15. C. M. Goethe, "The Influx of Mexican Amerinds," *Eugenics: A Journal for Race Betterment* 1, no. 3 (December 1928), 6–9. For more information on Goethe, see Tony Platt, "Engaging the Past: Charles M. Goethe, American Eugenics, and Sacramento State University," *Social Justice* 32, no. 2 (100) (2005): 17–33, http://www.jstor.org/stable/29768305.

16. David Courtwright, "Terry, Charles Edward," in *American National Biography*, vol. 21, ed. J. A. Garraty, and M. C. Carnes (New York: Oxford University Press, 1999), 460–61; Elizabeth Fee, "Charles E. Terry (1878–1945): Early Campaigner Against Drug Addiction," *American Journal of Public Health* 101, no. 3 (2011): 451. doi:10.2105/AJPH.2010.191171.

17. C. E. Terry, "Six Months of the Harrison Act," *American Journal of Public Health* (October 1916): 1087–92.

18. For more on the bureau, see The Rockefeller Foundation: A Digital History, "Bureau of Social Hygiene," https://rockfound.rockarch.org/bureau-of-social-hygiene.

19. Charles Edward Terry, *A Further Study and Report on the Use of Narcotics, Under Provisions of the Federal Law in Six Communities in the United States of America for the Period of July 1, 1923 to June 30, 1924* (New York: Bureau of Social Hygiene, 1927), 36.

20. "Estimated Average Annual Drug Addiction Among Violators of the Harrison Narcotic Act, 1922–1928," table, reprinted in Bingham Dai, *Opium Addiction in Chicago* (Montclair, NJ: Patterson Smith, 1970), 39.

21. Elaine Carey, *Women Drug Traffickers: Mules, Bosses, and Organized Crime* (Albuquerque: University of New Mexico Press, 2014).

22. John C. Williams, *The Protectors: Harry J. Anslinger and the Federal Bureau of Narcotics* (Newark: University of Delaware Press, 1990).

23. Michael Omi and Howard Winant, *Racial Formation in the United States: From the 1960s to the 1990s* (New York: Routlege 1994).

24. Phil Nicolas and Andrew Churchill, "The Federal Bureau of Narcotics, the States, and the Origins of Modern Drug Enforcement in the United States, 1950–1962, "*Contemporary Drug Problems* 39, no. 4 (December 1, 2012), 595–640.

25. Carey, *Women Drug Traffickers*, 49–52.

26. See for example, "Weeds That Cause Insanity," *Washington Post*, June 15, 1914. Carlota (1840–1927) was the wife of Emperor Maximilian, who was executed by Mexican Republicans in 1867.

27. "Plants Cause Madness," *Washington Post*, May 9, 1913.

28. Mayor's Committee on Marihuana, *The Marihuana Problem in the City of New York* (Lancaster, PA: Cattell Press, 1944), 3. See also report at Schaffer Library of Drug Policy, http://www.druglibrary.org/schaffer/library/studies/lag/lagmenu.htm.

29. Carey, *Women Drug Traffickers*; Diaz, *Border Contraband*; Sergio Corrado and Francesca Realacci, "The Business Relationship Between Italy's Mafia and Mexico's Drug Cartels," *InsightCrime: Investigation and Analysis of Organized Crime*, June 19, 2014, http://www.insightcrime.org/news-analysis/the-business-rela tionship-between-italys-mafia-and-mexicos-drug-cartels.

30. S. C. Peña, Special Employee to Commissioner of Customs, July 7, 1945, Drug Enforcement Administration, Subject Files of the Bureau of Narcotics and Dangerous Drugs, 1916–1970, RG 170, Box 161, National Archives II, College Park, MD, (hereafter DEA–BNDD).

31. Carey, *Women Drug Traffickers*.

32. Harry J. Anslinger and William F. Tompkins, *The Traffic in Narcotics* (New York: Funk and Wagnalls, 1953), 257. Anslinger and Tompkins argued that there were one hundred fifty thousand to two hundred thousand narcotics addicts in the United States before 1914, most of them women.

33. Campbell, *Using Women*. Nancy D. Campbell and David Herzberg, "Gender and Critical Drug Studies: An Introduction and an Invitation," *Contemporary Drug Problems* (November 2017): 251–64, https://doi.org/10.1177/0091450917738075.

34. Price Daniel was a senator from Texas from 1953 to 1957. He then was the governor of the state. In the 1950s, Mexican heroin accounted for 90 percent of the heroin in Texas.

35. US Congress Hearings Before the Subcommittee on Improvements in the Federal Criminal Code of the Committee on the Judiciary, Illicit Narcotics Traffic, United States Congress, 84th Congress (Washington, DC: Government Printing Office, 1956), 2–3. The hearings were held in three of Canada's largest cities. The format was similar to those in the United States in which medical doctors, politicians, policing agents, and addicts appeared before the committee.

36. Christopher Ray McCormick, Chris McCormick, and Len Green, *Crime and Deviance in Canada: Historical Perspectives* (Toronto: Canadian Scholar's Press, 2005), 359–60.

37. McCormick, McCormick, and Green.

38. For a discussion of McCarthyism, see Ellen Schrecker, *Many Are the Crimes: McCarthyism in America* (Boston: Little, Brown, 1998); Richard M. Fried, *Nightmare in Red: The McCarthy Era in Perspective* (New York: Oxford University Press, 1990).

39. Price Daniel to Óscar Rabasa and Carlos Franco Sodi, October 1, 1955, reprinted in Hearing Before the Subcommittee on Improvements in the Federal Code of the Committee on the Judiciary, United States Senate, 84th Congress. Illicit Narcotics Traffic: Austin, Dallas, Forth Worth, Houston, and San Antonio, Texas (Washington, DC: Government Printing Office, 1956), (hereafter Illicit Narcotics Traffic).

40. For an analysis of agency in drug use and trafficking, see Shaylih Muehlamn, "The Gender of the War on Drugs," *Annual Review of Anthropology* 47 (2018): 315–30.

41. Illicit Narcotics Traffic, 25. Anslinger also noted that before the enforcement of narcotics laws in the United States, the number of female narcotics users outnumbered male users by four to five times.

42. The case of Marilyn Grant, a nurse, smuggled marijuana in a sanitary pad that she made. Her case was sensational. Illicit Narcotics Traffic, 2599.

43. Illicit Narcotics Traffic, 2391. The numbers of those arrested from 1948 to 1955 that Laws provided were "Distribution as to sex: male offenders, 149, female 30, a total of 179. Distribution as to race: Anglo American 81; Latin American, 62; and colored, 36."

44. Illicit Narcotics Traffic, 2392.

45. Special Witness Travis Schnautz, Austin File, Box 27, RG 170; DEA-BNDD.

46. Special Witness Travis Schnautz.

47. Illicit Narcotics Traffic, 2397.

48. Special Witness Travis Schnautz, Austin File, Box 27, RG 170, DEA-BNDD.

49. Illicit Narcotics Traffic, 2397.

50. Nancy Campbell, J. P. Olsen, and Luke Walden, *The Narcotics Farm: The Rise and Fall of America's First Prison for Drug Addicts* (New York: Abrams, 2008). See also their documentary by the same name at http://www.narcoticfarm.com/t2_film.html.

51. US Bureau of Labor Statistics, CPI calculator, https://data.bls.gov/cgi-bin/cpicalc.pl.

52. Carey, *Women Drug Traffickers*. Since the 1940s, Borderlands drug traffickers routinely guaranteed delivery on the US side of the border.

53. As a comparison, in the 1970s, undercover New York Police Department narcotics officers only received up to $1500 for a buy in a sting operation.

54. Illicit Narcotics Traffic, 2400–2401.

55. "Narcotics Traffickers—San Antonio, Texas," Daniel Committee File, Box 9, RG 170, DEA-BNDD.

56. Simona's sister, Victoria Terrazos, ran fronts for stolen goods, and she was a recognized San Antonio crime boss who appears to have played a small role in the drug business. Her brother-in-law Tony Davila was a recognized drug supplier and smuggler.

57. Illicit Traffic in Narcotics, 2433–35.

58. Sam Quinones, *Dreamland: The True Tales of American's Opiate Epidemic* (New York: Bloomsbury Press, 2015); Beth Macy, *Dopesick: Dealers, Doctors, and the Drug Company that Addicted America* (New York: Little, Brown, 2018).

59. Illicit Traffic in Narcotics, 2401.

60. Richard Delgado, "The Law of the Noose: A History of Latino Lynching," *Harvard Civil Rights-Civil Liberties Law Review* 44 (2009): 297–312. William Carrigan and Clive Webb, *Forgotten Dead: Mob Violence Against Mexicans in the United States, 1848–1928* (New York: Oxford University Press, 2013); Monica Muñoz Martínez, *The Injustice Never Leaves You: Anti-Mexican Violence in Texas* (Cambridge, MA: Harvard University Press, 2018). See also *Refusing to Forget*, https://refusingtoforget.org/.

61. Gema Kloppe-Santamaria, "Lynching, Religion, and Politics in Twentieth Century Puebla," presented at the Latin American History Workshop, New York, April 17, 2015, Columbia University.

62. Carrigan and Webb, *Forgotten Dead*, 70–75.

63. Carey, *Women Drug Traffickers*.

64. See Anslinger and Thomkins, *The Traffic in Narcotics* and Will Oursler, *The Murderers: The Shocking Story of the Narcotic Gangs* (New York: Farrar, Straus, and Cudahy, 1961).

65. Illicit Traffic in Narcotics, 2423–30. The mother was referred to as "an undisclosed witness."

66. "Gangland Style Slaying Get Eye of Law Men," *San Antonio Express* (August 13, 1976): 10; Henry Travis Schnautz Jr., Plaintiff-appellant, v. Dr. George J. Beto, Director, Texas Department of Corrections, Defendant-appellee, 416 F.2d 214 (5th Cir. 1969). See also Graeme Thomson, *Willie Nelson: The Outlaw* (London: Virgin Books, 2007), 151.

CHAPTER SEVEN: BASEBALL AND THE CATEGORIZATION OF RACE IN VENEZUELA

1. Miguel Montefusco, "Cuando el poder negro asombró a Caracas," *Deportes* (Caracas) 2, no. 33 (January 28, 1980): 19–21; "Jackie Robinson's 1945 Tour of Venezuela," *Finding Baseball*, April 30, 2016, accessed June 12, 2018, Findingbaseball.blogspot.com; Daniel Crespo Varona, "El gran negocia de la pelota," *Bohemia* (Caracas), 702–6 (September 12, 1976): 26–29.

2. William F. McNeil, *Black Baseball Out of Season: Pay for Play Outside of the Negro Leagues* (Jefferson, NC: McFarland & Company, 2007), 170–75.

3. Luis López, "Grover 'Deacon' Jones: La estrella que más brilla en la liga occidental," *Momento* (Caracas) 340 (January 20, 1963): 58–60; see Sayuri Guthrie-

Shimizu, *Transpacific Field of Dreams: How Baseball Linked the United States and Japan in Peace and War* (Chapel Hill: University of North Carolina Press, 2012).

4. "Los Astros del último campeonato," *Deportes* 2, no. 35 (February 25, 1980): 8–10.

5. Author's interview with Simon Piña, July 15, 2006, Caracas; author's interview with Nicolás Hidalgo, July 15, 2006, Caracas.

6. Luis F. Angosto-Ferrández, "From 'café con leche' to 'o café, o leche': National Identity, *Mestizaje* and Census Politics in Contemporary Venezuela," *Journal of Iberian and Latin American Research* 20, no. 3 (2014): 373; David M. Guss, *The Festive State: Race, Ethnicity, and Nationalism as Cultural Performance* (Berkeley: University of California Press, 2000), 58–59.

7. Winthrop Wright, *Café con leche: Race, Class, and National Image in Venezuela* (Austin: University of Texas Press, 1990), 122.

8. See for example, Michael E. Donoghue, *Borderland on the Isthmus: Race, Culture, and the Struggle for the Canal Zone* (Durham, NC: Duke University Press, 2014); Jana K. Lipman, *Guantanamo: A Working-Class History Between Empire and Revolution* (Berkeley: University of California Press, 2008).

9. Oscar Chamosa, "Indigenous or Criollo: The Myth of White Argentina in Tucumán's Calchaquí Valley," *Hispanic American Historical Review* 88, no.1 (2008): 71–106.

10. Mario Valdéz, "Luis 'Camaleón' García, una leyenda del béisbol venezolano," *NoticieroDigital.com*, December 22, 2017, accessed September 10, 2018, http://www.noticierodigital.com/forum/viewtopic.php?t=89978.

11. G. Ender and G. Gonzalez, *El fenómeno Caracas-Magallanes (Una perspective sociológica)*, Comunicaciones, Universidad Central de Venezuela, 2002; Carlos D. Cárdenas Lares, *Leones de Caracas, crónica de una tradición* (Caracas: Fondo Editorial Cárdenas Lares, segunda edición, 1996); Rosa Virginia Fagundez Guedez, "El fanatismo Caracas-Magallanes: un negocio tan redondo como la pelota," Tesis de grado, Escuela de Comunicación Social, Universidad Central de Venezuela, 1999.

12. Eleazar Díaz Rangel, *El béisbol en Venezuela* (Caracas: Libros de Hoy, 1967), 53–64.

13. Zaidi Goussot, "Las bellas en el deporte," *Deportes* 3, no. 66 (May 3, 1981): 35–41. See Marcia Ochoa, *Queen for a Day: Transformistas, Beauty Queens, and the Performance of Femininity in Venezuela* (Durham, NC: Duke University Press, 2014); Elizabeth Gackstetter Nichols, *Beauty, Virtue, Power, and Success in Venezuela, 1850–2015* (Lanham, MD: Lexington Books, 2016); César Batiz and Jhon Lindarte, "Miss Venezuela, la cara bonita de la decadencia," *Nueva Sociedad* 255 (2015): 145–53.

14. "Lo más importante de 1974 en el Mundo del Espectáculo," *Meridiano* (Caracas) 1425, (January 5, 1975), 7–8.

15. "La CVP está triste: ¿Que le pasa a la CVP?" *Indiscreta* (Caracas) 3, no. 146 (July 1990): 28.

16. "La CVP está triste; George Reid Andrews, *Afro-Latin America, 1800–2000* (New York: Oxford University Press, 2004), 199.

17. Elizabeth Fraterrigo, *Playboy and the Making of the Good Life in Modern America* (New York: Oxford University Press, 2009), 170.

18. See *Cuentos Prohibidos*, 110; *Sexy Jeans*, 44; *Tabú en Español*, 16; *Supergirl en Español*, 15. Each was published in the late 1970s or early 1980s with no bibliographical information.

19. "El Paraíso de las Américas. United States Virgin Islands," *Hombre del Mundo* 8, no. 4 (April 1983): inside cover; "Para esos momentos . . . Ballantine's," *Hombre del Mundo* 8, no. 4 (April 1983): 12; Malvina E. Bush, "Idi Amin: el sanguinario dictador que ayer eliminó miles de personas, vive hoy en el exilio dorado que le brinda la Arabia Saudita,"*Hombre del Mundo* 8, no. 4 (April 1983): 17; "La invasion de las supercomputadoras japonesas: ¿Que significa este fenómeno para la industria electrónica de occidente?" *Hombre del Mundo* 8, no. 4 (April 1983): 38–39; Oscar R. Orgallez, "Las curaciones sorprendentes de los medicos-sacerdotes del Tibet: ¿Ciencia o milagro?" *Hombre del Mundo* 8, no. 4 (April 1983): 68–70; Y. H. "Seis rubias 'Made in USA,'" *Momentos* 343 (Feburary 10, 1963): 10–12.

20. Amy Shearn, "How Little League Prepares Kids for Work," *JSTOR Daily*, March 31, 2017, https://daily.jstor.org/when-little-league-invented-why/.

21. Michael H. Carriere, "'A Diamond is a Boy's Best Friend': The Rise of Little League Baseball, 1939–1964," *Journal of Sport History* 32, no. 3 (2005): 351–78.

22. "Niñitos, a jugar! La organización Criollitos de Venezuela enseñó lo que se puede hacer cuando hay deseo y responsabilidad," *Deportes* 6, no. 151 (September 8, 1984): 44–45; Berna Iskandar, "Criollitos de Venezuela. Semillero de Talentos del Béisbol," *Espacio Familiar* (Caracas) 8 (April 2007), Espaciofamiliar.net/articulo.asp?id=6455.

23. "Criollitos de Venezuela," *La Nación deportes* (San Cristóbal), November 8, 2015, https://lanaciondeportes.com/noticias/criollitos-de-venezuela/.

24. Lisa Glebatis Perks, "Sox and Stripes: Baseball's Iconic American Dreams," *Communication Quarterly* 60, no. 4 (2012): 448; Robert Elias, "The National Pastime Trade-Off: How Baseball Sells US Foreign Policy and the American Way," *International Journal of the History of Sport* 28, no. 17 (2011): 2506–26; S. Elizabeth Bird and Robert W. Dardenne, "Myth, Chronicle, and Story: Exploring the Narrative Qualities of News," ed. James W. Carey, *Media, Myths, and Narratives: Television and the Press* (Thousand Oaks, CA: Sage, 1988), 67–86.

25. Michael L. Butterworth, "Pitchers and Catchers: Mike Piazza and the Discourse of Gay Identity in the National Pastime," *Journal of Sport & Social Issues* 30, no. 2 (2006): 144; Nick Trujillo, "Hegemonic Masculinity on the Mound: Media Representations of Nolan Ryan and American Sports Culture," *Critical Studies in Mass Communication* 8, no. 3 (1991): 290–308.

26. Samuel O. Regalado, "Hey Chico! The Latin Identity in Major League Baseball," *NINE: A Journal of Baseball History and Culture* 11, no. 1 (2002): 16–24.

27. Nelson Morante, "La cueva de los Mellizos es muy tranquila para un Latino," *Sport Gráfico* (Caracas), 6–7; Mario Requena, "Antonio la nueva arma latina," *Deportes* 2, no. 52 (October 20, 1980): 12–13; "Kingman y Armas: La ponderosa lucha por un reinado," *Deportes* 6, no. 151 (September 8, 1984): 40–43.

28. "Idolos formados . . . y en formación de nuestro beísbol profesional," *Bohemia* (September 12, 1976): 52–56; G. Becerra Mijares, "Armas, Trillo y Salazar los ases," *Deportes* 3, no. 54 (November 17, 1980): 3–6; author's interview with Rafael Osío Cabriles, July 28, 2006, Caracas.

29. Anthony Cotton, "Marcano Trillo es caliente pero no 'perro caliente'" *Deportes*, 2.52 (October 20, 1980): 16–17.

30. Zaidi Goussot, "Cuando las grandes ligas quedan pequeñas," *Deportes*, 3.53 (3 November 1980): 12–15.

31. "Concepción: Superó la adversidad para ser super-estrella," *Deportes*, 2.31 (December 31, 1979): 3–7.

32. "Concepción"; Luis Carlos, Martín Ascanio, and Orlando Lara, *Venezuela, olimpismo, y sociedad* (Caracas: Instituto Nacional de Deporte, 2006), 116.

33. Francisco Morales, "Pompeyo Davalillo y su debut en el béisbol professional," *Deportes* 6, no. 151 (September 8, 1984): 18.

34. Morales, 18.

35. Nelson Martínez, *Cosas que pasan. Juegos, anécdotas y curiosidades para recordar*, vol. 2 (Caracas: Jaru, 2003), 70.

36. Jairo Cuba, "Luis Aparicio: La nave volvera al mar abierto," *Deportes* 2, no. 35 (February 25, 1980): 16–18.

37. Paul Sullivan, "Hall of Famer Luis Aparicio Skips All-Star Tribute Because of Unrest in Venezuela," *Chicago Tribune*, July 11, 2017, http://www.chicago tribune.com/sports/baseball/whitesox/ct-luis-aparicio-all-star-tribute-venezuela -20170711-story.html.

38. Jane Juffer, "Who's the Man? Sammy Sosa, Latinos, and Televisual Redefinitions of the 'American' Pastime," *Journal of Sport & Social Issues* 26, no. 4 (2002): 344.

39. As they had for decades with reference to Simón Bolivar, the Venezuelan media sometimes cast Chávez as an unusually strong and adept athlete. Zaida Montesinos, "Bolivar Deportista," *Deportes* 5, no. 118 (May 30, 1983): 28–31.

40. Giles Harrison-Conwill, "The Race toward *Caraqueño* Citizenship: Negotiating Race, Class, and Participatory Democracy," *Annals of the American Academy of Political Science* 637 (2011): 177.

41. Gisela Kozak Rovero, "Revolución Bolivariana: políticas culturales en la Venezuela Socialista de Hugo Chávez (1999–2013)," *Cuadernos de Literatura* 19, no. 37 (2015): 38–56; Yasmín Carolina Corrales González, "Más allá de darle al pilón: Avances, tensiones y limites del movimiento social afrovenezolano durante el proceso politico bolivariano (2000–2011)," master's thesis, Estudios Latinoamericanos, Universidad Andina Simón Bolivar, Quito, 2016; Krisna Ruette Orihue-

la, "'Somos Afro-Socialistas': Marcos de acción colectiva y etno-racialización del movimiento rural afroyaracuyano en Veroes-Venezuela," *Tabula Raza* 21 (2014): 351–68; Jesús M. Herrera Salas, "Ethnicity and Revolution: The Political Economy of Racism in Venezuela," *Latin American Perspectives* 32, no. 2 (2005): 72–91; Cristóbal Valencia, *We Are the State!: Barrio Activism in Venezuela's Bolivarian Revolution* (Tucson: University of Arizona Press, 2015), 161–84; Richard Gott, *Hugo Chávez and the Bolivarian Revolution* (New York: Verso, 2000), 11–13.

42. Daniel Fridman and David Sheinin, "Wild Bulls, Discarded Foreigners, and Brash Champions: U.S. Empire and the Cultural Constructions of Argentine Boxers," *Left History* 12, no. 1 (2007): 52–77; Kath Woodward, "Rumbles in the Jungle: Boxing, Racialization, and the Performance of Masculinity," *Leisure Studies* 23, no. 1 (2004): 13; Michael Donoghue, "Roberto Durán, Omar Torrijos, and the Rise of Ithsmian Machismo," ed. David M. K. Sheinin, *Sports Culture in Latin American History* (Pittsburgh: University of Pittsburgh Press, 2015), 17–38; David M. K. Sheinin, "Boxing in the Making of a Colombian *Costeño* Identity," *Sports Culture*, 139–60.

43. Nelson Contreras, "Luis Primera busca un milagro" *Deportes* 3.54 (November 17, 1980): 68–70.

44. Author's interview with Rafael Liendo, July 10, 2006, Turmero.

45. Author's interview with Simón Piña, May 12, 2018, Caracas.

46. "Pambelé en problemas con el Fisco," *Meridiano* (Caracas) 1624 (January 4, 1975): 8–9; Ignacio Amador de la Peña, *Luces sobre el ring* (Cartagena: Industrias Técnicas Gráficas, 1986), 75.

47. Carlos Cárdenas Lares and Giner García, *Venezolanos en el Ring* (Caracas: Torino, 1993), 77.

48. Lares and García, 78.

49. Lares and García, 80; Alfredo Fuentes R., "'Lumumba' Sueña Con Betulio," *Clinch: Revista Venezolana de Box*, 1 (nd, 1977): 24–25.

50. Simon Piña, "Hace 40 años Luis 'Lumumba' Estaba se coronó campeón mundial minimosca," *Solo Boxeo*, September 19, 2015, https://www.soloboxeo.com/2015/09/19/hace-40-anos-luis-lumumba-estaba-se-corono-campeon-mundial-minimosca/.

51. Author's interview with Juan José Landaeta, July 11, 2006, Turmero; author's interview with Yober Ortega, July 11, 2006, Turmero.

52. Carlos G. Girón, "Edwin Valero: A Fearless Champion, Pathetic Addict, and Cowardly Assassin," *Bleacher Report*, n.d. [2010], https://bleacherreport.com/articles/380961-edwin-valero-fearless-champion-pathetic-addict-and-cowardly-assassin; Quique Peinado, "Edwin 'El Inca' Valero: un chavista, un adicto, un enfermo . . . un asesino," *Marca*, April 21, 2010, http://www.marca.com/2010/04/21/mas_deportes/otros_deportes/1271843552.html; Martín Padrino, "España contra Venezuela (bis)," *Aporrea*, April 24, 2010, accessed July 14, 2018, https://www.aporrea.org/tiburon/a99494.html; Cecilio Canelón, "Contra todos los racismos,"

Misión Boves, June 7, 2010, http://misionboves.blogspot.com/2010/06/contra-to
dos-los-racismos.html.

53. At age sixteen, Jackson Melián signed for $1.6 million with the New York
Yankees (1996); at age seventeen, José Vicente Salinas for $1.2 million with the
Atlanta Braves (1998); at age eighteen, Guillermo Quiroz for $1.3 million with
the Toronto Blue Jays (1998); at age sixteen, Francisco Rodríguez for $950,000
with the Anaheim Angels (1998); and at age sixteen, José Miguel Cabrera for $1.8
million with the Florida Marlins (1999). Franklin Guerra Castro, "La contratación
de peloteros en Venezuela y la importancia periodística de ese proceso," Tesis de
grado, Escuela de Comunicación Social, Universidad Central de Venezuela, 2004,
78; "¿Cómo se fabrica una grande liga?" *El Nacional* (Caracas), July 12, 1998, B2;
Hilmar Rojas, "Millonario a los 16," *El Nacional,* July 9, 1999, B3; "1,2 millones de
dólares recibió prospecto criollo," *El Nacional,* July 8, 1998, B3.

54. "Texas firmó a prospecto venezolano," *El Universal* (Caracas), April 25,
1997, Section 2, 3.

55. Steve Fainaru, "La globalización del béisbol impone una nueva forma de
esclavismo," *El Nacional,* October 31, 2001, B3.

56. Cristóbal Guerra, "¿El béisbol? ¡Yo no leo deportes!" *El Nacional,* June 4,
1997, B3.

57. Ernesto Campo, "'Caracas es mayoría y sin fraude,'" *El Nacional,* December
5, 2007, C1.

CHAPTER EIGHT: MAKING THEIR OWN MAHATMA

The author would like to thank Paulina Alberto, Tariq Ali, Benjamin Bryce,
Antoinette Burton, Marcelo Kuyumjian, Antonio Luigi Negro, Anadelia Romo,
and David Sheinin for their wonderful insights and suggestions.

1. Philip Joseph Deloria, *Playing Indian* (New Haven, CT: Yale University
Press, 1998); Marc A. Hertzman, "Brincando de índio . . . e muito mais: atravessando espaço (e tempo) com os Oito Batutas, dentro e fora da cidade," in *Negros
nas cidades brasileiras (1890–1950),* ed. Ana Barone and Flávia Rios (São Paulo:
Intermeios, 2019).

2. Milton Araújo Moura, "Cinema, fantasia e Carnaval em Salvador (1945–
1970)," *Revista FSA (Teresina)* 11, no. 2 (June 2014): 98–125.

3. Anísio Félix, ed., *Filhos de Gandhi: a história de um afoxé* (Salvador: Gráfica
Central, 1987). In addition to these interviews, I use a number of previously unmentioned textual sources, many of which are newspaper articles I located using
the digitalized collection and search tools hosted by Brazil's Biblioteca Nacional
(http://bndigital.bn.gov.br/hemeroteca-digital/). Searching for "Gandhi" turned
up a surprising number of hits and indicate the rich, untapped material about
Gandhi's reception and significance in Brazil.

4. Even while critiquing Filhos de Gandhy for their own essentialisms and
distortions, Shukla engages in some of the same, describing, for example, "the hot

and sensuous streets of Brazil" and asserting, "For outsiders as well as for Brazilians, the flavour of the country, the passion of what it means to be a true Brazilian, can be summed up by three words: samba, carnival and soccer." Pravina Shukla, "Afro-Brazilian Avatāras: Gandhi's Sons Samba in South America," *Indian Folklore Research Journal* 1, no. 1 (May 2001): 36, 39, 42, 44.

5. Shukla, 36.

6. Isis Costa McElroy, "A Transdiasporic Paradigm: The Afoxé Filhos de Gandhy," in *Religion, Theatre, and Performance: Acts of Faith*, ed. Lance Gharavi (New York: Routledge, 2012), 128.

7. See Introduction of this volume.

8. C. R. Boxer, *The Portuguese Seaborne Empire, 1415–1825* (London: Hutchinson, 1969); Ananya Chakravarti, *The Empire of Apostles: Religion, Accommodation and the Imagination of Empire in Modern Brazil and India* (New Delhi, India: Oxford University Press, 2018).

9. In 1870, the politician and writer Aureliano Cândido Tavares Bastos denounced a proposal to attract "coolies," arguing that Brazil should learn from the French, Spanish, and English experiences and avoid "the error of importing Indians and Chinese." Tavares Bastos, *A provincia: estudo sobre a descentralisação no Brazil*, Second (São Paulo: Companhia Editora Nacional, 1937), 276–77; Jeffrey Lesser, *Negotiating National Identity: Immigrants, Minorities, and the Struggle for Ethnicity in Brazil* (Durham, NC: Duke University Press, 1999), 20–21.

10. Ananya Chakravarti, "Peripheral Eyes: Brazilians and India, 1947–1961," *Journal of Global History* 10 (2015): 122–46.

11. For a critical overview, see Florencia E. Mallon, "The Promise and Dilemma of Subaltern Studies: Perspectives from Latin American History," *The American Historical Review* 99, no. 5 (December 1994): 1491–515.

12. José C. Moya, "A Continent of Immigrants: Postcolonial Shifts in the Western Hemisphere," *Hispanic American Historical Review* 86, no. 1 (2006): 24.

13. Chakravarti, "Peripheral Eyes."

14. Chakravarti, 145–46; Moya, "A Continent of Immigrants," 24.

15. Chakravarti, "Peripheral Eyes," 124.

16. Chakravarti, 122.

17. As Jerry Dávila shows, Brazilian foreign policy during the era is not easily pigeonholed. Even under the control of a right-wing dictatorship in the 1960s and 1970s, Brazil pursued relationships with recently decolonized African nations. Jerry Dávila, *Hotel Trópico: Brazil and the Challenge of African Decolonization, 1950–1980* (Durham NC: Duke University Press, 2010).

18. Scott Ickes, *African-Brazilian Culture and Regional Identity in Bahia, Brazil* (Gainesville: University Press of Florida, 2013), 27; Anadelia A. Romo, *Brazil's Living Museum: Race, Reform, and Tradition in Bahia* (Chapel Hill: University of North Carolina Press, 2010), 149–50.

19. For national overviews, see Antonio L. Negro and Fernando T. Silva, "Trabalhadores, sindicatos e política (1945–1964)," in *O Brasil republicano*, vol. 3, ed. Jorge Luiz Ferreira and Lucília de Almeida Neves Delgado (Rio de Janeiro: Civilização Brasileira, 2003); Salvador A. M. Sandoval, *Os trabalhadores param: greves e mudança social no Brasil, 1945–1990* (São Paulo, SP: Editora Atica, 1994).

20. Thomas E. Skidmore, *Politics in Brazil, 1930–1964: An Experiment in Democracy* (London: Oxford University Press, 1967), 66–67, 111.

21. Antonio L. Negro, "'Não trabalhou porque não quis': greve de trabalhadores têxteis na Justiça do Trabalho (Bahia, 1948)," *Revista Brasileira de História* 32, no. 64 (2012): 104. See also Antonio Sérgio Alfredo Guimarães, "A formação e a crise da hegemonia burguesa na Bahia (1930–1964)" (master's thesis, Universidade Federal da Bahia, 1982), 105–15.

22. Félix, *Filhos de Gandhi*.

23. Ickes, *African-Brazilian Culture*, 15.

24. Antonio Risério, *Uma história da cidade da Bahia* (Rio de Janeiro: Versal Editores, 2004), 503.

25. Anadelia A. Romo, "Writing Bahian Identity: Crafting New Narratives of Blackness in Salvador, Brazil, 1940s–1950s," *Journal of Latin American Studies* 50, no. 4 (November 2018): 805–32.

26. Félix, *Filhos de Gandhi*.

27. Paulina L. Alberto, *Terms of Inclusion: Black Intellectuals in Twentieth-Century Brazil* (Chapel Hill: University of North Carolina Press, 2011), 282–83.

28. Félix, *Filhos de Gandhi*.

29. Kenneth Knowles, "The Post-War Dock Strikes," *The Political Quarterly* 22, no. 3 (1951): 266–90.

30. McElroy, "A Transdiasporic Paradigm," 142–43.

31. Félix, *Filhos de Gandhi*.

32. Governo do Estado da Bahia, *Desfile de afoxés* (Salvador: IPAC: Fundação Pedro Calmon, 2010), 46.

33. Raul Giovanni da Motta Lody, *Afoxé* (Rio de Janeiro: Ministério da Educação e Cultura, 1976), 6–9.

34. Moura, "Cinema, fantasia e Carnaval," 116.

35. Félix, *Filhos de Gandhi*.

36. Félix; See also Moura, "Cinema, Fantasia e Carnaval."

37. Félix, *Filhos de Gandhi*.

38. For overviews, see Edison Carneiro, *Folguedos tradicionais* (Rio de Janeiro: FUNARTE, 1982), 101–4; Ickes, *African-Brazilian Culture*, 172–80; Lody, *Afoxé*.

39. Kim D. Butler, *Freedoms Given, Freedoms Won: Afro-Brazilians in Post-Abolition São Paolo and Salvador* (New Brunswick, NJ: Rutgers University Press, 1998), 177–89.

40. Ickes, *African-Brazilian Culture*, 173.

41. Félix, *Filhos de Gandhi*.

42. Félix.

43. Carneiro, *Folguedos tradicionais*, 102–3.

44. Félix, *Filhos de Gandhi*.

45. This is not to say that "caste" is never used in Brazil, but "class" is much more common, and given the context, the choice seems significant.

46. Félix, *Filhos de Gandhi*.

47. Félix.

48. Félix.

49. Moura emphasizes this point, which is also evident throughout the interviews compiled by Félix. Félix, *Filhos de Gandhi*; Moura, "Cinema, fantasia e Carnaval," 115.

50. Félix, *Filhos de Gandhi*.

51. Félix.

52. Félix.

53. Before parading, the stevedores met with the leadership of their syndicate and, despite their fears, seem to have avoided any run-ins with authorities. Today, both spellings—"Gandhi" and "Gandhy"—are used.

54. Antonio Risério, *Carnaval Ijexá* (Bahia: Corrupio, 1981), 52.

55. There is little work about his influence in Latin America, but elsewhere we know much more. Among others, see Ashwin Desai and Goolam Vahed, *The South African Gandhi: Stretcher-Bearer of Empire* (Stanford, CA: Stanford University Press, 2016); Ramachandra Guha, *Gandhi Before India* (New York: Vintage, 2015); Isabel Hofmeyr, *Gandhi's Printing Press: Experiments in Slow Reading* (Cambridge, MA: Harvard University Press, 2013); Ramin Jahanbegloo, *The Global Gandhi: Essays in Comparative Political Philosophy* (Abingdon, Oxon: Routledge, 2018); Nico Slate, *Colored Cosmopolitanism: The Shared Struggle for Freedom in the United States and India* (Cambridge, MA: Harvard University Press, 2012).

56. Vijay Prashad, "Waiting for the Black Gandhi: Satyagraha and Black Internationalism," in *From Toussaint to Tupac: The Black International since the Age of Revolution*, ed. Michael O. West, William G. Martin, and Fanon Che Wilkins (Chapel Hill: University of North Carolina Press, 2009), 179.

57. Prashad, 179.

58. Book Forum, "The South African Gandhi: Stretcher-Bearer of Empire," *Journal of Natal and Zulu History* 32, no. 1 (2018): 100–118.

59. Faisal Devji, "The Undertaker," *Journal of Natal and Zulu History* 32, no. 1 (2018): 103.

60. Devji, 103.

61. Jon Soske, "Myth and the Archive: Reading Mandela's Gandhi," *Journal of Natal and Zulu History* 32, no. 1 (2018): 110.

62. Soske, 111.

63. Soske, 111.

64. Prashad, "Waiting for the Black Gandhi," 179.

65. Prashad. See also Slate, *Colored Cosmopolitanism*, esp. 42–47.

66. For a larger discussion of Black intellectual thought and debates, see Alberto, *Terms of Inclusion.*

67. Félix, *Filhos de Gandhi.*

68. Prashad, "Waiting for the Black Gandhi," 184.

69. Ashwin Desai and Goolam Vahed, *The South African Gandhi: Stretcher-Bearer of Empire* (Stanford, CA: Stanford University Press, 2016).

70. Mário Andrade, "Manhã," *Para Todos,* August 25, 1928.

71. "Luís Carlos Prestes," Dicionário Histórico-Biográfico Brasileiro (Fundação Getúlio Vargas) UOL Educação, https://educacao.uol.com.br/biografias/luis-carlos-prestes.htm.

72. Jorge Amado, *O cavaleiro da esperança: vida de Luíz Carlos Prestes* (São Paulo: Livraria Martins, 1942).

73. "Curiosidades," *Lusitania,* June 16, 1929.

74. Stuart Hall and Sut Jhally, *Race the Floating Signifier* (Northampton, MA: Media Education Foundation, 2002).

75. "Dois symbolos contradictorios da tactica de dirigir as multidões," *A.B.C.,* March 21, 1925.

76. "No maravilhoso paiz dos 'Rajahs,'" *Correio Paulistano,* September 19, 1921.

77. "Pedido em favor de 'leader' socialista Gandhi," *Diario de Pernambuco* Recife (January 9, 1924): 1. Such labels could be remarkably elastic, especially among the sometimes choppy currents that connected Brazil to India and the British Empire. A newspaper in Rio reprinted an article from the London-based socialist *Labour Leader,* which noted that followers "blindly obeyed" Gandhi and the Indian Muslim activist Shaukat Ali. "A situação nas Indias," *Correio Da Manhã,* November 20, 1920.

78. Félix, *Filhos de Gandhi.*

79. Félix.

80. Félix.

81. Joseph S. Alter, *Gandhi's Body: Sex, Diet, and the Politics of Nationalism* (Philadelphia: University of Pennsylvania Press, 2000), 4. Other scholars have offered more critical interpretations. For example, Anshuman Mondal shows how Gandhi was part of a larger "symbolic articulation of womanhood in nationalist discourse—a discourse for the most part composed by men, in which female agency is effaced or circumscribed." Anshuman Mondal, "The Emblematics of Gender and Sexuality in Indian Nationalist Discourse," *Modern Asian Studies* 36, no. 4 (October 2002): 936n62.

82. For helpful introductions to the complex histories and historiographies of Gandhian gender politics, see Mondal, "The Emblematics of Gender and Sexuality"; Bhikhu C. Parekh, *Colonialism, Tradition, and Reform: An Analysis of Gandhi's*

Political Discourse, rev. ed. (New Delhi: Sage Publications, 1999), 191–227; Sujata Patel, "Construction and Reconstruction of Woman in Gandhi," in *Ideals, Images, and Real Lives: Women in Literature and History*, ed. Alice Thorner and Maithreyi Krishna Raj (Mumbai: Published for Sameeksha Trust by Orient Longman, 2000), 257–87.

83. Wlamyra Ribeiro Albuquerque, "Esperança de Boaventuras: construções da África e africanismos na Bahia (1887–1910)," *Estudos Afro-Asiáticos* 24, no. 2 (2002): 215–45; Butler, *Freedoms Given, Freedoms Won*.

84. Lody, *Afoxé*, 3.

85. Moura, "Cinema, fantasia e carnaval."

86. Moura, 117.

87. Cláudio Tuiuti Tavares, "Afoché: ritmo bárbaro da Bahia," *O Cruzeiro*, May 29, 1948.

88. Tavares, 59, 62.

89. João José Reis, *Slave Rebellion in Brazil: The Muslim Uprising of 1835 in Bahia*, trans. Arthur Brakel (Baltimore: Johns Hopkins University Press, 1995).

90. Lody, *Afoxé*, 24.

91. "Afoxé Filhas de Gandhy." Facebook, https://www.facebook.com/afoxe .filhasdegandhy/; Daniela Gonçalves, "Filhas de Gandhy: Paz e Empoderamento Feminino Afoxé," RedBull, July 23, 2017, https://www.redbull.com/br-pt/fil has-de-gandhy.

92. In one especially evocative example during a property dispute in 1945, residents in Pelourinho, an area of Salvador named for the public whipping post used to punish slaves, paid homage to the Chilean poet, Communist, and then congressman Pablo Neruda. By evoking Neruda, the residents of an area prominently associated with Brazil's slave past crossed the artificial lines that often separates Brazil and the African diaspora from Spanish America. This very local manifestation of a broader regional connection is suggestive of broader forces. Raquel Oliveira Silva, "O PCB e comitês populares democráticos em Salvador (1945–1947)" (master's thesis, Universidade Federal da Bahia, 2012), 96.

93. Petilda Serva Vazquez, "Intervalo democrático e sindicalismo (Bahia, 1942–1947)" (master's thesis, Universidade Federal da Bahia, 1986), 137. There is a developed literature on Rio's Black port workers. See for example, Erika Arantes, "O porto negro: trabalho, cultura e associativismo dos trabalhadores portuários no Rio de Janeiro na virada do XIX para o XX" (PhD diss., Universidade Federal Fluminense, 2010); Maria Cecília Velasco e Cruz, "Puzzling Out Slave Origins in Rio de Janeiro Port Unionism: The 1906 Strike and the Sociedade de Resistência dos Trabalhadores em Trapiche e Café," *Hispanic American Historical Review* 86, no. 2 (May 1, 2006): 205–45; Kit McPhee, "'A New 13th of May': Afro-Brazilian Port Workers in Rio de Janeiro, Brazil, 1905–18," *Journal of Latin American Studies* 38, no. 1 (2006): 149–77.

94. Vazquez, "Intervalo democrático," 138.

95. "Preparando a Folia," *O Imparcial*, February 9, 1935.

96. Nelson de Souza Carneiro, "Uma poetisa . . . ," *O Imparcial*, August 14, 1935.

97. Rachel Prado, "A India," *O Imparcial*, September 23, 1935.

98. "Conflicto Italo-Abyssinio," *O Imparcial*, July 27, 1935.

99. "Febronio virá para a Bahia?," *O Imparcial*, February 11, 1935.

100. Carlos Augusto Calil, "Aí vem o Febrônio!," *Teresa: Revista de Literatura Brasileira* 15 (2015): 107.

101. Calil, 103.

102. Calil, "Aí Vem." The book by Gandhi that Febrônio read may have been *Hind Swaraj* (Indian Home Rule), translated into English in 1910. Notably, though, "Apart from an enthusiastic reception in the United States," writes Tripid Suhrud, "*Hind Swaraj* remained marginal and unread, even as Gandhi himself came to be internationally feted." There are passing references to the text in Brazilian newspapers during the 1930s, and Portuguese-language translations of Gandhi's other writings appeared much later. It also might have been Romain Rolland's 1924 French-language biography of Gandhi, which was sold in Brazil as early as 1928. Though not accessible to Febrônio in 1935, Gandhi's autobiography, *The Story of My Experiments with Truth* was published in Portuguese in 1945, four years before the creation of the Filhos de Gandhy. It is, of course, also possible that he had not actually read a book by Gandhi and instead read or learned about him through other means. "Feira de livros," *O Malho*, September 22, 1928; Mahatma Gandhi, *Cartas a Ashram*, trans. Rachel de Andrade Campos (São Paulo: Hemus, 1971); Mahatma Gandhi, *Gandhi e a não-violência*, ed. Thomas Merton, trans. O. S. B. Emmanuel (Petrópolis: Vozes, 1967); M. K. Gandhi, *Memórias: histórias de minhas experiências com a verdade*, trans. Livio Xavier (Rio de Janeiro: J. Olympio, 1945); "Gandhi: Sua Extranha Personalidade," *O Jornal*, August 5, 1935; Cecília Meireles, "A experiencia da verdade," *Diário de Notícias*, October 3, 1931; Romain Rolland, *Mahatma Gandhi: Édition nouvelle augmentée d'une postface* (Paris: Librairie Stock, 1924); Tridip Suhrud, "Hind Swaraj: Translating Sovereignty," in *Ten Books That Shaped the British Empire: Creating an Imperial Commons*, ed. Antoinette Burton and Isabel Hofmeyr (Durham, NC: Duke University Press, 2014), 153–67.

103. María Josefina Saldaña-Portillo, *The Revolutionary Imagination in the Americas and the Age of Development* (Durham, NC: Duke University Press, 2003).

104. For a similar call, focused on India and Africa, see Antoinette M. Burton, *Brown over Black: Race and the Politics of Postcolonial Citation* (Gurgaon, India: Three Essays Collective, 2012).

CHAPTER NINE: READING THE CARIBBEAN AND UNITED STATES THROUGH PANAMANIAN *REGGAE EN ESPAÑOL*

1. David McCullough, *The Path between the Seas: The Creation of the Panama Canal, 1870–1914* (New York: Simon & Schuster, 1977).

2. "The musical style known as 'dancehall' derives its name from the Jamaican dance hall, a cultural institution that has historically nurtured all major genres of that country's recorded popular music. Although dancehall first emerged in the late 1970s as a distinct style, its real explosion occurred in the early 1980s, coinciding with the widespread use of digital music technology by Jamaican record producers." Colin A. Palmer, ed., *Encyclopedia of African-American Culture and History*, vol. 2, 2nd ed. (Detroit: Macmillan Reference, 2006), 576–77.

3. Mento is a style of Jamaican folk music that characterized the Jamaican music scene before World War II. Ska is a hybrid of R&B and mento musical forms that featured shuffling rhythms, accented on the second and fourth beats, a chopped guitar or piano sound, and a loose horn section. By 1966, following American R&B's evolution into gospel-inspired soul music, the ska style gave way to slower rhythms called "rock steady," after the Alton Ellis hit "Get Ready to Rock Steady." Timothy Berg, "Mento," *St. James Encyclopedia of Popular Culture*, vol. 4, ed. Sara Pendergast and Tom Pendergast (Detroit: St. James Press, 2000), 194–96.

4. Petra Rivera-Rideau, *Remixing Reggaetón: The Cultural Politics of Race in Puerto Rico* (Durham, NC: Duke University Press, 2015), 33.

5. Lisa Shaw, *Tropical Travels: Brazilian Popular Performance, Transnational Encounters, and the Construction of Race* (Austin: University of Texas Press, 2018).

6. Lara Putnam, *Radical Moves: Caribbean Migrants and the Politics of Race in the Jazz Age* (Chapel Hill: University of North Carolina Press, 2013), 14.

7. Putnam, 37.

8. Putnam, 123.

9. Transnationalism "refers to the movement of ideas, people, and capital across national borders in the modern global era . . . [and] emphasizes the connections and flows between different nation-states, territories, and regions in the world," Vernadette González, "Transnationalism," *Encyclopedia of Race and Racism*, ed. John Hartwell Moore (Detroit: Macmillan Reference, 2013), 155.

10. Michael Omi and Howard Winant, *Racial Formation in the United States: From the 1960s to the 1990s* (New York: Routledge, 1994); Will Kymlicka, *Politics in the Vernacular: Nationalism, Multiculturalism and Citizenship* (Oxford: Oxford University Press, 2000).

11. "Folkloric cumbia is in duple meter and usually performed at a slow-to-medium tempo by a small ensemble featuring several drums (bombo, llamador, alegre), a wooden scraper (guacharaca), and shakers (guaches or maracas) playing a characteristic three-strike pattern, and flutes, either the vertical gaitas or the transverse caña de millo. The diatonic accordion, imported from Germany at the end of the nineteenth century, also found its way into cumbia repertoire," Juan C. Agudelo, *Encyclopedia of Latin American Popular Music*, ed. George Torres (Santa Barbara, CA: Greenwood, 2013), 133.

12. Melissa González, "Panama," in *Encyclopedia of Latin American Popular Music*, ed. George Torres (Santa Barbara, CA: Greenwood, 2013), 293.

13. The "mejorana" is a Panamanian folkloric musical genre that is sung and danced. In certain regions and on festive occasions, it is sung while dancing at the same time, and in others, such as in the Canajagua region, it is only sung. It is interpreted with two rustic and basic instruments, built by artisans, who are generally the best performers; it is called mejorana (today the term has been popularized as "mejoranera"), to differentiate it from Mejorana and the Socavón or Bocona. "La mejorana parte del folclor," *La Estrella de Panamá* (digital edition), July 13, 2013, http://laestrella.com.pa/opinion/mejorana-parte-folclor/23491425.

14. González, "Panama," 274.

15. Juan Humberto Manzzo Quintero, *Los archivos infranqueables de Yoni* (Panamá: Comité Nacional del Centenario, 2004), 10.

16. Antonio Cornejo Polar, "Mestizaje, Transculturation, Heterogeneity," in *The Latin American Cultural Studies Reader*, ed. Alicia Rios del Sarto and Abril Trigo (Durham, NC: Duke University Press, 2004), 117.

17. Fernando Ortiz, *Contrapunteo cubano del tabaco y del azúcar* (Madrid: Cátedra, 2002).

18. Peter Szok, *La última gaviota: Liberalism and Nostalgia in Early Twentieth-Century Panamá* (Westport, CT: Greenwood, 2001), 99.

19. Szok, 94.

20. Olmedo Alfaro, *El peligro antillano en la América Central* (Panama: Imprenta Nacional, 1924) 7.

21. Michael Conniff, *Black Labor on a White Canal: Panama, 1904–1981* (Pittsburgh: University of Pittsburgh Press, 1985), 4.

22. Peter Szok, *Wolf Tracks: Popular Art and Re-Africanization in Twentieth-Century Panama* (Jackson: University Press of Mississippi, 2012), 150–51.

23. Petra Rivera-Rideau, *Remixing Reggaetón: The Cultural Politics of Race in Puerto Rico* (Durham, NC: Duke University Press, 2015), 31.

24. Rivera-Rideau, 31–32.

25. George Priestley, "Antillean-Panamanians or Afro-Panamanians?: Political Participation and the Politics of Identity during the Carter-Torrijos Treaty Negotiations," *Transforming Anthropology* 12, no. 1-2 (2008): 53.

26. Priestley, 55.

27. The 1964 flag riots reference a series of events that took place on January 9, 1964, which resulted from decades-long tensions between native Panamanians and Zonians, or Americans residing within the US-controlled Canal Zone. These tensions led to a series of anti-US riots, which resulted in an evacuation of the US embassy in Panama City, widespread looting, and dozens of deaths.

28. Michael Conniff, *Black Labor on a White Canal: Panama, 1904–1981* (Pittsburgh: University of Pittsburgh Press, 1985), 145. The Hay–Bunau-Varilla

Treaty (November 18, 1903) was an agreement between the United States and Panama that granted exclusive canal rights to the United States across the Isthmus of Panama in exchange for financial reimbursement and guarantees of protection to the newly established republic.

29. Sabia McCoy Torres, "Just ask mi 'bout Brooklyn: West Indian Identities, Transgeographies, and Living Reggae Culture," (PhD diss., Cornell University, 2015), 3. Panamanian and Panamanian West Indian culture is widespread in Brooklyn, New York. Panamanians annually celebrate Panamanian culture and heritage at the Panamanian Day Parade in Brooklyn (Desfile de los Panamaneños en Brooklyn). The Day of Independence Committee of Panamanians in New York, Inc. started the parade twenty-two years ago to celebrate the connection between American and Panamanian culture in the United States, and prides itself as the "largest Panamanian Parade in the World out of the Republic of Panama." Held annually in Brooklyn in October, it celebrates Panamanian and Panamanian West Indian Culture in the diasporic community of New York.

30. Torres, "Just ask mi 'bout Brooklyn," 5.

31. Torres, 94.

32. Torres, 97.

33. "Get Smart" was broadcast on WNYU (89.1) FM from 1979 to 2004. Patricia Meschino, "Philip Smart, Celebrated Reggae Producer/Engineer, Dead at 61," Billboard, March 14, 2014, https://www.billboard.com/biz/articles/news/5937500/philip-smart-celebrated-reggae-producerengineer-dead-at-61.

34. Wayne Marshall, "Hearing Reggaeton's African American Address," in *African Diaspora in the Cultures of Latin America, the Caribbean, and the United States*, ed. Persophone Braham (Newark: University of Delaware Press, 2016), 129–30.

35. Patricia Meschino, "Philip Smart."

36. "El General," TioTeo.com, June 6, 2015, accessed October 22, 2018, http://www.tioteo.com/blog/el-general/.

37. John Otis, "Dressed in an olive-green military uniform, a lanky Panamanian . . . ," UPI, June 7, 1993, https://www.upi.com/Archives/1993/06/07/Dressed-in-an-olive-green-military-uniform-a-lanky-Panamanian/5252170490636/.

38. Now called Arena Roberto Durán.

39. For more on Black identity politics and red devil buses (*diablos rojos*), see Peter Szok, *Wolf Tracks: Popular Art and Re-Africanization in Twentieth-Century Panama* (Jackson: University Press of Mississippi, 2012).

40. Christoph Twickel, "Reggae in Panama: Bien Tough," in *Reggaeton*, ed. Raquel Z. Rivera, Wayne Marshall, and Deborah Pacini Hernández (Durham, NC: Duke University Press, 2009), 103.

41. Twickel, 82.

42. Brooklyn is home to hip-hop music and has produced iconic figures from the 1980s onward, including Big Daddy Kane, Busta Rhymes, the Notorious B.I.G., Lil' Kim, Mos Def, Talib Kweli, and Jay-Z. Big Daddy Kane is a Brooklyn

MC who undisputedly defined the term "lyricist" in the world of hip-hop. Trevor Tahiem Smith Jr. was born in East Flatbush, Brooklyn, to Jamaican parents and is better known by his stage name Busta Rhymes. Born Christopher George Wallace in 1972, Notorious B.I.G. was raised in Clinton Hill, Brooklyn, and was one of the most famous Brooklyn rappers until his untimely death in 1997. Lil' Kim, born Kimberly Denise Jones is a rapper, songwriter, and record producer. Mos Def, born Dante Terrell Smith in Brooklyn, is a famous hip-hop artist, activist, and actor. Talib Kweli grew up in Park Slope, the son of an English professor and an adminis-trator in the CUNY system. He has long been an activist and advocate for justice. In 2011, Kweli founded Javotti Media, his independent label, which is based in Brooklyn. Torres, "Just ask mi 'bout Brooklyn," 3–5.

43. George Andrews Reid, *Afro-Latin America: 1800–2000* (Oxford: Oxford University

Press, 2004), 183.

44. George Priestley and Alberto Barrow, "The Black Movement in Panamá: A Historical and

Political Interpretation, 1994–2004," *Souls* 10, no. 3 (2008): 232.

45. Priestley, "Antillean-Panamanians or Afro-Panamanians?", 55.

46. Twickel, "Reggae in Panama: Bien Tough," 105.

47. Wayne Marshall, "Dem Bow, Dembow, Dembo: Translation and Transna-tion in reggaeton," *Lied und populäre Kultur / Song and Popular Culture: Jahrbuch des Deutschen Volksliedarchivs* 53 (2008): 133.

48. Marshall, 139.

49. Underground music in Puerto Rico emerged in the 1980s and encompassed reggae and rap music that projected the environment of an invisible youth culture: drugs, violence, poverty, love, and sex. "Underground was indeed often vulgar and violent. Sex, marijuana, and guns figured prominently in many of its lyrics." Ra-quel Z. Rivera, Wayne Marshall, and Deborah Pacini Hernández, eds., *Reggaeton* (Durham, NC: Duke University Press, 2009), 111. Wayne Marshall et al., "Intro-duction: Reggaeton's Socio-Sonic Circuitry," in *Reggaeton*, 10–11.

50. Peter Szok, "Renato Sets it Straight: An Interview on the Diffuse Roots of Reggaeton," *El Istmo: Revista virtual de estudios literarios y culturales centroameri-canos* 21 (2010): 1–12, http://istmo.denison.edu/n21/articulos/10-szok_peter_inter view_form.pdf.

51. Sonja Stephenson Watson, "Interview with Renato," Panama City, Panama, June 15, 2015.

52. Szok, "Renato Sets it Straight."

53. Ifeoma Nwankwo, "The Panamanian Origins of Reggae en Español: Seeing History through 'Los ojos café' of Renato. Interview by Ifeoma C. K. Nwankwo," in *Reggaeton*, 90.

54. "Muevela—Chicho Man & Pepito Casanova 'Panameña,'" https://www .youtube.com/watch?v=tKyyyIDEnVE.

55. José A. Corella, *Panamá: Algo de lo Nuestro* (David, Chiriquí: República de Panamá, 2001), 102.

56. Peter, "Renato Sets it Straight."

57. Peter Manuel and Michael D. Largey, *Caribbean Currents: Caribbbean Music from Rumba to Reggae* (Philadelphia: Temple University Press, 2016), 10.

58. "The interaction between the minister and congregation is facilitated by call and response, a traditional practice in which the minister makes a statement (a call) and members of the congregation reply (response), indicating that they agree, understand, identify with, or have heard the statement, whether it be an exhortation, instruction, or general information," Lisa J. Green, *African American English: A Linguistic Introduction* (Cambridge: Cambridge University Press, 2002), 147.

59. "America performed by Renato 'God Bless America,'" YouTube video, uploaded by meneaitomania, June 22, 2007, http://www.youtube.com/watch?v=pEX7wjmTIdI.

60. "Oye . . . yo voy a viajar" (Listen ladies and gentlemen, this is for you. I am Central American, listen my friend, this is for all the *latinos,* the South Americans don't remain behind and I am even going to visit Chile).

61. "America," [by the artist Renato, on the album *Party Hardy Baby! Dance Til You Drop Hits Vol. 1*], YouTube video uploaded by Renato & Raphael, November 6, 2015, https://www.youtube.com/watch?v=eKMzgfEZTB8.

62. Mary Louise Pratt, *Imperial Eyes: Travel Writing and Transculturation* (New York: Routledge, 2002).

CHAPTER TEN: THE TORTUOUS ROAD TOWARD THE BUILDING OF A MOSQUE IN BUENOS AIRES

I wish to acknowledge financial support from the Thyssen Foundation and the Humboldt Foundation for the research and writing of this article. I would also like to thank the S. Daniel Abraham Center and the Elías Sourasky Chair, both at Tel Aviv University, for their support.

1. On Menem's Middle East policy, see Ornela Fabani, *Los gobiernos de Menem y el conflicto palestino israelí: ¿un quiebre del tradicional patrón de equidistancia?* (Madrid: Universidad Complutense de Madrid, 2013); Magdalena Carrancio, "Señales de una diplomacia presidencialista: Argentina y los países de Medio Oriente y Norte de África," in *La política exterior argentina: 1998–2001. El cambio de gobierno: ¿impacto o irrelevancia?* (Rosario: Ed. CERIR, 2001), 251–70; Magdalena Carrancio, "Las repercusiones del conflicto del Medio Oriente en la política exterior argentina," in CERIR, *La política exterior argentina, 1994–1997* (Rosario: Ed. CERIR, 1998), 149–73; Paulo Botta, "Argentina e Irán entre 1989 y 1999: Entre las sombras de los atentados terroristas y el cambio de política exterior argentina," *Araucaria* 14, no. 28 (2012): 155–78.

2. On Menem's social and economic policies, see Celia Szusterman, "Carlos Saúl Menem: Variations on the Theme of Populism," *Bulletin of Latin American Research* 19, no. 2, (April 2000): 193–206; Kurt Weyland, "Neopopulism and Neoliberalism

in Latin America: How Much Affinity?," *Third World Quarterly* 24, no. 6 (December 2003): 1095–1115; Marcos Novaro, "La década del menemismo," in *Entre el abismo y la ilusión Peronismo, democracia y mercado*, ed. Juan Carlos Torre, Marcos Novaro, Vicente Palermo and Isidoro Cheresky (Buenos Aires: Norma, 1999).

3. In his most recent book, Peter Wade views racial thinking as a historically constituted and ever-shifting assemblage. See Peter Wade, *Degrees of Mixture, Degrees of Freedom: Genomics, Multiculturalism, and Race in Latin America* (Durham, NC: Duke University Press, 2017).

4. Federico Finchelstein, *From Fascism to Populism in History* (Oakland: University of California Press, 2017), xii; Ernesto Semán, "Comparing Trump to South American Authoritarians Reveals a Dangerous Misunderstanding of Democracy," *Washington Post*, February 20, 2018, https://www.washingtonpost.com/news/made-by-history/wp/2018/02/20/stop-comparing-trump-to-south-american-dictators-hes-actually-far-worse; A. Dirk Moses, Federico Finchelstein, and Pablo Piccato, "Juan Perón Shows How Trump Could Destroy Our Democracy without Tearing It Down," *Washington Post*, March 22, 2017, https://www.washingtonpost.com/posteverything/wp/2017/03/22/juan-peron-shows-how-trump-could-destroy-our-democracy-without-tearing-it-down/; Jack Schwartz, "Will Donald Trump Be America's Own Juan Perón?," *Daily Beast*, last updated April 11, 2017, https://www.thedailybeast.com/will-donald-trump-be-americas-own-juan-peron.

5. There is a vast bibliography on Populism in Latin America. For two useful collection of essays, see Cynthia J. Arnson and Carlos de la Torre, eds., *Latin American Populism in the Twenty-First Century* (Baltimore: Johns Hopkins University Press, 2013); Michael L. Conniff, ed., *Populism in Latin America*, 2nd ed. (Tuscaloosa: University of Alabama Press, 2012).

6. Raanan Rein, "From Juan Perón to Hugo Chávez and Back: Populism Reconsidered," in *Shifting Frontiers of Citizenship: The Latin American Experience*, ed. Mario Sznajder, Luis Roniger, and Carlos Forment (Boston: Brill, 2012), 289–311.

7. This paragraph is based on my "Melting the Pot? Peronism, Jewish-Argentines and the Struggle for Diversity," in *Making Citizens in Argentina*, ed. Benjamin Bryce and David M. K. Sheinin (Pittsburgh: University of Pittsburgh Press, 2017), 102–18.

8. Lila Caimari, *Perón y la Iglesia Católica* (Buenos Aires: Ariel, 1995); Raanan Rein, *Populism and Ethnicity: Peronism and the Jews of Argentina* (Montreal: McGill-Queen's University Press, 2020), chapter 2.

9. See Orestes D. Confalonieri, *Perón contra Perón* (Buenos Aires: Editorial Antygua, 1956).

10. Leonardo Senkman, "Etnicidad e inmigración durante el primer peronismo," *Estudios Interdisciplinarios de América Latina y el Caribe* 3, no. 2 (julio-diciembre de 1992): 5–39; Mónica Quijada Mauriño, "De Perón a Alberdi: selectividad étnica y construcción nacional en la política inmigratoria argentina," *Revista de Indias* 7, no. 195/196 (January 1992): 867–88.

11. Hamurabi F. Noufouri, *La justicia estética de Evita y el orientalismo Peronista* (Buenos Aires: Cálamo de Sumer, 2013), 105, 115.

12. Quoted in Marcos A. Viquendi, "Los sirio-libaneses frente a la política nacional en el marco del primer peronismo (1946–1955)" (unpublished master's thesis, UNTREF, 2017), 8.

13. Carolina Biernat, *¿Buenos o útiles?: la política inmigratoria del peronismo* (Buenos Aires: Biblos, 2007), 118–23.

14. Eduardo Elena, "Argentina in Black and White: Race, Peronism, and the Color of Politics, 1940 to the Present," in *Rethinking Race in Modern Argentina*, ed. Paulina L. Alberto and E. Elena (Cambridge: Cambridge University Press 2016), 186–87.

15. Section 89 in the 1994 constitution stated instead that "To be elected President or Vice President of the Nation it is necessary to have been born in the Argentine territory, or to be the son of a native born citizen if born in a foreign country." On the previous constitutional change, see Raanan Rein, *Argentine Jews or Jewish Argentines? Essays on Ethnicity, Identity, and Diaspora* (Boston: Brill, 2010), chapter 7.

16. See Raanan Rein and Ariel Noyjovich, *Los muchachos Peronistas árabes* (Buenos Aires: Sudamericana, 2018). On Argentina's relations with the Middle East in this period, see Lily Pearl Ballofet, *Argentina and the Golbal Middle East* (Stanford, CA: Stanford University Press, 2020); Ignacio Klich, "Equidistance and Gradualism in Argentine Foreign Policy Toward Israel and the Arab World, 1949–1955," in *The Jewish Diaspora in Latin America: New Studies on History and Literature*, ed. David Sheinin and Lois Baer Barr (New York: Routledge, 1996), 219–38.

17. Lilia Ana Bertoni, "La inmigración sirio-libanesa en América Latina. De Turquía a Buenos Aires. Una colectividad nueva a fines del siglo XIX," *Estudios Migratorios Latinoamericanos* 9, no. 26 (Abril 1994): 68; Hamurabi Noufouri, *Del Islam y los árabes: acerca de la percepción argentina de lo propio y lo ajeno* (Buenos Aires: Cálamo de Sumer, 2001).

18. Domingo Faustino Sarmiento, "Prevenciones e insinuaciones de Peuser y Crespo," *El Diario*, January 5, 1888, in Juan José Sebreli, *La Cuestión judía en la Argentina* (Buenos Aires: Editorial Tiempo Contemporáneo, 1973), 59–60.

19. See Benjamin Bryce's chapter, "Asian Migration, Racial Hierarchies, and Exclusion in Argentina, 1890–1920," in this volume.

20. "La inmigración japonesa," *La Prensa*, February 17, 1910, quoted from Bryce, "Asian Migration."

21. "Los Turcos en Buenos Aires," *Caras y Caretas*, March 1, 1902.

22. Steven Hyland Jr., *More Argentine Than You: Arabic Speaking Immigrants in Argentina* (Albuquerque: University of New Mexico Press, 2017), 72–79.

23. Domingo F. Sarmiento, *Facundo or Civilization and Barbarism* (London: Penguin, 1998).

24. Sandra McGee Deutsch, "Insecure Whiteness: Jews between Civilization and Barbarism, 1880s–1940s," in *Rethinking Race in Modern Argentina: Shades of*

the Nation, ed. Eduardo Elena and Paulina Alberto (New York: Cambridge University Press, 2016), 25–52.

25. See Bryce, "Asian Migration." The English-language daily the *Standard* argued on February 3, 1912, that "the British position is that since Turkish Asiatics not of the Caucasian but Semitic race, and Moslems, as well as Moors, Algerians, Egyptians and other non-Europeans not so closely related to the white races as the Indo-Germanic people of Northern India, are admitted, there is no reason why these not quite so dark Aryans should be rejected." Quoted from Bryce, "Asian Migration."

26. 27. Eva Perón, "Discurso pronunciado por la señora Eva Perón en el homenaje rendido por la colectividad árabe," Buenos Aires, August 30, 1950.

28. Juan Domingo Perón, "Discurso a residentes libaneses," *Obras completas: Juan D. Perón*, (Buenos Aires), August 9, 1951.

29. The number of the so-called nipo-argentinos on the eve of World War II was estimated at some six thousand people, much smaller than the number of Japanese immigrants in Brazil or Peru. See Daniel Masterson with Sayaka Funada-Classen, *The Japanese in Latin America* (Urbana: University of Illinois Press, 2004), 146–47.

30. Juan Domingo Perón, "En la inauguración de la sede de la Organización Israelita Argentina," *Obras completas: Juan D. Perón* (Buenos Aires), August 20, 1948, 339.

31. Juan Domingo Perón, "Ante miembros de la colectividad japonesa," *Obras completas: Juan D. Perón*, (Buenos Aires), May 29, 1951, 365; A similar message was transmitted to a group of Japanese parliamentarians who came on a visit to Argentina. See "Recibió el Presidente de la República a dipuados japoneses que visitan al país," *El Argentino*, October 24, 1953. On the political integration of Argentines of Japanese origins during the Peronist decade, such as the national congressman, Angel Kiyoshi Gashu, see Raanan Rein, Aya Udagawa, and Pablo Vázquez, "Los muchachos peronistas japoneses: The Peronist Movement and the Nikkei," in *Migrants, Refugees, and Asylum Seekrs in Latin America*, ed. Raanan Rein, Stefan Rinke, and David M. K. Sheinin (Boston: Brill, 2020), 264–90.

32. Marcos A. Viquendi, "Los sirio-libaneses frente a la política nacional," 31.

33. Ariel Noyjovich and Raanan Rein, "'For an Arab There Can Be Nothing Better Than Another Arab': Nation, Ethnicity, and Citizenship in Peronist Argentina," in *The New Ethnic Studies in Latin America*, ed. Raanan Rein, Stefan Rinke, and Nadia Zysman (Boston: Brill, 2017), 78–98.

34. *El Día*, September 26, 2000. According to the Imam Mahmud Hussein, director of the Centro de Altos Estudios Islámicos de Buenos Aires, the cultural center included in the mosque, the latter "is not the only one in the world of these characteristics, since there is one in Rome and one in Madrid which are rather similar, at least among those that I know but this is a little larger."

35. Fabani, *Los gobiernos de Menem y el conflicto palestino israelí*, 58. Jorge Vanossi, a former member of the national congress, was among the very few politicians to oppose the initiative of Menem, claiming that this was a personal decision taken

by the president without previously consulting with the authorities of the capital city to which the land belonged (email exchange Jorge Vanossi to Julián Blejmar, November 17, 2017. I thank Julián Blejmar for sharing his exchange with Vanossi with me).

36. *La Nación*, October 30, 1999; *Página/12*, November 13, 1999.

37. Yusef Abboud, "Los árabes musulmanes," in *Sirios, libaneses y argentinos: fragmentos para una historia de diversidad cultural argentina*, comps. Hamurabi Noufouri (Buenos Aires: Fundación Los Cedros, 2004).

38. Steven Hyland Jr., "'Solemn Expression of Faith': Muslims and Belonging in Peronist Argentina, 1946–1955," *Latin Americanist* 61, no. 2 (June 2017): 115–44.

39. "Porqué se hará una mezquita en Buenos Aires," *Al-Istiqlal*, April 1, 1950; Julio Naput, "Una mezquita en la Capital Federal," *Al-Istiqlal*, April 15, 1950.

40. Ibrahim Hallar, "Fue colocada la primera piedra de una mezquita," *La Nación*, May 7, 1950.

41. Christina Civantos, *Between Argentines and Arabs: Argentine Orientalism, Arab Immigrants, and the Writing of Identity* (Albany: State University of New York Press, 2006), chapter 3.

42. Jeffrey Lesser, *Negotiating National Identity: Immigrants, Minorities, and the Struggle for Ethnicity in Brazil* (Durham, NC: Duke University Press, 1999).

43. Christina Civantos, "Custom-building the Fictions of the Nation Arab-Argentine Rewritings of the Gaucho," *International Journal of Cultural Studies* 4, no. 1 (March 2001): 69–87. Interestingly enough, Sephardi Jews, especially Moroccan Jews, also have a claim to Spanish identity, pointing to the ties of language, music, food, and memory that bound them to medieval Spain. See McGee Deutsch, "Insecure Whiteness."

44. Juan Domingo Perón, "En la ceremonia realizada en el Salón Blanco," *Obras completas: Juan D. Perón* (Buenos Aires), September 18, 1950.

45. "Bajo el cielo de un barrio porteño, Caballito, la primera mezquita elevará su grave cúpula," *El Laborista*, May 5, 1950; "Tendrán en pleno Caballito una gran mezquita los fieles de Alá," *La Razón*, May 6, 1950; "Fue colocada ayer la piedra básica de la mezquita de Buenos Aires," *La Prensa*, May 7, 1950.

46. With the end of the brutal military regime of the 1970s, two mosques were built in Buenos Aires: At-Tahuid was inaugurated in the Floresta neighborhood in 1983, sponsored in part by the Islamic Republic of Iran, and Al Ahmad, in 1985, in the San Cristobal neighborhood.

47. Fatima Rajina, "Islam in Argentina: Deconstructing the Biases," *Journal of Muslim Minority Affairs* 36, no. 3 (August 2016): 394–412.

48. *Clarín*, August 28, 2000.

49. Arslan, a Druze native of Mount Lebanon, did not leave Argentina after the collapse of the Ottoman Empire and became an Argentine citizen in 1921. See Ignacio Klich, "Argentine-Ottoman Relations and Their Impact on Immigrants from

the Middle East: A History of Unfulfilled Expectations, 1910–1915," *Americas* 50, no. 2 (October 1993): 177–205; Paulo Botta, "Las relaciones diplomáticas y con-sulares entre la República Argentina y el Imperio Otomano," in *Presença Árabe na América do Sul*, org. Paulo Daniel Farah (Sao Paulo: Ediciones BibliASPA, 2010): 17–46; Pablo Tornielli, "Hombre de tres mundos. Para una biografía política e intelectual del emir Emín Arslán," *Revista Tunecina de Estudios Hispánicos* no. 2 (2015): 157–81.

50. *Página/12*, November 13, 1999; *Clarín*, September 25, 2000.

51. *Página/12*, September 26, 2000.

52. *Página/12*, November 13, 1999.

53. *Clarín*, August 28, 2000.

54. Carrancio, "Las repercusiones del conflicto," 163.

55. Luis Gasulla, *El negocio político de la obra pública: De la patria contratista a Menem. De los noventa a Kirchner. De CFK a Macri* (Buenos Aires: Sudamericana, 2016).

56. *Clarín*, September 26, 2000.

57. Elena, "Argentina in Black and White," 187.

58. Christina Civantos, "Ali Bla Bla's Double-Edged Sword: Argentine President Carlos Menem and the Negotiation of Identity," in *Between the Middle East and the Americas: The Cultural Politics of Diaspora*, ed. Evelyn Alsultany and Ella Shohat (Ann Arbor: University of Michigan Press, 2013), 108–29.

59. Carl Solberg, *Immigration and Nationalism: Argentina and Chile, 1890–1914* (Austin: University of Texas Press, 1970), 20.

CHAPTER 11. BURIED

1. *Damiana Kryygi*, 8:40. The director and narrator, Alejandro Fernández Mou-ján, reads directly from a Spanish translation of Charles de la Hitte and Herman ten Kate, *Notes ethnographiques sur les Indiens Guayaquis* (La Plata: Anales del Mu-seo de La Plata, 1897). When the film quotes directly from primary source mate-rial, I use the archaic prose of the translation from French to Spanish to English (given in subtitles). For the remaining quotes, I translated from Spanish to English. For the translations from French to English, I was assisted by Henry Coomes. With the German-language sources and translations, I was assisted by Timo Schaefer. I am grateful to anthropologist Warren Thompson for extensive conversations on the Ache. Thanks to Alejandro Fernández Mouján for sharing important primary source documents and for allowing me to interview him. Thanks also to Julia Irion Martins for her assistance in reading the scene in the basement of the Museo de La Plata and for her efforts on an early draft.

2. The literature on colonial anthropology and photography is well-developed. As a starting point, see Deborah Poole's work cited below, and Zahid R. Chaud-hary, *Afterimage of Empire: Photography in Nineteenth-Century India* (Minneap-olis: University of Minnesota Press, 2012); Elizabeth Edwards, *Anthropology and*

Photography, 1860–1920 (New Haven, CT: Yale University Press, 1992); Amos Morris-Reich, *Race and Photography: Racial Photography as Scientific Evidence, 1876–1980* (Chicago: University of Chicago Press, 2016).

3. Records of the Bureau of Insular Affairs (Record Group 350), 1868–1945, US National Archives and Records Administration, https://www.archives.gov/research/guide-fed-records/groups/350.html.

4. Deborah Poole, "An Image of 'Our Indian': Type Photographs and Racial Sentiments in Oaxaca, 1920–1940," *Hispanic American Historical Review* 84, no. 1 (2004): 37–82 (quotes from pp. 45 and 40–41).

5. Jens Andermann, *The Optic of the State: Visuality and Power in Argentina and Brazil* (Pittsburgh: University of Pittsburgh Press, 2007), 203.

6. Robert Lehmann-Nitsche, "Über die langen Knochen der südbayerischen Reihengräberbevölkerung" (PhD diss., Ludwig-Maximilians-Universität, 1894).

7. Irina Podgorny, "Lehmann-Nitsche, Robert," *Complete Dictionary of Scientific Biography* (Detroit: Charles Scribner's Sons, 2008), http://www.encyclopedia.com/science/dictionaries-thesauruses-pictures-and-press-releases/lehmann-nitsche-robert. See also, Kathrin Reinert, *Indianerbilder: Fotografie Und Wissen in Peru Und Im La Plata-Raum von 1892 Bis 1910* (Wiesbaden, Germany: Springer VS, 2017), 273; Sandra Carreras, "Der Forscher Und Seine Sammlungen: Robert Lehmann-Nitsche Im Deutsch-Argentinischen Wissenschaftlichen Netzwerk," 9–19, n.d.

8. Andrew Zimmerman, *Anthropology and Antihumanism in Imperial Germany* (Chicago: University of Chicago Press, 2001), 63–65.

9. Zimmerman, 87.

10. Zimmerman, 91.

11. Zimmerman, 88.

12. Reinert, *Indianerbilder*, 278.

13. For a brilliant study of this museum, see Irina Podgorny, *El sendero del tiempo y de las causas accidentales: Los espacios de la prehistoria en la Argentina, 1850–1910* (Rosario: Prohistoria Ediciones, 2009), 194.

14. IAI, N-0070 b 684, Brief von Herman Frederik Carel ten Kate and Robert Lehmann-Nitsche vom 01.02.1897. Cited by Reinert, 278.

15. Robert Lehmann-Nitsche, "Revelamiento Antropológico de Una India Guayaquí," *Revista del Museo de La Plata* 15, no. 2 (1908): 91–99; quote from p. 91.

16. Lehmann-Nitsche, 91.

17. Lehmann-Nitsche, 92.

18. *Damiana Kryygi*; Lehmann-Nitsche, "Revelamiento," 92–93.

19. Lehmann-Nitsche cites C. Röse, which he writes as Roese: "Roese, *Beiträge zur europäischen Rassenkunde und die Beziehungen zwischen Rasse und Zahnverderbnis. Archiv für Rassen-und Gesellschaftsbiologie*, III, 1905, Sept, p. 18," ("Revelamiento," 98). See Oskar v. Hovorka-Wien in *Zentralblatt für Anthropologie*, December 1907, 147–48, http://www.digi-hub.de/viewer/!toc/DE-11-002123515/42/-/.

20. Lehmann-Nitsche, "Revelamiento," 97.

21. A classic on this topic is Stephen Jay Gould's *The Mismeasure of Man* (New York: W. W. Norton, 1981).

22. Hans Virchow, "Der Kopf Eines Guajaki-Mädchens," in *Zeitschrift Für Ethnologie*, 40, 1908; Katrin Koel-Abt and Andreas Winkelmann, "The Identification and Restitution of Human Remains from an Aché Girl Named 'Damiana': An Interdisciplinary Approach," *Annals of Anatomy—Anatomischer Anzeiger* 195, no. 5 (2013): 393–400.

23. Virchow, "Der Kopf Eines Guajaki-Mädchens."

24. Reinert, *Indianerbilder*, 274.

25. Reinert, 71.

26. Gastón R. Gordillo, cited by Reinert, 102–3. On indigenous labor in the sugar mills of Jujuy, see Gastón Rafael Gordillo, "The Bush, the Plantations, and the 'Devils': Culture and Historical Experience in the Argentinean Chaco" (PhD diss., University of Toronto, 1999), https://tspace.library.utoronto.ca/bitstream/1807/13281/1/NQ41162.pdf.

27. Lehmann-Nitsche, "Revelamiento Antropológico," 54, quoted by Marcelo Valko, "Prólogo," in Colectivo GUIAS, *El Familiar: Del Ingenio La Esperanza al Museo de La Plata* (La Plata: De la Campana, 2011), 11.

28. Reinert, *Indianerbilder*, 291.

29. Reinert, 291.

30. In interpreting this image, I draw on Deborah Poole, "An Excess of Description: Ethnography, Race, and Visual Technologies," *Annual Review of Anthropology* 34 (2005): 159–79. I get the Stocking quote from Poole, 162.

31. Lehmann-Nitsche, "Revelamiento Antropológico," 55; cited by Colectivo GUIAS in *El Familiar*, 86.

32. Andermann, *Optic of the State*, 45.

33. Historian William Fysh gives historical flesh to ahistorical notions of spectatorship; see "'The Little Crystal Eye Would Not Blink': Jean Rouch and the Camera Eye Witness," *Screen* 59, no. 4 (Winter 2018).

34. Jessica Stites Mor, *Transition Cinema: Political Filmmaking and the Argentine Left since 1968* (Pittsburgh: University of Pittsburgh Press, 2012), 3.

35. "Ley 25.517 y su Decreto Regl. 701," *Restitución de cuerpos humanos a pueblos originarios* (blog), November 21, 2001, https://restituciondecuerpos.wordpress.com/ley-nacional-25-5172001-y-su-decreto-reglamentario-7012010/.

36. Susana Margulies, María Julia, y Alejandro Fernández Mouján, "Damiana exige un nombre: Kryygi. La realización de un film entre docencia e investigación antropológica y cine documental." Ponencia presentada al IV Congreso Latinoamericano de Antropología, México DF, 7 al 10 de octubre, 2015.

37. Margulies, Julia, and Fernández Mouján.

38. Osvaldo Bayer, "Kryygi," *Página* 12, February 18, 2012, https://www.pagina12.com.ar/diario/contratapa/13-187811-2012-02-18.html.

39. Bayer was not alone in this reading of the repatriation of Damiana Kryygi's remains. After the release of the film, one newspaper offered a similar synopsis, "'Damiana' denuncia la historia de humillación de los pueblos originarios en Paraguay," *Télam*, May 19, 2015, http://www.telam.com.ar/notas/201505/105620-cine-alejandro-fernandez-moujan-damiana.html.

40. Film critic María Moreno places *Damiana Kryygi* alongside Albertina Carri's *Los rubios* as a film that moves beyond the "pornography of torture"; see "Cuento con cuatro científicos y una indita," *Página* 12, August 26, 2015, https://m.pagina12.com.ar/diario/contratapa/13-280174-2015-08-26.html.

41. "Preguntas sobre *Damiana Kryygi*," Alejandro Fernández Mouján to Kevin Coleman, personal communication, December 23, 2017.

42. Roger Koza, "Las vueltas del perpetuo movimiento del cine," *Clarín*, December 30, 2015, https://www.clarin.com/rn/escenarios/vueltas-perpetuo-movimiento-cine_0_S1x2hRuPmx.html.

43. Damiana Kryygi's remains were buried in Cazaapá, far from where she was captured. She was near Encarnación when a group of settler colonists killed her family and took her away. Decades later, a subgroup of the Ache, one that had been an enemy of Damiana Kryygi's community, claimed her as their own and buried her remains within their territory. While space does not permit a recounting of the decimation of the Ache and the fragmentation of their ancestral territory, I wish to briefly make two points, neither of which is raised in the film. First, the surviving Ache and the Argentine anthropologists did not have the option of returning her remains to the community from which she came. Second, the real ethnolinguistic barriers and enmity that characterized relations between these different Ache groups in previous generations had, by the 2000s when this film was made, been partially subordinated to an emerging notion of a Pan-Ache community. These two factors combined such that, 114 years after she was captured, the Ache of Ypetimí buried Damiana Kryygi in the Caazapá National Park. For different anthropological perspectives on the Ache and their history, see Warren M. Thompson, "'Goethe of the Jungle': Friedrich C. Mayntzhusen's Apprenticeship and Travels, 1900–1949" (2018, manuscript under review); Kim Hill and A. Magdalena Hurtado, *Ache Life History: The Ecology and Demography of a Foraging People* (New York: Aldine de Gruyter, 1996); Pierre Clastres, *Chronicle of the Guayaki Indians*, trans. Paul Auster (New York: Zone Books, 1998); Richard Arens, ed., *Genocide in Paraguay* (Philadelphia: Temple University Press, 1976). For more on how GUIAS coordinated with the Federación Nativa Ache de Paraguay (FENAP), see Margulies, Julia, and Fernández Mouján, "Damiana exige un nombre."

44. This is like a "duration photograph," a term that Walter Benn Michaels credits to artist Owen Kydd. See Walter Benn Michaels, "The Force of a Frame: Owen Kydd's Durational Photographs," *Nonsite.org*, March 14, 2014, http://nonsite.org/feature/the-force-of-a-frame.

45. Enrique Pérez Balcedo, "Hace 133 años era fundado el Hospital de Melchor Romero," *Oesteplatense*, April 6, 2017, http://oesteplatense.com.ar/nota/1901/hace_133_anos_era_fundado_el_hospital_de_melchor_romero.

46. For more on this, see Benjamin Bryce, *To Belong in Buenos Aires: Germans, Argentines, and the Rise of a Pluralist Society* (Stanford, CA: Stanford University Press, 2018). On German scientists in Paraguay, see Bridget María Chesterton, "Paraguay Guazú: Big Paraguay, Carlos Fiebrig, and the Botanical Garden as a Launching Point for Paraguayan Nationalism," in *The Chaco War: Environment, Ethnicity, and Nationalism* (New York: Bloomsbury, 2016), 91–111.

EPILOGUE. OVERCOMING THE NATIONAL

1. "What it Means to Be 'Black in Latin America,'" *NPR (National Public Radio)*, July 27, 2011, https://www.npr.org/2011/07/27/138601410/what-it-means-to-be-black-in-latin-america.

2. "Estvo seis horas detenida por la policia aeronáutica," *Clarín* (Buenos Aires), August 24, 2002, https://www.clarin.com/sociedad/mujer-denuncio-discriminaron-negra_0_SJ6xCfEeCKe.html.

3. Sergio Gómez, "Maldición eternal a quien lea esas páginas," *Página/12*, July 28, 2002, https://www.pagina12.com.ar/diario/suplementos/radar/9-290-2002-07-28.html.

4. "What it Means to Be 'Black in Latin America,'" *NPR*.

5. Mae Ngai, *Impossible Subjects: Illegal Aliens and the Making of Modern America* (Princeton, NJ: Princeton University Press, 2004).

6. Steve Carmody, "Flint Leaders Ramp Up 2020 US Census Campaign," *Michigan Radio*, January 24, 2020, https://www.michiganradio.org/post/flint-leaders-ramp-2020-us-census-campaign.

7. Amanda Burgess-Proctor, "Intersections of Race, Class, Gender, and Crime: Future Directions for Feminist Criminology," *Feminist Criminology* 1, no. 1 (2006): 27–47; Andrea Romo Pérez, "The Experiences of Black and Colombian Female Offenders with the Police in Ecuador: Understanding Minorities' Intersecting Identities," *Feminist Criminology* 14, no. 3 (2017): 330–48.

8. Michelle Ye Hee Lee, "Donald Trump's False Comments Connecting Mexican Immigrants and Crime," *Washington Post*, July 8, 2015, https://www.washingtonpost.com/news/fact-checker/wp/2015/07/08/donald-trumps-false-comments-connecting-mexican-immigrants-and-crime/.

9. Alma Guillermoprieto, "In the New Gangland of El Salvador," *New York Review of Books*, November 10, 2011, https://www.nybooks.com/articles/2011/11/10/new-gangland-el-salvador/.

10. Dara Lind, "MS-13, Explained," *Vox*, February 5, 2019, https://www.vox.com/policy-and-politics/2018/2/26/16955936/ms-13-trump-immigrants-crime.

11. Thomas B. Esdall, "We Aren't Seeing White Support for Trump for What It Is," *New York Times*, August 28, 2019, https://www.nytimes.com/2019/08/28/opinion/trump-white-voters.html.

12. Thomas Sugrue, *The Origins of the Urban Crisis* (Princeton, NJ: Princeton University Press, 2014).

ABOUT THE CONTRIBUTORS

Benjamin Bryce is assistant professor in the Department of History at the University of British Columbia. He is the author of *To Belong in Buenos Aires: Germans, Argentines, and the Rise of a Pluralist Society* (Stanford University Press, 2018). He is also the co-editor of *Making Citizens in Argentina* (University of Pittsburgh Press, 2017) and *Entangling Migration History: Borderlands and Transnationalism in the United States and Canada* (University Press of Florida, 2015).

David M. K. Sheinin is professor of history at Trent University and Académico Correspondiente of the Academia Nacional de la Historia de la República Argentina. His most recent books are *Migrants, Refugees, and Asylum Seekers in Latin America*, co-edited with Stefan Rinke and Raanan Rein (Brill, 2020) and *Making Citizens in Argentina*, co-edited with Benjamin Bryce (University of Pittsburgh Press, 2017).

Marc A. Hertzman is associate professor of history at the University of Illinois in Urbana-Champaign. He is the author of *Making Samba: A New History of Race and Music in Brazil* (Duke University Press, 2013) and *Refazenda* (Bloomsbury, 2020).

Waskar Ari-Chachaki is associate professor of history and ethnic studies/Latin American studies at the University of Nebraska. He is the author of *Earth Politics: Coloniality, Religion and Bolivia's AMP Indigenous Intellectuals, 1921–1971* (Duke University Press, 2014).

Lara Putnam is professor of history at the University of Pittsburgh. She is the author of *Radical Moves: Caribbean Migrants and the Politics of Race in the Jazz Age* (University of North Carolina Press, 2013) and *The Company They Kept: Migrants and the Politics of Gender in Caribbean Costa Rica, 1870–1960* (University of North Carolina Press, 2002).

Alexander Dawson is associate professor of history at SUNY Albany. He is the author of *The Peyote Effect: From the Inquisition to the War on Drugs* (University of California Press, 2018), *First World Dreams: Mexico Since 1989* (Zed Books, 2006), and *Indian and Nation in Revolutionary Mexico* (University of Arizona Press, 2004).

Stephen E. Lewis is professor and chair of the Department of History at California State University, Chico. He is the author of *Rethinking Mexican Indigenismo: The INI's Coordinating Center in Highland Chiapas and the Fate of a Utopian Project* (University of New Mexico Press, 2018) and *The Ambivalent Revolution: Forging State and Nation in Chiapas, Mexico, 1910–1945* (University of New Mexico Press, 2005).

Elaine Carey is professor of history and dean of the College of Humanities, Education, and Social Sciences at Purdue University Northwest. She is the author of *Plaza of Sacrifices: Gender, Power, and Terror in 1968 Mexico* (University of New Mexico Press, 2005) and *Women Drug Traffickers: Mules, Bosses, and Organized Crime* (University of New Mexico Press, 2014).

Sonja Stephenson Watson is dean of the AddRan College of Liberal Arts, interim dean of the School of Interdisciplinary Studies and professor of Spanish at Texas Christian University. She is the author of *The Politics of Race in Panama: Afro-Hispanic and West Indian Literary Discourses of Contention* (University Press of Florida, 2014), the forthcoming book *Globalization, Transnationalism, and Hybrid Identity in Panamanian reggae en español* (University Press of Florida), and the forthcoming co-edited volume with Lori Celaya, *Transatlantic, Transcultural, and Transnational Dialogues on Identity, Culture, and Migration*.

Raanan Rein is the Elías Sourasky Professor of Latin American and Spanish History and vice president of Tel Aviv University. Rein is the author of numerous books and articles. His most recent book is *Populism and Ethnicity: Peronism and the Jews of Argentina* (McGill-Queen's University Press, 2020). Rein is a member of Argentina's National Academy of History, and former president of the Latin American Jewish Studies Association (LAJSA). The Argentine government awarded him the title of Commander in the Order of the Liberator General San Martín for his contribution to Argentine culture.

Kevin Coleman is associate professor of history at the University of Toronto. He is the author of *A Camera in the Garden of Eden: The Self-Forging of a Banana Republic* (University of Texas Press, 2016), and co-editor (with Daniel James) of *Capitalism and the Camera* (Verso Books, 2021). He is principal investigator in the open-access digital humanities project, *Visualizing the Americas*, https://visualizingtheamericas

.utm.utoronto.ca. He is currently working on a documentary film called *The Photos We Don't Get to See.*

Julia Irion Martins is a PhD candidate in comparative literature and screen arts and cultures at the University of Michigan.

INDEX

Abreu, Bobby, 127
Ache (Guayaquí/Guayaki), 192–213
afoxé, 140–58
African Americans, 17, 111, 114–16,
    119, 121, 124, 126, 149, 174–75,
    214–18
African Venezuelans, 121, 123–25
Afro-Argentines, 21, 22, 36, 215
Afro-Brazilians, 10, 143, 140–58
Afro-Dominicans, 134
Afro-Hispanics, 162–63
Afro-Peruvians, 6
Aguirre Beltrán, Gonzalo, 5, 96–98
al-Said, Muhammad, 185–87
"Al tambor de la alegría" (1918), 161
Alberto, Paulina, 13
Alcaldes Mayores Particulares (AMP),
    37–39, 43, 47–55
Álvarez, Mario Roberto, 189
Alomar, Roberto, 133
Alsina, Juan, 24, 27, 28
Álvarez, Mario Roberto, 188–89
"América" (1987), 175
American Dream, 128
Anderson, Sparky, 131
Andrade, Mário de, 151–52, 157
Anslinger, Harry J., 106, 108, 110–15,
    119–20
anthropology, 18, 32, 75, 78, 84, 88,
    93, 96, 99–101, 104, 157, 162,
    192–98, 202–13
anti-Semitism, 180, 190
Aparicio, Luis, 124, 130, 132–33, 137

Arab Argentines, 18, 177–91
Argentina, 7, 8, 10, 11, 13, 14, 18, 19,
    20–36, 123–24, 135, 137, 151,
    177–213, 215–17, 219
argentinidad, 179
Arias, Arnulfo, 164
Armas, Antonio, 124, 127, 129–30
Arendt, Hannah, 70–72
Argentina, 7, 8, 10, 11, 13, 18, 19, 20–
    36, 123, 124, 135, 137, 151, 177–91,
    193–213, 215, 216, 217, 219
Arguedas, Alcides, 38, 41, 45
assimilation, 24, 29, 35, 43, 48, 53, 55,
    79, 84, 89, 91, 92, 94, 97–104, 163,
    181–84, 189, 190
Ávila Camacho, Manuel, 112
Aymaras, 13, 14, 37–55

Babalôtim/Babalotinho, 146, 154
Barbados, 65, 68, 75, 101, 159, 260,
    162
barbarism, 45, 82–83, 113, 182, 207
Bayer, Osvaldo, 206–7
Becker, Marc, 13
Blanco Chataing, Luis Jesús, 121
Boas, Franz, 79, 86, 196
Bolivia, 9, 13–15, 16, 17, 37–55, 151,
    202, 203, 216
Bolivarian Revolution, 134
Bracero Program, 10, 112, 118
Brazil, 5–7, 10–13, 23–24, 140–58,
    160, 186, 188, 195, 208, 214, 219
British West Indies, 6, 15, 56–73

Brooklyn, New York, 58, 114, 165–66, 169, 218
Bunge, Carlos Octavio, 21, 22
Bureau of Indian Affairs (BIA), 74, 75, 78–85, 88
Bureau of Social Hygiene, 109, 115
Busch, Germán, 53
Bustamante, Ramón "Pucho," 166
Butler, Kim, 14

C & C Music Factory, 168
Campanella, Roy, 121
Canada, 10, 22, 23, 27, 34, 56, 60, 62, 65, 67, 75, 100, 108, 111, 113, 169
Candomblé, 143, 145–47
Cárdenas, Lázaro, 80, 83, 95
Cardona, Ricardo, 135
Carty, Rico, 129
Carew, Rod, 129, 132, 133
Carneiro, Edison, 6, 143
Carneiro, Nelson de Souza, 156
Carnival, 8, 17, 140–58
Carrasquel, Alfonso, 124
Carter-Torrijos Treaties (1977), 165
Casanova, Pepito, 171–72
Centro Cultural Islámico Custodio de las Dos Sagradas Mezquitas Rey Fahd, 185
cephalic index, 196, 199, 202
Cervantes, Antonio "Kid Pambelé," 135
Cervecería de Caracas, 121, 132
Chaco War, 39, 44, 48
Chávez, Hugo, 133–34, 137, 216
chavismo, 133, 134, 137, 216
Chayanta, massacre of (1927), 46
Chicho Man, 164, 171–72
Chile, 9, 129, 168, 175, 215, 218
China/Chinese immigrants, 20–36, 94–95, 107, 111, 115, 142, 147, 183
cholos/cholas, 38, 40–42, 44–47, 49
Chorote, 202
Ch'utas, 44–47
Churchill, Winston, 60
Cincinnatti Reds, 123, 129–31

Citizens of the United Kingdom and Colonies (CUKC), 70, 72
Clemente, Roberto, 129
Cold Crush Brothers, 167
Cold War, 9, 70, 127–28, 143, 206, 208, 218
Collier, John, 75, 78–79, 82, 84–86, 89, 95
Colombia, 25, 59, 63, 64, 87, 123, 124, 125, 135, 161, 167, 169, 216, 217
communism, 13–14, 72, 78, 80, 83, 85, 143, 148, 150, 151, 152, 155
Concepción, David, 123–24, 129–32, 135, 138
Cordão Emulos de Gandhi, 156
Costa Rica, 15, 58, 59, 61, 63, 64, 160
crime, 101, 106, 108, 110–15, 118–20, 156, 157, 182, 207, 217, 218
criollos, 17, 121–39, 163
Cuba, 13, 15, 58, 59, 62, 63, 64, 122, 129, 132, 137, 160, 162, 214
cumbia, 161

Daddy Yankee (Ramón Luis Ayala Rodríguez), 170,
Daniel Commission Report on Illicit Narcotics Traffic (1955), 107, 113–19
Daniel, Price, 107, 113–19
Davalillo, Pompeyo, 132
De la Rúa, Fernando, 188–89
"Dem Bow" (1990)/"Son Bow" (1991), 166, 169–70
Derby, Lauren, 12
deviance, 16, 106–9, 112, 113, 117, 120, 127, 157, 169, 217
Diana, Pablo, 180
diaspora, 7, 10, 11–14, 17, 18, 59, 140, 141, 146, 149, 150, 161, 165, 169, 176, 186, 191
Díaz, Baudillo, 124, 130
Dihígo, Martín, 132
Do Alto, Hervé, 13
Dominican Republic, 6, 59, 121, 129, 134

Domingues, Petrônio, 10
dress codes, 32, 40–43, 45, 46, 47, 51, 92, 173

Earle, Rebecca, 17
Ecuador, 13, 217
Edsall, Thomas B., 218
education, 39–40, 46–55, 65, 78, 80, 85, 87, 94–98, 101–2, 104, 128, 164, 169, 173, 180, 198, 201
Egypt, 34, 94, 152, 185–87
Ejército Zapatista de Liberación Nacional, 102
El General (Edgardo Franco), 162, 164–72
El Maleante, 164
Eller, Anne, 6
Ellis, Michael F., 166–67
Embaixada Africana (African Embassy), 145
Empire Windrush, 57, 71
Escoté Montilla, Ricardo, 138
Estaba, Luis "abuelito" "Lumumba," 135–37
Estado Novo, 143, 151, 157
Ethiopia, 67, 156
eugenics, 15, 71, 104, 109
exotic, 29, 32, 126, 153, 154

Faiz, Zuhair, 189
Falcão, Ildefonso, 142
Febrônio Índio do Brasil, 156–58
Federación de Entidades Árabes Argentinas, 185
Federación Femenina Local (Bolivia), 42
Federación Nativa Aché del Paraguay, 206
Federación Obrera Local (Bolivia), 45
Federal Bureau of Narcotics (FBN), 106, 111–13, 116
Feldman, Heidi, 6
femicide 137
Fermín, Claudio "El Negro," 125
Fernández de Kirchner, Cristina, 216

Fernández Mouján, Alejandro, 18, 192–213
Ferrer, Ada, 6
Flanagan, John W., 120
Frankfurt Agreement, 196
Freyre, Gilberto, 142, 157

Galeano, Diego, 10, 11
Gamio, Manuel, 93–94, 96, 102
García, Luis "Camaleón," 124
Gates, Henry Louis, Jr., 214–16
gaucho, 182, 186–87
Gerchunoff, Alberto, 186
German Anthropological Society, 196
Gilroy, Paul, 5, 6
Gomes, Flávio, 10
Gómez, Sergio, 215
Graham, Jessica, 13, 14
Grenada, 58, 66, 67, 68, 159
Grinberg, Keila, 11
Guerra, Cristóbal, 139–40
Gunga Din (1939), 145, 147, 154

Haiti, 12, 126, 164
Hallar, Ibrahim, 186–87
Harrison Narcotics Act (1914), 107, 112
Hay-Buanu-Varilla Treaty (1903), 165
Hearns, Tommy, 135
Herskovits, Melville, 5
Heilman, Jaymie, 13
Hindus, 25, 29, 33–35, 141, 145
hip-hop, 162, 167–68, 170, 173
hispanidad, 163–64
Hollywood, 135, 144, 145
Hoover, J. Edgar, 113
Hoyos, Alejandro M., 180
Huichols, 87–89
hybridity, 17, 45, 134, 159–62, 168, 170–73, 175–76

India, 8, 22, 20–36, 141–58, 159
Indian Reorganization Act (IRA, 1934), 79, 85, 86

Jamaica, 10, 34, 58, 61–64, 70, 71, 149, 159–72, 176,
James, C.L.R., 5, 10
Japan/Japanese, 7, 20–36, 126, 142, 179, 181, 183, 184, 186, 219
Jesús de Machaca, massacre of (1921), 46
Jethroe, Sam, 121
Jews, 18, 70, 94, 177–86, 189–90
Johnson-Reed Act (1924), 62, 72
Jones, Claudia, 70, 72

Korn, Alejandro, 198, 199, 212
Koza, Roger, 208

La Castañeda mental asylum, 110
La Corporación Criollitos de Venezuela ("Los Criollitos"), 127–30, 134, 138–39
ladinos, 97–99
La Hitte, Charles de, 192–94, 197, 205, 208
Lamadrid, María Magdalena, 215
language, 5, 7, 25, 29, 31–36, 41, 43–47, 49, 54, 63, 80, 92, 96, 105, 133, 143, 161, 166, 169, 170, 172, 176, 181, 182, 190, 215
Las Estrellas del Caribe, 121
Las Estrellas Negras, 121–23
Las Estrellas Venezolanas, 121
Latinos, 112, 115, 124, 129, 131, 133–34, 166, 175, 219
Leal, Luis, 130
Lenin, V.I./Leninism, 148, 151, 157, 158
literacy, 46, 49, 52, 53, 58, 97
Little League Baseball, 127–28, 138
Lebanese, 28, 180–86
Lehmann-Nitsche, Robert, 18, 195–205, 207, 208, 210–13
Lesser, Jeffrey, 7
Liga Venezolana de Béisbol Profesional (LVBP), 121–24, 130, 132, 134, 138, 139
Lowe, Lisa, 5, 8

Maduro, Nicolás, 216
Major League Baseball (MLB), 121–24, 127, 129–34, 138–39, 172
Mandela, Nelson, 149
Mara Salvatrucha gang (MS-13), 217–18
Marley, Bob, 159
Marryshow, T. A., 66–71
Marshall, T. H., 57, 69–72
Martin, Rudolf, 197
masculinity, 17, 129, 132, 151–55
Matory, J. Lorand , 11
Matos, Fabio, 166
Meireles, Cecília, 142
Menem, Carlos Saúl, 18, 177–81, 184–85, 187–91
mento, 159
mercachifles, 178
mestizaje or mestizos, 6, 15, 16–18, 21, 22, 36, 38, 41–44, 46–47, 51, 55, 84, 89, 91–105, 123, 134, 163, 168, 178, 206, 216, 218
Mexico, 6, 9, 15–16, 34, 43, 59, 74–120, 122, 134, 216, 217
Miranda, Carmen, 144
Miss Venezuela competition, 124–25
Molina Enríquez, Andrés, 93, 103
modernity, 5, 6, 10, 13, 16, 23, 38, 40–47, 52, 55, 56, 60, 69, 71, 73, 76, 78, 82–84, 86–89, 91–95, 97, 99, 102, 103, 104, 151, 159, 179, 203
"Mohammedan Malays," 107
Montreal Expos, 131
Movimiento Popular Neuquino, 184
Muévela (1989), 171–72
Museo de La Plata, 18, 192–213
Museo de las Memorias, 209
música típica, 161
Muslims, 18, 41, 141, 154, 158, 177–91
Mussolini, Benito, 152, 156

Nando Boom (Fernando Brown), 162, 164, 165, 166,
Narcotics Control Act (1956), 113

national identity, 9, 12, 91, 94, 104, 124, 132, 134, 160–61, 164, 169, 218
nationalism, 17, 93–95, 161, 163, 169, 186, 190
Navajos, 75, 82, 84
Navegantes de Magallanes, 124, 132–33
Negro leagues, 121
Neruda, Pablo, 215
Nina Rodrigues, Raimundo, 5
Nivaclé, 202
Noriega, Manuel, 166

Oliva, Tony, 129
Organización Israelita Argentina, 183
Orientalism, 17, 141, 144, 151–55, 190
Ortiz, Fernando, 5, 162
Ottoman Empire/Ottomans, 25, 28, 30–36, 41, 181–83, 188, 190–91

Palestinians, 28, 94, 185, 186
Pan-American indigenist project, 16, 77–78, 96, 99, 103
Panama, 4, 15, 17, 56, 58, 59, 61–65, 68, 78, 122, 126, 129, 137, 159–76, 215
panameñidad, 161,
Pândegos da África (African Merry-makers), 145
Paraguay, 18, 44, 192–213, 216
Peralta, Santiago M., 180
Pérez, Carmen Victoria, 125
Pérez, Tony, 131, 131
Peronism, 18, 177–91, 205
Peru, 6, 12, 23–24, 43, 204, 214, 215, 216, 218
Petrullo, Vincent, 75–76, 85–86
peyote, 15, 75–77, 79, 85–89
Philippines, 7, 107
Pilagá, 202
Pinochet, Augusto, 168
Plessy v. Ferguson, 122, 216
police, 37, 41–43, 51, 107, 111, 113–16, 143, 147–48, 150, 157, 164, 168, 182, 189, 217

populism, 4, 50, 57, 62, 68, 71, 95, 177–91
pornography, 125–26
Porras, Belisario, 163
Prado, Rachel, 156
Prestes, Luis Carlos, 151
Price Daniel Commission hearings, 107, 113–19
Primera, Luis, 135
Prohibition era (1920–33), 108–10
Puente Luna, José Carlos de la, 7
Puerto Rico, 129, 167–71

q'aras, 39, 44
Quechuas, 39, 44, 45, 47
Queens, New York, 218
Quintana, Mirima, 125

rabiblancos, 168
Ranke, Johannes, 195, 196
reggaetón, 170–71
religion, 15, 17, 31, 35, 39, 47–48, 50, 51–54, 76, 79, 84–88, 92, 94, 129, 143–47, 156, 158, 162, 172, 177–91, 194
Remón-Eisenhower Treaty (1955), 164
Renato (Leonardo "Renato" Aulder), 164, 167, 170, 172–75
Robinson, Jackie, 121
rock steady, 159
Rockefeller, John D., 109
Roma people, 27, 29, 31, 34
Romero, Julio, 184

Saadi, Vicente Leónidas, 184
Saavedra, Bautista , 37, 46
Salazar, Luis, 124, 130–31, 135
Salazar Viniegra, Leopoldo, 110–11, 114
Salvatore, Ricardo, 10
Sanders, James E., 7
Santa Cruz, Nicomedes de, 6, 143
Santos, Manoel José dos, 146
Sapag, Felipe, 184
Saracho, Juan Misael, 46

Sarmiento, Domingo Faustino, 181, 182
Saudi Arabia, 177, 188–89
Schnautz, Travis, 107, 115–16, 118–20
Scott, R.C., 116–19
segregation, 12, 14, 37–44, 53, 121–24, 129,
Seijas, Tatiana, 6
sexuality, 118, 125–29, 138, 153, 157, 166, 167, 169, 172–75, 198, 200
Sheppard, John Ben, 117
Sierra, Justo, 93
Sikhs, 8, 27–28, 31–34, 144
ska, 159
South Asia/South Asians, 6–8, 14, 20–36, 140–58, 183, 217
Sosa, Sammy, 134
Spanish-American War (1898), 107
stevedores, 8, 17, 144, 146, 148, 150, 155, 157
streetcars, 38, 40
Syrians, 28, 31–35, 177, 180–87, 190

Tamayo, Franz, 45
tamborito, 161, 172
Tannenbaum, Frank, 4
Tarahumaras, 75, 87
ten Kate, Herman, 194, 197–99, 205, 208–9
Terry, Charles Edward, 109–11, 115
Texas Rangers, 138
The South African Gandhi: Stretcher-Bearer of Empire, 149–50
Thompson, Dennis "the Menace," 166
Thurner, Mark, 7
Tigres de Aragua, 132
Tinsman, Heidi, 9
Toba, 202
Torrijos, Omar, 165, 168–69
track and field, 123, 124
transculturation, 17, 160–62, 169–76
transnational turn, 3, 5, 10, 11
Trillo, Jesús Manuel Marcano "El Indio" "Manny," 124, 130
Trinidad, 34, 61, 66, 67, 68, 70, 71, 123, 159, 160, 162, 164–67

Trouppe, Quince, 121
Trump, Donald J., 74, 106, 178, 217–18
Trump, Fred, 218
Tseltal Mayas, 16, 91, 92, 96, 97, 99
Tsostil Mayas, 16, 91, 92

Ugarte, Manuel, 21, 22
United States, 9–13, 15–17, 18, 22, 24–27, 56, 58, 62, 68, 70, 74–90, 103–20, 121–39, 150, 155, 156–76, 178, 188, 195, 208, 209, 214, 216–19
Urrutia, Matilde, 215

Valenzuela, Fernando, 133
Valero, Edwin "El Inca," 136–37
Van Deusen, Nancy E., 7
Vargas, Getúlio, 143
Vasconcelos, José, 91, 94, 103, 104
Venezuela, 12, 15, 17, 56, 59, 63, 66, 72, 121–39, 216–17
Vézina, Catherine, 10
Viera de Valero, Jennifer Carolina, 136–37
Villamizar Durán, Gustavo, 128,
Villarroel, Gualberto, 53
Virchow, Rudolf, 196, 200–201
Vizcaya, Bernardo, 121
Vizquel, Omar, 127
Voekel, Pamela, 4, 10

Whiteness, 6, 16, 20–36, 38, 39, 104, 106, 124, 126–29, 151, 178, 187, 190, 217
Weinstein, Barbara, 11
white flight, 127
Wichí, 202
Wickham, Clennell, 65, 66, 69, 70

Yánez, Miurka, 124
Yasser, Juan, 187
Young, Elliot, 4, 10